British Rail Main Line Locomotives

Specification Guide

British Rail Main Line Locomotives

Specification Guide

Pip Dunn

The Crowood Press

First published in 2013 by
The Crowood Press Ltd
Ramsbury, Marlborough
Wiltshire SN8 2HR

www.crowood.com

© Pip Dunn 2013

**British Library Cataloguing-in-Publication
Data**
A catalogue record for this book is available
from the British Library.

ISBN 978 1 84797 547 8

The right of Pip Dunn to be identified as
the author of this work has been asserted
by him in accordance with the Copyright,
Designs and Patents Act 1998.

ACKNOWLEDGEMENTS

The following have contributed with
checking facts and answering numerous
e-mails to clarify facts: Mark Alden, Nigel
Antolic, Alan Baylis, Paul Britton, Keith Bulmer,
Neil Burden, John Chalcraft, Adrian Curtis,
Jon Dunster, Glenn Edwards, John Goodale,
Simon Grego, Simon Hartshorne, Mark Holley,
Ian Horner, Ian McLean, Russell Saxton,
John Stephens, Martin Street, Paul Taylor,
Steve Thorpe and contributors to the
fourfooteightandahalf forum.

My thanks also go to my wife Victoria and
daughter Harriet for their unerring support.

If you have any comments, amendments,
additions or clarifications to this book,
please e-mail the author at
pip.dunn@eastfieldmedia.com

Typeset by Shane O'Dwyer, Bristol, Avon

Printed and bound in India by Replika Press

ABBREVIATIONS

Companies and Organizations

AEI	Associated Electrical Industries	GWR	Great Western Railway
BARS	British American Railroad Services	HB	Hunslet Barclay
BL	Brush Loughborough	HT	Hanson Traction
BOR	Boden Rail	HNRC	Harry Needle Railroad Company
BP	Beyer Peacock	IC	InterCity
BR	British Rail (British Railways before 1965)	LHGS	LH Group Services
		LMS	London Midland Scottish Railway
BSC	British Steel Corporation	LNER	London North Eastern Railway
CE	Civil engineers	ME	Mechanical Engineering
DBS	DB Schenker	MLR	Main Line Rail
DBSP	DB Schenker Poland	MR	Merlin Rail
DCR	Devon & Cornwall Railways	NB	North British
DRS	Direct Rail Services	NCB	National Coal Board
ECR	Euro Cargo Rail	NR	Network Rail
ECT	Ealing Community Transport	NRM	National Railway Museum
EE	English Electric	NSE	Network Southeast
EWS	English Welsh and Scottish Railway	RMS	RMS Locotec
FGBRf	First GB Railfreight	RT	Railtrack
FLHH	Freightliner Heavy Haul	RTC	Railway Technical Centre Derby
FLI	Freightliner Intermodal	RVEL	Railway Vehicle Engineering Limited
FLP	Freightliner Poland	SR	Southern Railway
FMR	Fragonset Merlin Rail	TOC	Train Operating Company
FOC	Freight Operating Company	TOPS	Total Operating Processing System
FR	Fragonset Railways	WCR	West Coast Railways
GBRf	GB Railfreight		

Regions

AR	Anglia Region	SR	Southern Region
ER	Eastern Region	ScR	Scottish Region
LMR	London Midland Region	WR	Western Region
NER	North Eastern Region		

Measurement

AC	alternating current	kN	kilonewton
cm	centimetre	kW	kilowatt
DC	direct current	lb	pound
ft	feet	ltr	litre
gal	gallon	m	metre
bhp	horsepower	mm	millimetre
in	inch	mph	miles per hours
km/h	kilometres per hour	V	volt

Other Abbreviations

DE	diesel electric	MW	multiple working
DH	diesel hydraulic	NB	non-boilered
D/H	dual heat	OHLE	overhead line equipment
ED	electro diesel	RHTT	railhead treatment train
ETH	electric train heating	SH	steam heating
ETS	electric train supply	TDM	time division multiplex
LED	light-emitting diode		

contents

preface

This book is aimed at identifying the major detail differences and livery variations that have appeared on the ex-BR and privatized main-line diesel and electric fleets. Back in 1982, David Strickland produced a book for the Diesel and Electric Group called the *Locomotive Directory*, with a sub-heading 'every single one there has ever been'. It's a valuable text for anyone interested in the history of the BR fleet. Obviously it is now thirty years old, and therefore not only out of date, but also out of print. If you haven't got a copy it's worth trying to get one from Amazon or eBay, or at a second-hand bookshop. It has been a useful book for me, as a railway writer, over the years, and it is the aim of this book not only to bring that text up to date, but also to expand it.

I have not covered the shunters nor some of the more obscure prototypes, as these were not owned by BR and did not experience much in the way of changes such as liveries and modifications.

This book covers Class 14s to 92s. The main specification statistics are given, and the details of variations, aided by photographs where appropriate. It is especially aimed at modellers and those with an interest in the differences that have occurred to the BR fleet over the years. The level of detail is difficult to pitch, so in the main it is the major detail differences that affect locos and where known that are listed, and relevant minor details.

Liveries are a minefield, especially in the 1960s and early 1970s in the transition from green to blue. Some classes are well documented, such as the Class 52s and Class 42s/43s, but other types are not, such as the 20s, 31s and 37s. The work of livery expert Russell Saxton has been used as a base for much of the livery research.

The specifications are in imperial as well as metric, with figures rounded up where there is the odd fraction of an inch or a horsepower. Dual-braking dates are taken from the Strickland book, aided with dates reported in the mainstream railway press at the time.

The information in this book has been brought together by painstaking research through my library, and by trawling the Internet looking at pictures.

Use of Flickr has been a key component in unearthing great pictures to offer more information, as have some of the numerous railway groups on Facebook.

But I am not naive or arrogant enough to say it's either 'perfect' or 'comprehensive', and that is because there will be livery changes and modifications that we may not ever know about, simply because no one took any notice of them in the 1960s. So this book is a sort of 'work in progress' – a first edition, perhaps – and any updates, corrections or clarifications are welcome. They can be e-mailed to me at pip.dunn@eastfieldmedia.com.

It is also a book that is aimed to be used in conjunction with other texts – *see* the bibliography at the end – although I recommend as an invaluable starting point the Roger Harris collection – *The Allocation History of BR Diesel and Electrics* (3rd edition) – and also David Clough's two books *Diesel Pioneers* and *British Rail Standard Diesel of the 1960s*, which are well worth reading. Colin Marsden's *Modern Traction Locomotive Directory* is also a useful companion, as are his bi-monthly partwork magazines *Modern Locomotives Illustrated*. I would strongly recommend acquiring these texts.

There have been a lot of changes to the fleet since Strickland's book, most notably privatization of the railways – some authors have yet to come to grips with the end of BR! Some still refer to locos 'having been scrapped when they have not officially been withdrawn', but in fact the way that the status of vehicles is changed today is wholly different to the way it was in BR days. In the BR era locos were either active, stored or condemned, and could move between these statuses. Even a loco 'condemned' – effectively its useful life over and waiting for disposal – could, if the business demanded it, be returned to traffic. In fact the word 'withdrawn' was often misused, and being 'withdrawn' from traffic was quite different to being condemned! Nowadays locos are not withdrawn or condemned as such, they are simply moved into pools for component recovery or disposal.

In comparison, this is effectively the same as being moved into a stored unserviceable pool, since they are unser-

viceable once components have been removed – while moving into a pool for disposal is the same as being condemned, their useful life with their current owner being effectively over. Their physical scrapping is often not recorded on TOPS, and locos that have been broken up can actually remain on TOPS for several years after they were disposed of.

Some operators choose not to 'condemn' locos as such, and they may stay in yards for decades slowly being stripped with no chance of ever running again, yet some enthusiasts do not accept they are withdrawn. Even some locos regarded as preserved are anything but, and 'stored' is a more appropriate description of their status.

It is not the aim of this book to show pictures of every livery, or to record every minor modification – to do so would need twice as many pages and twice the budget – but through the pictures I hope to give you at least a flavour for the changes that have happened to the loco fleet in the last six decades. I have used a selection of BR era, privatized era and preservation images to show the differences that have occurred over that time. As a rule I have tried to use pictures not published before, although this has not always been possible. Changes that happened in the 1960s often went unnoticed because rail enthusiasts at the time were rarely interested in the diesels. The period from 1968–75 is in many ways even worse, as many enthusiasts simply 'packed up', and it wasn't until the rundown of the Class 52s was well under way *circa* 1975 that many enthusiasts came back into the hobby, and younger ones came into the hobby afresh.

The internet has been a wonderful tool in researching this book, and has thrown up much new information – in fact new things came to light as I was preparing it, so it is inevitable that some things may have been overlooked or omitted. If there are any omissions or errors, or anything you would like to correct or clarify, then please do get in touch via the aforementioned e-mail.

All information is understood to be correct to 31 January 2013.

Pip Dunn, Spalding, February 2013

part I
Introduction

the scope of this book

This book details all BR, ex-BR and privatized railway diesel and electric main line Classes from 14 to 92. Unlike many books, I have deliberately divorced 21s and 29s (the latter a rebuild of the former), and the same applies to the 30/31s, 47/48s, 47/57s and 71/74s; likewise there are separate chapters for the 24/25s, 26/27s, 44/45/46s and other types, which although similar, are different. However, just to make it more confusing, subclasses are kept under the one banner. Bizarrely, there are a lot more differences between a 37/0 and a 37/9 than there are between a 44 and a 45! But it was not me who chose the subclasses!

Not included are shunters (Classes 01–13), while only those prototypes that gained a classification (so, in effect, 1200 *Falcon*) are included. DP2, *Deltic*, D0260 *Lion*, *et al* are not, nor are the Class 80s testbed electric locos, and the HST prototype power cars – and besides, there were not a lot of detail differences of livery changes for these.

Also out are the Eurotunnel rescue and maintenance locos – they are restricted as to where they can work, and so are not nationwide locos. Nor are the French 22200 locos that worked into the UK on Channel Tunnel freights in the mid-1990s, or the EWS Class 21 Vossloh B-B locos. For a start, all these locos are out of gauge for Network Rail. With this in mind, locos that run only over HS1 or do not get beyond the Channel Tunnel are excluded, so if Alstom Prima or Siemens Vectron locos start using this route, they too are omitted. Anything from Northern Ireland is also excluded – as we are looking at British Rail and the ex-British Rail.

The Class 68s are also out simply because these are yet to be built, so there's hardly a lot you can say about their detail differences or liveries!

Foreign locos that have moved to the UK for use at preserved railways or industrial sites are also excluded – not that there are many.

Included are those locos that have run on the UK national network but have been moved abroad, such as 58s, 66s, 86s, 87s and the like.

details and differences

For BR, and the subsequent train operators, knowing which locos had train heating and what train brakes they had was of great importance in order to allocate the right locos to the right trains.

Other smaller detail changes were also of relevance, such as which locos could be fitted with snowploughs and which had headlights, as these factors affected the day-to-day operating practices, which differed from region to region and in some cases even from route to route.

For enthusiasts, detail differences were important for their hobby while others just found them interesting. In 1978 the first Platform 5 pocket book appeared, which listed the main differences such as brakes and heating, and other key things which could affect where a loco might, or might not, be seen working.

For modellers, knowing the detail differences can be the difference between a poor model, a good model or a stunning model. I have seen models of Railfreight grey Class 20s with disc headcodes incorrectly numbered as 20186, or 'regimental' Deltics with Finsbury Park white windows, all of which are incorrect. Of course, a modeller is free to do as they wish, but if you are spending hundreds of pounds in attempting to make a superb model, then surely attention to detail is important?

And also – and this is where I hope this book will help and even inspire – it is always nice for modellers to try something different. You only have to look at some of the excellent models in *Hornby Magazine*, *Rail Express* or *Model Rail* to see what is achievable. Getting the details for those models 'spot on' is the difference between a good model and an excellent model.

PERIODS

At one time there was BR, and then there wasn't! That's fine, but referring to Heritage locos as 'privately owned' is erroneous, because in reality, everything is privately owned. Just because a loco doesn't run on the national network doesn't mean it doesn't exist and carries on its life.

But of course, it's not as simple as that. So for argument's sake, all the information that refers to a loco only in 'preservation' is noted. For example, there have been two Railfreight grey Class 50s, 50149 in BR days (and again in preservation) and 50017 only in preservation. However, those preserved locos that have run on the main line in new, old or revised liveries are deemed to be part of the national fleet. And I say this because nearly all of them have done work for rail operators, be it a Deltic for Virgin, a Western for Colas or a Class 33 for the Valley Lines.

So just to add on this argument, 50017 was not LMS crimson (solely) 'in preservation': it was LMS crimson while passed to run on Railtrack (as was).

LIVERIES

It would be a sensible thing to say, so far as liveries are concerned, simply 'don't go there', because the history of liveries could fill a book in its own right. In short, diesel locos started in green with grey roofs and red bufferbeams, but some were all-over green, others two-tone green, and the AC electrics were painted in a light blue, known as 'Electric Blue'.

Then came small yellow warning panels, followed by full yellow ends, which on some locos went round to cover the side window frames, but on other locos did not. Then came BR blue, which was meant to be with full yellow ends, but again, some locos had small panels. Some fleets had yellow side window frames, and some, such as the 26s/27s, started without them but ended up with them.

Livery codes

B	BR blue
BR	BR 'Large Logo' blue
BRB	BR 'Large Logo' blue with black roof
BSB	British Steel light blue
C	Civil Engineers' 'Dutch'
CT	Civil Engineers' 'Dutch' with Transrail logos
D	Departmental grey
DC	DRS 'Compass'
DB	Deutsche Bahn red
DR	DRS blue
EW	EWS maroon/gold
F	Two-tone grey
FA	Trainload Construction
FC	Trainload Coal
FD	Railfreight Distribution
FE	Railfreight Distribution 'European'
FF	Freightliner grey
FG	Railfreight General grey
FLH	Two-tone grey with Loadhaul logos
FM	Trainload Metals
FML	Two-tone grey with Mainline Freight logos
FO	BR Railfreight grey
FP	Trainload Petroleum
FR	BR 'red stripe' Railfreight grey
FT	Two-tone grey with Transrail logos
GWR	GWR green
Gy	BR green with small yellow panels
GY	BR green with full yellow ends
IC	InterCity
ICE	InterCity Executive
ICM	InterCity Mainline
LB	'Laira' blue
LNE	LNER apple green
LH	Loadhaul black/orange
ML	Mainline Freight blue
My	Maroon with small yellow panels
ND	Revised dark NSE blue
NO	Original NSE red/white/blue
NV	Revised NSE red/white/blue
R	Parcels red/grey
RDZ	Trial Railfreight Distribution grey
RTC	Railway Technical Centre red/blue
RX	Rail Express Systems
SNCB	Belgian Railways turquoise
SNCF	French Railways 'sybic' grey/orange
SR	BR ScotRail
WC	West Coast Railways maroon

Sector liveries started in the 1980s: InterCity and Railfreight then Network SouthEast, Departmental and Parcels (later Rail Express Systems). Virtually every livery had its variations in style, application, numbers, positions of nameplates and so on.

The creation of shadow freight companies and franchises, and then the birth of the privatized railway, has led to further new liveries, often with a myriad of variations and alterations. As TOCs change ownership, so do the liveries. And there has also been the start of retro liveries as BR, and then the sectors, and the TOCs/FOCs painted some locos in the liveries of past.

In this book I have tried to cover as many of the major and minor livery styles as possible, but there will always be a debate as regards variations, especially where branding and positions of numbers and the like are concerned. And it's not helped when BR had a livery called 'Mainline' for a version of InterCity, only to be followed a few years later by Mainline Freight!

While liveries are explained in full, to save space when referring to emblems, numbers, plaques and the like, livery codes are used (*see* table *Livery Codes*).

NUMBERS

Numbers are another total minefield! As a rule, green diesel locos had serif-style numbers with a D prefix. From 1968 D prefixes were officially dropped, but many locos did not have them painted out. Serif font was retained for BR maroon Class 42/43s.

The BR blue era heralded a new font – the BR corporate font – and in theory this was applied to all blue locos and to new classes such as the 50s and 73/1s. However, some blue locos had serif font numbers, especially Classes 20, 22, 26, 27, 42 and 43. It would be nearly impossible to record every variation as regards numbers – fonts, size, prefixes and so on – but any additional information would be welcomed by the author.

Class 52s had cast numberplates, while Class 35s and the Class 81–86 AC electric fleets had separate raised aluminium numerals, the latter changing to transfer numbers when renumbered under TOPS. Renumbering into TOPS started as early as November 1971 when E26050 became 76050, and AC and DC electrics were the first locos to receive the new five-digit numbers, with 45101 the first diesel in March 1973. Renum-

bering was slow throughout 1973, but early 1974 saw a concerted effort for locos to be given their new numbers.

The exceptions were the 35s and 52s, which were not renumbered on account of their cast numbers and short life expectancy. The last loco renumbered was 125, which became 45071 in December 1975: it had been out of traffic for a year being rebuilt after a major collision. By then, some renumbering of TOPS locos had started. A few early renumberings – especially at Scottish depots – saw the old serif font numerals used incorrectly, but these were soon changed.

In 1979, Glasgow Works outshopped any Scottish Region loco with slightly larger numbers, and then from 1983 any loco overhauled there – regardless of allocation – gained the larger numbers. The practice ended in 1985 when Railfreight livery was applied to 20s and 26s. These numbers are bigger than the standard BR blue livery numerals, but much smaller than those large numbers applied as part of the 'Large Logo' livery.

Some locos gained these larger numbers even though they had not been outshopped from Glasgow, so the locos listed are simply those which had the larger numbers, regardless of who applied them. A few locos also ran with smaller than standard numbers – these are also listed where appropriate.

BR BADGES

Locos in BR green had the lion and wheel emblem or the coaching stock emblem (Class 14/52).

The familiar BR double arrow appeared in 1964 on D1733 and was adopted across the fleet as locos were painted blue. Some green locos, especially Classes 15 and 31, and Deltic D9010, carried the double arrow on green.

The size of BR double arrows varied, with at least three different sizes before the advent of the 'Large Logo' livery. For many classes there were inconsistencies as to whether the number went above or below the BR badge on the cabside. Other locos had the badges on the cabsides, some had them on the bodyside, some in the middle and some behind the cabs. One loco at least, D8048, even ran with a reversed BR double arrow for a period, and some ran without arrows. The arrows were slowly dropped from rolling stock in the late 1980s as sectorization started.

EMBLEMS

Reference is made to emblems: these are the depot trademark emblems applied from 1981. It started with Eastfield depot applying West Highland terrier emblems to its locos, Haymarket followed in 1984 with its castle symbol, and Inverness did likewise with its Highland stag. All were on the bodysides or cabsides. Although these started off as unofficial logos, they were soon allowed by the BRB.

Some more 'unofficial logos' were often painted, such as the Wigan pie, the Westbury horse, the Canton sheep and the Toton hare, but these are not included in this book as they were not proper stickers.

CAST DEPOT PLAQUES

The emblem themes were officially adopted from 1987, with cast diamond plaques for depots and stabling points, which were fitted to locos as they were painted into Trainload and 'Dutch' liveries. Where known, these are listed. These are actually one of the greatest challenges to source, and I would be lying if I said I have got them all. I doubt I have, because some were swapped and others 'stolen' and so may have only been on a loco for a very short period. If there are any that are omitted, please let me know via pip.dunn@eastfieldmedia.com

DEPARTMENTAL STRIPES

In 1988, BR's Departmental sectors started to brand their locos with cabside stripes: red for the Research Centre locos, grey for the mechanical engineers' pool, and, most commonly, yellow for the civil engineers' locos. Application ceased in 1989 and when locos were repainted they lost them, although many had them until withdrawal.

HEADCODES

Trains have been classified according to their importance since the days of steam, with the aim of allowing signallers to award priority: they did not want a fast express train stuck behind a slow goods train or an all-stations-stopping local passenger train. To assist signallers, trains would display their priority via a set of four lamps arranged in different patterns. When diesels came in these lamps were replaced by lights fixed on the loco front, and covered by hinged folding white discs with holes cut into them so the lights could still be seen: the train crew would open the discs to display the train classification, and fold them to hide the lights if required.

In 1961, trains were given a reporting number based on four characters. The first was a number to indicate priority: 1 for an express passenger train, 2 for a local passenger train, 3 for an express parcels or mail train, 4 for a 75mph freight train, 5 for an empty stock train, 6 for a 60mph freight, 7 for a 45mph freight, 8 for a 35mph freight and 9 for an unfitted, 25mph freight train. The second character was a letter to denote destination: E for Eastern Region, M for London Midland Region, N for North Eastern Region, O for Southern Region, S for Scottish Region and V for Western Region; later L for Anglian Region was introduced. Other letters were used for trains which stayed within one region.

The last two characters were numbers to differentiate between trains – usually, but not always, the lower the number the earlier in the day the train, and the higher the number, the later the train in the timetable. So 1V01 was an express destined for the Western Region, and typically early in the day while 2S76 was a local train destined for the Scottish Region, probably in the early evening. Where it was felt there would be no confusion to signallers, the regional letters might be used elsewhere, so O headcodes were also used for Edinburgh-Glasgow shuttles.

Once this system was introduced there was a move to switch from the folding disc system to a panel which displayed the reporting number lit by four bulbs. These included four roller blinds of the appropriate letters and numbers, which the traincrew were meant to wind round to display the reporting number and so assist signallers.

Throughout this book there will be references to discs and four-character headcodes. The latter are also further complicated by different styles. The early diesel designs had centre communication doors on the front that allowed traincrew to move between locos when double headed via corridor connection. They were fitted to some, or all, of Classes 21–31, 37, 40, 41, 44 and 45. The disc system was fine on these locos, the two central discs being fitted to the doors. When roller blind headcodes were introduced, initially some locos had them split into two boxes, one either side of the communication doors. Referred to as 'split boxes', they were fitted to some or all of Classes 22, 37, 40 and 45 from new, and retro-fitted to some 22s and all of the 41s.

Other locos had their roller-blind headcodes in one-piece boxes above the cab to allow the communication doors to be retained, referred to as roof-mounted boxes in this book. That was the case for some Class 24s, 30s and 31s and all Class 25s, 27s and 50s (although the 50s and many of the 25s did not have communication doors).

It was soon discovered that the communication doors were rarely used and more trouble than they were worth. They were shelved during the production of Classes 25, 37, 40 and 45, and instead, with a clean front end available, a single four-character headcode panel could be incorporated, referred to as a centre-panel. No 25s had centre-panels on their cab fronts, they all had them on the cab roof for ease. On the Class 14s, 42s, 43s, 52s, some 45s and some 46s the centre-panels were actually split into two portions, and these are referred to as split centre-panels.

Centre-panels were fitted from new to all 17s, 29s (bar one), 35s, 47s, the sole 53, 55s, 81–86s and to some Class 20s, 37s and 40s, while retro-fitted to a single Class 21, all Class 23s, seven Class 40s, a 44 and many 45s.

Class 33s, 71s, 73s and 74s had two-character Southern Region roller blinds, which were between the cab windows. This system was retained after 1976, and the locos did not have the roller blinds removed (*see* table *Headcodes*).

POST-HEADCODES

Although disc headcodes were superseded, most locos fitted retained them for many years afterwards.

Only a handful of locos lost discs for four-character headcodes, such as the 23s when refurbished, and all but one of the 21s when converted to 29s (and

	Discs	Split panels	Centre-panels	Split-centre panels	No headcodes	Changes
14				D9500–55		
15	D8200–43					
16	D8400–09					
17			D8500–8616			
20	D8000–8127		D8128–8199, D8300–27			See text
21	D6100–57		D6109			
22	D6300–33	D6300/02–58				See text
23	D5900–09		D5900–09			See text
24	D5000–5113		D5114–150 (on roof)			See text
25			D5151–5299, D7500–7677 (on roof)			
26	D5300–46					See text
27			D5347–5415 (on roof)			
28	D5700–19					
29	D6123		See text			
30	See text		See text			
31	See text		See text			
33			D6500–97+			
35			D7000–7100			
37		D6700–6818	D6819–6999, D6600–08			See text
40	D200–324	D325–344	D260–266, D345–399			See text
41	D600–604	D600–604				See text
42	D800–813			D800–832/866–870		
43				D833–865		
43 HST					43002–198	
44	D1–10		D9			See text
45		D11–30, 68–107	See text	See text		See text
46			D138–193	D138–173		See text
47			D1100–1111, D1500–1999			See text
50			D400–449 (on roof)			
52				D1000–73		
53			1200			
55			D9000–21			
56					56001–135	
57					See text	
58					58001–050	
59					59001–005, 59101–104, 59201–206	
60					60001–100	
66					66001–957	
67					67001–030	
70					70001–020/099	
70 DC	20001–03		See text			
71			E5001–24+			
73			E6001–49+			See text
74			E6101–10+			
76	E26000–57					
77	E27000–06					
81			E3001–23/96/97			
82			E3046–55			
83			E3024–35/98–100			
84			E3036–45			
85			E3056–95			
86			E3101–3200			See text
87					87001–035/101	
89					89001	
90					90001–050	
91					91001–031	
92					92001–046	

+ Two character roller blind headcodes, other headcodes are for four characters

The discs as a rule folded horizontally, the exceptions being the Class 21, 22s and 29s, which folded vertically.

one 21 after a collision), while the WR was keener on the change and switched all its disc-fitted 22s, 41s and 42s to roller blinds, apart from D6301. Haymarket also converted seven disc Class 40s to centre-panels. D9 was given a head-code panel after a collision in 1969, but only at one end and it retained discs at the other. It was only in the late 1970s that BR started to remove discs, purely because they were redundant. Several Class 20s, 31s and 40s lost them, and these are detailed in the text.

Displaying train-reporting numbers was discontinued from 1973, although some regions kept them until 1976. Initially the intention was that headcodes would be wound round to display 0O00. The Class 50s and 52s often had theirs wound round to show their loco numbers, such as 5O39 or 1O15.

The first replacement of headcode was a black sheet with two white dots over the two outermost lamps that were used to illuminate the characters. Deltic 9009 was the first loco to have this modification, in late 1972, before headcodes were officially abolished. This change is called the domino headcode, and was later seen on some Class 20s, 25s, 27s, 31s, 37s, 40s, 44009 (one end only), 45s, 46s, 47s, 50s, D1023, 55s, 81s, 82s, 83s and 86s.

In 1976, 55016 emerged from overhaul with its headcode box plated over with metal, painted yellow and fitted with two opaque lenses over the lamps. This modification was duly applied to many locos, as detailed in their chapters.

Other locos had yellow panels, but instead of opaque lenses they had protruding white lights, while headcode boxes were removed totally from some locos; again, these differences are detailed in the text.

Some locos, especially Class 45–47s, have lost their cab-front headcode panels in favour of a flush end. Some of the more unusual changes were on Class 37s, with some split-box locos having centre-boxes fitted (and one, D6772, having this change at one end only), while even as late as 1990, when Laira overhauled some split-box 37s it removed the boxes, but rather than give them a refurbished look, the instruction was to fit centre-panels!

HEADLIGHTS

Spotlamps are the small, car-style headlights fitted to some Class 26s, 37s, 47s and 86s. Sealed beam headlights are the small, black, rubber-mounted headlights applied to some Class 47s, 56s, 86s, 87s. The Class 50s and some 56s had larger, sealed beam lights in round metal frames fitted flush into the body.

The BR 'standard' headlight is the sealed beam headlight in a square frame fitted to some Class 08, 09s, 20s, 26s, 31s, 33s, 37s, 45/1s, 47s, 56s, 58s, 73s, 86s, 87s. Some locos carried more than one style of light, and some even differed between the two ends.

Non-standard lights, such as those on industrial Class 14s, are detailed as such.

BRAKES

Despite air-brake technology being available, the fact that the majority of the coaches and wagons dated from the steam era and were vacuum-braked (v), BR chose to build all main-line diesels in the 1950s and 1960s with vacuum train brakes. Dual – vacuum and air – train brakes (x) were fitted from new to Class 33s, 50s, 71s, 73s, 81s–86s and some Class 20s, 25s, 47s.

All Class 37s, 45–47s and 55s were converted to dual brakes, along with the majority of Class 20s, 26s, 27s, 31s and 52s, and many Class 25s, 40s and 76s. Classes 56–60, 66–67, 70, 87, 89–92 were air-braked only from new (a). Some Class 20s, 31s, 33s, 37s, 47s, 73s and 86s have since been converted to air brakes only, while a handful of locos have come full circle and been converted back from air only to dual-braked, mainly to haul heritage rolling stock.

Classes that remained vacuum-braked only were 15–17/21–24/28–30/35/41–44, while some Class 14s have been converted to dual-brake operation in industrial and preserved railway roles. All Class 30s were converted to Class 31s (*see* table *Braking Systems*).

WHEEL ARRANGEMENTS AND BOGIES

With the exception of the Class 14s, all locos in this book rely on two bogies, one at each end. The 14s have a fixed frame with six wheels connected by coupling rods, and hence use the Whyte system of designation used for steam locos, namely 0-6-0 (no pony wheels, six driving wheels and no trailing wheels).

The bogie designation tells the number of axles and which are powered: A = 1, B = 2 and C = 3. If suffixed by an o it implies powered, so Bo is a two-axle bogie with both axles powered by a traction motor. The number 1 implies an unpowered axle, while diesel hydraulics, which do not use traction motors, are simply B-B or C-C, depending on whether they are two- or three-axle bogies.

The Class 31s and 41s, which had unpowered centre axles, have two A1A bogies. The Class 40s and 44–46s had four-axle bogies, of which the lead axle was unpowered, hence they have two 1Co bogies.

When TOPS was introduced, every loco was meant to display a data panel that gave the basic facts about it – its type, weight, brake force, route availability (RA) and maximum speed. It also showed the loco's brakes, be it vacuum-, dual- or air-braked. The first type of data panels had the brakes listed as AB, VB or AB-VB. This Class 25 sports the first type of data panel, and still has its worksplate; these were soon removed and now command high prices at auctions. PDC

The revised data panel had a section on the top right, which was meant to have A, V or X on it to denote the loco's train brakes, although this was often left blank, as shown here. They also had an ETH index, which was left blank if the loco was boilered or non-boilered. These panels were in BR blue, though later clear versions with black lettering were applied to locos in different liveries. PDC

Braking Systems

	New v	New x	New a	Converted x	Converted a	Back to x from a
14	56			7		
15	44					
16	10					
17	117					
20	217	11		203	28	
21	58					
22	58					
23	10					
24	151					
25	315	12		137		
26	47			33		
27	69			35		
28	20					
29	20					
30	263					
31	263			235	4	
33		98			2	1
35	101					
37	309			308	37	
40	200			125		
41	5					
42	38					
43	33					
43 HST			197			
44	10					
45	127			127		
46	56			56		
47	207	305		204	208	8
50		50			1	1
52	74			70		
53	1				1	
55	22			22		
56			135			
57			33			
58			50			
59			15			
60			100			
66			455			
67			30			
70			21			
70 DC	3					
71		24				
73		49			15	
74		10				
76	58			21	9	
77	7				6	
81	25			22		
82	10			8		
83	15			15		
84	10			10		
85	40			40		
86		100			87	
87			36			
89			1			
90			50			
91			31			
92			46			

Wheel Arrangements

Wheel arrangement	Classes
0-6-0	14
A1A-A1A	30, 31, 41
B-B	22, 35, 42, 43
Bo-Bo	15, 16, 17, 20, 21, 23, 24, 25, 26, 27, 29, 33, 43 (HST), 67, 71, 73, 74, 81, 82, 83, 84, 85, 86, 87, 90, 91
Bo+Bo	76
Co-Bo	28
C-C	52
Co-Co	37, 47, 48, 50, 53, 55, 56, 57, 58, 59, 60, 66, 70, 70DC, 77, 89, 92
1Co-Co1	40, 44, 45, 46

The Class 76s had their bogies coupled together and hence were Bo+Bo, while the Class 28s were unique in having a three-axle bogie at No. 1 end and a two-axle bogie at No. 2 end, and so became the only Co-Bo class.

ENDS AND SIDES

Each loco has a No. 1 end and a No. 2 end and an A side and a B side. The No. 1 end is usually the end with the main radiator grilles. On most classes it is easy to differentiate between the two, although Class 52 and the 55s are notoriously difficult.

A sides and B sides vary in design between classes, especially the electric classes, although they tend to be fairly uniform – externally at least – on most diesel classes.

STANDARD BUFFERBEAM LAYOUT

Bufferbeam layouts might look complicated, but as a rule they conform to a standard pattern. With the drawhook in the middle, to the left of it was the vacuum-brake pipe and to the right the steam-heat pipe (if fitted). Air-brake pipes were always to the right of the drawhook, fitted above any steam-heat pipes. These always had a red painted opening cock, although these were sometimes painted white in the early days of dual-braking.

To the right of the steam-heat pipe/ air-brake pipe was the main reservoir pipe (yellow head) and the loco air-control pipe (white head), which was much thinner. These were duplicated on the left-hand side to the left of the vacuum-brake pipe.

details and differences

Multiple Working

Class	MW at construction	Later developments
14	Not fitted	
15	Blue Star	
16	Red Circle	
17	Red Diamond	Some changed to Blue Star
20/0	Blue Star	
20/3	DRS system	
20/9	Blue Star	
21	Red Circle (D6100–37), Blue Star (D6138–57)	
22	Orange Square (D6300–05), White Diamond (D6306–57)	
23	Blue Star	
24	Blue Star	
25	Blue Star	
26	Blue Star	
27	Blue Star	
28	Red Circle	
29	Red Circle	
30	Red Circle (D5500–19), Blue Star (D5520–5699, D5800–62)	
31/0	Red Circle	
31/1	Blue Star	
31/4	Blue Star	
33/0	Blue Star	
33/1	Blue Star	Duplicate waist-level pipes
33/2	Blue Star	
35	Yellow Triangle	
37/0	Blue Star	DRS system on 37038/059/069, 37218/259
37/3	Blue Star	
37/4	Blue Star	Dual Blue Star and DRS system on 37402/405/409/419/423/425
37/5	Blue Star	Dual Blue Star and DRS system on 37667/688
37/6	Blue Star at conversion	Dual Blue Star and DRS system on 37601/603/604, DRS system only on 37602/605–612
37/7	Blue Star	
37/9	Blue Star	
40	Blue Star	Jumpers removed from some (*see* text)
41	Red Circle	
42	Within Class only (D800–02), White Diamond (D803–832/866–70 only)	Jumpers removed, refitted to D803/04/07/08/14/16/19/22–29/31/32/66–70
43	White Diamond	Jumpers removed
43 HST	Within Class only	
44	Blue Star	Removed from all
45/0	Blue Star	Removed from all
45/1	Blue Star	Removed from all
46	Blue Star	Removed from all
47/0	Not fitted	Green Circle on some (see text), 47258 fitted with Blue Star push-pull operation only

Class	MW at construction	Later developments
47/2	Green Circle	
47/3	Not fitted	Green Circle on some (see text), 47370/379 trial system
47/4	Not fitted	Green Circle on some (see text)
47/6	Not fitted	
47/7a	Not fitted	Green Circle on some (see text)
47/7b	Not fitted	Green Circle on some (see text)
47/8	Not fitted	Green Circle on some (see text)
47/9	Not fitted	
47/9	Blue Star	47971/974-976, for push-pull operation only
50	Orange Square	
52	Not fitted	
53	Blue Star	Removed
55	Not fitted	
56	Red Diamond	
57	Not fitted	Green Circle on 57002–004/007–012
58	Red Diamond	
59	GM system	
60	Within Class only	
66	GM system	
67	GM system	
70	Within Class only	
70 DC	Not fitted	
71	Not fitted	
73	Blue Star with duplicate waist-level pipes	
74	Blue Star with duplicate waist-level pipes	
76	Not fitted	76006–016/021–039 within class only (AO and XO locos only)
77	Not fitted	
81	Not fitted	
82	Not fitted	
83	Not fitted	
84	Not fitted	
85	Not fitted	
86/0	Not fitted	Within Class only and Class 87
86/1	Not fitted	TDM
86/2	Not fitted	TDM
86/3	Not fitted	Within Class only and Class 87
86/4	Within Class only and Class 87	TDM
86/5	TDM	
86/6	Within Class only and Class 87	TDM
86/7	TDM	
86/9	TDM	
87	Within Class only and some Class 86s	TDM
89	TDM	
90	TDM	
91	TDM	
92	Within Class only	

Early pilot scheme locos had the main res and loco air-control pipe under the bufferstocks, but these were repositioned next to them closer to the middle on later production locos, and some, but not all, of the pilot scheme machines often had these similarly repositioned when dual-braked.

MULTIPLE WORKING

Multiple working (MW) was a system that allowed two or three locos to work together under the control of one driver. Pluggable cables mounted on the front were connected between locos, and would allow the application of power or the brakes to the rear loco(s) as soon as the driver activated them on the loco he was controlling. These jumper cables were generally fitted on the bufferbeam on the early loco designs, though later designs such as the 50s, 56s, 58s, 86s and 87s had them fixed on the cab fronts.

The most commonly used system, Blue Star, had the jumper cable on the right of the drawhook; this was fitted on to the bufferbeams, and the cable itself was then looped round under the bufferstocks and the jumper head clipped into a socket when not in use. The jumper receptacle was on the left hand of the bufferstock and to the left of the vacuum-brake pipe, but to the right of the main res/loco air control pipes. When two locos were working in multiple (or in 'multi', as was the common term used by staff), one jumper was unclipped and taken out of its holding socket and plugged into the receptacle: it was not necessary for both jumpers to be used.

On Red Circle (Classes 16/21/29/30/41) and White Diamond (Classes 22/42/43) locos, the receptacle was on the right of the drawhook and the jumper cable on the left, but on Yellow Triangle (Class 35) and Red Diamond (Class 17) the jumpers were similar to Blue Star. From the Class 50s, in 1967, the jumpers were mounted on the loco fronts and this was continued on Class 87, then 56, 86 and 58. All these had the jumper on the left and the receptacle on the right.

Lots of locos ran for periods with their multiple working isolated or removed. All Classes 44–46s had the equipment removed. Some Class 40s, mostly those allocated to ScR depots, had it removed – or to be more accurate, isolated, as it was just a case of taking the jumper cables off. In some cases it was later refitted. Most of the Class 50s were built with the wiring in place but the jumpers not fitted, though later it was fitted to all the fleet.

Some locos, like the 47s and 86s, were not fitted with MW at construction, but it was fitted to some locos later in their lives. The Class 47s had just a receptacle for the MW on the cab front, in between the headcode box marker lights, but the cable was stowed in the cab or engine room.

SNOWPLOUGHS

Brackets to allow fitting of three-piece miniature snowploughs to bufferbeams were fitted to some diesels from new. These comprised a centre plough and

Snowploughs

Locos	Brackets from new	Brackets fitted later	Locos	Brackets from new	Brackets fitted later
14	No		52	No	
15	No		53	No	
16	No		55	No	
17	Yes		56	No	
20	20028–034/070–127/129–228		57	No	57602–605
21	D6138–57		58	Yes	None ever carried ploughs
22	D6336–48	D6322/28	59	No	
23	No		60	Single-piece ploughs fitted	
24	D5114–32	See text	66	No	
25	See text	See text	67	No	
26	26021–046	26018	70	No	
27	27001–023	See text	70 DC	No	
28	No		71	No	
29	No		73	No	73212/213 (one end only)
30	No		74	No	
31	No	See text	76	No	
33	Yes		77	No	
35	Yes		81	No	
37	No	See text	82	No	
40	No		83	No	
41	No		84	No	
42	No		85	No	
43	No		86	No	
43 HST	No		87	No	
44	No		89	No	
45	No		90	No	
46	No		91	No	
47	No	See text	92	No	
50	Yes	See text			

two side ploughs, which were independently detachable. Many locos only had ploughs fitted for the winter or at least had the centre plough detached in summer when it was unlikely to be needed.

Initially the brackets were fitted to Scottish Region locos, namely some Class 20s, 21s, 24s, 26s and 27s, though later Classes 17, 20, 22, 33, 37, 50 and 58 were built with them regardless of the region they were intended for operation. Some Class 22s, 24s, 25s, 26s, 27s, 31s, 37s, 47s and 73s were retro modified with the brackets. To date, a Class 58 has never carried ploughs, while the only two 73s fitted with them were done so at one end only.

Class 60s were built with new single-piece snowploughs which were retained all year round.

NAMES

Names bestowed on locos are listed, including some 'unofficial' names, namely those applied by Tinsley on Class 31/37/45/47s, and Thornaby on its Class 20s. Names are shown as they appear on locos, so uppercase or lower case (except in captions, where they are in lower case regardless of style).

As a rule, names are in the BR corporate style, introduced in 1977. Those

names on Class 40s, 41s, 42s, 43s, 52s, 55s, 76s and 77s were in upper case and differed in fonts. The early Western Region named Class 47s were also in upper case, D1660–64 having them in the same style as Class 52s, while D1665–77 had them in GWR style.

In more recent times, nameplate fonts have changed immeasurably and it is not possible to list all the different styles, typefaces and the like. Some locos have crests or plaques above, below or even to the side of the nameplates and some locos have had them incorporated in the plate itself.

In the late 1987s, BR's InterCity sector opted for polished stainless-steel nameplates, often referred to as 'tin plate' names. These did not last long and were mainly fitted to 43s, 90s, 91s and a single 47. When GNER named its Class 43s and 91s it did so using transfers, but these have all since been removed.

Many locos, especially freight locos, have had names in company logo styles; this is especially true of some 47s and 60s. Other companies have introduced their own unique style, such as Virgin and Fragonset, although more recently there has been a tendency for preference for the old BR corporate-style font to be used. Locos often did not carry their names for their full lives.

TRAIN HEATING

Diesels were initially built with either no train heating (NB – no boiler) or steam heating (SH); a few were built from new with electric train heating (ETH), and some had dual heating (D/H) from new. Those with no heating are often referred to as 'non-boilered'.

Each ETH loco has an index rating, as does each coach: the higher the rating, the more power is required to provide heating/train supply to it. The loco can only provide ETH if its index does not exceed the total of the indexes of the coaches it is to heat. The lowest ETH index was twenty-eight on the Class 27/2s and thirty on the 37/4s. The general level was sixty-six, but the 33s and 50s were lower (at forty-eight and sixty-one). Some 47s had their ETH index uprated to seventy-five for 'sleeper' trains, while the earlier electrics had sixty-six, which was then increased to ninety-five for the 87s, 90s and 91s: these often hauled heavier trains of air-conditioned stock, which required more power. Having no train heating meant locos could not heat any passenger coaches, hence making them 'freight only', certainly for the winter.

Again, most early diesel types had a separate steam-heating system provided

When BR started naming again in 1977 it used its corporate font for nameplates. Variations started to appear in the 1980s, and the privatized companies have developed all manner of fonts. However, the standard style is still favoured today for the majority of nameplates. 87032 was named Kenilworth *on 9 May 1978, and retained the plates until early 2003, when it was renamed.* PIP DUNN

Train Heating			
Class	Train heat at construction	Notes	Current status (main-line fleets only)
14	NB		
15	NB	Through steam pipes	
16	NB	Through steam pipes	
17	NB	Through steam pipes	
20	NB	Through steam pipes on D8000–127	NB
21	SH		
22	SH		
23	SH		
24	SH	D5102–11 lost their boilers, others had them isolated	
25	SH on D5176–5237, D7568–97, rest NB	D5179–82, D7592 had their boilers removed, most others had their boilers isolated. NB locos had through steam pipes	
26	SH	26001–008/010/011/014/015/021/023–029/ 031/032/034–043/046 had their boilers removed at refurbishment. Boiler isolated on 26013	
27	SH on all bar D5370–78 NB	D5374 had a boiler fitted in 1971. Boilers were removed from 27038/042 and 27201–212, which were converted to ETH only, which was then removed. Some other locos had their boilers isolated	
28	SH		
29	SH		
30	SH		
31	SH	Removed from many locos. Seventy converted to ETH, of which 31401–423 were initially D/H then converted to ETH only. ETH was isolated on some 31s, which became Class 31/5s, later reinstated on those reverting to Class 31/4s. Remaining SH locos had their boilers removed at refurbishment or isolated	ETH on 31452/454/459, through ETH wiring on 31601/602, remainder NB
33	ETH	Isolated on some and removed from 33029, 33207	NB
35	SH		
37	SH on most (*see* text)	Thirty-one converted to ETH, boilers removed or isolated on all others	ETH on 37402/405/409/419/423/425, remainder NB
40	SH	Removed from many and isolated on others. D255 had ETH for a trial, but removed	Boiler isolated
41	SH	Isolated on some	
42	SH	Isolated on some	
43	SH	Isolated on some	
43 HST	ETH		ETH
44	SH	All removed	
45	SH	Fifty converted to ETH only, some remaining locos had their boilers isolated	
46	SH	Isolated on some	
47	D/H on D1500–19, D1960/61, NB on D1782–1836/1875– 1900, SH on remainder	Many steam-heat locos converted to D/H or ETH only, others had boilers isolated and eventually removed from most	NB on 47/0 and 47/3s, ETH on all 47/4, 47/7 and 47/8s
48	SH		
50	ETH		ETH
52	SH	Isolated on some locos	NB
53	SH	Isolated	
55	SH	All converted to D/H, boilers later isolated on 55008/018	ETH

Class	Train heat at construction	Notes	Current status (main-line fleets only)
56	NB		NB
57	NB (57/0), ETH (57/3 and 57/6)		NB (57/0), ETH (57/3 and 57/6)
58	NB		
59	NB		NB
60	NB		NB
66	NB		NB
67	ETH		ETH
70	NB		NB
70 DC	SH		
71	ETH		
73	ETH	Removed from 73212/213	ETH except on 73212/213
74	ETH		
76	SH on E26046–057	Boilers later isolated, then removed from most	
77	SH	All bar one converted to ETH only in the Netherlands	ETH
81	ETH		ETH
82	ETH		ETH
83	ETH		ETH
84	ETH		ETH
85	ETH	Isolated on Class 85/1s	ETH
86	ETH	Isolated on Class 86/5s, 86/6s, 86/9s	ETH, isolated on Class 86/5, 86/6 and 86/9
87	ETH		ETH
89	ETH		ETH
90	ETH	Isolated on Class 90/1s	ETH
91	ETH		ETH
92	ETH		ETH

by a removable boiler – a throwback to the steam era – often referred to as a steam generator. This was operated by the secondman and was used to generate steam, which was then pumped through the coaches. The system was often ineffective, and failures on boilers were commonplace in the 1960s.

ETH was more reliable and effective, but at the time of the early diesels there was little rolling stock that was compatible. ETH is also referred to as 'Electric Train Supply' (ETS) to take into account that as newer air-conditioned coaches came into use the ETH was used to power the air-conditioning and later also the central door locking (CDL) and other features such as ovens. For the sake of consistency throughout, this book refers to ETH rather than ETS.

SH was phased out in the late 1970s, but it was 1987 when the last steam-heated trains ran. Those locos with redundant boilers had them either removed or 'isolated' but kept inside the locos to keep its weight correct.

Those which had their boilers removed often had replacement ballast weights to keep the locos' overall weight correct.

Some locos built without train heating had through steam pipes fitted. These were to allow a 'no-heat' loco to work in multiple with a steam heat loco and still allow the steam to get through to the coaches. It was another rarely used feature and the pipes were removed in the late 1960s or early 1970s, although two Class 20s, 20045/085, had them refitted in 1983 when a need to double-head on the West Highland line with Class 37s was identified. This only lasted for that year and the pipes were removed when the locos were next overhauled.

REFURBISHMENT

For the scope of this book, 'refurbishment' is deemed to be work above and beyond an overhaul. Classes widely regarded as being refurbished are 23, 26, 31, 37 and 50, and this usually featured such extensive work as rewiring, replating of bodywork, changes to major components and removal of redundant equipment.

In the case of the Class 23s the headcodes changed from disc to panels, while the Class 50s had a lot of equipment changed and were physically noticeable by their new headlights.

The Class 31s lost their bufferbeam skirting and had their headcodes plated over, while the Class 26s had their front ends stripped of all but two marker lights and two tail-lights. Refurbished Class 37s had their main generators changed to alternators, as well as other differences to their nose ends.

Several Class 27s were also refurbished, but there were no major differences to unrefurbished (dual-braked) 27s. 55016 was also refurbished, but aside from yellow headcode panels, later fitted to other 55s, it was not distinguished as 'refurbished'. The DRS Class 20/3s are refurbished locos, again because the physical differences are there for all to see.

Of course it could be argued that 29s are refurbished Class 21s and Class 57s are refurbished Class 47s, and to a degree there is some element of truth in that, but because they were given new engines and new classifications, for the scope of this book 29s and 57s are 'new build', just using second-hand parts such as bodies and bogies.

1957 BR number range:	D9500–55
Former class code:	6/1
Built by:	BR Swindon
Year introduced:	1964–65
Wheel arrangement:	0-6-0
Weight:	50 tons
Height:	10ft (3.05m)
Length:	34ft 7in (10.54m)
Width:	8ft 8in (2.63m)
Wheelbase:	15ft 6in (4.72m)
Wheel diameter:	4ft (1.22m)
Min. curve negotiable:	3 chains
Maximum speed:	40mph (64km/h)
Engine type:	Paxman 6YJX 'Ventura'
Engine output:	650bhp (486kW)
Power at rail:	480bhp (358kW)
Tractive effort:	30,910lb
Brake force:	31 tons
Route availability:	2
Transmission type:	Hydraulic – Voith L217u
Fuel tank capacity:	338gal (1,521ltr)

The last loco built by Swindon for BR was Class 14 D9555. Now preserved, it shows off the original look of a Class 14 with vacuum brakes and split-centre headcode panels. The loco has wasp stripes on its doors, which could be opened for access to the internal running gear. PIP DUNN

THIS IS WITHOUT doubt one of the hardest fleets on which to offer concrete information about its detail differences, mainly because all the changes happened after its BR days. All fifty-six locos were uniform in their short BR lives, and all were withdrawn so quickly there was hardly any time to change them. That was not the case for those sold to industry, as some were repainted while others remained in BR green. Furthermore some were renumbered, others were not; some had single headlights fitted, and others twin headlights; a number had headcode panels painted over, others had headlamps fitted in them. Some lost their train vacuum brakes as the pipes were removed. In preservation/industry several have been upgraded with dual train brakes.

DETAIL DIFFERENCES

All had split-centre headcodes, one on each of the opening doors on the nose ends. In preservation D9524/39 have had domino headcodes. D9504/29 have their headcode boxes removed. Some NCB and BSC locos had their headcodes painted over, but the glass panels were retained.

All were vacuum-braked, but D9504/05/15/16/20/23/24/29/31/34/48/49 have been converted to dual brakes in preservation/industry.

Headlights were fitted to many in industrial use. Single nose end headlights were fitted to at least D9515/26/48, and twin nose end headlights to at least D9507/16/20/23/32/33/37/39/42/48/49/51/53. Single square nose-end headlights were fitted to D9504/05, while those with headlights in headcode panels were at least D9504/25/39. D9553 had roof-mounted flashing orange lights. On their bufferbeams, the Class 14s used by BSC had additional lifting points fitted and two clips mounted for storing a shunter's pole when not in use.

LIVERIES

All were new in British Railways green with wasp stripes on the nose ends. The cabs were light green. The BR carriage emblem was applied on the cabsides above the numbers. Bufferbeams were yellow.

BR green: D9500–55
NCB blue+: D9500/04/13/14/17/18/21/27/28/31/35/36/40/55. It is possible that D9508/11/32 were also repainted in BSC blue
Export yellow+: D9505/15/48/49
BP light green+: D9524+
Railfreight*: 14021 (ex-D9521)
BR blue: D9524*/29+
BR blue with yellow cabs: 14901* (ex-D9524)
Maroon: D9523*

+ industry; * preservation

MINOR VARIATIONS

Large numbers D9553* Gy, cast BR Emblems: D9537*/39* G, cast number panels: D9516*/37*/39* G, D9523* My.

Some NCB locos had wasp stripes on their bufferbeams.

NAMES

D9505 *Michlow*+
D9531 *ERNEST**
D9534 *Eccles*+

RENUMBERINGS

BR No.	User	Number
D9500	NCB	9312/92
D9502	NCB	9312/97
D9503	BSC	8411/25
D9504	NCB	2233/506
D9507	BSC	8311/35
D9508	NCB	9312/99
D9510	BSC	8411/23
D9511	NCB	9312/98
D9512	BSC	8411/24
D9513	NCB	D1/9513
D9514	NCB	9312/96
D9515	BSC	8411/22
D9516	BSC	8311/36
D9517	NCB	9312/93
D9518	NCB	9312/95
D9520	BSC	8311/24
D9521	NCB	9312/90
D9523	BSC	8311/25
D9524	British Petroleum	8 144–8
D9525	NCB	2233/507
D9527	NCB	9312/94
D9528	NCB	9312/100
D9529	BSC	8411/20

D9530	Gulf Oil	D9530
D9531	NCB	D2/9531
D9532	BSC	8311/37
D9533	BSC	8311/26
D9535	NCB	9312/59
D9536	NCB	9312/91
D9537	BSC	8311/32
D9538	Shell Mex	160
D9539	NCB	8311/30
D9540	NCB	2233/508
D9541	BSC	8411/26
D9542	BSC	8311/27
D9544	BSC	8311/11
D9545	NCB	9312/101
D9547	BSC	8311/28
D9548	BSC	8411/27
D9549	BSC	8311/33
D9551	BSC	8311/29
D9552	BSC	8411/21

D9553	BSC	8311/34
D9554	BSC	8311/38
D9555	NCB	9107/57

NOTES

D9505 was exported in 5/75 to Belgium and scrapped in 1999.

D9515/48/49 were moved to Hunslet, Leeds and regauged for 5ft 6in track in 12/81 and exported 6/82. Moved to various sites in Spain and D9515/48 understood to have been scrapped 10/02 and D9549 in 1999.

D9530 was sold by Gulf Oil to NCB 10/75 for use at Mardy Colliery.

D9534 was exported to Belgium 5/75. Resold 5/76 to Brescia, Italy. Understood to have been scrapped 10/05.

D9538 was used as a depot shunter at Cardiff Canton 3/70. Sold to Shell Mex 4/70 and planned to be fitted with flame-proofing, but this was too costly, and it was resold to BSC Ebbw Vale. Moved to Corby 4/76 for spares.

D9544 is not thought to have worked for BSC, and was used for spares for the fleet; D9545 likewise for the NCB.

RIGHT: *D9551 is now preserved, but spent a spell in industrial use, during which time it gained nose-end dual headlights; otherwise it still has an as-built look, albeit missing its BR emblems.* PIP DUNN

BELOW: *Class 14s sold to industry and then preservation have appeared in different liveries. D9523 sports the maroon livery applied by BR to some Class 42s and 52s, as well as a cast Class 52-style numberplate. The loco is also dual braked, as signified by the red-capped pipe on the right of the drawhook.* PIP DUNN

specifications

1957 BR number range:	D8200–43
Former class codes:	D8/1, later 8/5
Built by:	Yorkshire Eng. Co & BTH Ltd
Introduced:	1957–61
Wheel arrangement:	Bo-Bo
Weight (operational):	68 tons
Height:	12ft 6in (3.81m)
Width:	9ft 2in (2.79m)
Length:	42ft (21.3m)
Min. curve negotiable:	3½ chains
Maximum speed:	60mph (96km/h)
Wheelbase:	31ft (9.45m)
Bogie wheelbase:	8ft 6in (2.59m)
Bogie pivot centres:	22ft 6in (6.86m)
Wheel diameter:	3ft 3in (0.99m)
Route availability:	4
Brake force:	31 tons
Engine type:	Paxman 16YHXL
Engine horsepower:	800bhp (597kW)
Power at rail:	627bhp (468kW)
Tractive effort:	37,500lb
Main generator type:	BTH RTB10858
Auxiliary generator type:	BTH RTB7420
No. of traction motors:	4
Traction motor type:	BTH 137AZ
Gear ratio:	65:16
Fuel tank capacity:	400gal (1,800ltr)

ABOVE: 8207 in 1970 shows a Class 15 in final BR guise, in green with full yellow ends. It retains its through-steam pipe hose next to the Blue Star MW. The loco has headcode discs. RAIL PHOTOPRINTS
BELOW: One of the four Class 15s converted to static ETH generators for pre-heating trains, ADB968001. The ETH jumper can be seen on the right hand of the bufferbeam, and the receptacle to the right of the left-hand buffer. This loco was the former D8233 and the only surviving Class 15, currently undergoing restoration. PDC

ANOTHER CLASS WHICH showed few detail differences in its short BR career. All were delivered in BR green, all later had small yellow panels added, and some later had full yellow ends.

Some had BR double arrows, although none were ever repainted into BR blue. All had steam pipes from new, but some lost these.

The major change affected the four locos converted to ETH generators, which had ETH jumpers fitted and were renumbered.

All were withdrawn by 1971 after working solely on the Eastern region.

DETAIL DIFFERENCES

All had disc headcodes. Snowplough brackets were not fitted, nor were headlights. The four locos which had ETH cables fitted had them in place of multiple working cables. Of these, D8237 (968002) also had additional ETH boxes mounted on its nose front.

LIVERIES

All were new in all-over BR green with red bufferbeams. Small yellow warning panels were applied to all locos, while full yellow panels were applied to D8200/ 01/03–05/07/09–11/13–22/24–29/31/ 34–37/39/40/43 and ADB968003.

Number styles varied. The serif style was used from new, but some had these with the D prefix dropped (8221), while others had corporate-style numbers, some with D prefixes (D8213/29/34), some without (8229).

D8200/02 had large white numbers on the nose ends above the small yellow panels.

8213/26/28/29/31/34–36/38/40/42/ 43 all had BR double arrows in BR green, and these varied in size. D8243, as ADB968000, was repainted in all-over lime green with full yellow ends.

BR green: 8200–43
BR green with small yellow panels: 8200–43
BR green with full yellow ends: D8200/ 01/03–05/07/09–11/13–22/24–29/31/ 34–37/39/40/43, ADB968003

BUILD BATCHES

D8200–09 were the first batch, part of the modernization plan pilot scheme. They were ordered in 1955 and delivered 1957–58. D8210–43 were ordered in 1958 and delivered in 1959–61.

RENUMBERINGS

None were numbered under TOPS, but 8203/33/37/43 were taken into Departmental use and became ADB986003/ 001/002/000 respectively.

class 16

ANOTHER PILOT SCHEME batch, similar to the Class 15 in design and using the same engine. No repeat orders for this batch of ten locos from the North British Glasgow factory were received, hence detail differences between the class were restricted to liveries.

DETAIL DIFFERENCES

All had disc headcodes, but snowplough brackets were not fitted, neither were headlights.

LIVERIES

All were new in all-over BR green with red bufferbeams. Small yellow warning panels were applied to all locos, while full yellow panels were known to have been applied to at least D8400–03/06–08. D8404/09 may have been likewise, but this is unconfirmed. D8405 was scrapped with small yellow panels. D8408 had square yellow panels for a period. D8403 had BR double arrows applied.

BR green: D8400–09
BR green with small yellow panels: D8400–09
BR green with full yellow ends: D8402/03/06/07

BUILD BATCHES

D8400–09 was the only batch, as part of the modernization plan pilot scheme. They were ordered in 1955 and delivered in 1958, and withdrawn by 1969.

8207 in 1970 shows a Class 15 in final BR guise, in green with full yellow ends. It retains its through-steam pipe hose next to the Blue Star MW. The loco has headcode discs.
RAIL PHOTOPRINTS

specifications

1957 BR number range:	D8400–09
Former class codes:	D8/2, later 8/4
Built by:	NBL Ltd
Introduced:	1958
Wheel arrangement:	Bo-Bo
Weight (operational):	68 tons
Height:	12ft 6in (3.81m)
Width:	8ft 9in (2.67)
Length:	42ft 6in
Min. curve negotiable:	3½ chains
Maximum speed:	60mph (96km/h)
Wheelbase:	28ft 6in (12.95m)
Bogie wheelbase:	8ft 6in (2.59m)
Bogie pivot centres:	20ft (6.1m)
Wheel diameter:	3ft 7in (1.09m)
Route availability:	4
Brake force:	42 tons
Engine type:	Paxman 16YHXL
Engine horsepower:	800bhp (597kW)
Power at rail:	627bhp (468kW)
Tractive effort:	42,000lb
Main generator type:	GEC WT881
Auxiliary generator type:	GEC
No. of traction motors:	4
Traction motor type:	GEC WT441
Gear ratio:	75:15
Fuel tank capacity:	400gal (1,800ltr)

class 17

specifications

AFTER CONCERN OVER the visibility of other Type 1 designs, when the locos were being driven bonnet leading, BR chose to look at a replacement from Clayton featuring a cavernous central cab with two low bonnets, each housing a Paxman engine: the Class 17. Sadly it ordered 117 locos without testing a prototype, and ultimately they proved woefully unreliable, so much so that 100 more EE Type 1s were ordered: the Class 17s were all laid up by 1971, less than a decade after the first loco had appeared. One was sold for industrial use and has since been preserved.

DETAIL DIFFERENCES

All had centre-panel headcodes. All had snowplough brackets, and locos noted with three-piece snowploughs were D8505/30/41/43/57/65/71/74/80/81/87/

1957 BR number range:	D8500–616
Former class codes:	D8500–87, 9/18
	D8588–616, 9/19
Built by:	D8500–87 Clayton D8588–616 Beyer Peacock
Introduced:	1962–65
Wheel arrangement:	Bo-Bo
Weight (operational):	68 tons
Height:	12ft 8in (3.86m)
Width:	8ft 10in (2.69m)
Length:	50ft 7in (15.42m)
Min. curve negotiable:	3½ chains
Maximum speed:	60mph (96km/h)
Wheelbase:	36ft 6in (11.12m)
Bogie wheelbase:	8ft 6in (2.59m)
Bogie pivot centres:	28ft (8.53m)
Wheel diameter:	3ft 4in (1m)

Brake force:	35 tons
Engine type:	D8500–85/88–616: two Paxman 6ZHXL
	D8586/87: two Rolls-Royce D
Engine horsepower (total):	900bhp (671kW)
Power at rail:	602bhp (448kW)
Tractive effort:	40,000lb
Main generator type:	D8500–87: GEC WT800 D8588–616: Crompton Parkinson
Auxiliary generator type:	D8500–87: GEC WT D8588–616: Crompton Parkinson
No. of traction motors:	4
Gear ratio:	66:15 (17/1, 17/2); 81:13 (17/3)
Traction motor type:	GEC WT421
Fuel tank capacity:	500gal (2,250ltr)

23

91, 8601/06–08/16, but others may have carried them. Some ran with only one or two parts of their snowploughs from time to time. All had Red Diamond multiple working from new, but many were converted to Blue Star. D8586/87 had raised bonnets to accommodate the larger Rolls-Royce engines.

LIVERIES

All were delivered in BR green with half yellow panels, red bufferbeams and lighter green cabs. D8502/04/06/08/15/28/30/36/39/46/48/49/51/52/58/59/61–63/72/79/81/86/89/92–94/97/98,8601/02/04/07/08/10/12–16 all had full yellow nose ends applied. BR blue was applied to D8500–03/07/10/12–15/20–27/29/32/34/35/38/40/42/43/45/50/51/56/57/64–67/71/73/74/77/80/82–85/98,8606.

D8568 was painted in Castle Cement grey in 1977, while D8512 was painted in all-over BR blue with no yellow panels when in departmental use.

BR green with small yellow panels: 8500–99, 8600–16

BR green with full yellow ends: 8502/04/06/08/15/28/30/36/39/46/48/49/51/52/58/59/61–63/72/79/81/86/89/92–94/97/98, 8601/02/04/07/08/10/12–16

BR blue: 8500–03/07/10/12–15/20–27/29/32/34/35/38/40/42/43/45/50/51/56/57/64–67/71/73/74/77/80/82–85/98, 8606.

BUILD BATCHES

The first eighty-eight were ordered in April 1961, with delivery starting in 1962. The last two of this batch were fitted with Rolls-Royce engines so became Class 17/2s, the first eighty-six being Class 17/1. A second batch, D8588–8616, was ordered in July 1962 – the same time that D8500 was being unveiled. These were built by Beyer Peacock and became the Class 17/3s. The delivery of the first 17/3 was in March 1964, so before the last of the first batch of locos, May 1964 for D8585 and February 1965 for D8587.

NUMBERS

None was renumbered under TOPS, but two were renumbered as part of an extended role in Departmental use, D8521/98 becoming S18521/98.

THESE SINGLE-CAB LOCOS became BR's standard Type 1 freight design, built over several batches, the first twenty as part of the pilot scheme programme. 228 were delivered between 1957–62 and 1966–8.

They were based on the ScR, LMR, ER and NER, and because of concerns when running bonnet-leading had to be double-manned when running solo; however, usually the locos are found operating in pairs, nose to nose.

The Class 20s have proved very reliable, and a handful are still in traffic today with many operators, including main-line registered locos with DRS and GB Railfreight.

DETAIL DIFFERENCES

The locos had no train heating, but D8000–127 had through-steam pipes from new, which remained until dual braking, although the bufferbeam hoses were removed from the late 1970s. Sometimes a blanking plate was fitted over the end of the pipe. 20052 still had its pipe as late as 1978. In 1983 20045/085 had them refitted for a short period.

All disc locos initially had ladders fitted to the bodyside at their nose ends, but these were soon removed.

MW was Blue Star, although the DRS Class 20/3s had the unique DRS system of MW. Of these, 20311/314 have been modified to run using Blue Star. 20131 ran in traffic with no multiple working at the cab end in 1982. Others ran for short periods with either a jumper or the receptacle missing.

D8000–199, D8300–16 were vacuum-braked from new, D8317–27 were dual-braked from new. All were later dual-braked apart from 20003/012/014/017/018/024/027/033/038/074/079/091, 20109. The 20/3s, 20/9s and 20056/066, 20168 have been converted to air brakes only.

Westinghouse brake pipes were fitted to D8085/86, which meant two additional pipes aside of the drawhook. These were removed in the early 1970s.

Dual-brake dates: 8002/11/15/36/39/83, 8111/14/15/22/37/38/44–46/49/50/52–56/62/64/65/67/74/75/91 (1971); 8179/84 (1972); 20116/123, 20216 (1974); 20009/035/062/064/076/089, 20118/

ABOVE: In as-built condition, D8028 sports all-over BR green with a red bufferbeam. It features the bodyside ladder fitted to early Class 20s as well as snowploughs and a tablet catcher. The ladders were soon removed as a result of concerns about staff climbing on locos as more high-voltage overhead power lines were built for the railway. PDC

LEFT: Immaculate despite being three years old, in July 1965 D8123 shows an as-built Scottish Region Class 20. The MW is angled on the bufferbeam and it retains a through-steam pipe and connecting hose. It has a tablet catcher recess, with no tablet fitted; only D8028–034 ever ran with the equipment fitted. BILL WRIGHT

specifications

TOPS number range:	20001–228, 20301–308, 20301–315, 20901–906
1957 BR number range:	D8000–D8199, D8300–D8327
Former class codes:	D10/3, then 10/3
Built by:	English Electric Vulcan Foundry (D8000–19/35–49/128–199, 8300–27) or Robert Stephenson & Hawthorns (D8020–34/50–127)
Years introduced:	1957–68 1986 (20301–308) 1995–98 (20301–315) 1989 (20901–906)
Wheel arrangement:	Bo-Bo
Weight:	73 tons
Height:	12ft 8in (3.86m)
Length:	46ft 9in (14.26m)
Width:	8ft 9in (2.66m)
Wheelbase:	32ft 6in (9.90m)
Bogie wheelbase:	8ft 6in (2.59m)
Bogie pivot centres:	24ft (7.31m)
Wheel diameter:	3ft 7in (1.09m)
Min. curve negotiable:	3½ chains (70.40m)
Engine type:	English Electric 8SVT Mk 2
Engine output:	1,000bhp (746kW)
Power at rail:	770bhp (574kW)
Tractive effort:	42,000lb
Maximum speed:	75mph (120km/h)
Brake force:	35 tons
Route availability:	5 (6 – 20306–315)
Main generator type:	EE819-3C
Auxiliary generator type:	EE911-2B
Traction motor type:	EE526/5D (D8000–49), 526/8D (D8050–199, D8300–27)
No. of traction motors:	4
Gear ratio:	63:17
Fuel tank capacity:	380gal (1,727ltr), 640gal (2,909ltr): 20301–305; 1,090gal (4,909ltr): 20306–315; 1,040gal (4,727ltr): 20084, 20902/903/905

ABOVE LEFT: Built with vacuum brakes but converted to dual brakes, 20025 shows off the nose end of a production series Class 20 built for English depots. On the right, the MW jumper is fixed halfway up the side of the bufferbeam, however on Scottish locos and on those from the headcode box batch, this was moved to the top right of the bufferbeam. The loco does not have snowplough brackets. ANDY HOARE

ABOVE RIGHT: Aside from the livery change, vacuum-braked 20058, seen in 1981, is essentially in as-built condition. It has had its through-steam pipe removed, the hole of which can be seen to the right of the drawhook. Its loco control and main reservoir pipes remain under the bufferstocks. When the loco was dual-braked, these were moved in between the bufferstocks and the MW equipment. ANDY HOARE

124/125 (1975); 20066/086, 20201/203 (1976); 20200/202/204–207 (1977); 20069/ 097, 20127/139/148/171/198/199 (1982); 20004/008/016/019/022/025/026/029– 031/037/041–044/046/048/049/054/ 055/061/063/065/067/068/070/072/088/ 092–096/098, 0100/102/107/110/112/ 113/119/121/126/129/140/143/160/166/ 176/181/182/189/192/193, 20208/211/ 212/228 (1983); 20001/005–007/013/ 021/028/032/034/040/045/047/051– 053/056–058/060/071/073/075/078/ 080–082/085/087/099, 20101/103/105/ 106/117/120/128/130/131/133–136/ 142/151/157–159/161/168/172/173/ 177/178/180/183/186/188/190/194–197, 20209/210/213/214 (1984); 20010/020/ 023/059/077/084/090, 0104/108/132/ 141/163/169/170/185/187, 20215 (1985).

Several 20s have lost their vacuum brakes, namely 20041/060/083, 20101, 20219/225, when converted to 20/9s in 1989, 20035/063, 20139, 20228 when overhauled for CFD in 1992, 20047/ 084/095, 20120/127 in 1995 when converted to 20/3s followed by 20042/075, 20102/104/117/128/131/187/190/194 in 1998.

20056/066, 20168 had their vacuum-brake exhausters isolated and their vacuum pipes removed – essentially making them air only – when overhauled by HNRC for industrial use in 2007 (20056/066) and 2004 (20168). They would be relatively easy to return to dual-brake operation, if so required by the operator.

SNOWPLOUGHS

D8028–34/70–199, D8300–27 had snowplough brackets. Usually ploughs were only fitted at the cab end, except in Scotland where they were often fitted at both ends. As a rule all three pieces were fitted, but some had the centre plough removed for ease of coupling. Others have been in traffic with just one or two parts of the three-piece set. Noted with ploughs have been 20028/ 031–034/071/073/075/079/080/083/ 084/086/088/089/094/096/099, 20100/ 101/104/110/111/113/114/116/117/121/ 123/125–127/129/131/134/135/137–139/ 141/143/146/148/149/151/152/154/ 156/159/160/161/166/169–171/175– 177/179/186–195/197/199, 20202/203/ 208/209/214/216/222/226–228, DRS 20303–305, 20901/905.

HEADCODES

Discs were fitted to D8000–127. Several had these removed, usually at overhaul. Those with discs removed were 20001*/ 008*/010/016/047/052*/071/075/076*/ 082/084/087/090/096*, 20104/113/117*/ 122. Those with three missing discs were 20073*, 20901*/902* while locos with just one missing disc were 20061*/094* (* at cab end only.)

Centre panels were fitted to D8128– 199, D8300–27. These were changed to dominos from the mid-1970s. 20133/158 ran with dominos while still in BR green.

Some had their nose-end panels removed. Those with indented marker lights were 20163/170, while 20228 had two protruding white side lights, and 20203 had a yellow-painted metal headcode plate (in the same style as Class 37s and 55s). 20132 had a black-painted metal headcode plate at No. 2 end.

In industrial use, 20168 now has yellow headcode plates at both ends, while HNRC's 20905 has this feature at No. 1 end only.

20139, 20228 and 20906 lost their cab-end headcode panels when overhauled for CFD or Lafarge.

HEADLIGHTS

High intensity headlights were fitted at No. 2 end to 20007/075/092/096, 20102/ 107/110/118/127/128/131/132/142/154/ 169/179/184/187/189/192/193/198/199, 20201–204/208/213/217–223/225–227, 20901–906, and to No. 1 end on 20007/ 075/092/096, 20107/118/128/131/132/ 142/169/187/189, 20219/227, 20901– 906.

Bmac lights were fitted to DRS's 20301–315, and more recently to HNRC's 20056/066, 20906.

LIVERIES

D8000–177 were delivered in all-over BR green, with small yellow panels applied from new to D8110–77, and retro applied to the rest of the fleet. D8178–

99, D8300–27 were new in BR blue with full yellow ends.

Several had full yellow ends on green. All later went to blue except 20014. Some Scottish locos, when repainted into BR blue, did not have the wrap-around yellow nose – at least 8080/93/95, 8100/110/117 were so noted in the late 1960s.

In 1985 Railfreight livery appeared for the first time, and in 1988 two-tone grey (without Trainload Coal logos) was applied to 20088, a livery that 20031/096, 20901/905 have since carried in private ownership.

Hunslet Barclay grey appeared on the 20/9s from 1989, while two were painted in Central Services livery in 1993 and four in BRT grey.

BR green: D8000–109
BR green with small yellow panel: D8000–177 (D8110–77 from new)
BR green with full yellow ends: D8002/04/05/09/12–29/31/33/35/37/45–47/56–59/63/64/69/74/75/80, 8128–33/37/38/40/41/44–47/49–56/58/59/62–65/67–77
BR blue: 20001–013/015–228
BR blue with white cab roofs: 20122/172/173

BR blue with red solebar: 20028/055/070, 20106/172–174
BR blue with red solebar and white cab roofs: 20028/070, 20172/173
BR blue with red cab: 20160
Red stripe Railfreight: 20010/023/059/077/090, 20104/108/118/122/132/137/138/141/156/163/165/170/175, 20215/227
Red stripe Railfreight (no logos): 20118/132/137/165
Two-tone grey (BR): 20088
Two-tone grey (HNRC): 20096, 20901/905
Two-tone grey (preserved): 20031
Hunslet Barclay grey: 20901–906
Central Services: 20092, 20169
RFS grey: 20001/047/048/056/084/088/095, 20102/105/107/108/113/120/127/133/145/159/166/175/194
RMS Locotec grey: 20107
DRS blue with grey bonnet roof: 20301–305
DRS blue with black bonnet roof: 20306–315, 20905
DRS Compass: 20301–305/308/309/312/314
DRS blue (unbranded): 20301/302/304/305
DRS blue with red solebar: 20901–904/906
CFD orange: 20035/063, 20139, 20228
BR blue with BRT logos: 20075, 20128/131/187
BRT grey: 20075, 20128/131/187
Blue Circle Cement: 20168
Lafarge white/green: 20168
Corus yellow: 20056/066
Tata blue: 20066
Waterman Railways: 20042, 20188
MC Metals grey: 20189

A comparison picture of the different ends of Class 20s. On the left is dual-braked 20175, while on the right is 20218, one of eleven Class 20s built with dual brakes. These eleven locos, 20217–227, were noticeable by the metal patch on their cab fronts. They also had a similar patch on the other side of the cab on the right-hand side under the window. This panel was to provide access to the myriad of pipe connections on the bottom of the train brake controller underneath the driver's desk. Note the angled positioning of the MW jumpers, a feature on both Scottish 20s and centre-panel 20s. ANDY HOARE

ABOVE LEFT: *A comparison picture of the two cab window styles on the Class 20s, taken in February 1989: 20044 has the smaller windows and the original position of the MW jumper, while 20112, originally a Scottish loco, has deeper windows and the MW jumper mounted higher up, on the bottom of the cab. 20044 has St Rollox numbers, 20112 has standard size numbers.* PDC
ABOVE RIGHT: *20071 has the Scottish bufferbeam layout, hence its ability to sport a full set of snowploughs. It has had its headcode discs removed.* PDC

Tinsley green: 20030/064
Tinsley green (preserved): 20110/166
Metropolitan Railway maroon: 20227
Dark blue: 20205
BR green half yellow panels (preserved only): 20189, 20214
Russian black: 20188
GB Railfreight: 20901/905
Lafarge white: 20906
London Underground red: 20189
London Underground white: 20227

NUMBERS AND BADGES

All had their numbers under the cabsides, either below or above a BR badge, and from the 1980s, with the BR badge moved to the bodyside. There was no rule, and the different styles of badges, be they small or large, under or above the numbers, varied.

Bodyside numbers were applied in the early 1970s to 8034/41/90/99/100/102/112/117, 20032/041/058/081.

The incorrect serif font in BR blue on the cabside was on 8001/10/11/77/95, 8127, 20039, 20116, while the incorrect serif font in BR blue on the bodyside was applied to 8034/76, 8112.

Larger 8in numbers were applied from the late 1970s, mainly to locos overhauled at Glasgow Works, to 20004/006/007/013/019/020/025/028/037/040/043–045/049/059/063/067/069/070/076/078/080/081/083/085/086/089/092/095–099, 20100–106/110/111/114/117/119–121/124/126–128/130/139/144/146/148/149/169/171/179/184/187/189/197–199, 20201–206/210–219/221–226.

Large bodyside numbers were applied by Thornaby to 20008, 20172, while front-end TOPS numbers were also on 20118/165/172/173.

Front-end three-digit numbers were unofficially applied to 20053, 20169, while 20090 had 90 on its cab front in small black numbers for a short period in the early 1990s. Three-digit 088 numbers were applied to 20088 when painted in two-tone grey.

20170/175 had small cabside numbers (the former just had the 170 part of its number small and on one side only) while in Railfreight grey.

THE DIFFERENT BATCHES

There were four main batches of Class 20s. The first comprised the twenty pilot scheme locos, D8000–19, which had oval

buffers from new, although some, but not all, were changed to round variants. All had through-steam pipes.

The next batch was D8020–27/35–69 built for English depots, and these followed the same bufferbeam style as the pilot scheme locos, with main reservoir and loco air-control pipes below the bufferstocks.

D8028–34/70–127 were built for Scottish depots and differed by having deeper side windows, recesses in the cabside for fitting to token catching equipment, snowplough brackets, and a revised layout of bufferbeam pipes. The multiple working was angled on the bufferbeam with the jumper head mounted on the cab front as opposed to the right of the right-hand bufferstock. The loco air control and main reservoir pipes were moved to the sides of the snowplough brackets, which flanked the drawhook.

The fourth batch was D8128–99, D8300–27 which, as well as having headcode panels, also had the Scottish style

of bufferbeam layout – with snowplough brackets – but the English-style shallower windows. They had no tablet recesses and no through-steam pipes.

CABSIDE CHANGES

After collisions, 20115/122 had their deep windows changed to standard size. When dual-braked, some of the 'English' locos had their main reservoir and loco air control pipes moved to the side of the bufferstocks as opposed to underneath them, but the MW jumpers remained as they were. These locos also lost their steam pipes when dual-braked.

From new, D8317–27 had large rectangular metal plates on their front cabs and to the below right of the headcode panels, and a similar panel on the other side of the cab below the small vertical window on the right-hand side. This panel was to provide access to the pipes on the bottom of the train-brake controller underneath the driver's desk.

20172 shows the results after a visit from Thornaby depot's painters: a red solebar, large bodyside numbers, a white cab roof, a kingfisher emblem and an unofficial name, Redmire. The cabside numbers were later removed, while other locos had coloured kingfisher emblems. PDC

Fifteen Class 20s were refurbished for DRS in three batches. The first five locos were done by Brush and were restricted to 60mph (96km/h), the next six and final four were overhauled by Wabtec and still capable of 75mph (120km/h). On the right, 20305, in original DRS livery, stands next to 20314. The first five 20/3s did not have the MW receptacle on their cabs, but this was modified, and can clearly be seen as an addition to 20305. PIP DUNN

ABOVE LEFT: 20163 sports Railfreight grey livery and has had its headcode box removed at No. 1 end and two marker lights indented into the nose end, one of only two Class 20s to look like this. PDC

ABOVE RIGHT: Four Class 20s were sold to private French operator Chemins de Fer Départmentaux and overhauled in 1992. They featured new light clusters, had lost their vacuum brakes and headcodes, and had their MW jumpers repositioned on the right-hand side. All later returned to the UK, and one has been scrapped. 2004, formerly 20228, shows the new look in August 1998. PIP DUNN

When overhauled for Corus steel in 2006, HNRC's 20056/066 had windows fitted to their cab doors; 20906, for use with Lafarge, is likewise.

Tablet recesses were plated over in the 1970s, although at least 20028–034/ 070–074/076–078/080/081/083/085/088/ 090/091/093/095/097/098/20100–105/ 107/108/113/117/119/123/125/127 had tablet recesses when in BR blue, while 20075 had them with TOPS numbers in BR green.

OTHER DETAIL DIFFERENCES

Extra side-mounted saddle fuel tanks were fitted to 20084 in 1985 and later to Hunslet 20902/903/905 and DRS 20301–315.

When new, D8000–05 did not have the vertical curved handrails on the cab ends, but these were soon retro-fitted. They were missing off 20096 and 20123 for periods, and partly missing from 20052.

At No. 1 end, all locos had two vertical grab poles above the bufferbeam, but on 20011/015/032/072, 20216–228 these differed by being two horizontal grab handles fitted on to the bufferbeam.

In 1987, 20114/127/138 were fitted with RETB for working on the West Highland lines, and with a large aerial on their nose ends. When their WHL role ended, these were removed, but 20138 kept the arm of the aerial for a period thereafter.

EMBLEMS

Emblems were on the nose-end bonnet doors, although 20145 (dog) and 20186

(salmon), after door swaps, had them midway along the body. Door swapping by maintenance staff also led to some Railfreight locos having BR blue doors and vice versa.

Small West Highland terrier: 20007/ 009/015/022/035/037/039/042–044/ 048/063/064/067/069/076/083/086/ 089/095/097, 20100–102/110/111/114– 116/118/119/122/125–127/137–139/ 144–146/148/149/151/152/154/156/ 171/175/179/181/184/189/191–193/ 198/199, 20201–206/208/211–213/216– 218/226/228 B; 20138 FR

White castles: 20009/029/080/093, 20148/149, 20203–206/208/211–213/216 –226 B; 20227 FR

Red castles: 20069 B

Salmon: 20020/048, 20122–126/171/ 179/186 B; 20122 FR

White kingfishers: 20028/070, 20172– 174 B; 20122/137/165 FR

Coloured kingfishers: 20008/070, 20119/144/174 B; 20118/122/137/156/ 165 FR

Yellow DCE stripes: 20005/029/032/ 034/042/048/054/063/070/072/086/ 099, 20124/147/160/176/195, 20217 B

Grey MEE stripes: 20146, 20204 B

RFS roundels: 20087 B; 20138 FR

RENUMBERINGS

D8000 became 20050, D8001–049 became 20001–049 (to keep the batch with 526-5D traction motors together). D8050 became 20128, D8051–127 became 20051–127, D8128 became 20228 and D8129–199, D8300–27 became 20129–227.

In 1986 eight locos were renumbered in the 20/3 series by BR because of modified brake valves for working Tunstead limestone trains. They reverted to their original identities later in 1986/87. Six were renumbered in the 20/9 series for weedkilling trains with Hunslet Barclay in 1989.

DRS chose the 20/3 series for its fleet of refurbished locos, which were modified in their different batches – 20301– 305 at Brush Loughborough, 20306–311 at Wabtec Doncaster, and 20312–315 also at Wabtec Doncaster.

20023	20301[1]
20059	20302[1]
20134	20303[1]
20168	20304[1]
20172	20305[1]
20173	20306[1]
20194	20307[1]
20196	20308[1]
20041	20904[2]
20060	20902[2]
20083	20903[2]
20101	20901[2]
20219	20906[2]
20225	20905[2]
20042	20312[3]
20047	20301[3]
20075	20309[3]
20084	20302[3]
20095	20305[3]
20102	20311[3]
20104	20315[3]
20117	20313[3]
20120	20304[3]
20127	20303[3]

RFS provided twenty Class 20s, fifteen of its own and five hired from preservation groups, for working the trains which laid the track in the Channel Tunnel. All were repainted in RFS grey. The locos were modified by having headlights on their cab and nose roofs, and exhaust scrubbers to contain exhaust emissions when working in the Tunnel. These have been removed in this 1993 view of 2014 (20048) and 2011 (20001). PIP DUNN

Six Class 20s were converted to 20/9s after sale to Hunslet Barclay for use on weedkilling trains. 20902 shows off its saddle fuel tanks to give it an extended range between refuelling. It has the standard BR high-intensity headlight fitted under the headcode. The bottom three discs have been removed, but the top one is retained. PIP DUNN

20128	20307[3]	20108	2001[4]	20107	HO10[6]
20131	20306[3]	20113	2003[4]		
20187	20308[3]	20120	2009[4]	20056	81[7]
20190	20310[3]	20127	2018[4]	20066	82[7]
20194	20314[3]	20133	2005[4]		
		20145	2019[4]	20219	3[8]
20001	2011[4]	20159	2010[4]		
20047	2004[4]	20166	2015[4]	
20048	2014[4]	20175	2007[4]	
20056	2012[4]	20194	2006[4]	
20084	2002[4]			
20088	2017[4]	20035	2001[5]	
20095	2020[4]	20063	2002[5]	
20102	2008[4]	20139	2003[5]	
20107	2013[4]	20228	2004[5]	
20105	2016[4]			

[1] Class 20/3 conversion by BR – modified brake valves
[2] Class 20/3 conversion for DRS – refurbished locos
[3] Class 20/9 conversion for Hunslet Barclay for weedkilling trains
[4] RFS locos for Channel Tunnel tracklaying
[5] CFD (France) locos
[6] RMS Locotec
[7] Corus/Tata Steel
[8] Lafarge

NAMES

20028	*Bedale*[+]
20030	*RIVER SHEAF*[+]
20064	*RIVER ROTHER*[+]
20070	*Leyburn*[+]
20075	*Sir William Cooke*
20118	*RIVER DON*[+]
20118	*Saltburn-by-the-Sea*
20122	*Cleveland Potash*
20128	*Guglielmo Marconi*
20131	*Almon B. Strowger*
20132	*Barrow Hill Depot*
20137	*Murray B. Hofmeyr*
20165	*Henry Pease*
20168	*Sir George Earle*
20172	*Redmire*[+]
20173	*Wensleydale*[+]

After Hunslet Barclay 20s ceased working weedkilling trains, they were all sold to DRS, which overhauled them and returned them to traffic. 20905 was the last to be treated, although despite being reactivated did not go on to work for DRS and was part of a deal which saw all six 20/9s sold to HNRC. In July 2003, 20905 shows off its DRS livery. The loco has a domino headcode, a standard BR high intensity headlight and saddle fuel tanks. It is now air-braked only. PIP DUNN

LEFT: 20901 was originally 20101, and apart from the livery is very much in original as-built condition. Modifications have been the loss of its vacuum brakes and removal of its centre bottom disc to allow space to fit the headlight. Some ScR 20s had these headlights fitted by BR and saw this disc and lamp removed and the headlight fitted centrally in its place. 20901 is in the first style of DRS livery but with a red solebar. The loco remains in traffic with GBRf, although is owned by HNRC. PIP DUNN

RIGHT: HNRC's 20168 Sir George Earle *is on long-term hire to Lafarge. Initially it was painted in Blue Circle yellow, white and blue, but in June 2008 it was repainted into Lafarge green and white. It also has its headcode panels plated over and white LED marker lights fitted at both ends. It has a camera on its nose end to allow single manning when being driven bonnet first. Another modification, not visible here, is the fitting of a silencer to drown out the familiar whistling nose. The loco is also air-braked only.* ANTHONY HICKS

20187	*Sir Charles Wheatstone*	
20301	*Max Joule 1958–99*	
20305	*Gresty Bridge*	
20310	*Gresty Bridge*	
20311	*Class 20 'Fifty'*	
20901	*NANCY*	
20902	*LORNA*	
20903	*ALISON*	
20904	*JANIS*	
20905	*IONA*	
20906	*GEORGINA*	
20906	*KILMARNOCK 400*	

⁺ unofficial painted named. 20301 also carried a plaque *Furness Railway 150*

REFURBISHMENT

RFS: RFS acquired twenty Class 20s for a contract to provide traction to CTTG, which laid the track for the Channel Tunnel in 1992/93. They were given light overhauls, but the only changes were the fitting of square spotlamps on the nose and cab ends, and 'scrubbers' on their roofs so the exhaust fumes were transferred into tanks on wagons and not emitted in the tunnel. All were painted in RFS grey.

CFD: 20035/063, 20139, 20228 were sold to French operator Chemins de Fer Départementaux in 1992 and overhauled at Crewe. Modifications included removal of the vacuum brakes, removal of headcodes – discs or boxes – at both ends, the fitting of French Railway light clusters, and moving the multiple working jumper cabs on the buffer-beam.

Renumbered 2001–2004, 2003/04 were recognizable as former headcode box locos at No. 2 end, as the top lip that had surrounded the headcodes remained. All were painted in orange, white and turquoise livery. They worked in France for a decade, but in 2005 all returned to the UK.

DRS: The first five DRS Class 20/3s differed very visibly. The vacuum brakes were removed, leaving a hole on the bufferbeam, as was the Blue Star MW. Cabs and nose ends were 'shaved', with the headcodes, handrails, marker lights and headlights removed. In their place were Bmac light clusters above the bufferbeams, and new aluminium window frames. A cab-to-shore radio pod was fitted in a frame on to the curved cab roof.

On the nose end, a MW jumper socket was fitted in the middle of the nose. The second batch of ten locos also had a multiple working jumper cable on the cab front plus an additional headlight fitted at the top of the cab, in between the windows. These features were retro-fitted to 20301–305.

On the cabsides, the windows were replaced by new, square-cornered windows, which were all the same size regardless of the size of the windows on the locos before refurbishment. In more recent times, aerials have been added on the cab fronts above the left-hand window.

HNRC: The refurbished HNRC 20s for industrial use have seen a number of changes. 20168 was modified for use by Lafarge in 2004. It was fitted with a nose-end camera to allow single manning when running nose first. It was also fitted with an engine silencer to reduce the noise. Initially painted in Blue Circle Cement livery, it has since been repainted into Lafarge livery and now has its domino headcodes replaced by yellow panels with white LED lamps.

20056/066 were prepared for Corus and had their discs removed (but the BR tail-lights retained); they have had new light clusters fitted under the cab windows and on the nose ends, and have roof-mounted flashing orange lights and nose-end cameras. The cab doors have had windows fitted, the vertical cab-front handrails were removed, and 20066 has slightly larger cabside windows.

20906 has also been prepared for Lafarge and has lost its headcode boxes for flush ends, and Bmac lights have been fitted. It has oval buffers, enhanced footsteps for accessing the cab, and dual cab handles, with a duplicate set at the bottom of the door.

class 21

1957 BR number range:	D6100–57
Former class codes:	As built – D11/2, later 11/4 De-rated – D10/1, later 10/4
Built by:	NBL Ltd
Introduced:	1958–60
Wheel arrangement:	Bo-Bo
Weight (operational):	73 tons
Height:	12ft 7in (3.84m)
Width:	8ft 8in (2.64m)
Length:	51ft 6in (15.69m)
Min. curve negotiable:	4½ chains
Maximum speed:	75mph (120km/h)
Wheelbase:	37ft (11.28m)
Bogie wheelbase:	8ft 6in (2.59m)
Bogie pivot centres:	28ft 6in (8.69m)
Wheel diameter:	3ft 7in (1.09m)
Route availability:	5
Brake force:	42 tons
Engine type:	NBL/MAN L12V18/21
Engine horsepower:	Original: 1,000bhp (746kW): D6100–09 Modified: 1,100bhp (821kW): D6110–57
Power at rail:	Original: 816bhp (609kW): D6100–09 Modified: 890bhp (664kW): D6110–57
Tractive effort:	45,000lb
Main generator type:	EE WT880
Auxiliary generator type:	EE WT761
No. of traction motors:	4
Traction motor type:	EE WT440
Gear ratio:	64:15
Fuel tank capacity:	360gal (1,620ltr)

THE CLASS 21s WERE another pilot scheme batch of ten locos, this time from North British. Again a repeat order – for forty-eight locos – was placed before the initial batch had been delivered. The locos were split into three batches: the pilot scheme ten, D6100–09; another twenty-seven, D6110–37; and a final batch, D6138–57. The first thirty-eight were intended for Great Northern use, the last twenty for Scottish use, although all soon found their way north of the border.

D6100–03/06–08/12–14/16/19/21/23/24/29/30/33/34/37 were later rebuilt as Class 29s.

DETAIL DIFFERENCES

All were built with discs. D6109 was converted to centre panels in the same style as Class 29s. All were vacuum-braked, and none converted to dual brakes.

Snowplough brackets were fitted on D6138–57, and all carried them at various times as they were used on routes north of Aberdeen.

The first thirty-eight had Red Circle MW, the last twenty had Blue Star. Train heating was via a Spanner Mk 1 boiler.

LIVERIES

All were new in all-over BR green with red bufferbeams. Yellow panels were added to all the fleet, apart from D6127, which was withdrawn in 1962 after a serious fire and never repaired. None received full yellow ends, and just D6109 was repainted into BR blue.

All had their numbers in serif font. None are thought to have lost their D prefixes by virtue of their early withdrawal.

BR green: D6100–57
BR green with small yellow panels: D6100–26/28–57
BR blue: D6109

ABOVE: One of the second batch of Class 21s (D6110–37) in its original guise, apart from the addition of a yellow warning panel. The loco – which is vacuum-braked, has steam heating and uses Red Circle MW – was not converted to a Class 29, and was condemned in December 1967. RAIL PHOTOPRINTS

BELOW: BR green D6117 is in as-built condition, aside from the addition of small yellow warning panels. JIM BINNIE

The messy nature of the bodyside of a Class 22 is clear in this view of D6339 in BR blue. It has the incorrect serif-style numbers, still with D prefixes as well as snowplough brackets, a relatively rare feature on a Class 22. The MW has also been moved to an angular position, to help shunters when uncoupling when snowploughs were carried. RAIL PHOTOPRINTS

Specifications	
1957 BR number range:	D6300–57
Former class codes:	D6300–05: D10/2A, later 10/4A D6306–57: D11/5, later 11/4A
Built by:	NBL
Introduced:	1959–62
Wheel arrangement:	B-B
Weight (operational):	65–68 tons
Height:	12ft 10in (3.91m)
Width:	8ft 8in (2.64m)
Length:	46ft 9in (14.25m)
Min. curve negotiable:	4½ chains
Maximum speed:	75mph (120km/h)
Wheelbase:	34ft 6in (10.52m)
Bogie wheelbase:	8ft 6in (2.59m)
Bogie pivot centres:	23ft (7.01m)
Wheel diameter:	3ft 7in (1.09m)
Route availability:	4
Brake force:	29 tons
Engine type:	MAN L12V18 21A: D6300–05 MAN L12V18 21B: D6306–57
Engine horsepower:	Original: 1,000bhp (746kW): D6300–05 Modified: 1,100bhp (821kW): D6306–57
Power at rail:	Original: 816bhp (609kW): D6300–05 Modified: 890bhp (664kW): D6306–57
Tractive effort:	40,000lb: D6300–05 38,000lb: D6306–57
Transmission type:	Voith LT306r
Fuel tank capacity:	450gal (2,025ltr)

SIMILAR TO THE Class 21s, the 22s were a diesel hydraulic version of the North British Type 2 for the Western Region. The small B-B Type 2s were built in two main batches: D6300–05 were pilot scheme locos, and D6306–57 production series locos. Various detail differences exist among the fleet, as well as a myriad of livery variations.

DETAIL DIFFERENCES

Discs were fitted to D6300–33 and split headcodes to D6334–57 at construction, and split boxes were retro-fitted to D6300/02–33. Of these, D6302/05/06/17/24/26/30 had large protruding boxes mounted on to the nose ends, while the others had them in the same style as those locos that had them from new – flush with the front of the body. D6323 ran for a while retaining the two central discs on the communication doors while having its headcode boxes plated over.

Several had snowplough brackets, D6336–48 from new, but they were also retro-fitted to at least D6322/28, the former after an accident rebuild. This also saw the MW jumpers and receptacles mounted on angled plates to assist shunters gain access to the MW equipment when ploughs were carried.

All were vacuum-braked only, and none converted to dual brakes. Multiple working was Orange Square for the pilot scheme locos, which could only work in multiple with each other and with D600–04 (but not with D800–02). The rest had White Diamond MW, also compatible with D803–70.

Train heating was a Spanner Mk 1 boiler on D6300–05, and a Clayton or Stones boiler on D6306–57.

When new, the 22s had vertical handrails under their windscreens, but some locos had these changed to horizontal, namely at least 6308/10/12/19/20/22–27/30/31/33.

LIVERIES

New in all-over BR green were D6300–36, while D6337–57 had yellow panels from new. D6334–36 were the only locos fitted with headcode panels to run in all-over green. Half yellow ends were applied to at least D6300/01/05/11–12/15/21–23/25/27, and with discs to at least D6302/04–13/15/17/19–21/23/2426/30/31 with headcode panels. Only D6312/31 ran in BR green with full yellow ends. 6323/52 are thought to be the only 22s to run in green without D prefixes.

BR blue with small yellow panels was seen on 6300/03/14/27 (which all had BR arrows on the bodysides as opposed to on the cabsides) and BR blue with full yellow ends was applied to 6300/02/08/14/18/19/22/25/26/28/30/32–34/36–40/42/43/48/52/54/56. None ran in maroon.

In blue, the positioning and size of the BR double arrow badges varied, as did the fonts, with some blue locos having serif font numbers, both with and without the D prefix. Some had their numbers above the BR badge – 6318/25 above small badges and D6302/22/28/32–34/36/37/39/40/42/43/54 above medium-sized arrows, while 6308/19/26/29/38/48/52/56 had their numbers below medium-sized arrows and no D prefixes.

BR green: D6300–36
BR green with small yellow panels: D6302/04–13/15/17/19–27/30/31/37–57
BR green with full yellow ends: D6312/31
BR blue with small yellow panels: D6300/03/14/27
BR blue: D6300/02/08/14/18/19/22/25/26/28/30/32–34/36–40/42/43/48/52/54/56

This view of 6308 shows the final look of a Class 22, in BR blue with correct font numbers and no D prefix. However, very few of the fifty-eight Class 22s ever reached this stage. All 22s retained communication doors. This loco was originally built with headcode discs, but was changed to split panels in the late 1960s. It is in remarkably good condition, yet it was commonplace for the type to be running round with panels missing from the solebars. DAVE THORPE

specifications

1957 BR number range:	D5900–09
Former class codes:	D11/1, later 11/3
Built by:	EE Vulcan Foundry
Introduced:	1959
Wheel arrangement:	Bo-Bo
Weight (operational):	74 tons
Height:	12ft 8in (3.86m)
Width:	8ft 11in (2.72m)
Length:	52ft 6in (16m)
Min. curve negotiable:	4½ chains
Maximum speed:	75mph (120km/h)
Wheelbase:	40ft 6in (12.34m)
Bogie wheelbase:	8ft 6in (2.59m)
Bogie pivot centres:	32ft (9.75m)
Wheel diameter:	3ft 7in (1.09m)
Route availability:	5
Brake force:	36 tons
Engine type:	Napier 'Deltic' T9: 29
Engine horsepower:	1,100bhp (821kW)
Power at rail:	768bhp (573kW)
Tractive effort:	47,000lb
Main generator type:	EE 835D
Auxiliary generator type:	EE 912
No. of traction motors:	4
Traction motor type:	EE 533A
Gear ratio:	63:17
Fuel tank capacity:	550gal (2,475gal)

ANOTHER SMALL FLEET of ten born out of the pilot scheme plan, these locos from English Electric used a single 9-cylinder Napier Deltic engine. Ultimately they proved unreliable, which led to no repeat orders, and while all were refurbished, reliability did not improve dramatically. A plan to re-engine D5901 with an EE unit was started but shelved, and the loco was returned to traffic with its Napier engine: with the fleet being small and non-standard, withdrawal was inevitable. One was retained and put into Departmental use until 1975; it was scrapped in 1977.

A plan to build a new Class 23 is currently under way using a surviving Napier T9 engine which is being fitted to an as-new body built from a 'cut and shut' Class 37 donor. This loco will be D5910 when completed.

DETAIL DIFFERENCES

When new, the locos had headcode discs. Once refurbished, these were removed and centre panels were fitted in the same style as Class 37s and 40s, although they had square corners as opposed to rounded ones.

All were built with Blue Star MW, train vacuum brakes, and steam heating from a Stone OK4616 boiler, and all retained these features to withdrawal.

The bogies were similar to those used on Class 20s, while the cab shared the same design as Class 37s and 40s, albeit with a much shorter nose.

LIVERIES

All were new in all-over BR green with a light grey solebar and roof and red bufferbeams. When refurbished they were in all-over BR green with small yellow warning panels. Full yellow ends were applied to D5903/08, while D5909 was the only loco to receive BR blue, with full yellow ends.

BR green: D5900–09
BR green with small yellow panels: D5900–09
BR green with full yellow ends: D5903/08
BR blue: D5909

RIGHT: In as-built condition, D5905 shows the original look of a Class 23 with headcode discs, communication doors and nose-end ladder. The cab design was similar to that used on the 37s and 40s, although the nose was much shorter. The bogies were similar to those used on Class 20s. RAIL PHOTOPRINTS

LEFT: D5907 is refurbished with centre panels and square corners, and with the tail-lights moved lower. It retains its bufferbeam skirts, steam heating, vacuum brakes and Blue Star MW. The loco is in two-tone green with a small yellow panel, but two locos had full yellow ends and one had BR blue livery. RAIL PHOTOPRINTS

THE CLASS 24 was another pilot scheme design, of which twenty locos were ordered for initial evaluation. They won several repeat orders totalling 151 locos of the Class 24 design and another 327 of the similar Class 25.

The 24 were a mixed traffic design for the ER, NER, LMR and ScR, although some started life on the SR as a stopgap until ETH stock was delivered to work with Class 33s. The first fifty were Class 24/0s, the remainder were 24/1s, which were five tons lighter. None were dual-braked, and the rundown of the fleet started in August 1975 (fourteen locos had been withdrawn by then due to accidents). The last were withdrawn by May 1979, apart from 24081, which lasted until October 1980.

DETAIL DIFFERENCES

Discs were fitted to D5000–5113, and later 24001–113, but from D5114 through to D5150, roof-mounted centre panels were fitted. All were vacuum-braked only and had Blue Star MW. The steam-heat boiler was either a Stones OK4616 or 4610, later removed from some locos.

24049/055 also ran with headcode boxes at No.2 and No.1 end only respectively (after replacement cab roofs were fitted) but both retained headcode discs at these ends. 24147/148 had headcode boxes from the later Class 25 design but without horns, while 24136/142/147 also ran for periods with the Class 25-style roof-mounted air horns.

specifications

TOPS number range:	24001–150
Original 1948 number range:	D5000–150
Former class codes:	D11/1, later 11/1 (24/00), D11/3, later 11/1A (24/1)
Built by:	BR Derby, Crewe, Darlington
Introduced:	1958–61
Wheel arrangement:	Bo-Bo
Weight (operational):	77–79 tons (24/0), 71–73 tons (24/1)
Height:	12ft 8in (3.86m)
Width:	8ft 10in (2.69m)
Length:	50ft 6in (15.39m)
Min. curve negotiable:	4½ chains
Maximum speed:	75mph (120km/h)
Wheelbase:	36ft 6in (11.13m)
Bogie wheelbase:	8ft 6in (2.59m)
Bogie pivot centres:	28ft (8.53m)
Wheel diameter:	3ft 9in (1.14m)
Route availability:	6
Brake force:	38 tons
Engine type:	Sulzer 6LDA28A
Engine horsepower:	1,160bhp (865kW)
Power at rail:	843bhp (629kW)
Tractive effort:	40,000lb
Main generator type:	BTH RTB15656
Auxiliary generator type:	BTH RTB7440
No. of traction motors:	4
Traction motor type:	BTH 137 BY
Gear ratio:	81:16
Fuel tank capacity:	630gal (2,835ltr)

ABOVE: A batch of nineteen Class 24s, D5114–32, were fitted with two spotlamps in the late 1960s for working lines north of Inverness, as seen on 5127 in BR blue. It has the roof-mounted headcode box and snowploughs. These lamps were car headlights acquired from local car-part traders. They were removed in 1975 and the holes plated over, while twelve Class 26s had the lights fitted circa 1976. JIM BINNIE
BELOW: Two Class 24s, 24049/055, built with disc headcodes, had the roof sections for later Class 24s fitted so ran with plated-over headcode boxes as well as retaining their discs. 24049 shows off this modification. PDC

D5114–132 were built with snow-plough brackets for use in Scotland, but at least 24077, 24134/135 also ran with snowploughs.

Twin spot headlights were fitted to D5114–32, of which D5115–121/123–130/132 were renumbered to 24115–121/123–130/132. These were removed *circa* 1975 and the holes plated over. This batch of locos – based at Inverness – also had recesses under the driver's side windows for the installation of tablet catching equipment, which was fitted to all this batch but later removed. All had bufferbeam skirts.

D5000–05 had split radiator grilles at No.1 end, a feature not continued on the rest of the class, although these grilles also appeared on 24006/025, 24134 following component swaps.

D5102–111 were converted for use on Consett iron-ore trains, and in order

to be able to power the air-operated doors on the wagons, had an additional air pipe fitted to the cab fronts. In this conversion the locos lost their train heating, and so their boiler water tanks under the battery boxes on the middle underframe were removed. Later, 24034/035/039/063, 24134 also lost their boiler water tanks when their boilers were isolated or removed.

Some had the grille over the steam heat boiler blanked over, although this was not necessarily a sign the locos had lost their boilers. D5114–132 had these plated over but with five slots added to allow air into the boiler, but on a reduced level. In the late 1960s/early 1970s, with more concerns about staff climbing on loco roofs near high voltage overhead lines, most locos had the three handles on the side of the locos (used for climbing up to fill the boiler water tank) plated over. The cant rail boiler water-filling port was also plated over, and the attachment for the hoses moved to behind a panel door on the bodysides.

The communication doors on the front were progressively removed and sealed in the late 1960s and early 1970s, although those withdrawn early did not receive this modification. At least 24015 was also scrapped with its doors still in place.

Two were converted as static carriage heaters, 24054 and 24142, and were modified with ETH jumpers fitted to their bufferbeams in the place where the multiple working jumpers had sat. They had a set of buttons mounted on all four sides of their bufferbeam skirts below the cabsides. Panels were added to their cabsides detailing what to do in the event of a fire on the locos.

LIVERIES

D5000 was new in all-over BR green with a thin waist-height white stripe. The rest of the fleet were the same, but with this stripe replaced by a thicker stripe at sole-bar level.

BR green with small yellow panels was applied to D5001–04/06–08/12/14/19/30/32/35/37–39/41/42/44/46/47/49/50/55/57/61/65–67/69–72/79/81/82/85/88/90/92/94/95/97, 5100/03/04/08/10/13/36/37/41/42/44/47.

Two-tone green was applied to D5005/37/38/72.

Three locos had full yellow ends on BR green, namely 24021/071/092. The transition to BR blue saw 5021 in blue with small yellow panels, while standard BR blue with full yellow ends was applied to 5000–04/06–42/44–50/52–87/89/91/94–99, 5100–21/23–35/37/40–50. Withdrawn in green were D5005/43/51/88/93, 5122/38/39, 24090/092, 24136.

24090/092, 24136 were the only TOPS numbered 24s not to go blue, while 24032/035/039/044/047/063/069/071/081/082, 24110 also ran in green with TOPS numbers but went blue later. Some 24s had BR arrow symbols on green livery; 5069/81/92, 5113 and possibly 5108.

When converted for Departmental use, 24061 was painted into Research Centre blue and red livery and numbered 97201.

In preservation, 24054 was painted in BR black by the East Lancashire Railway in 1997 and spent a short period in 2001/02 in Loadhaul colours. It has also run in BR blue with small yellow panels. D5032 has had spells in two-tone green in preservation.

BR green: D5000–150
BR green with small yellow panels: D5001–04/06–08/12/14/19/30/32/35/37–39/41/42/44/46/47/49/50/55/57/61/65–67/69–72/79/81/82/85/88/90/92/94/95/97, 5100/03/04/08/10/13/36/37/41/42/44/47
Two-tone green with small yellow ends: D5005/37/38/72
BR blue with small yellow panel: 24021
BR green with full yellow ends: D5021/071/092
BR blue: 24001–042/044–050/052–087/089/091/094–121/123–135/137/140–150

NAMES

97201	*Experiment*
D5032	*Helen Turner*
D5054	*Phil Southern*

BUILD BATCHES

D5000–29/66–75, D5114–50 BR Derby, D5030–65/76–93 BR Crewe, D5094–113 Darlington.

NUMBERS

All locos were numbered under TOPS, with the last three digits being retained with the exception of D5005/28/43/51/67/68/88/93, D5114/22/31/38/39/49: these were withdrawn prior to renumbering. This meant D5000 took the vacant 24005 number.

SUBSEQUENT RENUMBERINGS

When 24054 and 24142 were converted to carriage heaters they were renumbered ADB968008/009 respectively in 9/76.

24061 was taken into RTC use as a test train loco (to replace D5901) and was initially numbered RDB968007 (11/75) and later 97201 (8/79). It was withdrawn in 1987, having been the last 24 to run on the network by some seven years.

24107 was one of the small batch of Class 24s fitted with what looks like an air-brake pipe but is, in fact, an air pipe to control the opening of hoppers on certain wagons used on the Consett line. It is vacuum-braked and has lost its train heating boiler, hence the lack of a boiler water tank in between the bogies. The loco has discs, but production changed to headcode boxes from D5114, seven locos later. RAIL PHOTOPRINTS

One Class 24 was retained by BR for hauling test trains: 24061, which was renumbered 97201 and named Experiment. The loco was also painted in the RTC's livery of BR blue with a red upper bodyside. Sporting its old 5061 number the loco shows off its revised look. The loco is now preserved in BR green. PDC

class 25

specifications

TOPS number range:	25001–327	Bogie wheelbase:	8ft 6in (2.59m)
1957 BR number range:	D5151–D5299, D7500–677	Bogie pivot centres:	28ft (8.53m)
		Wheel diameter:	3ft 9in (1.14m)
Former class codes:	D12/1, later 12/1 (D7598-D7619 classified 12/1A)	Route availability:	5
		Brake force:	38 tons
Built by:	BR Darlington, Derby, Beyer Peacock Gorton	Engine type:	Sulzer 6LDA 28B
		Engine horsepower:	1,250bhp (933kW)
Introduced:	1961–67	Power at rail:	949bhp (708kW)
Wheel arrangement:	Bo-Bo	Tractive effort:	45,000lb
Weight (operational):	72 tons (25/0, 25/1), 76 tons (25/2, 25/3)	Main generator:	AEI RTB 15656
		Auxiliary generator:	AEI RTB 7440
Height:	12ft 8in (3.86m)	No. of traction motors:	4
Width:	9ft 1in (2.77m)	Traction motor type:	AEI 137BX (25001–025), AEI 253AY (25026–327)
Length:	50ft 6in (15.39m)		
Min. curve negotiable:	4 chains	Gear ratio:	79:18 (25/0), 67:18 (remainder)
Maximum speed:	90mph (144km/h)		
Wheelbase:	36ft 6in (11.13m)	Fuel tank capacity:	500gal (2,250ltr)

A DEVELOPMENT OF the Class 24s with the higher-powered B version of the Sulzer 6LDA engine, 327 locos were built from 1961–7 in four main types. The Class 25/0s were the same as the 24/1s but with the higher-powered engine. The Class 25/1s had GEC series one electrical equipment, with the 25/2s having series two GEC equipment, and the Class 25/3s having series three equipment.

There were two major body designs, with most of the locos having no train heating. Apart from three early withdrawals due to accidents, the rundown of the fleet started from December 1975, mostly with the 25/0s. 1980 saw withdrawals start on an almost regular basis, but it was March 1987 when the final locos were laid up. One was reinstated in 1990 for special trains, but it, too, only lasted until 1991. Several are preserved.

DETAIL DIFFERENCES

The most noticeable detail differences were the two distinct bodysides. The series one design was essentially the same as the Class 24s and featured bodyside grilles and nose-end communication doors, while the series two bodyside features all the air-intake grilles at cant rail height and no communication doors, allowing a full depth centre window and a full width front hand rail.

Locos with series one bodies were D5151–5232 and D7568–97, later 25001–082, 25218–247. D5151–75 featured

the same bufferbeam skirt as the Class 24s, dropped from D5176 onwards. These twenty-five locos became the Class 25/0s and externally were the same in appearance as a late series headcode box-fitted Class 24/1.

All were built with roof-mounted centre panels, of which 25001–025 did not have side air horns next to the headcode boxes, although 25006/008/010/015 did run with boxes from later 25s including the air horns. 25006 also had, at one end, the angled headcode box but without air horns.

Snowplough brackets were fitted to at least 25001/003/009/022/026–028/

031/032/035–044/052/059/076/080/082/083/088/097, 25109/113/119/138/142/144/146/149/191/196/198/199, 25200–205, 25223–227/235/239/244/260/271/283/289, 25305–307/313/315–319/321–327.

Stones 4610 boilers were fitted to all Class 25/1s apart from D5179–32 (25029–032) and to Class 25/2s 25083–087 and 25218–247, of which 25242 lost its boiler *circa* the early 1970s.

25083–087 were the only second two design locos to have train heating, although all 25s were built with through-steam pipes for double heading between freight and passenger locos.

ABOVE LEFT: 25001 shows the bufferbeam skirting fitted to Class 24s and the twenty-five Class 25/0s. The loco also has the original headcode box, now with a domino but still without side horns. The front-end communication doors have been removed and plated over. The loco has snowplough brackets, vacuum brakes only, and Blue Star MW. ANDY HOARE

ABOVE RIGHT: 25084 shows off the cab front of a series two Class 25. It is one of a batch of just five locos which had steam-heat boilers with this bodyshell – 25083–087; the boiler water tanks can be seen in between the bogies next to the fuel tank. The steam pipe on the front would not be a guarantee that this was a boilered loco, as several still had through-steam pipes, though not so many ran like this in BR blue. The headcode has yet to be changed to a domino, but is not showing 0O00 either. ANDY HOARE

The main difference between the Class 25/1, 25/2 and 25/3 subclasses was in their electrical equipment.

Headlights were fitted to 25035/059/067, 25278, 25321 in preservation, of which 25059/067, 25278 still retain them.

LIVERIES

All-over BR green was new on D5151–75 (the Class 25/0s), with red bufferbeams and a grey roof. From D5176 onwards small yellow panels were added. The series one bodyside locos had all-over green with a grey roof and solebar off-white stripe.

The series two locos were delivered in two-tone green with a lighter green lower half and the same darker green at the solebar, replacing the off-white stripe. These all had a small yellow panel and red bufferbeams. Anomalies were D5159, which ran in traffic with a trial orange warning panel in 1966, and D5153 which ran with a reflective strip at the bottom of its small yellow warning panel in 1967.

Locos in BR green with full yellow ends were D5155/66/69/69/75/78–82/86/88/90/93/96, 5203/04/08/11/12/19–21/24/27–43/45–48/51–66/68–71/73/76–82/84–86/88–94/96–99, 7500–12/14–27/29–34/36–43/45/46/50–61/63–65/68/71–98, 7601/02/07/10–12/15/16/18/19/24/26–29/32–37/44/45/49/52/55.

Locos which ran in green with TOPS numbers were 25006/036/038/040/043/053/058, 25102, 25202/203/218/248/251/252/260/261/278/279/285/294, 25305.

D7660–77 were new in BR blue, of which 7660/61 were new with small yellow panels, a livery also given to 7568.

All 25s were painted into BR blue, apart from accident-damaged early withdrawals 5278 and 7605.

The only major BR livery variation was on 25322, later 25912, which had wrap-around yellow ends to cover its cabside but did not have large logos, or numbers, or black window surrounds. It also had a grey roof.

After withdrawal in 1987, 25912 was taken on as a training loco and in 1990 was reinstated to traffic; it was brought out in BR green with full yellow ends and carrying its original number D7672.

One loco ran with black window surrounds, 25095, with its number on the cab front, but in mirror image style.

In 1983 three Class 25s were converted to mobile ETH locos, and renumbered ADB97250–252. The locos, formerly 25310/305/314 respectively, were repainted into the same livery as coaches with a grey upper half and a BR blue lower body, and did not have warning panels. 97250 had BR blue cabsides, but 97251/252 differed by also having a grey upper half on their cabsides. Of these, 97251/252 was later repainted in InterCity colours, with yellow panels.

In preservation, 25072 was repainted briefly in GWR green with cast 5222 GWR-style numberplates. 25035 was also painted in all-over maroon with a small panel, departmental grey and 'Dutch' grey/yellow liveries for a short spell, and in the case of the last two colour schemes, was renumbered 25735.

25040, with the series one body which had grilles on the side and communication doors on the cab fronts, leads a series two Class 25 with the much cleaner bodyside. The lead loco sports snowploughs, has a steam pipe and is vacuum-braked only. Also, compared with the 25/0, it has warning horns next to the headcode, which is displaying 0O00 prior to the implementation of domino headcodes. The loco also has a different arrangement of headboard clips as compared with 25001. ANDY HOARE

LEFT: *Three Class 25/3s were converted to mobile ETH units to provide train supply to air-conditioned coaches hauled by locos without ETH. They were used on the West Highland Line from 1983–85 until ETH Class 37/4s were delivered. 97252 shows the ETH jumpers on the bufferbeam. The locos could move under their own power but not while providing heat. They were painted in the same livery as coaches, and hence did not have yellow ends. After their use ended on the WHL, they were used by InterCity on charter trains.* PDC

BR green: D5151–75
BR green with small yellow panels: D5151–5299, D7500–7659
BR green with small orange warning panel: D5159
BR green with full yellow ends: D5155/66/69/69/75/78–82/86/88/90/93/96, 5203/04/08/11/12/19–21/24/27–43/45–48/51–66/68–71/73/76–82/84–86/88–94/96–99, 7500–12/14–27/29–34/36–43/45/46/50–61/63–65/68/71–98, 7601/02/07/10–12/15/16/18/19/24/26–29/32–37/44/45/49/52/55
BR blue with small yellow panels: D7568, D7660/61
BR blue: D5151–5277/79–99, 7500–7604/06–77
BR blue with wrap-around yellow ends and grey roof: 25322, 25912
BR green (special): 25912
BR blue and grey (no yellow ends): 97250
BR blue and grey (no yellow ends) with great upper cabsides: 97251/252
InterCity: 97251/252

NUMBERS

Large Glasgow numbers were carried by 25028/046/062/065/072/075/083–086, 25109, 25226/230/231/234 B

NAMES

Apart from the three ETH conversions, ADB97250–252, 'named' Ethel 1–3, only one Class 25 was named by BR – reinstated D7672 (25322/912), christened *Tamworth Castle* in 1989. Several appeared with unofficial names in 1986/87.

25034	*Castell Aberystwyth/Aberystwyth Castle*
25035	*Castell Dina Bran*
25058	*Castell Criccieth/Criccieth Castle*
25109	*Castell Trefaldwyn/Montgomery Castle*
25201	*Castell Y Bere*
25265	*Castell Harlech/Harlech Castle*
25278	*Castell Powys/Powis Castle*
25313	*Castell Y Waun/Chirk Castell*
25322	*Tamworth Castle*

In preservation the following have been named, all with cast plates apart from 25322, which has a painted name.

D5185	(25035)	*Castell Dina Bran*
D7541	(25191)	*The Diana*
D7523	(25173)	*John F Kennedy*
D7535	(25185)	*Mercury*
D7628	(25278)	*Sybilla*
25265		*Castell Harlech/Harlech Castle*
25322		*Tamworth Castle*

BUILD BATCHES

D5151–85, D5223–32, D7578–97 BR Darlington
D5186–222, D5233–299, D7500–77, D7598–623, D7660–77 BR Derby
D7624–59, Beyer Peacock Gorton.

DATES DUAL-BRAKED

All were built with vacuum brakes, although dual braking started in 1967, with D7658–69 (25308–319) having dual brakes from new.

Dates for subsequent dual braking were 7568/71/72/86/93/96 (1968); 7576/78–84/90/91, 7600/01/06/07/26/29/33/35/36/39/45/46/50/75 (1971); 7651/74/76/77 (1972); 7587/92/95/97, 7604/16/32/34/38/47 (1973); 25032/036/051/053/054/057/058/060/095, 25154/196–199, 25200–207/249/265/268/269/277/278/287/298, 25303/305 (1974); 25048/099, 25155, 25259 (1975); 25088/097, 25109/120 (1976); 25028/044/059/072/077/079/082/089, 25106/113/117/145/175/178/183/184/194, 25227/239/244/258/262, 25307/322/323 (1977); 25033/035/049/050/064/076/078, 25173/176/181/182/185/191/193, 25208/210–213/235, 25320/321 (1978); 25037, 25189/190/192, 25209 (1979).

NUMBERS

Locos were renumbered in series:

D5151–75	25001–025 (Class 25/0)
D5176–231	25026–081 (Class 25/1)
D5232–99	25082–149 (Class 25/2)[+]
D7500–97	25150–247 (Class 25/2)
D7598–677	25248–327 (Class 25/3)[+]

[+] D5278 and 7605 were withdrawn due to accidents, so 25128 and 25255 were left vacant.

SUBSEQUENT RENUMBERINGS

As ETHELs, 25310/305/314 became ADB97250–252 in 1983, and carried their numbers with and later without the ADB.

25131 was renumbered 97202 for a brief role in Departmental use. In 1985, twelve Class 25/3s were given 'E-exams' with the view to a life extension, and these were renumbered in the 25/9 series:

25901	25262
25902	25268
25903	25276
25904	25283
25905	25286
25906	25296
25907	25297
25908	25307
25909	25309
25911	25315
25911	25316
25912	25322

25908/912 were due to be renumbered ADB968026/027 for their roles as static training locos, but neither had these numbers applied.

ABOVE: After withdrawal, all three ETHELs congregated at Inverness prior to being sold for scrap. 97252 shows off its InterCity livery, while 97250 retains its original coaching stock blue and grey livery; 97251, also in InterCity livery, is behind in this 1993 view. The ETH jumpers can be seen on the bufferbeams. The ETHELs worked in multiple with Class 37s on the sleepers and were not crewed. They did not have fire-suppressant equipment fitted. PIP DUNN

LEFT: A Class 25/3 with series two body in original condition, albeit now dual-braked. The loco, D7659, is non-boilered but sports a through-steam pipe, which was typical of these locos when built. PIP DUNN

BELOW: The Class 25/0s visually looked the same as later Class 24s. They were all non-boilered, although this view of D5159 from April 1967 shows the through-steam pipe fitted to the subclass. This loco ran with a unique orange panel as BR tried various methods to improve the visibility of diesel locos for trackworkers. Eventually BR opted for full yellow ends, with high intensity headlights not being a fleet-wide requirement until 1993. BILL WRIGHT

specifications

TOPS number range:	26001–046
1957 BR number range:	D5300–46
Former class codes:	D11/4, later 11/6 (Class 26/0), 11/6A (Class 26/1)
Built by:	Birmingham RCW
Introduced:	1958–59
Wheel arrangement:	Bo-Bo
Weight (operational):	75–79 tons
Height:	12ft 8in (3.86m)
Width:	8ft 10in (2.69m)
Length:	50ft 9in (15.47m)
Min. curve negotiable:	5 chains
Maximum speed:	75mph (120km/h)
Wheelbase:	39ft (11.89m)
Bogie wheelbase:	10ft (3.05m)
Bogie pivot centres:	29ft (8.84m)
Wheel diameter:	3ft 7in (1.09m)
Route availability:	5 (26/1), 6 (26/0)
Brake force:	35 tons
Engine type:	6LDA28A
Engine horsepower:	1,160bhp (865kW)
Power at rail:	900bhp (671kW)
Tractive effort:	42,000lb
Main generator type:	CG391-A1
Auxiliary generator type:	CAG 193 1A
No. of traction motors:	4
Traction motor type:	CP171-A1 (Class 26/0), CP171 D3 (Class 26/1)
Gear ratio:	63:16
Fuel tank capacity:	500gal (2,250ltr)

Fresh out of works after refurbishment, 26005 shows the new-look front end for 26s at the time, with all discs removed and the two central white marker lights removed and plated over. The communication doors would have been removed and plated over at an earlier overhaul. The loco retains oval buffers and pipes below the bufferstocks, as was the case on 26/0s. This was one of the seven 26s dual-braked in 1967. Note also the larger Glasgow St Rollox 'trademark' 8in numbers. ANDY HOARE

THE CLASS 26 was another pilot scheme design of twenty locos, then a repeat order for twenty-seven more was placed, followed by another sixty-nine of a similar design which became the Class 27s.

The pilot scheme locos were initially used in London on Great Northern lines, but the second batch were for Scottish use, although the first twenty all joined them from 1960.

A refurbishment programme was undertaken in 1981–86, and thirty-three were treated. The last were condemned in October 1993, but thirteen are preserved.

DETAIL DIFFERENCES

All were built with Stones boilers, but D5300–06 lost them in 1967 when they were dual-braked. From 1982, several had their boilers isolated, which meant the steam-heat pipe was removed. Sometimes this was just the end hose, leaving the on/off cock in situ, in other cases both pipe and cock were removed to leave a hole in the steam pipe, which was sometimes plated over.

Boilers were removed from 26010/011/014/015/023/025 while they were still vacuum-braked; when locos were dual-braked, those with boilers lost them. From 1982–86 locos to lose their boilers were 26008/010/011/014/015/021/023–029/031/032/034–043/046 as they were refurbished. Locos that retained boilers until withdrawal were D5328, 26009/012/013/016–020/022/030/033/044/045, of which 26013 had an isolated boiler.

All 26/1s had snowplough brackets, and all carried them at times. In 1975, 26018 was fitted with brackets, but this modification was not replicated on any other 26/0. The loco kept its multiple working and pipes in the standard 26/0 position. Not all locos carried snowploughs all year round, and all ran for periods without ploughs – which were painted black in green, and yellow in BR

A clear demonstration of the different window designs on the two Class 26 subclasses. On the left is 26008 with droplight windows, and on the right is 26040 with sliding windows. The 26/1 was built with a table recess under this window but it has been plated over; the MW jumper head is also mounted on the bottom of the body as opposed to on the bufferbeam of a 26/0. Both locos, in common with all 26s, have had their cab door windows plated over, though 26040 also shows signs of a temporary repair. ANDY HOARE

blue. It was commonplace for locos to run with just side ploughs, or occasionally with a side plough missing.

The 26/1s also had a revised multiple working layout with the jumpers mounted on to the bufferbeam in an angular fashion and the jumper receptacle socket fitted on the cab front, while the main reservoir and loco air-control pipes were to the side of the drawhook.

D5300–19 had droplight-style cab-side windows, while D5320–46 had sliding windows. Tablet recesses were fitted to D5320–46 – at least D5321/29/30/36/41/42/44 had the equipment fitted, and at least 5343/44 and 26021/035/037/041 had the tablet recesses in BR blue. 26001–008/010/011/014/015/019 had their droplight windows changed to sliding windows.

All 26s had Blue Star MW, which was retained until withdrawal. On the Class 26/0s the MW jumpers were mounted flat on to the bufferbeam, as was the jumper receptacle socket. The main reservoir and loco air-control pipes were underneath the buffers (which were oval). The 26/0s did not have snow-plough brackets from new, as they were built for use in England.

HEADCODES

Class 26s were built with discs. Some unrefurbished locos had discs on their side removed after works visits, namely 26030/032/036/043, while 26046 lost all its discs at No. 2 end after an accident.

When refurbished, discs were removed from 26001–008/010/011/014/015/021/023–029/031/032/034–043/046. When the side discs were removed, the white sidelights were retained, but at refurbishment any centre white lamps were removed.

In 1992, 26001/007 were returned to original green livery as D5301/00 with small yellow panels. This saw discs refitted, but unlike the originals, they were not flush on to the body and were mounted on frames fitted to the body.

HEADLIGHTS

In 1976, Inverness depot fitted twin spotlights to 26015/022/030/032/035/038/039/041-043/045/046 for working on the Kyle line, which had several unprotected level crossings. Strangely, a 26/0 was selected, 26015 (which did not have snowploughs), but the other eleven were 26/1s. Some had the lamps fitted quite wide apart, others had them closer together. Of these, the twin spotlights were mounted on backing plates on 26041.

Single spotlights were fitted to 26021/024/040/044, with 26040 retaining four discs and the other three losing their centre bottom disc. 26038/043 were later changed from twin lights to single spotlamps.

The only loco with just two centre discs retained was 26036, while those with two centre discs and twin spotlights were 26030/032/043. The only loco to have no discs and twin spotlights

ABOVE: 26045, in typical Highland Class 26/1 guise, with a full set of snowploughs and twin spotlamps fitted. The communication doors have been plated over but discs retained. ANDY HOARE

BELOW: One of the original pilot scheme locos, 26004, heavily modified having been first dual-braked and then refurbished. The loco now sports Trainload Coal livery and has had its droplight windows changed to the sliding type on 26/1s. It also has round buffers. PIP DUNN

was 26046 (at No. 2 one end only), while 26043 had two side discs and twin spotlights removed, plated over and a single spotlight fitted; 26038 was the same, but with four discs.

In 1992/93, high intensity headlights were fitted to refurbished 26003/005/006/008/032/036/037, just above the bufferbeam.

REFURBISHMENT

D5300–06 (26007/001–006) were dual-braked in 1967, and also fitted with slow speed control.

From 1981 a refurbishment programme started, in which vacuum-braked locos were upgraded with dual brakes; if they retained a boiler, it was removed at this time. Any retained head-code discs were also removed, as were the centre white lights behind the discs. Spotlamps were also removed from 26015/032/035/038/039/041–043/046.

Dates for refurbishment were 11/81 (26004), 02/82 (26001), 05/82 (26003/005), 12/82 (26007), 09/83 (26028*), 10/83 (26027*), 03/84 (26039*), 04/84 (26023*/029*/046*), 05/84 (26015*), 09/84 (26042*), 10/84 (26014*), 11/84 (26021*), 12/84 (26011*/024*/036*), 05/85 (26043*), 07/85 (26026*FR), 08/85 (26010*FR/031*FR), 10/85 (26034/035* FR), 12/85 (26006FR/041*FR), 01/86 (26008*FR/032*FR), 02/86 (26040*FR), 03/86 (26037*FR), 04/86 (26002FR), 05/86 (26038*FR), 07/86 (26025*FR).

* loco dual-braked at the same time
FR loco repainted into Railfreight livery

Locos not refurbished were D5328, 26009/012/013/016–020/022/030/033/044/045.

While twelve Class 26s had twin spotlamps fitted in the mid-1970s, four had single spotlamps fitted in the early 1980s. 26021 shows this modification, and also the fact it has lost its bottom discs, yet retains the other three. The loco is in original condition, vacuum-braked and boiler fitted, but it was later refurbished. PDC

In March 1979, 26043 shows off its full Inverness look, with snowploughs and twin spotlamps. Refurbishment included fitting the air tanks for the air brakes under the body between the bogies in the place of the boiler water tank, which was removed along with the steam-heat boiler. DAVE THORPE

LIVERIES

All were delivered in all-over BR green, with small yellow panels later applied. Only D5335 had full yellow ends on green. All later went to blue.

At first, blue locos were given full yellow front ends with no wrap-arounds on the window frames. In the early 1970s the yellow was extended around the side window frames. At about the same time, the cab door windows were plated over and this led to a variety of permutations, with some locos having yellow window frames with cab door windows retained, others having blue window frames with cabside windows plated over.

In 1985 Railfreight livery was applied, and from 1988, two-tone grey with Trainload Coal logos was applied to the first eight locos. 'Dutch' Civil Engineers appeared in 1991, and in 1992 the first two locos were repainted back into BR green.

BR green: D5300-46
BR green with half yellow end: D5300-46

BR green with full yellow end: D5335
BR blue: 26001–046, D5328
'Red stripe' Railfreight: 26001–008/010/026/031/032/034/035/037/038/040/041
Trainload Coal: 26001–008
'Dutch': 26001–005/007/011/025/026/035/036/038/040/043
BR green (special): 26001/007

Minor Variations

BR blue with full yellow end wrap-round side windows: 26001–046

Blue cab doors with window frames, no yellow surrounds: 5302/03/05–10/12–16/18^/20–22/24/26/29/33/34/36/38/39/42–46, 26006

Cab doors with windows, yellow surrounds: 5300/27, 26010/021

Cab door windows plated over, no yellow surrounds: 5312^/17/18^/28

Cab door windows plated over, blue plates, yellow back frame: 26034

Cab door windows plated over, yellow surrounds: 5304, 26001–046

D numbers under cabsides (in blue): 5300/03/04/09*/10*/12*/13*/14*/15–18/20/22/23/24*/26/28/29/33/34/38/43*/44*/45*/46*

D numbers on bodysides (in blue): 5305/07*/27/36*/42

* D prefix retained
^ numbers in a serif font with double arrows on cab doors

NUMBERS

Large Glasgow numbers were applied to 26001–008/010/011/014/015/019/021/023–046 B.

EMBLEMS

White Inverness stags: 26025/032/037/038/040/042 B

Yellow Inverness stags: 26008/032/034/035/037/038/040–042 B

Red Haymarket castles on cabsides: 26003/023 B

White Haymarket castles: 26001–007/011/014/015/021/023/024/027–029/033/036/039/040/042/043/046 B

Small West Highland terriers: 26027/036/039 B: 26025 FR

Large West Highland terriers: 26023/024 B; 26025/026/031/032/034/035/038/040/041 FR

Cast Eastfield plaques: 26003–006/008 FC; 26001/002/004–007/011/025/026/035/036/040/043 C

Yellow DCE stripes: 26011/023/024/028 B; 26025/035 FR

Grey MCE stripes: 26011/043 B

BUILD BATCHES

All were built by BRCW at Smethwick. D5300–19 were pilot-scheme locos, and the repeat order was D5320–46. The latter were for Scottish use and so had a number of the aforementioned detail changes.

Part way through the refurbishment programme, Railfreight livery was implemented and 26040 shows off this scheme with a red solebar. The flush front is clear, with just two marker lights retained. The loco fuel tank remains below the batteries in between the bogies, but the boiler tank is removed. Snowploughs are retained, and the loco sports a large West Highland terrier emblem. PDC

RENUMBERINGS

All were numbered under TOPS with the last digits being retained with the exception of D5328, which was withdrawn prior to renumbering. To keep locos together in numeric batches, D5300 became 26007, D5307 became 26020, and D5320 took up the vacant 26028 number.

NAMES

26001   *Eastfield*

Sectorization in 1987 saw the remaining Class 26s, all now refurbished, split between the Railfreight and Departmental sectors. In 1991 the latter started to repaint its 26s into its grey and yellow livery, known as 'Dutch' livery as it was similar to the colours used by Netherlands State Railways. 26035, sporting a cast diamond West Highland terrier plaque, was one of fourteen Class 26s so repainted. The first loco, 26026, had the top of its communication door painted yellow, the remainder had them black. PDC

IN THE SAME way that Class 25 was a development of Class 24, Class 27 was an 'enhanced' Class 26, also using the uprated 1,250bhp Sulzer 6LDA28B engine. The locos used the same bodyshell, but had headcode boxes, not discs. They also used GEC electrical equipment rather than Crompton Parkinson.

Like the 26s, they were all eventually concentrated on the Scottish Region, although some were allocated to English depots until 1970. Despite a refurbishment programme being started in the mid-1980s, the last was laid up in August 1987, with their Class 26 stablemates outliving them by six more years. Eight are preserved.

DETAIL DIFFERENCES

All had roof-mounted headcodes that were later changed on most – but not all – to dominos, but some briefly ran with white panels: examples of this are 27001/005/009/014/017–021/024/025/ 028/037/041/043, 27101/102/104/105/ 107/109/112, 27202/204/206–209/211. At least D5383, 27006/013/015/031/035/ 039/044 were withdrawn with roller blind headcodes still in place.

D5347–69 had snowplough brackets from new, and most others had them fitted later. It was, generally, the boiler-fitted 27/0s that carried them, but over the years the following are known to have carried them: 27001–025/030/032/ 041/045/050–052/065, 27204/207.

D5347–69 were fitted with recesses under their driver's side windows for the fitting of tablet-catching equipment – though there is no evidence to suggest that any actually had the equipment fitted. The recesses were plated over, although often not until the 1970s, and 27006/013/015 still had them when scrapped. Many ran in TOPS numbers with them, including 27004/010–015.

D5347–69 had sliding cabside windows, all others had droplight-style windows. All cab doors had droplight windows.

27007/008 both had their centre front cab window plated over at No. 2 end, although the latter had it changed back to a window when refurbished. At least 27005/021, 27105/109 ran for periods with at least one yellow plated-over cab door window in the same style as Class 26s, so presumably a Class 26 door.

All were built with centre communication doors although all were removed and plated over, apart from on D5383.

LIVERIES

The 27s were delivered in all-over British Railways green with a grey roof, and window frames extending over the top of the communication doors. Buffer beams were red, and there was an off-white body stripe at waist height.

At least D5370/72/80 were painted in two-tone green. Small yellow panels were applied from new to D5379

specifications

TOPS number range:	27001–066, 27101–124, 27201–212
1957 BR number range:	D5347–D5415
Former class codes:	D12/3, later 12/6
Built by:	Birmingham RCW
Introduced:	1961–62
Wheel arrangement:	Bo-Bo
Weight (operational):	74–77 tons
Height:	12ft 8in (3.86m)
Width:	8ft 10in
Length:	50ft 9in (15.47m)
Min. curve negotiable:	5 chains
Maximum speed:	90mph (144km/h)
Wheelbase:	39ft
Bogie wheelbase:	10ft
Bogie pivot centres:	29ft
Wheel diameter:	3ft 7in
Route availability:	5
Brake force:	35 tons
Engine type:	Sulzer 6LDA28B
Engine horsepower:	1,250bhp (933kW)
Power at rail:	933bhp (696kW)
Tractive effort:	40,000lb
Main generator type:	GEC WT981
Auxiliary generator type:	GEC WT782
No. of traction motors:	4
Traction motor type:	GEC WT459
Gear ratio:	60:17
Fuel tank capacity:	500gal (2,250ltr: 27001–023/032–037/ 039–041/043/044), 600gal (2,700ltr: 27024–031/038/042), 685gal (3,083ltr: 27045–056), 970gal (4,365ltr: 27058/059/ 063–066, 27201–203/ 206–208)

BELOW: 27010 was one of the batch of twenty-three locos built for Scotland so has many features of the 26/1s, such as snowplough brackets. Like the 26s, the communication doors have long been removed. The 27s had a much cleaner look, with a roof-mounted headcode – now changed to dominos – and no discs. Unlike the 26s though, the 27s, as a rule, retained their cab door windows. The loco is vacuum-braked and sports snowploughs. ANDY HOARE

ABOVE: 27001 in its final guise – dual-braked, with domino headcodes, snowploughs, and sporting an Eastfield depot West Highland terrier logo. PDC

RIGHT: *27204 shows the ETH jumper on the cab front and the additional grilles cut in its bodyside to improve airflow to the Deutz donkey engine that was fitted to provide the ETH. One of the bodyside windows is also opened to improve airflow; on many locos these were removed to leave a square hole in the bodyside.* BILL ATKINSON

BELOW: *It was also common practice for Class 27s of all three subclasses to run with some windows removed, leaving a hole in the bodyside to aid ventilation to the engine room. However, 27032 still caught fire, which brought about its withdrawal. While many 27s caught fire, they were in the main caused by issues with heavy braking on freight trains igniting dirt on the bogies.* PDC

onwards, and retro painted on D5347–78. 5347/49/50/55/56/58/61/70–72/76–80/84/85/90/98, 5402–06 later had full yellow ends on BR green, and some had the yellow extended to cover the window frames on the side. 27001/024 ran in this livery with TOPS numbers.

All apart from D5383 were repainted into BR blue, and 5389 ran from September 1966 to 1970 in BR blue with a small yellow panel. Some, including at least 5351/52/54–56/59/62/89/95, 5401/15, ran in BR blue with full yellow ends but blue side window frames – though from the early 1970s, the window frames went yellow.

Livery variations were then few and far between, and mainly centred on the positioning and fonts of the numbers, although in 1983, 27056 appeared with a white stripe along its solebar.

BR green: D5347–78
BR two-tone green: D5370/72/80
BR green with small yellow panels: D5347–5415
BR green with full yellow ends: 5347/49/50/55/56/58/61/70–72/76–80/84/85/90/98, 5402–06, 27001/024
BR blue with small yellow panels: 5389
BR Blue: 27001–056/058/059/063–066, 27101–124, 27201–212
BR blue with white solebar stripe: 27056

EMBLEMS

Small West Highland terriers: 27001/003/008/020/022–026/029/030/032/034/037/038/040–042/045–049/052/054–056/058/059/063/066, 27103, 27206–208 B
Large West Highland terriers: 27059 B
White castles: 27002/004/010/012/014/017/018/023/032/036/040/047/049/051–055/059, 27204/206–208 B
Red castles: 27017/064 B
White stags: 27005/020/037/042/049–051/064/065 B
Yellow stags: 27003/008/014/020/021/029/032/037/049–053/064/065 B
Larger (8in) numbers: 27001–005/007/008/010/012/016–030/032–034/036–038/040–042/045–047/049–056/058/059/063–066, 27101–103/105–109, 27203–208/210–212 B

BUILD BATCHES

The 27s were built in three batches: D5347–69 for the Scottish Region, D5370–78 for North-Eastern Region, and D5379–5414 for the London Midland Region. All locos later moved to the ScR (except D5383).

MAJOR MODIFICATIONS

All were built with vacuum brakes, but thirty-five were dual-braked, namely 5374/86/87/91–94/99, 5403/04/07–12 (1971); 5380/88/97, 5400/01 (1972); 5396/97 (1973); 27041 (1975); 27034/038/042 (1976); 27001/003/005/008/024–026 (1983). Those converted to dual brakes in 1971–73 were also modified for push-pull operation.

All were built with Stones steam-heat boilers except D5370–78. Of these, D5374 was fitted with a boiler in 1971 when converted to a Class 27/1, leaving 5370–73/75–78 to become 27024–031.

Boilers were removed from 27103/113–117/119–124 when converted to ETH with an index of just twenty-eight. They were removed from 27038/042 in April 1985 when overhauled.

The last survivors had their boilers isolated in late 1986, although in many cases this was only on paper; 27001 'steamed' as late as May 1987.

Those converted from 27/1s to ETH were renumbered in the 27/2 series. Unlike other ETH conversions, the 27s did not have the power for the ETH tapped off the main generator, and instead separate Deutz donkey engines were fitted. Those converted were 27201–203/205/206/210 (1974); 27204/207–209/212 (1975); 27211 (1976).

27118 (ex-D5413) was originally selected for conversion to 27212. It was then deemed unsuitable for conversion so 27103 (D5386) was substituted. This meant 27118 took the now vacant 27103 number and returned to traffic with steam heating but with an ETH jumper holder on its front.

Removal of ETH was progressive from 1980, with 27201/202 being withdrawn with the equipment still in place. At first just the Deutz engines were isolated and then removed along with the ETH cables, but the jumper heads and receptacles retained. These were then removed in the early 1980s – 27206 still had them in January 1983, 27208 in May 1983 and 27207 in March 1984. They were removed leaving a mounting plate on the bottom right of the cab, which in turn was removed when some locos were overhauled, namely 27205/209/210/212 when they became 27059/063/064/066.

The 27/2s were noticeable not only for their ETH jumpers, which were mounted on the bottom lip of the cab front, but also on the side they had additional grilles. Looking from No. 2 end, on the right-hand side, one was in place of one of the four bodyside windows while additional two round grilles were fitted just above the solebar at No. 2 end. On the left-hand side, one was again fitted in place of a window, while another was midway up the body behind the cab door. These were to give improved airflow around the Deutz engines.

A refurbishment programme began in 1982 in which the locos were completely rewired, and if vacuum-braked, they were dual-braked. Locos refurbished were 27056 (1982), 27046/049/053–055/059 (1983), 27001/003/005/008/024–026/052 (1984), 27038/042 (1985).

NUMBERS

Class 27 renumbering was complicated. All were built as 27/0s and twenty-four converted to push-pull 27/1s, but prior to TOPS. These became 27101–124, of which 27101 had previously been one of the batch of nine non-boilered locos.

With D5383 condemned in 1966, renumbering started at 27001–044 and 27101–124, but the 27/1s were selected 'at random'.

Soon after the 27/1s had been created, twelve were selected for conversion to ETH, 27201–212. These were meant to be 27113–124, but 27118 was shelved for conversion so 27103 took its place and 27118 took the now vacant 27103 slot.

After the end of the push-pull operations, the 27/1 and 27/2s were to be renumbered back into the 27/0 series, with 27045–056 for the 27/1s and 27057–066 for the remaining 27/2s (27201/202 having been condemned).

27203 was also withdrawn prior to taking its allotted 27057 number, and in the event 27206–208 never gained their 27060–062 numbers as they were not overhauled.

The full Class 27/0 renumbering is as follows:

5347	27001		
5348	27002		
5349	27003		
5350	27004		
5351	27005		
5352	27006		
5353	27007		
5354	27008		
5355	27009		
5356	27010		
5357	27011		
5358	27012		
5359	27013		
5360	27014		
5361	27015		
5362	27016		
5363	27017		
5364	27018		
5365	27019		
5366	27020		
5367	27021		
5368	27022		
5369	27023		
5370	27024		
5371	27025		
5372	27026		
5373	27027		
5374	27101	27045	
5375	27028		
5376	27029		
5377	27030		
5378	27031		
5379	27032		
5380	27102	27046	
5381	27033		
5382	27034		
5383	-		
5384	27035		
5385	27036		
5386	27103	27212	27066
5387	27104	27048	
5388	27105	27049	
5389	27037		
5390	27038		
5391	27119	27201	
5392	27120	27202	
5393	27121	27203	
5394	27106	27050	
5395	27107	27051	
5396	27108	27052	
5397	27109	27053	
5398	27039		
5399	27110	27054	
5400	27111	27055	
5401	27112	27056	
5402	27040		
5403	27122	27204	27058
5404	27113	27207	
5405	27041		
5406	27042		
5407	27114	27208	
5408	27115	27209	27063
5409	27116	27210	27064
5410	27123	27205	27059
5411	27117	27211	27065
5412	27124	27206	
5413	27118	27103	27047
5414	27043		
5415	27044		

When the ETH was removed from Class 27s, the jumpers were taken off and the jumper head left in place. These were then removed, leaving the mounting plate, which in turn was removed from refurbished locos, namely 27059/063/066. The mounting plate is visible in this picture of 27047. This loco had an interesting history: as 27118 it was selected for ETH conversion, and while the jumpers were added, it was then decided it was not suitable so 27103 took its place to become 27212. 27118 then became 27103 and retained its ETH cable for a while and then its mounting plate until withdrawal, by which time it was numbered 27047. PDC

SUBSEQUENT RENUMBERINGS

After withdrawal, 27207 was renumbered ADB68025 (incorrectly, as it should have been ADB968025), for use as a training loco at Eastfield. This role was then taken on by 27024, which was renumbered ADB968028.

specifications

1957 number range:	D5700–19
Former class codes:	D12/1 later 12/5
Built by:	Metropolitan Vickers
Introduced:	1958–59
Wheel arrangement:	Co-Bo
Weight (operational):	97 tons
Height:	12ft 8in (3.86m)
Width:	9ft 3in (2.82m)
Length:	56ft 8in (17.27m)
Min. curve negotiable:	3½ chains
Maximum speed:	75mph (120km/h)
Wheelbase:	42ft 7in (12.98m)
Bogie wheelbase:	Bo: 8ft 6in (2.59m) Co: 12ft 3in (3.73m)
Bogie pivot centres:	32ft 4in (9.86m)
Wheel diameter:	3ft 4in (1.02m)
Route availability:	8
Brake force:	35 tons
Engine type:	Crossley HSTV 8
Engine horsepower:	1,200bhp (895kW)
Power at rail:	942bhp (703kW)
Tractive effort:	50,000lb
Main generator type:	Met Vic TG4204
Auxiliary generator type:	Met Vic TAG
No. of traction motors:	5
Traction motor type:	Met Vic 137 BZ
Gear ratio:	15:67
Fuel tank capacity:	510gal (2,295ltr)

THE CLASS 28 comprised a fleet of twenty pilot scheme locos with a three-axle bogie at No. 1 end and a two-axle bogie at No. 2 end: it was thus the only Co-Bo design to run on the UK rail network. These locos proved relatively unsuccessful, and no repeat orders were gained. A plan to re-engine them with EE units was discussed, but dropped. One was taken into Departmental service, enabling it to last long enough to be preserved.

DETAIL DIFFERENCES

Locos were fitted with discs, although unlike most classes they were mounted on frames, which were then affixed to the cab front. They had Red Circle MW and vacuum brakes only. Heating was via a Spanner Mk 1 boiler.

They were refurbished in 1961/62, and lost their wrap-round front windows for standard flat windows and a wider cab pillar.

LIVERIES

All were new in BR green, and all then had half yellow panels added. Only two ran in green with full yellow ends, D5707/08, and just one loco, D5701, was painted in BR blue.

BR green: D5700–19:
BR green with small yellow panels: D5700–19
BR green with full yellow ends: D5707/08
BR blue: D5701

RENUMBERINGS

D5705 was taken into Departmental use and renumbered S15705 for hauling test trains. It was replaced by 1973 and moved to Wales as stationary train heat boiler, and renumbered DB968006. Its new role enabled it to last long enough to be preserved.

RIGHT: Just one Class 28 survives, D5705, which is undergoing restoration at the East Lancashire Railway. The loco sports a full set of headcode discs plus Red Circle MW and a steam pipe. The 28s had their windows changed in the early 1960s: originally they wrapped round the side slightly, but they were changed to give a bigger pillar and to leave the windows flat on the front. Communication doors were also a feature.
PIP DUNN

Pictures of the sole BR blue Class 28 are exceptionally rare. This June 1968 view of the loco in its last month of service shows the unusual bogie and bodyside arrangements of this 'oddball' class. The door for the driver at No. 2 end is some way from the cab itself. BILL WRIGHT

class 29

AFTER A TRIAL in which Class 21 D6123 was rebuilt with a Paxman Ventura engine, BR sanctioned another nineteen conversions in 1965. The work was done by BR at Glasgow. Locos selected were those from the first two batches of Class 21s, D6100–09 and D6110–37. None of the final batch of D6138–57 were rebuilt. Although superior to the 21s, the rebuilt locos – known as Class 29s – only lasted until 1971, and none were preserved. Like the 21s, they spent their careers working in Scotland.

DETAIL DIFFERENCES

The prototype conversion loco D6123 retained its headcode discs. The rest were fitted with centre panels, with square corners. In this change they lost their communication doors.

All were vacuum-braked and had Red Circle MW, and none were converted to dual brakes.

Heating was provided by a Spanner Mk 1 boiler.

None had snowplough brackets despite being allocated to the ScR.

Some had cleaner fronts, while others had traces where the communication doors had been removed, namely D6113/14/29/30.

The horn grilles were also at the bottom of two long oval vertical panels, and on D6108/12/23/24/29/32/37 these had rubber mountings, while on D6100/02/03/06–08/13/14/19/21/30 they were welded on.

Some had only small circular grilles covering their horns, such as D6102/03/06/14/21/23/30/32, while others had larger circular horn grille covers, namely D6100/07/08/12/13/19/24/29/37.

The Class 29s also had their windscreen wipers mounted below the windscreens, unlike the Class 21s which had them fixed above the windscreen.

LIVERIES

All were painted in BR two-tone green with small yellow panels. Some had full yellow ends, while a handful were painted into BR blue.

BR green with small yellow panels: D6100–03/06–08/12–14/16/19/21/23/24/29/30/33/34/37

BR green with full yellow ends: D6102/06/12/21/23/30/32

BR blue: 6100/07/08/19/24/29/37

NUMBERS

All initially had their numbers in serif font. Green locos known to have lost the D prefix are 6102/06/12/21/23/30/32.

Those repainted into blue varied. D6107 had standard corporate-style numbers with D prefixes on its

specifications

1957 BR number range:	D6100–03/06–08/12–14/16/19/21/23/24/29/30/33/34/37
Former class codes:	13/4
Rebuilt by:	BR Glasgow
Introduced:	1963–67
Wheel arrangement:	Bo-Bo
Weight (operational):	73 tons
Height:	12ft 7in (3.84m)
Width:	8ft 8in (2.64m)
Length:	51ft 6in (15.69m)
Min. curve negotiable:	4½ chains
Maximum speed:	80mph (128km/h)
Wheelbase:	37ft (11.28m)
Bogie wheelbase:	8ft 6in (2.59m)
Bogie pivot centres:	28ft 6in (8.69m)
Wheel diameter:	3ft 7in (1.09)
Route availability:	5
Brake force:	42 tons
Engine type:	Paxman 12YJXL
Engine horsepower:	1,350bhp (1,007kW)
Power at rail:	925bhp (691kW)
Tractive effort:	47,000lb
Main generator type:	EE WT880
Auxiliary generator type:	EE WT761
No. of traction motors:	4
Traction motor type:	EE WT440
Gear ratio:	64:15
Fuel tank capacity:	375gal (1,688ltr)

In dirty two-tone green, 6130 in 1970 in the last few months of Class 29 operations. The loco clearly shows the changes made when converted from a Class 21, namely the centre headcode panel with square corners, and the evidence of the former communication doors which were removed at conversion. It has Red Circle MW, steam heating and vacuum brakes only. RAIL PHOTOPRINTS

The first Class 21 converted to a Class 29, D6123: it retained its headcode discs instead of the centre panels, which were fitted to the following nineteen conversions. The loco, which has lost its D prefix, also shows the vertically folding discs which North British fitted to Class 21s and 22s as opposed to horizontal folding discs as fitted to other loco types. RAIL PHOTOPRINTS

bodysides behind all four doors. It had BR arrows on all four cabsides. D6108/ 19/24/29/37 had serif font D-prefixed numbers on all four cabsides with BR badges on all the cab doors. 6119/24/29 later had the D prefixes painted out. 6100 had standard corporate-style numbers with no D prefixes on its cabsides, and with BR badges on all the cab doors.

class 30

specifications

1957 BR number range:	D5500–D5699, D5800–62	Engine type:	Mirrlees JVS12T
Former class codes:	D12/2, later 12/2	Engine output:	1,250bhp (933kW), 1,600bhp (1,194kW): D5545, D5655–70; 2,000bhp (1,492kW): D5835
Built by:	Brush Ltd, Loughborough		
Years introduced:	1957–62	Power at rail:	1,050bhp (783kW)
Wheel arrangement:	A1A-A1A	Tractive effort:	42,000lb
Weight:	107–111 tons	Maximum speed:	90mph (144km/h)
Height:	12ft 7in (3.83m)	Brake force:	49 tons
Length:	56ft 9in (17.29m)	Route availability:	5
Width:	8ft 9in (2.66m)	Main generator type:	Brush TG160-48
Wheelbase:	42ft 10in (13.05m)	Auxiliary generator type:	Brush TG69-42
Bogie wheelbase:	14ft (4.26m)	Traction motor type:	Brush TM73-68
Bogie pivot centres:	28ft 10in (8.78m)	No. of traction motors:	4
Wheel diameter:	Powered: 3ft 7in (1.09m); Pony: 3ft 4in (1.02m)	Gear ratio:	64:17
		Fuel tank capacity:	650gal (2,954ltr)
Min. curve negotiable:	4½ chains (90.52m)		

THE CLASS 30 was another pilot scheme design of twenty locos; further orders were placed, which added another 243 to the fleet. All were built by Brush at its Loughborough works. Because of problems with the engines, D5677 was re-engined with an EE 12SVT unit in 1964, and it was decided to re-engine the whole fleet progressively from 1964 to 1969: these became Class 31s (*see* next section).

DETAIL DIFFERENCES

Discs were fitted to D5500–29/35/39/ 43/47/51/52/55/56/59/62, and roof-mounted headcode boxes to D5530–34/ 36–38/40–42/44–46/48–50/53/54/57/ 58/60/61/63–5699, 5800–62.

Snowplough brackets were not fitted, and all had a Spanner Mk 1 boiler and vacuum brakes.

The pilot scheme locos had Red Circle MW, while the production series locos had Blue Star. D5518 was converted to Blue Star at the same time as it was converted to a Class 31/1. All had centre communication doors.

LIVERIES

All were new in BR all-over green with a grey roof and off-white stripes at sole-bar level and midway up the bodyside. Bufferbeams were red. From D5832 onwards, yellow panels were applied from new. These were retro-applied to the fleet, although some may have been done when converted to Class 31s.

A trial Golden Ochre livery was applied to D5579, both without, and later with, a yellow panel, and a trial 'Electric' blue livery to D5578, again without, and later with, a yellow panel.

BR green: D5500–D5699, D5800–31

BR green with half yellow end: D5500–D5699, D5800–62
Electric blue: D5578
Golden Ochre: D5579
Electric blue with small yellow panel: D5578
Golden Ochre with small yellow panel: D5579

BUILD BATCHES

The fleet was built in two main batches, the first twenty pilot scheme locos, then the production series machines, although there was not one main order for 243 additional locos and instead batches were ordered in stages.

There were eight months between the arrival of D5500 and the 3 July 1958 order for another forty locos, D5520–59. These were followed on 3 December by another twenty locos, D5560–79. 21 April 1959 saw the biggest order, for seventy-five locos, D5580–5654, followed by twenty-five more on 15 August, D5655–79.

In January 1960 forty-six more locos were ordered, D5680–99 and D5800–25 (there was a gap in numbers as D5700–19 had been taken by the Class 28s); the final two orders in November and December 1960 were for ten locos numbers D5826–35, and twenty-seven numbered D5836–62.

MAJOR MODIFICATION DATES

The pilot scheme locos were 1,250bhp, while the production series locos were uprated to 1,365bhp. D5507 was temporarily uprated to 1,450bhp but later reverted to its specification output.

D5545, D5655–70 were uprated to 1,600bhp, and D5835 to 2,000bhp. The latter had a change to its bodyside by having an additional two grilles on its bodyside at No. 2 end.

Problems with the Mirrlees engine saw D5677 fitted with a trial EE engine in 1964. BR then opted to fit EE units to the entire fleet, with the pilot scheme locos usually the last to be treated – in fact pioneer D5500 was the last to be modified in 1969, so actually spent twelve years as a Class 30 and just seven (in traffic) as a 31/0. As locos were re-engined they changed from Class 30 to 31.

Dates for re-engining, and so conversion to Class 31s, were as follows:

D5677 (1964); 5525/27/34/40/41/46/53/
56/57/59/68/70/71/74/76/87/91/94,
5601/16/20/32/33/42/45/50/51/75/80/
81/84/86/87/97, 5840/41/44–46/48–50/
55/59 (1965); D5521/36/49/62/81/84/
90/93/95/96, 5602/04–06/08–11/13/14/
22/25–27/30/31/40/43/44/46/49/53/62/
64/65/67/73/76/78/83/85/88/89/91, 5800
–02/05/07/13/15/25/34/56/62 (1966);
D5518/20/32/37/48/51/55/61/66/80/85/
86/88/97/98, 5600/03/07/12/17/18/23/
24/28/35–38/47/48/54/58/60/63/66/68/
71/74/90/92–94/96/98/99, 5801/03/04/
06/08–12/14/16–24/26–33/37/38/42/
43/47/52/54/58 (1967); D5502–06/08/09/
13–15/17/19/22–24/26/29–31/33/35/
38/39/42–45/47/50/52/54/58/60/63–65/
67/69/72/73/75/77–79/82/83/89/92/99,
5615/19/21/29/34/39/41/52/55–57/59/
61/69/70/72/79/82/95, 5835/36/39/51/
53/57/60 (1968); D5500/01/07/10–12/
16/28 (1969).

No Class 30s were ever renumbered under TOPS.

ABOVE: Although this 1997 image of D5500 is a Class 31, it is restored to the original look of the twenty pilot scheme Brush Type 2s delivered in 1957–58 as Class 30s. All were withdrawn early in the mid-1970s, but D5500 survives in the NRM collection, and is in original external condition. It has since been repainted into BR blue. Internally, however, the loco is much changed from construction, with its Mirrlees engine replaced in 1969 by an EE engine, thus becoming a Class 31. PIP DUNN

RIGHT: There were no external differences between a Class 30 and a Class 31. D5847 therefore looks like a Class 31, but it still has its Mirrlees engine so it is a Class 30. BILL WRIGHT

specifications

TOPS Number range:	31001–019, 31101–327, 31400–469, 31507–569, 31601/602, 31970
1957 BR number range:	D5500–D5699, D5800–62
Former class codes:	12/2 (31/0), D14/2, then 14/2 (31/1)
Built by:	Brush Ltd, Loughborough
Years introduced:	1964–69
Wheel arrangement:	A1A-A1A
Weight:	107–111 tons
Height:	12ft 7in (3.83m)
Length:	56ft 9in (17.29m)
Width:	8ft 9in (2.66m)
Wheelbase:	42ft 10in (13.05m)
Bogie wheelbase:	14ft (4.26m)
Bogie pivot centres:	28ft 10in (8.78m)
Wheel diameter:	Powered: 3ft 7in (1.09m), Pony: 3ft 4in (1.02m)
Min. curve negotiable:	4½ chains (90.52m)
Engine type:	English Electric 12SVT
Engine output:	1,470bhp (1,097kW)
Power at rail:	1,170bhp (872kW)
Tractive effort:	42,000lb: 31101–116; 35,900lb: remainder
Maximum speed:	75mph (120km/h): 31001–019, 31101–116; 80mph (128m/h): 31117–327; 90mph (144km/h):
Brake force:	49 tons
Route availability:	5 (31/0, 31/1), 6 (31/4, 31/5)
Main generator type:	Brush TG160-48
Auxiliary generator type:	Brush TG69-42
Auxiliary ETH alternator type:	Brush BL100-30
Traction motor type:	Brush TM73-68
No. of traction motors:	4
Gear ratio:	64:17 (31001–019, 31101–116, 31418), 60:19 (31117–327, 31400–417/419–469)
Fuel tank capacity:	530gal (2,385ltr), 630gal (2,835ltr): 31178

AS TOPS WAS introduced the Brush Type 2s were being re-engined, and so the locos still with their original Mirrlees engines became Class 30s, and those converted with English Electric units became Class 31s. The Class 31/0s were the original pilot scheme locos, while the 31/1s were the production series locos. Pilot scheme D5518 went direct from a Class 30 to 31/1, the other nineteen pilot scheme locos went from 30 to 31/0, and the 243 production locos went from 30 to 31/1.

In 1972 a start was made on converting twenty-four locos to dual heat by upgrading them with ETH whilst retaining their boilers. They became the 31/4s, although 31424 was modified to ETH only. This programme finished in 1975, but in 1983 a major conversion programme for a further forty-four ETH locos – without steam heating – was made. Locos were also refurbished. When this programme finished, other 31/1s were refurbished as well, although the programme ended in 1988 leaving eighty-nine locos untreated (some of which had already been withdrawn and scrapped). Two further locos were converted to ETH to replace accident-damaged 31401/436, and they became 31400/469 to take into account the slightly different electrics on the first twenty-four ETH conversions.

In 1990 some ETH locos had the equipment isolated, and these became 31/5s, although some reverted back to ETH capability and regained their original 31/4 numbers. In 1999 two 31/1s were fitted with through ETH wiring and became 31/6s. A sole loco taken into the RTC fleet was renumbered from the 31/1 series initially into the 97/2 series, then into the 31/9 series.

DETAIL DIFFERENCES

The first locos built had discs, namely 31001–019, 31102/103/105–111/117/ 121/125/129/133/134/137/138/141/144, 31418. All others had headcode boxes. In the mid-1970s as communication doors were plated over, the two centre discs were removed; those locos which ran with just two headcode discs were 31102/103/105–111/117/121/125/129/ 133/134/137/138/141/144, 31418.

The remaining two discs were removed from refurbished 31102/105– 108/110/125/134/144, 31418/444/450/ 461.

Headcode boxes were fitted to 31101/112–116/118–120/122–124/126 –128/130–132/135/136/139/142/143/ 145–156/158–171/173–196/198–266/ 268–309/311–327, 31400–417/419–443/ 445–449/451–460/462–469, 31970. Of these, 31101 had previously carried discs as Class 30 D5518.

All headcode panels were changed to dominos, apart from 31150, the first withdrawal. 31187, at No. 1 end, had its domino panel changed to a yellow metal panel with opaque lenses in the early 1980s, while refurbished locos had metal panels in place of headcode panels.

31215 had its headcode box removed from No. 2 end while unrefurbished. No horn grille was added in its place, thus giving a completely curved cab roof. It had two white lamps added inside of its existing red tail-lights. It kept this look

The cluttered front end of an original unrefurbished Class 31 with all four headcode discs retained and the central communications doors still in place, albeit not in use. This is 31141 in 1980, which was dual-braked in 1973 but never refurbished, and hence retained the skirting around the bufferbeam until withdrawal. The loco has lost its train heating boiler. ANDY HOARE

when refurbished, except the white lamps moved to below the red tail-lights in the same style as an ex-disc refurbished 31. No. 1 remained unaffected.

Unrefurbished 31292 also had metal plates on both headcode boxes from the mid-1980s, painted blue in the same style as a refurbished loco.

Snowplough brackets were fitted to 31106/108/111/115/117/118/120/121/ 123/125/128/130/132/142/146/164, 31200/210/229/253/258/259/263/270/ 271/273/275, 31304/312/316–319.

The centre communication doors were removed from the late 1970s and replaced by a sheet of metal with two additional footwells. Some had plain panels without these footwells, and at least 31101/116/121/137/161/194,31269/ 280/283, 31401/412/414/420/422/465 were noted for periods running as such. 31148 ran for a period in the early 1980s with a recessed front panel with no centre footwells; this was removed when the loco was refurbished.

Recesses with tablet-catching equipment were fitted in the driver's cab doors from new to D5671–76 (31243–248), and after the equipment was removed the recesses remained until plated over at works visits in the mid-1980s. 31244/ 245 were withdrawn like this in 1982/ 86 respectively.

31178 had its fuel tank increased by 100 gallons by converting its boiler fuel tank for loco fuel.

The two Class 31/6s are standard refurbished 31/1s but fitted with through ETH wiring so they can work in multiple with an ETH Blue Star loco but not be the lead loco. 31452/454/459/468, 31601/602 also had fire-suppressant equipment to allow them to be on the rear of a train but unmanned and running.

Several Class 31s had an additional roof-mounted metal rim added around their fan which was meant to aid cooling. It was fitted to unrefurbished 31115/ 182/186, 31207/225/226/262/264/295, 31401–415/417–424. Of these, 31186 had (and still has, as 31601) a special version with reinforcing strips. Some locos later lost them – 31402/410/412/ 419/421 at least – while those on 31406/415 became damaged. 31182 retained its own on conversion to ETH as 31437. In 1989/90 this modification became standard, along with vertical grilles, for works overhauls of both 31/1s

A standard unrefurbished Class 31 with headcode boxes as opposed to discs. 31132 is vacuum-braked and non-boilered so has a very sparse bufferbeam. When refurbished, the bufferbeam skirting and the band around the middle of the loco were removed and the headcode panels plated over. PDC

and 31/4s, but it then stopped again after 1990.

Most refurbished 31s had their driver's side front cab windows strengthened, and this featured a more prominent metal window frame. At least 31106/ 119/135/165, 31206, 31400/403/414/ 416/425/427/429/430/432–435/437– 439/441–445/447/449/450, and 31601 were so fitted.

D5835, later 31302, had an additional two grilles at No. 2 end on one side only to allow additional cooling for its period as a Class 30 with an uprated Mirrlees engine. These were retained even after a standard EE engine was fitted.

HEADLIGHTS

From 1984, high-intensity headlights were fitted to 31446–455 at refurbishment; these were mounted to one side of the plated-over communication doors. Other locos to have headlights to the side of their doors at refurbishment were 31102/116/126/130/132/ 144/146/160/164/171/184, 31229/255/ 270/275/290/296, 31304/317/319/324, 31401/405/412/414/438/446–454, 31512/514/546–549/551–554. Later, as headlights became a standard fitment, they were fitted to the centre of the cab at the bottom of the front just above the bufferbeam; these were fitted to 31105–107/110/112/119/125/134/135/ 142/145/154/155/158/163/165/166/178/ 181/185/186/188/190/191/196/199, 31200/201/205/206/217/224/230/233/ 237/238/242/250/263/271/272/273/276/ 282/285/294,31301/306/308/327,31405/

407/408/410/413/417/420–423/427/ 434/439/442/459/461–463/465–468, 31519/524/530/531/533/537/538/541/ 544/545/556/558/563/568, 31601/602.

Strangely the headlight was removed from 31555, while some locos which had side headlights had them moved to the new centre bottom position.

LIVERIES

The Class 30s were in a mix of all-over BR green and BR green with small yellow panels when converted to Class 31s. Some 31s emerged in green with small yellow panels, and others in blue, while many went on to run in green with full yellow ends; these were D5513/18/20/ 22–25/27/29/32/34/37/40–42/44/46/47/ 51/53–76/79–86/88–92/94–98, 5600–27/ 29–34/36–38/42/44/45/47/48/50–53/ 55–57/60/61/63–65/67–82/84–95/97– 99, 5800–29/34/35/42/43/47/52/56.

BR blue: 31001–019, 31101–103/105– 266/268–327, 31400–469, 31507/514/ 516/522/526/533/537/538/544/545/546/ 548/549/552/556/558/563/569
BR blue with white roof: 31005/019, 31412/416/430
BR blue with white body stripe: 31309, 31404/405/409/411/413/416/424
BR blue with white cant rail stripes: 31277/281, 31323
BR blue with yellow side window frames: 31135
BR blue with red cab solebars and large badge: 31101
Railfreight: 31102/108/110/113/116/ 120/125/126/128/130/132/134/142–147/

LEFT: The first twenty-three Class 31s converted to ETH retained their steam-heat boilers so became dual-heat locos. They retained skirts and middle bands, and had their ETH jumpers on the front of the body. This is dual-heat 31415, which has the steam-heat pipe under the air-brake pipe in the same style as a dual-braked steam-heat 31/1. PDC

BELOW: Six Class 31s, D5671–76 (31243–248), had tablet-catching equipment fitted (for working on the Hugh Dyke branch near Grantham), and this was fitted in a recessed section on the cab doors, as seen clearly on 31248. Those refurbished lost these recesses, but 31244/245 retained them until withdrawal, as they were never overhauled. PDC

154/155/158–161/163/164/166/171/174/ 183–185/198/299, 31200/201/203/207/ 209/210/215/217/226/229/230/233/234/ 240/243/248/252/255/261/270/273/275/ 290/294/296/299, 31302/304/306/308/ 312/317/319/324

Red stripe Railfreight: 31105/107/112/ 119/135/149/159/165/178/180/181/186 –188/190/191/196, 31205/206/219/224/ 232/235/237/238/242/247/250/263/268/ 271/272/276/282/285/290, 31301/327

Trainload Coal: 31120/130/199, 31200/ 201/217/270/275/276, 31304/312/319/ 324

Trainload Petroleum: 31185/199, 31201/207/233/238/273, 31302/304/319

Trainload Construction: 31155, 31209/ 271/294/296

Railfreight Distribution: 31160

Two-tone grey: 31160, 31271

Departmental grey: 31113/166, 31308, 31412/417/417/424/431/451/453–455/ 457/461/462/465/466/468, 31511/530

InterCity 'Mainline': 31405/407/420/ 422/423/464

InterCity: 31454

Infrastructure yellow: 31116

Research centre red and grey with yellow cabsides: 97203

Research centre red and grey: 97204, 31970

Transrail: 31105

BR blue with yellow cabs and red cab solebars: 31413

'Dutch': 31102/105–107/110/112/113/ 116/119/125/126/134/135/142/144–147/ 154/158/159/163/166/174/178/181/185 –188/190/191/196, 31203/206/207/219/ 224/229/232/233/235/237/238/242/250/ 255/263/268/272/273/285/290, 31306/ 308, 31435/466, 31512/514/516/519/

524/526/530/531/533/537/541/544/546 –549/551–556/558/563/565/568/569

'Dutch' with green solebar: 31558

Regional Railways: 31270, 31410/421/ 439/455/465

Mainline Freight aircraft blue: 31407

'Dutch' Transrail: 31112

EWS: 31255, 31466

Fragonset: 31106/128/190, 31452/459/ 468

FM Rail: 31459

Railtrack: 31190, 31601

West Coast Railways: 31190

Wessex Pink: 31601

Network Rail yellow: 31105, 31233/ 285, 31465, 31602

BR green (special): 31110/165/190

BR blue (retro): 31106/128

Devon and Cornwall Railways: 31452, 31601

Golden Ochre (preservation): 31463

EMBLEMS

Small West Highland terrier: 31420 B

White kingfishers: 31277, 31323 B; 31327 FR

Coloured kingfishers: 31123, 31281/ 283 B

Stratford Sparrows: 31227, 31432 B; 31116/128, 31226 FO, 31219/224/234/ 240 FR

Cast depot plaques:

Bescot saddle: 31105/106/110/116/ 126/145–147/166/174/178/185/196, 31512/514/516/519/524/526/530/533/ 537/546/548/551/555/565 C

Crewe DMD cat: 31102/125/134/142/ 144/159/188, 31203/206/229/232/235/ 237/238/242/255/272/273/285/290 C, 31120/130/199, 31200/217/270/275/ 276, 31304/312/324 FC,

Immingham star: 31185/199, 31201/ 207/233/273, 31302/319 FP; 31531/541/ 544/547/549/552/553/556/558/569 C; 31294/296 FA,

Stratford sparrow: 31125/181/186/ 187/190/191/196, 31219/224/263 C; 31155, 31271/294 FA, 31294 F

Tinsley rose: 31160 FD

31430 ran with cast numberplates, painted red, on its bodyside behind the cabs from 1988.

Larger (8in) numbers: 31117/121, 31309, 31411/413/464, 31537 B; 31555 D; 31112, 31524/537 C
Black larger (8in) numbers: 31160 F
Large black numbers on front: 31311, 31544 B
Large white numbers on front: 31327 FR
Large white bodyside numbers: 31278/281/283 B
Small numbers: 31411, 97203 B; 31178 FR
Yellow DCE stripes: 31106/123/152/167, 31281/283/284/286, 31305/320, 31415/420/423/433–435/437/446/463/465, 31533 B; 31107/165/178/186/187/191, 31219/235/237/268/285 FR
Grey MEE stripes: 31131, 31260/264/286/292, 31415/465 B
Red RTC stripes: 31970 RTC
NSE branding: 31425 B
Regional Railways branding: 31233 C

NAMES

31102	Cricklewood
31105	Bescot TMD
31106	The Blackcountryman
31106	SPALDING TOWN
31107	John H Carless
31116	RAIL Celebrity
31128	CHARYBDIS
31130	Calder Hall Power Station
31146	Brush Veteran
31147	Floreat Salopia
31160	Phoenix*
31165	Stratford Major Depot
31190	GRYPHON
31201	Fina Energy
31203	Steve Organ GM
31233	Phillips Imperial
31233	Severn Valley Railway
31271	Stratford 1840-2001
31276	Calder Hall Power Station
31289	PHOENIX
31296	Amlwch Freighter/ Trên Nwyddau Amlwch (different plate each side)
31309	Cricklewood
31327	Phillips Imperial
31405	Mappa Mundi
31410	Granada Telethon
31413	Severn Valley Railway
31418	Boadicea*
31421	Wigan Pier
31423	Jerome K Jerome

31428	North Yorkshire Moors Railway
31430	Sister Dora
31435	Newton Heath Depot
31439	North Yorkshire Moors Railway
31444	Keighley & Worth Valley Railway
31452	MINOTAUR
31454	THE HEART OF WESSEX
31455	Our Eli
31459	CERBERUS
31468	The Engineman's Fund
31468	HYDRA
31530	Sister Dora
31544	Keighley & Worth Valley Railway
31558	Nene Valley Railway
31568	The Engineman's Fund
31601	BLETCHLEY PARK STATION 'X'
31601	THE MAYOR OF CASTERBRIDGE
31601	GAUGE 'O' GUILD
31602	CHIMAERA
31602	DRIVER DAVE GREEN

* Unofficial names

MAJOR MODIFICATION DATES

Dual-braking of the fleet began in 1968 but stopped in 1977; it was restarted in 1982 and was completed in 1987. No 31/0s were dual-braked.

Heating was initially provided by a Spanner Mk 1 boiler, but some locos were fitted with ETH, with an index of sixty-six. Twenty-four were done in 1972–75, and then another forty-four in 1984/85, with two subsequent conversions as replacements.

Boilers were removed from all refurbished locos, as well as from the following unrefurbished locos: 31101/109/118/121/123/124/138/141/167, 31212/

227/245/260/278/280/281/283/284/287–289/292/298, 31311/322.

Dates dual-braked: 5530/35/39/81/90/95/99, 5601/02/05/08/09/11/13/22/26/41/42/44/46/50-53/57/78 (1968); 5523/28/36/48/49/93, 5610/14/25/27/40/43/49/62/65/73/77/85, 5802/06/13/15/25/29/34 (1969); 5524/27/34/41/45/61/86, 5615/20/23/36/37/48/58/80/84, 5817/40/45/48/54/58 (1970); 5531/63/74/83/84/89/92, 5616/56/59/70/75/83, 5686/62 (1971); 5596, 5606/69/91/98 (1972); 5522/37/55/56/59/70/80/88, 5632/45/92, 5807/14/24/42/57 (1973); 31107/128/135/147/150/153/154/158/174/176/184, 31210/241/243/258/259/273/286/294, 31302/304, 31413/419–422 (1974); 31142/144/149/155/155/195, 31205/206/209, 31423/424 (1975); 31189, 31233/263/281/184 (1976); 31221/278 (1977), 31101, 31260/264, 31309 (1982); 31122/124/167, 31280/287–289/293, 31305/326, 31425–431 (1983); 31433/435–440/442/443/445/447/448/450–458/460 (1984); 31102/120/125/134/146/160/161/164/183, 31200/261/299, 31306/308/312/319/324, 31461–464/466/468 (1985); 31207/215/229/234/240/248/270/275/290/296 (1986); 31237/271 (1987).

Not dual-braked: 31001–019, 31103/111/136, 31214/244/254/262, 31313.

Refurbishment dates: 31425–432^ (1983); 31412/414/416/423/433–460^ (1984); 31108*/113/120*/126*/128/134*/143/145/147/154/156/158/159/161/166/174/198/199, 31200*/202/209/210/226/243/252/261/299, 31302/306/308*/

A refurbished 31/4, 31424, shows off the repositioned ETH jumper on the bottom right of the cab front. To the left can be seen the bottom of the frame which is now uncovered following the removal of the skirt. The headcode box has been plated over with opaque lenses added. 31424 was never dual heat. PDC

A refurbished 31/1 in Railfreight livery, 31252 shows the clean bufferbeam with steam pipe removed and a hole left under the air-brake pipe. These holes were sometimes plated over. Aside from the lack of an ETH box and the livery, the loco is the same as 31424. PDC

Spot-hire company Fragonset had a fleet of Class 31s in its short life. 31459 Cerberus is painted in its black livery with a maroon stripe and a grey roof. The loco is a standard refurbished 31/4 with a headlight above the bufferbeam; other locos had this light on the right of the cab front above the footwell. PIP DUNN

312ˆ, 31406/417/419/422/424/461–468ˆ (1985); 31102ˆ/116/126ˆ/130ˆ/132ˆ/142/ 144/146ˆ/155/160ˆ/163/164ˆ/171/183– 185, 31203/207/215ˆ/217/229/230/233/ 234ˆ/240ˆ/248ˆ/255/270ˆ/273/275ˆ/290/ 294/296, 31304/317ˆ/319/324, 31401/405/ 407–409/411/420 (1986); 31105/107/112/ 135/149/178/180/181/186–188/190/191/ 196, 31201/219/224/232/235/237ˆ/238/ 242/247/250/263/268/271ˆ/272/276/ 282, 31301/327, 31402/404/410/413/415/ 418/421/469ˆˆ (1987); 31106/119/165, 31205/206/285, 31403 (1988).

ˆ locos fitted with ETH at the same time; entered works as 31/1s
ˆ loco dual-braked at same time

Locos not refurbished: 31001–019, 31101/103/109/111/117/118/121–124/ 127/131/136/138/141/150/152/162/167/ 168/170/173/175/176/189/192/195, 31204/208/212/214/218/221–223/225/ 227/231/241/244/245/249/254/257/259/ 260/262/264/278/280/281/283/284/286 –289/292/293/298, 31305/309/311/313/ 314/320/322/323/326.

Locos unrefurbished before ETH conversion: 31114ˆ/115ˆ/129ˆ/133ˆ/ 137/139ˆ/140ˆ/148ˆ/153/157ˆ/169ˆ/172ˆ/ 177ˆ/179ˆ/182ˆ/193ˆ/194ˆ/197ˆ, 31211ˆ/ 213/216ˆ/220/228ˆ/236ˆ/239ˆ/246ˆ/251ˆ/ 253ˆ/256/258/265ˆ/266ˆ/269ˆ/274ˆ/277ˆ/ 279ˆ/291ˆ/295ˆ/297ˆ, 1300ˆ/303ˆ/307ˆ/310ˆ/ 315ˆ/316ˆ/318ˆ/321ˆ/325ˆ.

ˆ vacuum-braked only prior to ETH conversion

NUMBERS

Renumbering was not straightforward to TOPS because of the ETH programme. 5522 and 5697 had been allocated 31104 and 31267 respectively prior to being selected for the ETH conversion programme, but went from their D numbers to 31418/419 respectively. 31420– 424 all spent brief spells as TOPS 31/1s before being converted.

5518 was converted from a pilot scheme Class 30 straight to a 31/1 after collision, thus never being a Class 31/0 which in theory it should have been.

As more 31/1s were selected for ETH upgrading in the 1980s, these too became 31/4s. The transition to 31/5s was straightforward, just changing the 4 to a 5, so for example, 31407 became 31507. 31507/511/522/544/552/554/555/ 565/568 later changed back to ETH operation and so simply reverted to their original 31/4 number.

5500	31018		
5501	31001		
5502	31002		
5503	31003		
5504	31004		
5505	31005		
5506	31006		
5507	31007		
5508	31008		
5509	31009		
5510	31010		
5511	31011		
5512	31012		
5513	31013		
5514	31014		
5515	31015		
5516	31016		
5517	31017		
5518	31101		
5519	31019		
5520	31102		
5521	31103		
5522	31418		
5523	31105		
5524	31106		
5525	31107		
5526	31108		
5527	31109		
5528	31110		
5529	31111		
5530	31112		
5531	31113		
5532	31114	31453	31553
5533	31115	31466	
5534	31116		
5535	31117		
5536	31118		
5537	31119		
5538	31120		
5539	31121		
5540	31122		
5541	31123		
5542	31124		
5543	31125		
5544	31126		
5545	31127		
5546	31128		
5547	31129	31461	
5548	31130		
5549	31131		
5550	31132		
5551	31133	31450	
5552	31134		

5553	31135			5613	31190			5651	31225		
5554	31136			5614	31191			5652	31226		
5555	31137	31444	31544	5615	31192			5653	31227		
5556	31138			5616	31406			5654	31228	31454	31554
5557	31139	31438		5617	31193	31426	31526	5655	31229		
5558	31140	31421		5618	31194	31427		5656	31409		
5559	31141			5619	31195			5657	31230		
5560	31142			5620	31196			5658	31231		
5561	31143			5621	31197	31423		5659	31232		
5562	31144			5622	31198			5660	31233		
5563	31145			5623	31199			5661	31234		
5564	31146			5624	31200			5662	31235		
5565	31147			5625	31201			5663	31236	31433	31533
5566	31148	31448	31548	5626	31202			5664	31237		
5567	31149			5627	31203			5665	31238		
5568	31150			5628	31204			5666	31239	31439	
5569	31151	31436		5629	31205			5667	31240		
5570	31152			5630	31206			5668	31241		
5571	31153	31432		5631	31207			5669	31410		
5572	31154			5632	31208			5670	31242		
5573	31155			5633	31209			5671	31243		
5574	31156			5634	31210			5672	31244		
5575	31157	31424	31524	5635	31211	31428		5673	31245		
5576	31158			5636	31212			5674	31246	31455	31555
5577	31159			5637	31213	31465	31565	5675	31247		
5578	31160			5638	31214			5676	31248		
5579	31161	31400		5639	31215			5677	31249		
5580	31162			5640	31407	31507		5678	31250		
5581	31163			5641	31216	31467		5679	31251	31442	
5582	31164			5642	31217			5680	31252		
5583	31165			5643	31218			5681	31253	31431	31531
5584	31166			5644	31219			5682	31254		
5585	31167			5645	31220	31441	31541	5683	31255		
5586	31168			5646	31408			5684	31256	31459	
5587	31169	31457		5647	31221			5685	31257		
5588	31170			5648	31222			5686	31258	31434	
5589	31401			5649	31223			5687	31259		
5590	31171			5651	31224			5688	31260		
5591	31172	31420									
5592	31402										
5593	31173										
5594	31174										
5595	31175										
5596	31403										
5597	31176										
5598	31177	31443									
5599	31178										
5600	31179	31435									
5601	31180										
5602	31181										
5603	31182	31437	31537								
5604	31183										
5605	31404										
5606	31405										
5607	31184										
5608	31185										
5609	31186										
5610	31187										
5611	31188										
5612	31189										

Network Rail has four Class 31s in its fleet for working test trains, usually in push-pull fashion with DBSOs but sometimes top-and-tail with Class 31s/37s/73s. For their role on the Structure Gauging Train, 31233/285 have been fitted with cameras, mounted above the footwells, and additional lights at No. 2 end, seen to great effect in this view of 31233 in April 2011. ANTHONY HICKS

5689	31261		
5690	31262		
5691	31411	31511	
5692	31412	31512	
5693	31263		
5694	31264		
5695	31265	31430	31530
5696	31266	31460	
5697	31419	31519	
5698	31268		
5699	31269	31429	
5800	31270		
5801	31271		
5802	31272		
5803	31273		
5804	31274	31425	
5805	31275		
5806	31276		
5807	31277	31469	31569
5808	31278		
5809	31279	31452	31552
5810	31280		
5811	31281		
5812	31413		
5813	31282		
5814	31414	31514	
5815	31283		
5816	31284		
5817	31285		
5818	31286		
5819	31287		
5820	31288		
5821	31289		
5822	31290		
5823	31291	31456	31556
5824	31415		
5825	31292		
5826	31293		
5827	31294		
5828	31295	31447	31547
5829	31296		
5830	31297	31463	31563
5831	31298	97203	
5832	31299		
5833	31300	31445	31545
5834	31301		
5835	31302		
5836	31303	31458	31558
5837	31304		
5838	31305		
5839	31306		
5840	31307	31449	31549
5841	31308		
5842	31416	31516	
5843	31309		
5844	31310	31422	31522
5845	31311		
5846	31312		
5847	31313		
5848	31314		

5849	31315	31462	
5850	31316	31446	31546
5851	31317		
5852	31318	31451	31551
5853	31319		
5854	31320		
5855	31321	31468	31568
5856	31417		
5857	31322		
5858	31323		
5859	31324		
5860	31325	31464	
5861	31326	97204	31970
5862	31327		

DEPARTMENTAL CLASS 31s

Several Class 31s were used for Departmental purposes. In 1977–80, four Class 31/0s were converted to carriage heaters. They were 31002/008/013/014 which became ADB968014/016/013/015 respectively. 31007/012 were initially also earmarked for these roles, but were later shelved as better locos were used instead.

ADB968013/014 were painted in green with full yellow ends and white bodyside stripes, with BR double arrow badges. ADB968015 was in BR blue with a white stripe, while ADB968016 was in BR blue. They retained their full sets of headcode discs.

They were fitted with ETH jumpers and used at Great Yarmouth, Norwich, Colchester, Cambridge before being laid up in 1982/83, and dumped at March and Stratford. They were withdrawn

after an increase of ETH locos in general, and complaints from residents over the excessive noise from revving the engine to provide heat.

In July 1986, 31298 was acquired by the RTC as a replacement for 97201 (ex-24061) to haul test trains. It was renumbered 97203, and in March 1987 repainted into RTC red and blue livery. In April 1987 it caught fire and was withdrawn.

Its replacement was dual-braked 31326, which became 97204 in September 1987. It was also repainted into RTC livery, albeit slight different to 97203 by not having yellow lower cabsides. In August 1989 it was renumbered as 31970. It was withdrawn in December 1990.

NETWORK RAIL 31s

Network Rail owns four Class 31s, all painted in all-over yellow, and also hires others as required, one of which, 31602, was also repainted into yellow.

31233/285 have, at No. 2 end, a series of cab-mounted lights, three at roof level on the headcode box, and two at solebar level above the buffers. They also have cameras mounted in their cab fronts, in the panel that covered the old communication doors, above the footwells.

At No. 1 end, 31233/285 have additional boxes for plugging in cables to the test stock, but they have no camera. 31105 and 31465 remain as standard refurbished 31s, although all four are now air-braked only.

After withdrawal, four Class 31/1s were converted to static carriage pre-heaters for use in East Anglia. ADB968016 (ex-31008) was the last of the quartet, modified in October 1980, and based at Stratford. It was withdrawn from this role in late 1982. PDC

A DEVELOPMENT OF the BRCW Type 2, Class 33 uses the same body design as Classes 26/27, but with an 8-cylinder Sulzer engine, the 8LDA. Designed for the SR, they had dual brakes and ETH from new. There were initially two main types: the standard locos and twelve narrow-bodied locos for the gauge-restricted line to Hastings.

In 1966/67, nineteen were converted to push-pull use and became the 33/1s, leaving the remaining standard locos to be the 33/0s and the narrow locos to be the 33/2s. The Class 33/1s were originally to have been Class 34s.

DETAIL DIFFERENCES

All were built with two-character SR headcodes, which were retained throughout their lives. All had snow-plough brackets, but the following are known to have carried ploughs: 33001 –004/008/013/015–017/019/021/022/ 025–027/029/030/032/033/035/037/039/ 044/046–054/056–060/063/064, 33103/ 116, 33201/202/206–208/211/212 and before its conversion to a 33/1, D6511.

All were fitted with ETH (index 48), which was isolated on some locos in the late 1980s, and removed from 33029 and 33207 during overhaul. All were dual-braked from new, but 33029 and 33207 were converted to air only, although 33207 has since had its vacuum brakes reinstated.

All were fitted with Blue Star MW. The 33/1s had duplicate pipes on their cab fronts to allow them to work in push-pull mode, and multiple with SR Mk 1 EMU stock.

Cab-to-shore radio pods were fitted to the cab roofs of 33008/019/021/025/ 030/046/051/057/063, 33103/109/116, 33201/202/207/208.

HEADLIGHTS

High intensity headlights were fitted to 33002/008/009/012/019/021/023/025/ 029/030/035/042/046/050/051/063/064, 33101/103/109/116, 33201/202/207/208.

Tail-lights were removed from 33006 (r/h No. 1 end), 33013 (both No. 1 end), 33021 (both No. 2 end), 33025 (both No. 2 end), 33029 (both No. 2 end), 33043 (both No. 1 end), 33046 (both No. 2 end), 33051 (both No. 1 end), 33058 (all), 33059 (both No. 2 end), 33206 (both No. 2 end), 33207 (all).

LIVERIES

Green: D6500–97
Green half yellow end: D6500/01/ 03–97
Green full yellow end: 6501/03/06/ 10/18/50/53/59–64/56–58/66/70/71/73/ 75/76/82/84/96 and possibly 6572/81 as well
BR blue: 33001–065, 33101–119, 33201 –212
BR blue-white windows: 33023, 33101/ 105/119
BR blue with wrap-round yellow ends and grey roof: 33012/021
BR blue with grey roof: 33008/023/ 025/027/056
BR blue with black window frames: 33112
BR blue with grey roof and two thin bodyside white stripes: 33056

specifications

TOPS number range:	33001–065, 33101–119, 33201–212
BR 1957 number range:	D6500–97
Former class codes:	D15/1, later 15/6 (33/0), D15/2, later 15/6A (33/2)
Southern Region class code:	KA (33/0), KB (33/1), KA-4C (33/2)
Built by:	Birmingham RC&W
Years introduced:	1960–62
Wheel arrangement:	Bo-Bo
Weight:	77 tons, 78 tons (33/1)
Height:	12ft 8in (3.86m)
Length:	50ft 9in (15.47m)
Width:	9ft 3in (2.81m) (33/0+33/1), 8ft 8in (2.64m) (33/2)
Wheelbase:	39ft 0in (11.88m)
Bogie wheelbase:	10ft 0in (3.04m)
Bogie pivot centres:	29ft 0in (8.83m)
Wheel diameter:	3ft 7in (1.09m)
Min. curve negotiable:	4 chains (80.46m)
Engine type:	Sulzer 8LDA28A
Engine output:	1,550bhp (1,154kW)
Power at rail:	1,215bhp (906kW)
Tractive effort:	45,000lb
Maximum speed:	85mph (137km/h)
Brake force:	35 tons
Route availability:	6
Main generator type:	Crompton Parkinson CAG391-B1
Auxiliary generator type:	Crompton Parkinson CAG193-A1
ETH generator type:	Crompton Parkinson CAG392-A1
Traction motor type:	Crompton Parkinson C171-C2
No. of traction motors:	4
Gear ratio:	62:17
Fuel tank capacity:	750gal (3,410ltr)

The front end detail of 33044 is clear. The 33s were dual-braked and ETH-fitted from new, and also retained their two-character headcodes throughout their lives, so did undergo as many external changes as other classes. The loco sports a full set of snowploughs. The 33 has two Blue Star MW receptacles and used cables stowed in the locos' cabs to work in multiple. The ETH receptacle is on the left under the buffer. ANDY HOARE

BR green (retro): 33008/012, 33208
Mainline InterCity: 33115 (83301) – *see* below
Trainload Construction: 33021/033/042/050/051/053/056/063/064, 33202/204/207
Railfreight Distribution: 33203–206/211, 33302
Departmental grey: 33002/008/025/026/057/065, 33101/103/108/109/116/118, 33201
'Dutch': 33002/008/009/019/025/026/030/035/046/047/051/057/065, 33103/108/118, 33201/202/208
Dark NSE: 33035, 33114
Two-tone grey with Mainline logos: 33021/063, 33204/207
EWS: 33030
DRS: 33025/029/030, 33207
DRS minimodal: 33025/030
DRS unbranded: 33025/029, 33207
Fragonset: 33021, 33103/108, 33202
West Coast Railways: 33025/029, 33207
Parcels red: 33021
SWT blue: 33046 (it has never run in this livery)

No Class 33s ran in BR green with TOPS numbers, aside from retro repaint 33008

EMBLEMS

Yellow DCE stripes: 33004/009/015/022/040, 33110/114/117, 33201/208 B; 33008, 33110 Gy
Naval crests: 33025 B/D/C
Coats of arms: 33027/056 B (later on 33202/207 FA)

NAMES

33002	*Sea King*
33008	*Eastleigh*
33009	*Walrus*
33012	*Stan Symes*
33019	*Griffon*
33021	*Eastleigh*
33021	*Captain Charles*
33025	*Sultan*
33025	*Glen Falloch*
33027	*Earl Mountbatten of Burma*
33029	*Glen Loy*
33035	*Spitfire*
33046	*Merlin*
33047	*Spitfire*
33050	*Isle of Grain*
33051	*Shakespeare Cliff*
33052	*Ashford*
33056	*The Burma Star*
33057	*Seagull*

ABOVE: A standard Class 33/0 with side snowploughs retained, but the centre plough removed. 33008 Eastleigh was one of the first 33s named, and often ran with a grey roof and red bufferbeams. PDC
BELOW: In 1986 33008 Eastleigh was repainted into original BR green, and given that the 33s had been little changed from construction, the result was very authentic. The changes were a TOPS number, albeit in the correct font and the BR corporate-style names plates. For a period, as seen here, 33008 also ran with DCE yellow cabside stripes. PDC

33063	*R J Mitchell*
33065	*Sealion*
33103	*SWORDFISH*
33108	*VAMPIRE*
33109	*Captain Bill Smith RNR*
33112	*Templecombe*
33114	*Sultan*
33114	*Ashford 150*
33116	*Hertfordshire Railtours*
33202	*The Burma Star*
33202	*METEOR*
33207	*Earl Mountbatten of Burma*
33207	*Jim Martin*

CAST DEPOT PLAQUES

Eastleigh Spitfire: 33101/116 D, 33002/019/025/026/046/047/051/065, 33118 C, 33035, 33114 ND, 33116 B
Hither Green oast houses: 33051, 33116 B, 33050/063, 33207 FA, 33116 D, 33208 C, 33204/206/211 FD
Stewarts Lane Power station: 33202 C, 33204/206 FD

BUILD BATCHES

The 33s were built in two main batches, the standard locos D6500–85 and the narrow-bodied D6586–97. The 33/1s were converted from 33/0s.

MAJOR MODIFICATION DATES

In 1965, D6580 was converted to push-pull use and featured duplicate waist-level brake and MW pipes fitted to its cab fronts. The trials were successful, and D6511/13/14/16/17/19–21/25/27–29/31–33/35/36/38 were also converted. These also featured rubbing plates between the buffers, a modification retro-added to D6580.

BR overhauled Class 33s, but the only locos to have full refurbishment were DRS's 33029 and 33207, which were recognizable because they had no vacuum-brake pipes as they were air-braked only; they also lost their ETH. 33207 is now dual-braked again.

NUMBERS

D6500	33001	
D6501	33002	
D6502	–	
D6503	33003	
D6504	33004	
D6505	33005	
D6506	33006	
D6507	33007	
D6508	33008	
D6509	33009	
D6510	33010	
D6511	33101	
D6512	33011	
D6513	33102	
D6514	33103	
D6515	33012	
D6516	33104	
D6517	33105	
D6518	33013	
D6519	33106	
D6520	33107	
D6521	33108	
D6522	33014	
D6523	33015	
D6524	33016	
D6525	33109	
D6526	33017	
D6527	33110	
D6528	33111	
D6529	33112	
D6530	33018	ADB986030
D6531	33113	
D6532	33114	
D6533	33115	83301
D6534	33019	
D6535	33116	
D6536	33117	
D6537	33020	
D6538	33118	

One of the nineteen push-pull Class 33/1s, 33108 shows off the changes to the front end. Duplicate waist-level MW, loco air control and main reservoir pipes are fitted, and the vestibule rubbing plate is visible between the buffers. Just above these is a small plug socket for fitting a flashing light and bell unit to the locos when they travelled over the Weymouth Quay line. PDC

One of the more unusual liveries applied to a Class 33 was Post Office red to Fragonset's 33021 Eastleigh, seen in April 2001 complete with a Spitfire depot plaque and BR cast arrow. The loco has lost both its red tail-lights, which were often removed by BR after accident damage, and also shows the standard method of fitting high-intensity headlights to 33s by putting them centrally on the cab front. PIP DUNN

D6539	33021		D6543	33025
D6540	33022		D6544	33026
D6541	33023		D6545	33027
D6542	33024		D6546	33028

BELOW: 33202 The Burma Star was one of the last EWS Class 33s, and was later sold to Fragonset Railways. In this September 1999 view, the 'Dutch' loco sports a full set of snowploughs and a headlight. PIP DUNN

ABOVE RIGHT: Preserved 33110 was painted in BR green with a small yellow warning panel, which was not prototypical for a Class 33/1, apart from D6580, which had a smaller yellow warning panel than that applied to 33110, which also has DCE stripes. The loco has since been repainted into Departmental grey. This illustration shows the duplicate brake pipes and MW cables attached to the front of this subclass. PIP DUNN

The last twelve Class 33s were built to a narrow body profile to allow them to travel along the gauge-restricted tunnels on the line to Hastings. D6586 (33201) leads push-pull 33109, and the difference between the loco widths is evident. The 33/2s were recognizable from the side at the solebar level, where there is definite slab-sidedness where the body joins the solebar, whereas the 33/0s and 33/1s had a clear change in profile. ANTHONY HICKS

D6547	33029	D6571	33053	D6595	33210	
D6548	33030	D6572	33054	D6596	33211	
D6549	33031	D6573	33055	D6597	33212	
D6550	33032	D6574	33056			
D6551	33033	D6575	33057			
D6552	33034	D6576	–			
D6553	33035	D6577	33058			
D6554	33036	D6578	33059			
D6555	33037	D6579	33060			
D6556	33038	D6580	33119			
D6557	33039	D6581	33061			
D6558	33040	D6582	33062			
D6559	33041	D6583	33063			
D6560	33042	D6584	33064			
D6561	33043	D6585	33065			
D6562	33044	D6586	33201			
D6563	33045	D6587	33202			
D6564	33046	D6588	33203	33302	33203	
D6565	33047	D6589	33204			
D6566	33048	D6590	33205			
D6567	33049	D6591	33206			
D6568	33050	D6592	33207			
D6569	33051	D6593	33208			
D6570	33052	D6594	33209			

SUBSEQUENT RENUMBERINGS

33205 was renumbered 33302 in September 1988, and 33203/206 were due to become 33301/303 as part of a dedicated pool of locos for Train Ferry shunting at Dover. The plan was soon shelved and 33302 reverted to 33205, and the other two renumberings did not take place.

For a period in Departmental use, 33018 was allocated the number TDB968030, but it did not carry this number.

33115 was also transferred to Departmental use as an unpowered test vehicle, and renumbered in the coaching stock series as 83301. In this role it was repainted into the InterCity Mainline livery.

From June 2002 to July 2005, DRS used a small fleet of Class 33s, with four in traffic. 33030 was acquired from EWS and overhauled by Railcare at Glasgow. The loco retains its vacuum-brake pipe, but it has these brakes isolated and is air-braked only. Aside from the livery and the headlight, it is still in as-built condition. PIP DUNN

33207 Jim Martin, now owned by West Coast Railways, is missing its tail-lights, and also has snowploughs and a headlight. It was converted to air brakes only and lost its ETH when owned by DRS (modifications also afforded to 33029), but recently had its vacuum brakes reinstated. Leading 33025 shows the difference in width between a 33/2 and a 33/2. RAIL PHOTOPRINTS

THE ONLY TYPE 3 diesel hydraulic design, these stylish 101 locos were built by Beyer Peacock in Gorton, Manchester. All were used on the WR, although they had booked jobs to the SR at Portsmouth.

Nicknamed Hymeks, all these mixed-traffic Type 3s had been withdrawn by 1975 as part of the plan to eliminate hydraulics from the BR fleet. Four survive in preservation.

DETAIL DIFFERENCES

All Class 35s had centre panels on their cab fronts, retained until withdrawal. D7017 has had dominos briefly in preservation. Snowplough brackets were fitted to all, and at least 7000/09/16/21/22/25/26/31 have carried them. Yellow Triangle MW was fitted, so 35s could only work in multiple with other 35s.

D7000–44 had a Stone OK4616 boiler, while D7045–100 used the Spanner Mk 3 for train heating.

D7000–02 were built with air horns under the bufferbeams, while the rest had them fitted to the cab roofs from new. D7000–02 were later modified to follow.

D7000–33 did not have headboard clips above the headcode panels. D7038 lost them after collision to its 'A' end.

Locos had their numbers on individual raised aluminium digits. In the final knockings of Hymek activity some locos ran with digits missing, and 7017 had its numbers applied in standard BR style transfers after all its digits were removed.

LIVERIES

The first nineteen were new in all-over BR green with a light green solebar stripe

specifications

1957 BR number range:	D7000–100
Former class codes:	D17/2, later 17/7
Built by:	Beyer Peacock
Introduced:	1961–65
Wheel arrangement:	B-B
Weight (operational):	74 tons
Height:	12ft 11in (3.94m)
Width:	8ft 9in (2.67m)
Length:	51ft 9in (15.77m)
Min. curve negotiable:	4 chains
Maximum speed:	90mph (144km/h)
Wheelbase:	36ft (10.98m)
Bogie wheelbase:	10ft 6in (3.2m)
Bogie pivot centres:	25ft 6in (7.77m)
Wheel diameter:	3ft 9in (1.14m)
Route availability:	6
Brake force:	33 tons
Engine type:	Maybach MD870
Engine horsepower:	1,740bhp (1,298kW)
Power at rail:	1,320bhp (985kW)
Tractive effort:	46,600lb
Transmission type:	Mekydro K184U
Fuel tank capacity:	800gal (3,600ltr)

LEFT: Hymek D7076 is preserved, but still in as-built condition, apart from full yellow ends on its two-tone green livery. The loco is vacuum-braked only and retains its Yellow Triangle MW, the codes for which can be seen on the bufferbeam. The Hymeks were withdrawn too early not only for dual braking, but also to lose their headcode panels, and all were withdrawn with four character roller-blinds in place. PIP DUNN

RIGHT: A fine view of a Hymek in BR days in February 1968; D7070 is in original guise with steam pipe next to the snowplough brackets. This is No. 2 end; note the numbers were individual digits screwed into the cabsides, while above the number is a slot for the driver to display a name badge. The horns on the first three 35s were not in the familiar roof position, but were later retro-fitted there. The 35s have Yellow Triangle MW, which meant they could only 'multi' with other Class 35s. BILL WRIGHT

and off-white window surrounds. Small yellow warning panels were added from D7019 and retro-applied to D7000–18.

Some BR green had full yellow ends and side window frames, namely D7000/09/13/14/18/20/23/31/75/84/92–94/97. It is possible that D7050 was similarly treated.

The transition to BR blue was convoluted. Three had all-over BR blue with small yellow panels, D7004/07/51, but soon the window frames reverted to off-white, and this was applied to several locos. Full BR blue with full yellow ends was bestowed on all bar 7002/03/05/06/08/13/14/20/21/24/25/54/60. Several went for scrap in green, several still only with half yellow panels when condemned.

Preserved 7017 was painted in 'Dutch' livery for a short period in 1991, renumbered 35017 and named *Williton*.

BR green: D7000–18:

BR green with small yellow panels: D7000–100

BR green with full yellow ends: D7000/09/13/14/18/20/23/31/75/84/92–94/97

BR blue with small yellow panels: D7004/07/51

BR blue with small yellow panels white windows: 7010/12/27/34/36/40/45–48/52/56/57/59/64

BR blue with full yellow ends: D7000/01/04/07/09–12/15–19/22/23/26–53/55–59/60–7100

'Dutch': 7017 (preservation only)

DEPARTMENTAL USE

Four Hymeks were transferred to Departmental use. 7055 was allocated the number DB968004, but never took up either the number or its role. 7089 was used as a static train heat loco at Laira, and allocated the number TDB968005, which was never applied.

7076/96 were taken into Departmental use as dead weight load banks and moved to Derby, where they spent spells at the test tracks at Eggington and Old Dalby, but neither were renumbered. Their role ended in the late 1970s, and while 7076 was preserved, 7096 was scrapped in early 1986, the last 35 to be broken up.

The operational preserved Hymeks tend to be much cleaner than BR days, so the symbols for the MW are clearer in this view of D7017. Like so many diesel classes withdrawn by the mid-1970s, changes were few and far between, mainly because the headcode boxes were never changed, air-braking was rarer, and new features such as headlights and aerials were still some way off being implemented fleet wide. PIP DUNN

Some Class 35s ran in traffic in BR blue with small yellow panels. The first three repaints had blue window frames, but soon BR opted for white window frames before full yellow ends were applied. D7056 shows off the livery to good effect. JIM BINNIE

THE FLEET OF Class 37s, which spanned 309 locos, was introduced from 1960–65, and a handful are still in traffic today. Over forty are also preserved.

Changes were made during construction from split to centre headcode variants, and from 1985 to 1989 a refurbishment programme was undertaken in which 135 locos changed to have alternators instead of generators. Thirty-one were also fitted with ETH at the same time. Six were re-engined as test-bed locos in 1986/87, with two new engine types under evaluation.

The fleet has undergone numerous changes over the years, with new numbers, liveries and cosmetic changes. As there were different locos to carry the numbers 37271–274, those marked ^ are the second locos to carry these numbers and not the original.

TRAIN HEATING

One of the biggest mysteries concerns which Class 37s were fitted with boilers, and which were not. This is mainly because so many lost their boilers early on in their lives for use in Class 47s, as BR decided that many 37s were for freight work. Although nothing official exists to substantiate the following, it is *believed* that D6700–D6938 were built with Clayton boilers, while D6939–99, D6600–08 were built without boilers but were capable of subsequent fitting if required. These later locos had through steam pipes.

Circa 1963 boilers were removed from forty-six locos in the D6819–74 batch and fitted to Class 47s D1636–81 after slight modifications. In 1964 the boilers were removed from the remaining ten of the D6819–74 batch, and also from D6893–D6938, and fitted to D1901–47, with nine spares retained. Boilers were removed from D6755–D57/59–74/76–80 in 1964, and fitted to D1977–99 and D1100.

In 1967/68 boilers were removed from D6701–10 and fitted to D6947/60–68. It was originally intended that D6959 was to receive a boiler, but D6947 was selected instead.

From 1972 further Eastern Region 37s had their boilers removed, 6700 being the first, so that by December 1976 only 37011/012/014/015/017–023/025–027/029/032–041/043/044/047/049–052/054/075/081/084–097/099, 37100–116/118/175–192, 37247/260–268 retained boilers, of which 37015/018–020/093/094, 37100 had them isolated.

These were isolated progressively, and were then removed, with the last operational boilers being in use in the spring of 1987. Some retained isolated boilers *in situ* to keep the locomotive's weight correct: for example, 37087 retained a boiler until its 2012 withdrawal.

ETH was fitted to 37401–431 in 1985/86 (index 30), and through-ETH wiring was fitted to 37601–612 in 1995/96, but it was never used and has since been removed following the locos' sale to DRS, with the exception of 37601/603/

A standard split-box unrefurbished 37/0, 37013 is vacuum-braked and non-boilered, while also not having snowplough brackets, leading to a relatively sparse bufferbeam. The skirts around the bufferstocks have been removed and the headcode panels changed to yellow panels, while the communication doors remain in situ – they were later removed from this loco. Headlights have yet to be fitted. ANDY HOARE

TOPS number range:	37001–308, 37310–384, 37401–431, 37503–521, 37601–612, 37667–699, 37701–719, 37796–803, 37883–899, 37901–906
1957 BR number range:	D6600–D6999
Former class codes:	D17/1, then 17/3
Built by:	English Electric, Vulcan Foundry or Robert Stephenson & Hawthorns
Years introduced:	1960–65
Wheel arrangement:	Co-Co
Weight:	102–108 tons, 120 tons (37/7 and 37/9)
Height:	13ft 1in (3.96m)
Length:	61ft 6in (18.74m)
Width:	8ft 12in (2.73m)
Wheelbase:	50ft 8in (15.44m)
Bogie wheelbase:	13ft 6in (4.11m)
Bogie pivot centres:	37ft 2in (11.32m)
Wheel diameter:	3ft 7in (1.14m)
Min. curve negotiable:	4 chains (80.46m)
Engine type:	English Electric 12CSVT 37901–904: Mirrlees MB275T 37905–906: Ruston RK270T
Engine output:	1,750bhp (1,304kW) 1,800bhp (1,340kW): 37901–906
Power at rail:	1,250bhp (932kW) 1,300bhp (940kW): 37901–906
Tractive effort:	55,500lb–62,680lb
Design speed:	90mph (144km/h)
Brake force:	50 tons 60 tons (37/7 and 37/9)
Route availability:	5 (7 Class 37/7 and 37/9)
Main generator type:	EE822-10G, EE822-13G or EE822-16J
Main alternator type:	Brush BA1005A (37796–803: GEC G564AZ)
Auxiliary generator type:	EE911/5C
Auxiliary alternator type:	Brush BA606A (37796–803: G658A, 659AZ or 658BY)
ETH alternator type:	Brush BAH701
Traction motor type:	EE538-1A or EE538-5A
No. of traction motors:	6
Gear ratio:	60:27 (37/0, 37/6) 53:18 (37/3, 37/4, 37/5, 37/7, 37/9)
Fuel tank capacity:	890gal (4,046ltr) or 1,690gal (7,682ltr)

An unrefurbished Class 37 in near original condition. The only changes made to 37036 in this view are a coat of BR blue, removal of the frost grille over the No. 1 end radiator panel, and the domino headcodes in the split panels. The communication doors remain, but a common modification among East Anglian 37s was the fitting of a bar across them to keep them closed. Some 37s had these doors removed and a flush panel fitted to reduce draughts. The loco, which retains its steam-heat boiler, was refurbished in 1985; it emerged as 37507, but has since been renumbered again and is still in traffic as 37605 with a flush front and Bmac lights. PDC

604. The 37/6s also had UIC cables which have been removed from all, bar 37602, since their sale to DRS.

HEADCODE PANELS

The Class 37s were built in two main batches, D6700–6818, with central communication doors and split headcodes, while from D6819 the doors were done away with, so centre panels were fitted.

Roller blinds were removed and domino headcodes fitted, and these were replaced by yellow metal panels or removed together. 37031/047/053/072–074/091 were changed from split boxes to centre panels (37072 at No. 1 end only)

All refurbished centre-panel 37s had the opaque rubber-mounted lenses on their headcode boxes replaced by white lamps, and these were also fitted to unrefurbished split-box 37013/023/062/066 and centre-box 37073, 37137/142/185/188/198, 37213/220/225/239/245/248/252/263/273^/280/293/294, 37332. The refurbished ex-split-box locos had their headcodes 'shaved off' and replaced by two inset white lamps. 37116 also had this modification in 1996. The exception was 37712 at No. 2 end, which had these lenses protruding slightly.

As well as a flush end with no doors, 37075 also had its boxes removed at No. 2 end and replaced by two protruding white lenses while keeping its standard

headcode boxes at No. 1 end. Other locos which lost split-boxes but retained their communication doors were 37006/019 (No. 1 end only) and 37065, 37100 at No. 2 end.

37204 and 37375 have both run with smaller opaque lenses at No. 1 end. In BR blue and 'Dutch' colours, 37038 ran with glass panels painted yellow, which was also a feature of 37029 when in DRS livery, while 37092 had one metal panel and one yellow-painted glass panel at No. 2 end when in BR blue. 37097 also had one domino and one yellow panel on its split-boxes at No. 2 end in BR blue before it was dual-braked.

HEADLIGHTS AND LAMPS

The first 37 to receive headlights was a trial on D6721/22 in 1966/67, where two flashing lamps were fitted above the buffers. The trial was deemed not to be a success and the lamps were removed.

In the 1970s it was common practice for any loco-hauled train along the Central Wales line to have a headlight. This usually meant a lamp fixed on a beam which was attached to the headboard clips on any loco in the 37120–238 batch, but the reality was it was usually one of the boiler-fitted batch of 37175–192. These were removable and interchangeable.

In the early 1980s, several 37s were transferred to Scotland for working on Highland Lines and were fitted with

small spotlamps. They were 37011/012/014/017/021/022/025–027/033/035/037/039/043/051/081/085/088/099, 37108/111/112/114/175/178/183/188/190–192, 37260–264. As a rule, on the centre-box locos they were above the headcode box, although 37264 ran for a period with it under the box. The split-box locos had them placed on the right-hand side of the communication doors in between the headcode boxes. The exceptions were 37011/014/017, which had them centrally overlapping the doors, of which 37014 was much lower than the other two. Those with plated over doors and spotlamps were 37025/035, 37108, the former duo having them centrally placed, the latter to the right. 37021, 37114 and 37263 had their lamps mounted on the top of the nose. ScR boiler-fitted locos which did not have spotlamps were 37049/090.

BR standard sealed beam-style headlights were fitted when locos were refurbished (37401–431, 37501–521, 37601–612, 37667–699, 37701–719/796–799, 37800–803/883–899, 37901–906) and then from the early 1990s they were added later to the rest of the unrefurbished fleet, namely 37003/004/008–010/012/013/015/019/023/025/026/029/031/032/035/037/038/040/042/043/045–049/051/053–055/057–059/063/065/066/068–075/077–080/083/087/088/092/095/097–099, 37100/101/104/106–111/113/114/116/127/128/131/133/137–142/144–146/152–154/156/158/162/165/167/170/174/175/178/184/185/188/191/194/196–198, 37201–203/207/209/211–223/225/227/229/230/232/235/238–242/244/245/248/250–252/254/255/258/261–264/271–274^/275/278/280/284/285/293/294/298, 37303/304/306/308, 37330–335/340/341/343/344/350–359/370–384. They were never fitted to 37011/062/096, 37260.

For centre-box locos these headlights were directly below the panel. For split-box locos their positioning varied, with the lights being placed centrally (overlapping the doors if they remained in place) on 37003/008/012/013/019/025/029/032/035/043/045/049/051/055/057–059/065/066/068–071/075/077/079/083/087/092/095/098, 37100/101/104/107/108–110/116, 37350/351/359, while they were on the right-hand door on 37004/009/010/013/015/023/026/037/038/040/042/046/048/054/063/072/078/080/088/097/099, 37106/111/113/114.

Bmac light clusters were fitted by DRS to 37038/059/069, 37218/259, 37423, 37602/605–612, while DRS has also replaced the lenses on 37229, 37402/405/409/419/422/425, 37510, 37667/682/688 with LEDs.

Split headcode boxes: 37001–119
Centre headcode boxes: 37120–308
Split-box converted to centre box: 37031/047/053/073/074/091
Split-box converted to centre box at No. 1 end only: 37072
Split-boxes removed (unrefurbished) at No. 1 end only: 37006/019
Split-boxes removed (unrefurbished) at No. 2 end only: 37065/075, 37100
Split-boxes removed (unrefurbished, flush end): 37116
Split-boxes removed (unrefurbished, DRS): 37038/059/069
Split-boxes removed (refurbished): 37001/005–007/014/016–018/020–022/024/027/028/030/033/034/036/039/041/044/050/052/056/060/061/064/067/076/081/082/084–086/089/090/093/094, 37102/103/105/112/115/117 (37501–521, 37601–609, 37701–719/796–799)
Centre boxes removed (refurbished): 37612
Class 37s retaining dominos prior to refurbishment: 37034/041, 37115 37135/171/181/183/187, 37206/208/233/236/243/247/265/266/268/269/270/273/274/276/277/279/282/286/288–291/295–297, 37300–302/305/307

NOTES: 37123/186 No. 1 end only, 37295 had dominos but was painted yellow; 37372 retained a black panel at No. 1 end until withdrawal in 2004.

NOSE-END CHANGES

All Class 37s were fitted with a cowling around the bufferstocks, known as skirts. These were removed progressively from the late 1979, and at the same time it was common practice to plate over the headcodes. However, some locos retained domino panels despite having their skirts removed, while other locos had yellow panels fitted while still retaining skirts.

Known to have retained skirts with yellow panels are 37001/003/004/007/009–012/015/025/029/032/035/039/040/048/051/053–055/063/065/068/070/073/074/076–079/083/092, 37102–105/111–113/114/119/144/147/155/157/167/190/

191/193/194/196/198, 37200/206/216/217/219/220/238/245/246/249/278/281/286 and 37123/186 at No. 2 end only. Those which lost their skirts but retained black dominos were 37022/038/087, 37115/123/135/142/159/171/181, 37204/220/225/233/242/247/289/290/294/295, 37300/372. This does not include those locos with black-painted headcode panels, which was common practice from the mid-1980s.

Some locos had their bufferbeams exposed further by the removal of the bottom lip of the nose ends, namely 37019/034, 37102/138/160, 37373, 37712.

Some split-box 37s had their doors removed and replaced with a panel in between, yet retaining headcode boxes. They were 37002/008/013/020/025/030–032/035/042/043/045/058/062/066/068/075/077/079/083/092/097/098, 37108/109/117, 37350–357/359. All split-box 37s which were refurbished lost their doors.

Split-box 37066 was seen in late 1974 running with one headcode box at No. 2 end plated over temporarily while retaining roller blinds on the other box, while 37323 ran in traffic in late 1989 with a damaged headcode box at No. 1 end.

The roof-mounted horns on 37332/334, 37677/680/686/688/697 were repositioned to in front of the cab windows, while those on 37401/425, 37670 were repositioned to the top middle of the nose ends – but those on 37425 were later repositioned into their correct roof-mounted position.

D6959–68 were fitted with an additional headboard clip on the top of their noses, and these were retained by 37401/421/422/430 after refurbishment, while 37426/427 also gained them. D6819–6938 had two headboard clips above the headcode.

37028 ran for a period with a metal bar across the full width of its communication doors at No. 2 end, while 37080/081, 37101/115 had a smaller bar across the middle of the doors at No. 2 end, and 37035/036/059/087, 37115 were likewise at No. 1 end.

Underslung tanks:
Boiler water tanks removed: 37001/100
Boiler water tanks removed for ERTMS: 97301–304 (37100/170/178/217)
Boiler water tanks converted to additional fuel tanks: 37002/003/005–009/015/020/029–032/042/045/058/059/061

–063/065–069/071–073/076/078/079/082/083/093/095/096/098, 37101/106/117/119/161–165/167/193–195/197–199, 37200/205/210/212–214/216/217/220/222–225/227–231/234–236/239/240/242–244/248/250/251/254/255/257/269–273/275–282/284–298/299, 37300–308, 37271–274^, 37401–431, 37501–521, 37601–612/667–699, 37701–719/796–799, 37800–803/883–899, 37901–906.

Snowplough brackets: 37011/012/014/017/021/022/025–027/030/031/033/035/037/039/040/043/051/081/085/099, 37108/111/112/114/121/123/128/133/135/151–154/156/169/170/174/175/177/178/180/182–188/190–199, 37200/201/205/206/208/209/211/212/214–219/221/222/226/228/229/232/235/240/242/246–252/254/258–264/267/275/278/283, 37330/334/379, 37401–431, 37503/505/510/514–521, 37601/667/669/670/674/676–678/682–685/688/689/694/695/697/698, 37706–708/711/719/797, 37803/883–885, 37906, 97301–304.

Sandite ports: Several locos were fitted with Sandite hoppers in the old boiler compartment. To fill the hoppers a port was fitted in the bodyside in an indented panel on 37503/505/516–518/520/521, 37667–670/673–680/682/684/685/688/689/692/694/695/698. On 37676/679/685 the ports have been plated over, but 37516 retains them. 37152 also had a side filler port behind a door.

LIVERIES

Green: D6700–30
Green half yellow end: D6600–08, 6700–6999
Green full yellow end: 6600–08, 6701/04–12/14–16/18/21–23/25/26/29–43/45/47–52/54–61/64/66/67/69/81/83/84/86/88/90–92/97–99, 6800–11/13–19/21/23/25/26/28/30/32/38–43/47–50/52/54/55/60/63/71/74/76/80/83/84/86–88/90–96, 6900–18/20–36/38–44/46–78/80–82/84–91/93–99.
BR blue: 37001–308
BR blue with wrap-round yellow ends, small BR badge: 37111/112
BR blue with wrap-round yellow ends and yellow doors: 37027
BR 'Large Logo': 37004/008/011/012/021/022/025–027/035/043/051/057/079/081/085, 37108/111/112/114/116/117/

128/146/152/153/174/175/183/188/191, 37209/260–262/264, 37311, 37401–431

BR blue with yellow bonnets, black window surrounds, large numbers and badge: 37116

BR blue with wrap-round yellow ends, large numbers, no badge: 37025

BR blue with wrap-round yellow ends, large numbers, small badge and blue bonnet: 37146

Railfreight: 37180/196, 37501–513, 37689–699, 37701–704/796–799, 37800 –803/894–899, 37901–906

Red stripe Railfreight: 37002/008/ 032/045/068/079, 37118/127/147/159/ 160/165/167/193/196/199, 37200/204/ 226/250/255/308, 37502/506/514–520, 37669–672/674–688

Railfreight General: 37104, 37673

Trainload Coal: 37049, 37131/139/ 165/167, 37212/213/222/223/229/235/ 239/274/278, 37308/332/374–376/380, 37689/692–699, 37701–704/796–799, 37800–803/887/889/894–899

Trainload Petroleum: 37035/078/080, 37138/145/184/188, 37215/220/232/248/ 273/280/294, 37350/359/382, 37418/421/ 428, 37505/521, 37667/668, 37705–712/ 712/715–717/719, 37883–885/887–893

Trainload Construction: 37043/080, 37138/144, 37211/214, 37354, 37411/ 414/422/425/427/429, 37676–684/686 –688, 37715

Trainload Metals: 37004/037/040/042/ 048/051/077/078/099, 37100/106/109– 111/138/145/190, 37201–203/227/241/ 248/250/255/275/284/293, 37312/381, 37423, 37501–521, 37667/668/671, 37710 –719, 37883–886, 37901–906

Railfreight Distribution: 37009/015/ 019/026/029/031/047/053/055/059/063/ 065/068/070/073/074/079, 37101/107/ 110/113/114/131/154/178/185/194/198,

37218/225/238/242/244/252/261/271/ 272/298, 37333/340/344/345/357/378, 37401/403/406/411–414/423, 37669–675

Two-tone grey: 37037/045/047/065/ 075/080, 37108/131/178, 37202/203/ 218/225/235/238/241/242/244/248/285/ 298, 37331/333–335/341/358/376/380, 37402/404/409/410/412/417/423/428, 37505/509, 37667/676–679/683/684/689, 37712, 37884/888, 37902/904

Two-tone grey with dark upper bodyside: 37402, 37601

Two-tone grey with lighter upper bodyside: 37167

Departmental grey: 37025/054/066/ 071/072/087/088/092/095/098, 37104/ 133/142/156/162/197, 37207/240/251/ 258/262/263

Departmental grey with small body-side Trainload Petroleum logos: 37162

InterCity 'Mainline': 37401/402/404/ 407/409/410/415–417/419/420/423/ 424/426/430/431

InterCity 'Mainline' with small cabside Trainload Petroleum logos: 37431

InterCity: 37152, 37221/251, 37505/510/ 518, 37683/685

'Dutch': 37003/010/012/023/025/035/ 038/043/046/049/054/058/066/069/ 071/083/087/088/092/095/097–099, 37104/106/114/133/140–142/146/153/ 146/158/165/170/174/175/184/185/188/ 191/196–198, 37201/207/211/221/230/ 232/240/245/254/255/258/263/264/274, 37351/370/372/375/377/379

'Dutch' Transrail: 37043/088, 37153/ 165/170/197, 37201/230/232, 37351

Regional Railways: 37414/418/420– 422/425/427/429

Mainline Freight aircraft blue: 37013/ 023/047/055/065/074/077, 37109/167/ 198, 37203/216/219/242/248/274/293, 37371/372/379, 37798, 37803

Mainline Freight aircraft blue unbranded: 37375

Two-tone grey with Mainline logos: 37042/048/051/077, 37109/137/194, 37203/220/222/227/293, 37380, 37703/ 705/709/715, 37800/890–892

Loadhaul: 37513/517, 37698, 37706/ 710, 37884

Loadhaul unbranded: 37516

Transrail: 37073, 37100/111/154/156, 37212/214/221/250, 37401/404/406/ 407/409–413/423/424/428/430, 37505/ 509, 37668–675/683/693/695/696, 37701/ 702/799, 37802/887/889/893/896–898, 37901/906

BR blue with Transrail logos: 37116

Eurostar: 37601–612

Eurostar with DRS branding: 37607–612

EW&S: 37040/051/057, 37109/114, 37220, 37370, 37415/416/418/419/427, 37503, 37668/682/684/688, 37704/706/707/717, 37801/883/885/886/895

EWS: 37042, 37174, 37298, 37401/405/ 406/408/410/411/413/417/421/422/426, 37520/521, 37667/669/670/694/695, 37703/712/714/716/797, 37893

EWS with black bonnets: 37425

Royal Scotsman: 37401/416/428

West Coast Railways: 37197, 37214/ 248/261, 37516, 37676/685, 37706/712

HNRC orange and grey: 37087, 37194

HNRC orange and grey with large numbers: 37515

DRS: 37029/038/059/069/087, 37194, 37218/229/259/261, 37510/515, 37602/ 605–612/667/688

DRS Compass: 37059/069, 37194, 37218/ 229/259/261, 37402/405/409/419/423/ 425, 37510, 37601–612/667/682/683/ 688

DRS unbranded: 37197

Ian Riley grey and green: 37197

DRS bought the twelve Eurostar Class 37s in three transactions, and progressively modified them. This is 37609: it has benefited from the cab modifications, which include fitting of Bmac lights, but the recesses where the old white marker lights were have yet to be plated over. It also retains its through ETH and UIC cables, which have now been removed. The loco is in the first style of DRS blue, which is now no longer on any 37/6s. PIP DUNN

Network Rail yellow: 37198, 97301 –304

GIF: 37702/703/714/716/718/799, 37800 –802/883–885/888/899

BR green (special): 37216/261, 37350, 37403/411

BR blue (special): 37219/275

Police: 37093

DB Schenker: 37419, 37670

EMBLEMS

Small West Highland terriers: 37011– 014/017/018/020/022/024/026/027/029/ 033/034/036/037/039/043/049/051/063/ 081/085/088/090, 37108/111–113/144/ 149/151/157/170–172/175/178/184/185/ 188/190–192, 37237/263/266/267/269/ 272/288/291/297/299, 37300 B; 37081, 37264 BR; 37118 FR; 37023 ML; 37405/ 410/411 EW; 37214/248; 37676/685 WC; 37069 DC; 37518 IC

Large West Highland terriers; 37008/ 011/012/021/022/025/027/035/043/051/ 079/081/085, 37111/117/175/188/191, 37264, 37401–414/422–425 BR

Motherwell salmons: 37024/034/037/ 038/040/099, 37108/110/125/133/139/ 145/146/148/155/184/190, 37281, 37312/ 313/322–324 B; 37026/051, 37108/111/ 152/188, 37264, 37310/311/320/325/ 326 BR; 37160, 37370/373/379 FR

White stags: 37056, 37263 B

Yellow stags: 37033, 37279 B; 37021/ 025/035, 37114/146/153/175/183, 37260– 262/264, 37414–421 BR; 37114, 37416/ 419 EW

White kingfishers: 37013/028/042/ 062/063/066/071/072/077/078/095, 37193 B; 37506/512/519 FR; 37506, 37693 FO; 37501 BSB

Coloured kingfishers: 37074, 37194 B; 37502–506/508/510/512–518/520 FR; 37503–505/508/510/512/513, 37693 FO; 37501 BSB; 37507/521, 37667/668 FM; 37069 F; 37417 ICM

Red Dragons 37180 B (headcode); 37426–431 BR (cabside), 37414/420 RR (headcode)

Stratford Sparrows: 37001/019/048/ 053/055/087/091, 37100/107/116/140/ 144/154/176/178, 37209/211/216/218/ 238/241, 37358 B; 37012, 37128 BR; 37350 GY; 37106, 37370/371/379 C; 37037/075 F; 37705–708, 37888/890 –892 FP; 37087, 37261 DR

Cornish Lizards: 37181, 37207 B

Cornish Railways branding: 37247 B

Cast Depot Plaques

Buxton mill stone: 37411/422, 37680/ 681/684/686–688 FA, 37683/684 F

Canton goat: 37213/235, 37698, 37702, 37887/898/899, 37220/273/280/294, 37350, 37521, 37667/668 FP; 37138, 37293, 37521, 37711/712, 37902/905/906 FM; 37702, 37802/887/889/898 FT; 37010/ 012/035/038/046/054/092/097/098, 37133/141/142/158/174/191/197, 37207/ 230/254/258/264, 37372 C, 37197, 37230 CT; 37293 FML; 37213, 37698, 37702, 37898 FC

Eastfield West Highland terrier: 37403 Gy; 37106/133/165/170/175/184/188, 37232/294 C; 37165, 37375/376, 37692 –694 FC; 37080, 37184/188, 37359, 37707 FP; 37080, 37380 F; 37403 FD; 37106 FM; 37232 CT

Immingham star: 37144 FA, 37138, 37382, 37418/421, 37505, 37706/707/ 712/717/719, 37883/884 FP; 37106, 37381 FM; 37058/071/083/095, 37104, 37221 C; 37104 D

Motherwell anvil and hammer: 37049 FC; 37051, 37190 FM; 37156, 37221, 37410 FT

Ripple Lane torch: 37708/709, 37887/ 888/890/892/893 FP

St Blazey lizard: 37411–413, 37669– 673/675 FD; 37412, 37673 F; 37412, 37669/ 670/672/673 FT; 37672 FR; 37417/420 ICM

Stewarts Lane power station: 37074/ 077, 37274^ ML, 37798; 37715 FA

Stratford sparrow: 37055, 37376 F; 37053/059, 37252 FD, 37023, 37242 ML, 37023, 37106/140 C

Thornaby kingfisher: 37504/506/507/ 510/511/514/521, 37667/668, 37716 FM; 37712 F; 37667 FP

Tinsley rose: 37015/026/029/047/053/ 055/059/065/073/079, 37131/194/198, 37252/271^/272^, 37333/344/381 FD; 37045, 37334/341 F; 37430 ICM

NUMBERS AND EMBELLISHMENTS

White 8in numbers: 37078, 37128/ 142, 37220/223 B; 37414 RR; 37263 D.

Black 8in numbers: 37008, 37165, 37248, 37352/353/355/356/370/371/373/ 378/379, 37679 FR; 37055, 37248, 37380 F

Large white bodyside numbers: 37033, 37312/313/321–324 B, 37204, 37506/ 514–520 FR; 37503/504/508/509/511– 513 FO; 37511 FM

Small numbers (where non-standard): 37219 B

Square numbers: 37081 BR

Four numbers: 37178 B

White numbers on cab roof: 37078 B

Hand-painted numbers: 37401–416 BR

White numbers on headcode panel: 37203 B (last three digits only)

Yellow DCE stripes: 37023, 37140, 37221 B; 37153 BR; 37263 C

White cant rail stripes: 37013/028/ 042/059/062/063/066/067/070/071/077/ 078/095/098, 37193 B

Thin white solebar stripes: 37012/014/ 017/022/037/039/081, 37111/112/178/ 192 B

Red solebar stripe: 37196 B

White window frames: 37064, 37243 B

Larger BR badges: 37142, 37263 D; 37219 B

NAMES

37003	*TIGER MOTH*^
37003	*Dereham Neatherd High School 1912–2012*
37008	*HORNET*^
37009	*TYPHOON*^
37012	*Loch Rannoch*
37013	*VAMPIRE*^
37023	*Stratford TMD*
37025	*Inverness Depot*
37026	*Loch Awe*
37026	*Shap Fell*
37027	*Loch Eil*
37032	*Mirage*
37037	*Gartcosh*
37037	*Loch Treig*
37043	*Loch Lomond*
37049	*Imperial*
37051	*Merehead*
37055	*RAIL Celebrity*
37057	*Viking*
37059	*Port of Tilbury*
37062	*British Steel Corby*
37066	*British Steel Workington*
37068	*Grainflow*
37069	*Thornaby TMD*
37071	*British Steel Skinningrove*
37073	*TORNADO*^
37073	*Fort William An Gearsaden*
37077	*British Steel Shelton*
37077	*HURRICANE*^
37078	*Teesside Steelmaster*
37079	*Medite*
37081	*Loch Long*
37087	*VULCAN*^
37087	*AVRO VULCAN B1 & B2*
37087	*Keighley and Worth Valley Railway*
37088	*Clydesdale*
37095	*British Steel Teesside*
37096	*SPITFIRE*^

37097	Old Fettercairn	37311	British Steel Hunterston	37420	The Scottish Hosteller
37099	Clydebridge	37312	Clyde Iron	37421	Strombidae
37107	FURY	37314	Dalzell	37421	The Kingsman
37108	Lanarkshire Steel	37320	Shap Fell	37422	Robert F Fairlie Locomotive
37111	Loch Eil Outward Bound	37321	Gartcosh		Engineer 1831-1885
37111	Glengarnock	37322	Imperial	37422	Cardiff Canton
37113	Radio Highland	37323	Clydesdale	37423	Sir Murray Morrison Pioneer of
37114	Dunrobin Castle	37324	Clydebridge		the British Aluminium Industry
37114	City of Worcester	37325	Lanarkshire Steel		1873-1948
37116	COMET	37326	Glengarnock	37423	Spirit of the Lakes
37116	Sister Dora	37332	The Coal Merchants'	37424	Glendarroch
37128	JUPITER		Association of Scotland	37424	Isle of Mull
37137	Clyde Iron	37343	Imperial	37425	Sir Robert McAlpine/
37152	British Steel Ravenscraig	37350	NATIONAL RAILWAY MUSEUM		Concrete Bob
37154	SABRE	37356	Grainflow	37425	Pride of the Valleys/Balchder y
37154	Johnson Stevens Agencies	37358	P&O Containers		Cymoedd
37156	British Steel Hunterston	37379	Ipswich WRD Quality	37426	Y Lien Fach Vale of Rheidol
37175	W S Sellar		Approved	37426	MT VESUVIUS
37178	METEOR	37401	Mary Queen of Scots	37427	Bont Y Bermo
37180	County of Dyfed Sir Dyfed	37401	The Royal Scotsman	37427	Highland Enterprise
37185	BUCCANEER	37402	Oor Wullie	37428	David Lloyd George
37185	Lea & Perrins	37402	Bont Y Bermo	37428	Loch Awe/Loch Long
37188	Jimmy Shand	37403	Isle of Mull	37429	County of Dyfed Sir Dyfed
37190	Dalzell	37403	Glendarroch	37429	Eisteddfod Genedlaethol
37191	International Youth Year 1985	37403	Ben Cruachan	37430	Cwmbrân
37194	British International Freight	37404	Ben Cruachan	37431	County of Powis Sir Powis
	Association	37404	Loch Long	37431	Bullidae
37194	NEIL WEBSTER 1957–2001	37405	Strathclyde Region	37501	Teesside Steelmaster
37196	Tre Pol and Pen	37406	The Saltire Society	37502	British Steel Teesside
37197	Loch Laidon	37407	Loch Long	37503	British Steel Shelton
37201	Saint Margaret	37407	Blackpool Tower	37504	British Steel Corby
37207	William Cookworthy	37408	Loch Rannoch	37505	British Steel Workington
37209	PHANTOM	37409	Loch Awe	37506	British Steel Skinningrove
37214	Loch Laidon	37409	Lord Hinton	37507	Hartlepool Pipe Mill
37216	Great Eastern	37410	Aluminium 100	37511	Stockton Haulage
37219	Shirley Ann Smith	37411	The Institution of Railway	37512	Thornaby Demon
37220	Westerleigh		Signal Engineers	37517	St Aiden's CE Memorial School
37229	The Cardiff Rod Mill	37411	Ty Hafan		Hartlepool Railsafe Trophy
37229	Jonty Jarvis	37411	The Scottish Railway		Winners 1995
	8.12.1998–18.3.2005		Preservation Society	37518	Fort William An Gearsaden
37232	The Institution of Railway	37411	CAERPHILLY CASTLE/	37521	ENGLISH CHINA CLAYS
	Signal Engineers		CASTELL CAERFFILI	37601	Class 37 'Fifty'
37235	The Coal Merchants'	37412	Loch Lomond	37610	The Malcolm Group
	Association of Scotland	37412	Driver John Elliott	37610	T.S (Ted) Cassady
37238	SPITFIRE II	37413	Loch Eil Outward Bound		14.5.61–6.4.08
37239	The Coal Merchants'	37413	The Scottish Railway	37667	Wensleydale
	Association of Scotland		Preservation Society	37667	Meldon Quarry Centenary
37248	Midland Railway Centre	37414	Cathays C&W Works 1846-1993	37668	Leyburn
37248	Loch Arkaig	37415	MT ETNA	37670	St Blazey T&RS Depot
37251	GLADIATOR	37416	MT FUJI	37671	Tre Pol and Pen
37251	The Northern Lights	37416	Sir Robert McAlpine/	37672	Freight Transport Association
37254	Driver Robin Prince MBE		Concrete Bob	37674	Saint Blaise Church 1445–1995
37260	Radio Highland	37417	Highland Region	37675	William Cookworthy
37261	Caithness	37417	RAIL Magazine	37676	Loch Rannoch
37261	Loch Arkaig	37417	Richard Trevithick	37682	Hartlepool Pipe Mill
37262	Dounreay	37418	An Comunn Gaidhealach	37684	Peak National Park
37275	Stainless Pioneer	37418	Pectinidae	37685	Loch Arkaig
37275	Oor Wullie	37418	East Lancashire Railway	37688	Great Rocks
37298	VICTOR	37419	MT PINATUBO	37688	Kingmoor TMD
37310	British Steel Ravenscraig	37419	Carl Haviland 1954–2012	37692	The Lass O' Ballochmyle

37692	DIDCOT DEPOT
37693	Sir William Arrol
37694	The Lass O' Ballochmyle
37698	Coedbach
37702	Taff Merthyr
37706	Conidae
37711	Tremorfa Steelworks
37712	The Cardiff Rod Mill
37712	Teesside Steelmaster
37713	British Steel Workington
37715	British Steel Teesside
37715	British Petroleum
37716	British Steel Corby
37717	Stainless Pioneer
37717	Maltby Lilly Hall Junior School Rotherham Railsafe Trophy Winners 1996
37717	St Margaret's Church of England Primary School City of Durham Railsafe Trophy Winners 1997
37717	Berwick Middle School Railsafe Trophy Winners 1998
37718	Hartlepool Pipe Mill
37799	County of Dyfed Sir Dyfed
37800	Glo Cymru
37801	Aberddawan Aberthaw
37884	Gartcosh
37886	County of Dyfed Sir Dyfed
37887	Caerphilly Castle/ Castell Caerffili
37888	Petrolea
37890	The Railway Observer
37892	Ripple Lane
37898	Cwmbargoed DP
37899	Sir Gorllewin Morgannwg County of West Glamorgan
37901	Mirrlees Pioneer
37902	British Steel Llanwern
37905	Vulcan Enterprise
37906	Star of the East
97304	John Tiley

* unofficial

Build Batches

D6700–68 (37119, 37001–068)	Vulcan Foundry	1960–62
D6769–95 (37069–095)	RSH Darlington	1962–63
D6796–6818 (37096–37118)	Vulcan Foundry	1962–63
D6819–28 (37283, 37120–128)	RSH Darlington	1963
D6829–58 (37129–158)	Vulcan Foundry	1963
D6859–68 (37159–168)	RSH Darlington	1963
D6869–78 (37169–178)	Vulcan Foundry	1963
D6879–98 (37179–198)	RSH Darlington	1963–64
D6899–6999, D6600–08 (37199–308)	Vulcan Foundry	1963–65

D6700–05 had dividing strips on the cant rail height air-intake grilles, but the rest of the VF locos did not. However, this feature was also implemented in the Darlington-built locos.

MAJOR MODIFICATION DATES

Dates for dual braking: 6854, 6960–68 (1967); 6820–25/27/29/31/35/36/85, 6941/43/44/47/54/78/85/89, 6604 (1968); 6712/18–20/24/27/37/43/44/55/56/86/89/91, 6826/28/30/32/34/39/60/61/63–69/71/72/74/75/78/79/88/90/93–95/97/99, 6800/02/08/09/11/12/15/16/26/59/69/73/75–77/79–84/86–88/90/91/93–95/97–99, 6600–02/05–08 (1969); 6733/47/49/52/59/69/70/72/74, 6876/77/80–84/86/87/91/92/98, 6901/06/10/21/24/31/33/34/56–58/72/96 (1970); 6722/34/39/41/57/60/67/73/77/78/81/95, 6803/05/08/12/15/16/18/33/37/38/41/43–53/55–57/59/70/89, 6903/05/07/19/32/36/55/70/71/74/92, 6603 (1971); 6764, 6873, 6937 (1972); 37140/142/158 (1973); 37010, 37242/245/246/249/250/252 (1974); 37001/006/016/026/030, 37111, 37204 (1975); 37002/004/007/008/014/080 (1976); 37015/021/031/042/045/050/068/076/084/085/088/094,

37119 (1977); 37009/029/032/038/048/051/053/054/063/079/092/096/098/099, 37101/102/106/107/110 (1978); 37011, 37114/117/162, 37213/223/227/248 (1982); 37025/035/040/046/065/071/087, 37104/109/113, 37218/220/238/240 (1983); 37066/075/083/097, 37100, 37214/217/222/229/230/239/251 (1984); 37003/023/058/062, 37196, 37235 (1985); 37005*/013/017*/028*/036*/061*/082*/090*/093*, 37225/228*/253* (1986)

* refurbished (and renumbered) when dual-braked

REFURBISHMENT

The refurbishment programme from 1985–89 saw the creation of several new subclasses. The first were the thirty-one Class 37/4s, selected at random from the 37258–308 batch, depending on which were next due a works overhaul.

The Class 37/5s started from 37501 upwards for split-box locos chosen randomly from 37001–119, and downwards from 37699 for centre-box locos.

The 37/7s were the same – up from 37701 for split-box and down from 37899 for centre-box locos. These were the same as 37/5s but with ballast weights for added adhesion.

While Brush alternators were used in the 37/4s, the plan had been for the 37/5s to have Brush alternators for some locos, 37501 onwards and 37699 downwards, and GEC alternators for others, 37599 downwards and 37600 upwards. In the event this was not pursued, but for the 37/7s it was, with 37701 upwards and 37899 downwards having Brush alternators, and 37799 downwards and 37800 upwards having GEC alternators. In the event, just eight locos, 37796–799 and 37800–803, had GEC equipment.

Dates refurbished: 37401–421 (1985); 37422–431, 37501–511, 37693–699, 37701/ 702/796–799, 37800–803, 37896–899, 37901/902/905/906 (1986); 37512–520, 37669–692, 37703–707, 37888–895, 37903/ 904 (1987); 37521, 37667/668, 37708– 715, 37883–887 (1988); 37716–719 (1989)

The detail differences between refurbished and unrefurbished locos were numerous. Apart from the changes to the headcode panels previously described (and then also applied to some unrefurbished locos), there were changes to their grilles.

On the nose end at No. 1 end, the two-piece grille was extended to the full length of the nose, although the left section closest to the end of the loco stopped short and a square fire extinguisher panel was added. At No. 2 end the full height two-piece grille remained, although, again, nearest the nose end the grille was cut back for another fire extinguisher panel.

On the 37/7 and 37/9s the window midway along the body was removed and plated over. Any locos which retained the frost grilles over the No. 1 end radiator grille had them removed. Most of these had been removed from 37/0s anyway, although some did retain them until withdrawal, such as 37203.

DRS has also had some of its locos overhauled with noticeable differences. Fitted with cab modifications inside and out, with Bmac lights, have been 37038/ 059/069, 37218/259, 37423, 37602/605– 612.

Some DRS locos were fitted with new multiple working and lost their Blue Star MW, while others retained Blue Star as well as having the DRS system, and others retained their Blue Star.

Blue Star only were 37029/087, 37194, 37229/261, 37510/515, 37682/683; DRS system only: 37038/059/069, 37218, 37259, 37602/605-612; Dual Blue Star and DRS systems: 37402/405/409/419/ 423/425, 37601/603/604/667/688. Additionally 37422 may also be modified to have both systems as part of its ongoing overhaul.

NUMBERS

Renumberings from D series was, with most locos, taking the last two digits for their new TOPS numbers, so D6701–99 became 37001–099, D6800–99 became 37100–199, with the exception that D6700 took the 37119 number to keep all the split-box locos together. D6900– 99 became 37200–299, with the exception of D6819 which took the 37283 number, as D6983 had been written off in an accident. D6600–08 became 37300 –308.

SUBSEQUENT RENUMBERINGS

All refurbished Class 37s were renumbered as detailed below, but there have been some subsequent renumberings. In 1986, Motherwell locos dedicated to iron ore trains were renumbered in the 37/3 series, from 37310 upwards. Only 37310–314/320–326 were done, the first five being centre-box locos, the other seven being split-box. They remained unrefurbished.

In 1988 the refurbishment programme was ended, but it was decided to fit some 37s with the same regeared bogies as used on refurbished locos, while giving them a light overhaul. These were numbered 37350–359 for split-box locos and 37370–381 for centre-box locos. Later 37330–335/340–345/382– 384 were added when the bogies from twelve Class 37/5s were swapped for conventional bogies to create the 37/6s.

Because of the new 37/3 subclass with regeared bogies it was decided to renumber the Motherwell 373xx locos back to their original identities. Also, with original 37/0 locos 37303/304/ 306/308 still in traffic (having not been selected to become 37/4s), to avoid any confusion among operating staff these were renumbered in the vacant 37271– 274 series, the original locos that had carried these numbers having been converted to 37/4s. These are marked with ^ in the text to signify it is the second 37271–274.

To further add to the story, 37145, which had been numbered 37313 for a period, then became 37382 when it was given regeared bogies. Then 37271/272 became 37333/334 when they recieved CP7 bogies.

The 37/6s, all of which are still in traffic, were Class 37/5s fitted with original 90mph bogies and planned for use on Eurostar trains, which never happened. All have been sold to DRS. 37360 has only run as such in preservation, while 37019 never took up its allocated 37342 number before withdrawal; 37101 did become 37345, but the renumbering was undertaken while the loco was stored and it never ran like this.

Finally, four 37/0s have been converted to Class 97/3s with ERTMS, but they are essentially, to all intents and purposes, still 37/0s.

37001	37707
37002	37351
37003	37360+
37005	37501
37006	37798
37007	37506
37008	37352+
37009	37340
37014	37709
37015	37341
37016	37706
37017	37503
37018	37517
37019	37342*
37020	37702
37021	37715
37022	37512
37024	37714
37026	37320+
37027	37519
37028	37505
37030	37701
37032	37353+
37033	37719
37034	37704
37036	37507
37037	37321+
37039	37504
37041	37520
37043	37354+
37044	37710
37045	37355+
37049	37322+
37049	37343
37050	37717
37052	37713
37053	37344
37056	37513

37060	37705	37160	37373	37270	37409
37061	37799	37161	37899	37271	37418
37064	37515	37163	37802	37271^	37333
37067	37703	37164	37675	37272	37431
37068	37356+	37165	37374+	37272^	37334
37076	37518	37166	37891	37273	37410
37079	37357+	37167	37383	37274	37402
37081	37797	37168	37890	37276	37413
37082	37502	37169	37674	37277	37415
37084	37718	37170	97302	37279	37424
37085	37711	37171	37690	37281	37428
37086	37516	37172	37686	37282	37405
37088	37323	37173	37801	37283	37895
37089	37708	37176	37883	37284	37381
37090	37508	37177	37885	37285	37335
37091	37358	37178	97303	37286	37404
37093	37509	37179	37691	37287	37414
37094	37716	37180	37886	37288	37427
37099	37324+	37181	37687	37289	37408
37100	97301	37182	37670	37290	37411
37101	37345*	37183	37884	37291	37419
37102	37712	37186	37898	37292	37425
37103	37511	37187	37683	37295	37406
37105	37796	37189	37672	37296	37423
37108	37325+	37190	37314+	37297	37420
37111	37326+	37192	37694	37299	37426
37112	37510	37193	37375	37300	37429
37115	37514	37195	37689	37301	37412
37117	37521	37199	37376	37302	37416
37118	37359	37200	37377	37303	37271^
37119	37350	37202	37331	37304	37272^
37120	37887	37204	37378	37305	37407
37121	37677	37205	37688	37306	37273^
37122	37692	37206	37906	37307	37403
37123	37679	37208	37803	37308	37274^+
37124	37894	37210	37693	37501	37601
37125	37904	37217	97304	37502	37602
37126	37676	37224	37680	37504	37603
37127	37370	37226	37379	37506	37604
37128	37330	37228	37696	37507	37605
37129	37669	37231	37896	37508	37606
37130	37681	37233	37889	37511	37607
37132	37673	37234	37685	37512	37608
37134	37684	37236	37682	37514	37609
37135	37888	37237	37893	37687	37610
37136	37905	37239	37332	37690	37611
37137	37312+	37243	37697	37691	37612
37143	37800	37246	37698		
37145	37313+	37247	37671		
37145	37382	37249	37903		
37147	37371	37253	37699		
37148	37902	37256	37678		
37149	37892	37257	37668		
37150	37901	37258	37384		
37151	37667	37259	37380+		
37152	37310+	37265	37430		
37155	37897	37266	37422		
37156	37311+	37267	37421		
37157	37695	37268	37401		
37159	37372	37269	37417		

+ later reverted to original number
^ second locos to carry 37271–274 numbers.
* loco allocated this number, but not applied

class 40

TOPS number range:	40001–199
BR 1957 number range:	D200–D399
Former class codes:	D20/1, later 20/3
Built by:	EE & RSH Ltd
Introduced:	1958–62
Wheel arrangement:	1Co-Co1
Weight (operational):	133 tons
Height:	12ft 10in (3.91m)
Width:	9ft (2.74m)
Length:	69ft 6in (21.18m)
Min. curve negotiable:	4½ chains
Maximum speed:	90mph (144km/h)
Wheelbase:	61ft 3in (18.67m)
Bogie wheelbase:	21ft 6in (6.55m)
Bogie pivot centres:	34ft 4in (10.46m)
Wheel diameter	Driving: 3ft 9in (1.14m) Pony: 3ft (0.91m)
Route availability:	6
Brake force:	51 tons
Engine type:	English Electric 16SVT Mk11
Engine horsepower:	2,000bhp (1,492kW)
Power at rail:	1,550bhp (1,156kW)
Tractive effort:	52,000lb
Main generator type:	EE822
Auxiliary generator type:	EE911-2B
No. of traction motors:	6
Traction motor type:	EE 526-5D
Gear ratio:	61:19
Fuel tank capacity:	710gal (3,195ltr)

THIS CLASS WAS another pilot scheme of ten locos, which won repeat orders for 190 more. Aimed to be a mixed traffic design, it was soon overtaken in design terms by locos with more power and a lighter weight. Based on the ER, NER, ScR and LMR, the 40s were nevertheless still in traffic until 1985 (and class pioneer 40122 was retained for three further years for charters), and 125 were upgraded with dual brakes. Built with steam heating, many locos lost this capability in the mid-1970s. Seven are preserved.

NOSE ENDS

D200–324 were built with discs, of which D260–66 were converted to centre panels. This meant that 40001–059/067–124 ran with TOPS numbers with discs.

Split boxes were fitted to D325–344, later 40125–144, while centre panels were new on D345–399 (40145–199) and retro-fitted to D260–266 (40060–066) from the mid-1960s.

All split and central panel 40s later had dominos fitted, apart from 40162/166/189/190.

There were several subsequent changes to the front ends. A yellow metal headcode panel was on 40158 (No. 2 end only), while a yellow plastic headcode panel was fitted on 40062 (No. 2 end only).

Flush fronts with communicating doors were removed from 40002 (No. 1 end), 40011 (No. 1 end), 40027 (No. 2 end), 40029 (No. 1 end), 40044 (No. 2 end), 40067 (both ends), 40086 (No. 1 end), 40095 (No. 2 end), 40098 (No. 1 end), 40111 (both ends), 40116 (No. 2 end), 40133 (No. 1 end), 40134 (No. 1 end), 40139 (No. 2 end), 40144 (both ends). 40058 was unique in having its door plated over at No. 1 with its discs removed.

Discs were removed from 40001/009/010/012/013/033/035/058/070/073/084/085/092/099, 40101/121. Odd discs were removed from 40028/078 (left-hand bottom No. 1 end), 40029/057 (left-hand and right-hand bottom No. 1 end), 40044 (centre bottom No. 2 end), 40056/084 (centre bottom No. 1 end), 40079 (left-hand bottom No. 2 end).

At No. 2 end, 40127 had a door fitted from a disc loco and retained this in between its split headcode, and ran like this with both 0O00 and domino headcodes, while 40131 was likewise but the discs and the lamps behind were removed, also at No. 2 end.

In the conversion of D260–266 to centre panels the locos were given square corners to their panels and no handrails, although 40060/061/065 later had the same rounded corners, leaving 40062–064/066 with the square corners, which were also fitted to 40167, presumably after collision repairs.

All disc locos initially had ladders fitted to their nose ends, but these were soon removed. An extra vertical handrail was fitted to D241/42/86 (40041/042/086) on the right of the nose, 40086 retaining this when fitted with a flush nose end.

Additional headboard clips were fitted at the bottom of the nose to 40145–150, while an extra lamp bracket below the headcode box was fitted to 40167/168/185, and a high, central lamp bracket was also fitted to split-box 40125/131–139.

The only loco to have a headlight is 40145, which also had radio aerials on the top of its nose.

TRAIN HEATING

All 40s were built with steam heating, with 40001–059/067–086, 40105–124 having a Stone 4625 boiler, while 40060–066/087–104/125–199 had a Clayton RO 2500.

ETH was fitted to D255 from new in January 1960 but was only used for trials

A rare picture of a TOPS blue named Class 40. In this November 1974 view, 235 has been renumbered 40035 while still retaining its original Apapa nameplates. The nameplates from 40s were removed in the early 1970s, with 40035 being the last to retain them, in March 1975. PDC

40009 displays a Class 40 with its headcode discs removed. It is also a vacuum-braked only, non-boilered loco, but retains its MW. PDC

096, 40104/129/132/140/174/182/189 (1974); 40002/006/007, 40124/133/135/137/169/176/181 (1975); 40113/136 (1977).

Not dual-braked were 40003/005/008–011/016–021/023/025/026/031/032/036/037/039–043/045/046/048/049/051/059/062/065/070/072/075/087–089/092/094, 40100–103/105–109/112–116/120/121/123/125/138/139/142/144/148/156/161/173/175/179/183/184/187/190/198.

Due to bogies swaps, some vacuum-braked locos ran with air-brake pipes; at least 40121/183 ran as such.

MULTIPLE WORKING

All had Blue Star MW. Unlike other classes, as well as the cables on the front of the bufferbeams, because they were on the bogies as opposed to the frame, the 40s' MW then had a side jumper to connect the MW from the bogie to the body.

In the late 1960s the ScR region removed the cables from its 40s (D260–66, D357–68); others which ran for periods without MW were 40004/012, 40103/133/148. It was refitted to some locos, namely 40064, 40168. Bogie swaps, however, often changed a loco's MW status, and locos may have MW cables at one end and not the other, or side MW cables and not the front jumpers or even just parts – such as the jumper or the receptacle – removed.

As far as can be ascertained, ScR-allocated 40048/072, 40101/123/142/173/184 did not lose their MW.

and demonstration and was removed *circa* April 1960.

Boilers were removed in the 1970s from 40001/002/004/008–010/020/022/036–038/040/046/073/079/082/088/091/094/096/099, 40115/121/130/131/133/135/137–140/145/152/169/170/177/178/180/183/192–196/199, while the boiler water tanks were also removed from 40001/008–010/020/022/036/037/073/079/082/091/092/094/096/099, 40115/121/131/135/137–140/145/152/169/170/177/180/183/192–196.

BRAKES

All 40s were built with vacuum brakes. The following were converted to dual brakes: 252/56/57/73/74/76/77/81/82/86, 345/52/53/94/99 (1969); 258/64/84/85, 346/49/50/54 (1970); 200/01/04/12/13/24/27/30/33/53/54/60/61/63/66–69/83, 319/30/55/57–60/63/64/68/70/71/77/78/80/88/97 (1971); 214/28/34/44/47/55/91/93/97–99, 328/51/62/66/67/85/93 (1972); 215/29/38/71/80/95, 310/11/17/18/26/27/31/34/41/43/47/65/72/86/91/92/95/96; (1973); 40022/035/050/090/

ABOVE LEFT: 40133, one of the batch of twenty with split headcodes, was also one of the few 40s to have its central communication doors removed and a flush panel fitted in their place to reduce draughts. In this 1983 view, it has also had its MW removed, although judging by the fact it still has a steam pipe on and the other ends looks to have its MW retained, this is more likely because it has had a bogie swap with an ex-ScR Class 40. The loco has no frost grille protecting its radiator at No. 1 end. RAIL PHOTOPRINTS

ABOVE RIGHT: D260-66 had their front end discs changed to centre panels in the early 1960s by the ScR. They differed by not having handrails above and to the side of the panels, and also by having square corners to the panels as opposed to the round edges on the factory-built centre-panel 40s. This modification is clearly shown on 40064, which also shows the bottom lip where the communication doors used to be – the nose of the later locos had a flat bottom. Unusually for a Haymarket 40, the loco has had its MW refitted. PDC

40069 had the bottom section of its bodywork cut away to give easier access to pipework, but the modification was not undertaken on any other locos. PDC

LIVERIES

BR green: D200–372
BR green with small yellow panels: D200–399
BR green with full yellow ends: 201/02/05/08–12/14/15/17/18/20–26/28–32/34–36/39/41–44/47/49/52–58/60/64–69/72–74/77–79/82–99, 300–20/23–55/57–59/61/63/66–69/71–87/89–99. Possibly 362.
BR blue: 40001–038/040–099, 40100–105/107–199
BR 'Large Logo' blue: 40145

D322, 40039 and 40106 were withdrawn in BR green.

After withdrawal, 40013 spent a period as a display loco, which saw short spells in BR blue with small yellow warning panels, and in BR blue with a white window frame at No. 1 end.

EMBELLISHMENTS

Gateshead crests: 40057/084
White headcode box trim: 40128/155
Red bufferbeams (blue): 40004/013/057/084/092, 40173, 97407

NAMES

D210	*EMPRESS OF BRITAIN*
D211	*MAURETANIA*
D212	*AUREOL*
D213	*ANDANIA*
D214	*ANTONIA*
D215	*AQUITANIA*
D216	*CAMPANIA*
D217	*CARINTHIA*
D218	*CARMANIA*
D219	*CARONIA*
D220	*FRANCONIA*

Several disc Class 40s had their communicating doors removed and plated over to give a flush front, with the discs retained. 40044 had this modification at No. 2 end only. This view of the loco on a curve shows how the bogies move when the locos go round corners. PDC

A centre-panel Class 40 prior to the fitting of dominos. 40169 is dual-braked, and although it retains a steam pipe and boiler water tanks between the bogies, the loco is 'no heat'. PDC

D221	*IVERNIA*	D225	*LUSITANIA*
D222	*LACONIA*	D227	*PARTHIA*
D223	*LANCASTRIA*	D228	*SAMARIA*
D224	*LUCANIA*	D229	*SAXONIA*

ABOVE: One of the seven Haymarket locos converted to centre panels from discs, 40062 also shows off its unique yellow headcode at No. 2 end. In common with many HA 40s, it has its MW removed. Because of the bogies the MW cables, which connected between locos, were then connected to the loco via cables on the side. The hole for the MW cables can be seen on the bogie side above the pony axle and on the front to the right of the steam-heat pipe. 40062 remained vacuum-braked and boiler-fitted until its demise in November 1981. PDC

RIGHT: The number of pipes on a Class 40 bufferbeam varied. Some were vacuum-braked only, had no steam-heat pipe, and even lost their MW. The 'busiest' bufferbeam, seen here on 40135, is a dual-braked loco with steam heating and MW. This image shows the side MW cables to good effect. PIP DUNN

D230	*SCYTHIA*
D231	*SYLVANIA*
D232	*EMPRESS OF CANADA*
D233	*EMPRESS OF ENGLAND*
D234	*ACCRA*
D235	*APAPA*
40145	*East Lancashire Railway*

The twenty-five locos named by BR had impressive nameplates with the name at the bottom and a circular section with the shipping line's flag inside a ship's wheel. Each had the shipping line (in upper case) under the name: these were Canadian Pacific Steamships (D210/32/33), Elder Dempster Lines (D212/34/35) and Cunard Lines (D211/213–25/27–31).

As the 40s were replaced on the WCML expresses, the nameplates were removed from the late 1960s, although the last was 40035 in March 1975. This meant some had their nameplates in blue, and some ran with them while having TOPS numbers.

In the early 1980s several of the names were unofficially reapplied in painted stencil style. At first they were just white lettering, but some had red panels and borders.

A comparison of front ends of two Class 40s. On the left, with all its discs folded down so covering their marker lights, is D200, while on the right is D345 with a centre panel and small yellow panel. Both locos are dual-braked. PIP DUNN

BR blue with cast nameplates: 211/
212/215/216/219/221/222/224–228/232
–235
**Green with TOPS numbers and cast
nameplates:** 40017/022
**Blue with TOPS numbers and cast
nameplates:** 40016/027/029/032/035
Painted names white: 40011–014/
017–019/022–024/027/028/032/035
Painted names red: 40012/013/015/
020/022/024/025/027/029/031/033/035

BUILD BATCHES

1958	D200–209	Vulcan Foundry
1959	D210–252/254	Vulcan Foundry
1960	D253/255–304	Vulcan Foundry
	D305–314	RSH Darlington
	D325–327	Vulcan Foundry
1961	D315–324	RSH Darlington
	D328–371	Vulcan Foundry
1962	D372–399	Vulcan Foundry

OTHER DETAIL DIFFERENCES

A number of variations and modifications affected the Class 40 fleet. Frost
grilles were removed from 40001–016/
018/020/022–029/031–040/042/046–
075/077–090/092–095/097/099, 40100–
104/106/108–133/135–139/141–176/179
–188/192–199.

A cut-away solebar was implemented
on 40069 to see if it would ease maintenance, but no further locos were
modified.

NUMBERS

Apart from D322, written off in 1967, all
Class 40s gained TOPS numbers. D200
took the 40122 slot, while the other locos
in the D2xx series became 400xx, and
D300–399 became 40100–199, with
the exception of D322.

Subsequent Renumberings

Four locos were reinstated in 1985 for
working infrastructure trains in connection with the Crewe station remod-
elling. They were renumbered into the
97/4 series, and the last remained in
traffic until 1987.

40060	97405
40135	97406
40012	97407
40118	97408

*One Class 40 is currently passed for main line running, D345/40145. In April 2003 it was running in
original green but with a full yellow nose end. The modifications for main-line running are the headlight
and the nose-end aerial plus the newer style yellow overhead warning flashes, but otherwise the loco
is as it would have been in the early 1970s, albeit perhaps a bit too clean.* PIP DUNN

*An original-look Class 40 in February 1968, D286 has all its discs folded down but an oil lamp added to the lamp iron. It also has an additional vertical
handrail on the nose end, a feature only carried by D241/42/86. The loco is vacuum-braked only with MW still in place.* BILL WRIGHT

THE CLASS 41s were a pilot scheme design of diesel hydraulic built by North British. No more orders were made, but their design led to the development of the Class 42/43s.

It is worth noting a quandary about the classification. Technically the TOPS classifications did not come into effect until 1 January 1968, two days after the last of these locos were withdrawn. They would have become Class 41s on TOPS had they lasted two days longer, but some refuse to call them Class 41s for that reason – they were all withdrawn when TOPS came into effect.

That said, they all *existed* when TOPS came in, so it is equally fair to say there were Class 41s, and just withdrawn Class 41s! It is also worth mentioning that the TOPS classifications had been decided before they were withdrawn and hence 41s was allocated to the D600s, but some historians will refer to them solely as the D600 class.

None were preserved, despite D601 remaining in a scrapyard as late as 1980.

DETAIL DIFFERENCES

All had Red Circle MW and vacuum brakes only. Discs were fitted from new, and at least D600/1 was fitted with two frames on their front for fitting headboards. These were later removed and WR three-character frames for trains reporting numbers were added later.

All five had train split-boxes added, keeping their communication doors. The dates of fitting of headcodes were

D602 (12/64), D603 (10/65), D601 (1/66), D604 (11/66), D600 (5/67).

A Spanner Mk 1 boiler was fitted for train heating.

LIVERIES

All were new in all-over BR green with a thin off-white stripe above the solebar and a grey roof and red bufferbeams.

All had half yellow panels added, while none had BR green with full yellow ends. BR blue with small yellow panels was only seen on one loco, D602 (from December 1966), while full BR blue with full yellow ends was treated to just D600 in May 1967 – only seven months before it was withdrawn. All locos had serif-style numbers, while D600 had four BR badges – one on each cabside – while D602 had its double arrows on the bodyside above the nameplates.

BR green: D600–04
BR green with small yellow panels: D600–04
BR blue with small yellow panels: D602
BR Blue: D600

NAMES

D600	*ACTIVE*
D601	*ARK ROYAL*
D602	*BULLDOG*
D603	*CONQUEST*
D604	*COSSACK*

1957 BR number range:	D600–04
Former class codes:	D20/2, later 20/4
Built by:	NBL Ltd
Introduced:	1958–59
Wheel arrangement:	A1A-A1A
Weight (operational):	118 tons
Height:	12ft 10in (3.91m)
Width:	8ft 8in (2.64m)
Length:	65ft (19.81m)
Min. curve negotiable:	4½ chains
Maximum speed:	90mph (144km/h)
Wheelbase:	50ft (15.24m)
Bogie wheelbase:	15ft (4.57m)
Bogie pivot centres:	35ft (10.69m)
Wheel diameter (driving):	3ft 7in (1.09m)
Wheel diameter (middle):	3ft 4in (1.02m)
Route availability:	5
Brake force:	88 tons
Engine type:	Two NBL L12V 18/21A
Total horsepower:	2,000bhp (1,592kW)
Power at rail:	1,700bhp (1,268kW)
Tractive effort:	50,000lb
Transmission type:	Voith L306r
Fuel tank capacity:	800gal (3,600ltr)

D601 ARK ROYAL shows the original look of a Class 41 with disc headcodes; all were later changed to chunky split panels mounted each side of the rarely ever used central communication doors. The loco does not have the frames for mounting GWR-style reporting numbers, but it does have two metal frames on the front to which headboards were affixed. RAIL PHOTOPRINTS

79

1957 BR number range:	D800–32/66–70
Former class codes:	D800–02: D22/1, later 22/1 D803–32/66–70: D20/1, later 20/1
Built by:	BR Swindon
Introduced:	1958–61
Wheel arrangement:	B-B
Weight (operational):	79 tons
Height:	12ft 10in (3.91m)
Width:	8ft 9in (2.67m)
Length:	60ft (18.29m)
Min. curve negotiable:	4½ chains
Maximum speed:	90mph (144km/h)
Wheelbase:	48ft 3in (14.71m)
Bogie wheelbase:	10ft 6in (3.2m)
Bogie pivot centres:	37ft 9in (11.61m)
Wheel diameter:	3ft 4in (1.02m)
Route availability:	6
Brake force:	35 tons
Engine type:	Two Maybach MD650: D800–29/31/32/66–70 Two Paxman 12YJXL: D830
Total horsepower:	2,000bhp (1,592kW): D800–02 2,200bhp (1,641kW): D803–29/31/32/66–70 2,400bhp (1,790kW): D830
Power at rail:	1,700bhp (1,268kW): D800–02 1,750bhp (1,306kW): D804–29/31/32/66–70 1,800bhp (1,343kW): D830
Tractive effort:	52,400lb
Transmission type:	Mekydro K104
Fuel tank capacity:	800gal (3,600ltr)

BASED ON THE German Railways V200 design, the first three locos were part of the pilot scheme plan and led to repeat orders, for thirty-five Class 42s and thirty-three Class 43s (see below). These B-B diesel hydraulics had very low overall weight, which meant they were popular for fast passenger use. They were allocated to the WR, though did reach Crewe, Shrewsbury and Birmingham on inter-regional trains. All were withdrawn by December 1972; two are preserved. Along with the Class 41s and 43s they were known as Warships.

DETAIL DIFFERENCES

Discs were fitted to D800–12 at construction, complete with a frame for three character GWR reporting numbers. From D813, split-centre boxes were fitted. D800–12 were retro-fitted with headcode boxes; D801 (6/63), D804 (8/63), D806 (10/63), D812 (1/64), D800/09 (2/64), D805/11 (3/64), D808 (12/64), D802/03/07 (2/65), D810 (9/65). These thirteen locos also had additional central red tail-lights below the top central headcode disc, in the middle of the nose; these were removed when headcode panels were fitted.

MW was complicated on the Class 42s. From new, D800–02 could only work in multiple with each other using a system similar to that in use on the V200s in Germany. D800 had its B-end jumper cables damaged in September 1959, and when it was stopped in January 1960 for a Heavy Intermediate repair, they were removed and it returned to traffic without MW in February 1960. D801 lost its MW at its Heavy Intermediate in March 1960, while D802 did likewise when released to traffic in June 1960. They could not work in multiple with any other locos, including D6300–05 and D600–04 (which were Red Circle).

White Diamond MW was fitted to D803–32/66–70. This was progressively removed in 1966 due to its unreliability

In March 1969, D817 FOXHOUND shows a typical Warship look for the late 1960s. The old maroon livery is retained, but has full yellow ends applied. The MW has been removed, which is identifiable by the metal plates to the top right of the steam heat pipe and to the left of the left buffer. Obscured by the buffer would be another plate to the right of the left buffer. RAIL PHOTOPRINTS

LEFT: The last Warship built, D870 ZULU, differed by having its horns mounted above its cab in a separate grille, as it was intended the loco would be fitted with ETH, a modification which never happened. The loco is in maroon with small yellow panel, its second livery, after green (without and then with a small yellow warning panel). It then had full yellow ends on maroon before being repainted into BR blue. RAIL PHOTOPRINTS

ABOVE RIGHT: D821 GREYHOUND is in all but original condition in the October 1998 view, being in all-over green with a split-centre headcode and MW fitted, the jumper for which is on the left-hand side on White Diamond locos. The loco retains its steam pipe, though its boiler is not operational. PIP DUNN

and because it was rarely used. In 1968/69 it was reinstated on D803/04/07/08/14/16/19/22–29/31/32/66–70 as pairs of 42s were diagrammed from May 1968 on some Paddington-Penzance trains. D866/70 lost their MW at one end by May 1971, but the others retained MW until withdrawal.

D870 was unique in having roof-mounted horn grilles above its cab windows. D803, after collision damage, had the two air-ventilation grilles under its headcode box, a feature normally exclusive to Class 43s.

D830 had oval offset exhaust ports on account of it being the only 42 fitted with Paxman engines as opposed to Maybachs. It was fitted with the different engines at construction, and this made it non-standard for its entire life. It was never fitted with Maybach engines and was an early withdrawal.

D800–12/66–70 had Spanner Mk 1 boilers, D813–17/19–32 had the Stones OK4616 boilers, while D818 had a Spanner Mk 3. Those locos with Stone Vapor boilers had the boiler room air-intake grilles cut horizontally into the body above the cantrail, but on one side only.

D800–02 had short, curved handrails when new, but the production series locos had longer, two-section handrails directly under each front cab window. D800–02 were later modified to follow suit at the same time their headcode boxes were fitted.

LIVERIES

All were new in BR green, and half yellow panels were added *circa* 1962/63 to all the fleet. The only two to have BR green with full yellow ends were D808/810. Maroon with small yellow panels was applied to D801/02/05/06/09/11–13/15/17/21/23/28/29/32/67/69/70, while full yellow ends on maroon were on D805/06/09/11/12/15/17/23/29/32/69/70.

BR blue with small yellow panels was on just 830/31, and standard BR with blue full yellow ends on 802–08/10–14/16/18–32/66–70. The positioning of badges and fonts varied in the blue era. Locos were meant to have corporate font numbers with a badge central on the bodyside, but some locos had badges on all four cabsides – D802–04/07/08/11/14/16/18–22/25–27/66/68 – while others had serif-style font

numbers – D802/04/07/11/14/16/18–21/26/27/68.

Some locos had the correct corporate font but four badges on the cabsides – 803/19/22/25/26/66 – and with – incorrect – D prefixes.

Those locos in the correct style with single badges underneath the nameplates and corporate font were 805/08/10–14/16/18/20/21/23/24/28/29/31/32/67–70.

Of the two locos in blue with small yellow panels, D830 had small, single BR badges above the nameplates and serif-style numbers, while D831 had four badges on the cabsides, and four sets of numbers on the bodysides.

In preservation, 821 has run in a version of the DB V200 maroon and black livery, renumbered V200.021 and named *WINDHUND*, while 832 has run in BR black, again a livery never previously seen before on 42s. These locos have also recreated liveries that were carried by other 42s, such as green with full yellow ends, green with very small yellow headcode panel frames, and BR blue with small yellow panels.

BR green: D800–32/66–70

BR green with small yellow panels: D800–32/66–70

BR green with full yellow ends: D808/810

Maroon with small yellow panels: D801/02/05/06/09/11–13/15/17/21/23/28/29/32/67/69/70

Maroon with full yellow ends: D805/06/09/11/12/15/17/23/29/32/69/70

BR blue with small yellow panels: D830/31

BR blue: D801–08/10–14/16/18–32/66–70

NAMES

D800	*SIR BRIAN ROBERTSON*
D801	*VANGUARD*
D802	*FORMIDABLE*
D803	*ALBION*
D804	*AVENGER*
D805	*BENBOW*
D806	*CAMBRIAN*
D807	*CARADOC*
D808	*CENTAUR*
D809	*CHAMPION*
D810	*COCKADE*
D811	*DARING*
D812	*THE ROYAL NAVAL RESERVE 1859–1959*
D813	*DIADEM*
D814	*DRAGON*
D815	*DRUID*
D816	*ECLIPSE*
D817	*FOXHOUND*
D818	*GLORY*
D819	*GOLIATH*
D820	*GRENVILLE*
D821	*GREYHOUND*
D822	*HERCULES*
D823	*HERMES*
D824	*HIGHFLYER*
D825	*INTREPID*
D826	*JUPITER*
D827	*KELLY*
D828	*MAGNIFICENT*
D829	*MAGPIE*
D830	*MAJESTIC*
D831	*MONARCH*
D832	*ONSLAUGHT*
D866	*ZEBRA*
D867	*ZENITH*
D868	*ZEPHYR*
D869	*ZEST*
D870	*ZULU*

Small replica ship's crests were fitted to D823 in October 1965. These were by the loco's number on the driver's cabs, and were retained when the loco was repainted from green to maroon and then on to blue. No other Warships carried this feature. D812 was originally to be named *DESPATCH*.

In preservation, the two surviving Class 42s have carried names of other 42s; also 821 has been named *HERZOGMANN*, *WINDHUND*, *CORNWALL* and *CHRIS BROADHURST*, while 832 was briefly named *COLIN MASSINGHAM*.

DEPARTMENTAL USE

832 was added to the Departmental fleet after it was retired from capital stock, and moved to Derby to act as a dead load on test tracks at Old Dalby and Eggington. It was not renumbered, although 97401 was at one point mooted for the loco, but never applied. Its role ceased in 1979, but it was sold for preservation.

870 was initially intended for a Departmental role, and even moved to Derby, but it had suffered minor collision damage and was therefore not deemed suitable.

818 was retained for spares for 832, and then remained on display at Swindon works until scrapped in late 1985.

1957 BR number range:	D833–65
Former Class Codes:	D22/2, later 22/2, 22/4
Built by:	NBL Ltd
Introduced:	1960–62
Wheel arrangement:	B-B
Weight (operational):	79 tons
Height:	12ft 10in (3.91m)
Width:	8ft 9in (2.67)
Length:	60ft (18.29m)
Min. curve negotiable:	4½ chains
Maximum speed:	90mph (144km/h)
Wheelbase:	48ft 3in (14.71m)
Bogie wheelbase:	10ft 6in (3.2m)
Bogie pivot centres:	37ft 9in (11.51m)
Wheel diameter:	3ft 4in (1.02m)
Route availability:	6
Brake force:	35 tons
Engine type:	Two NBL/MAN L1 2V1 8/21
Total horsepower:	2,200bhp (1,641kW)
Power at rail:	1,800bhp (1,343kW)
Tractive effort:	49,030lb
Transmission type:	Voith LT306r
Fuel tank capacity:	800gal (3,600ltr)

THE CLASS 43s were the final version of the Warship design, and like the Class 41s, were built by North British, although they had the same body design as the Class 42s. They had two MAN engines as opposed to Maybach units. All were B-B diesel hydraulics and exclusive to the WR in terms of allocation, but did venture to Crewe and Birmingham. All were withdrawn by 1971, and none were preserved.

DETAIL DIFFERENCES

All had split-centre boxes. MW was White Diamond, so the locos could work with other Class 43s and Class 42s D803–32/66–70. It was removed progressively from 1966, and the holes for the jumper cables plated over. All had Stones OK4616 boilers.

All 43s had two small grilles on their headcode boxes directly below the panels on the bottom left and right corners, although on 841/48 they were positioned centrally under each headcode panel. These grilles on 839 were square as opposed to round. They were removed from 849.

859 also had longer-than-standard vertical handrails on its nose front, the only Warship to do so. When 846 was rebuilt after a collision, it lost its central WR-style lamp iron and two headboard clips from A-end.

LIVERIES

BR green was applied to all the fleet, D833–65, and all had small yellow panels applied. Of these, 845 initially had just the frame of the headcode box painted yellow in 1961, along with a white cab roof. Proper half yellow panels were added to 845 in 1964.

No Class 43s had BR green with full yellow ends, but maroon, initially with small yellow panels, was bestowed on D834/38–40/42/44/48/55/57/58/61–63/65. Of these, 834/38/42 later had full yellow ends on their maroon livery.

None were ever painted in BR blue with small yellow panels, but most were painted in BR blue, namely 833–37/39/41–47/49–65 – just 838/40/48 were scrapped in maroon, 838 with a full yellow end.

864 also ran in BR blue with dark brown underframe panels, and was withdrawn as such.

In similar vein to the Class 42s, badge and number styles varied. Locos in the early version of BR blue with the – incorrect – style of four cabside badges and D prefixes in serif were D841/46/49/57/59/63/64.

Those with four cabside badges, D prefixes and corporate-style numbers were D835–37/43/49–51/53/60; the locos in, officially, the correct version of BR blue, with no D prefix and just bodyside badges below the nameplates and correct font numbers were 833–35/39/41–46/52–58/61/62/65.

To add to the confusion, D847 ran in blue with a small BR badge above its nameplate and serif-style numbers with D prefixes, while 864 also ran with four cabside badges and D prefixes on its serif numbers, but those numbers on the bodyside.

BR green: D833–65
BR green with small yellow panels: D833–65
Maroon with small yellow panels: D834/38–40/42/44/48/55/57/58/61–63/65

ABOVE: D835 PEGASUS in 1962 has already had its yellow warning panels added to its green livery. The loco retains its multiple working jumpers, though they were later removed. It also has an 83A shedplate fitted to its bufferbeam. It has split-centre headcodes which were hinged to allow easy access – indeed it is partially open in this view. RAIL PHOTOPRINTS

RIGHT: D852 TENACIOUS shows the relatively uncluttered bufferbeam layout of a Class 43 Warship, even while retaining the MW jumper. The loco, like all 43s, spent its entire life vacuum-braked and with steam-heat only. RAIL PHOTOPRINTS

Maroon with full yellow ends: D834/38/42

BR Blue: D833–37/39/41–47/49–63/65

BR blue with dark brown underframe: D864

NAMES

D833	PANTHER
D834	PATHFINDER
D835	PEGASUS
D836	POWERFUL
D837	RAMILLIES
D838	RAPID
D839	RELENTLESS
D840	RESISTANCE
D841	ROEBUCK
D842	ROYAL OAK
D843	SHARPSHOOTER
D844	SPARTAN
D845	SPRIGHTLY
D846	STEADFAST
D847	STRONGBOW
D848	SULTAN
D849	SUPERB
D850	SWIFT
D851	TEMERAIRE
D852	TENACIOUS
D853	THRUSTER
D854	TIGER
D855	TRIUMPH
D856	TROJAN
D857	UNDAUNTED
D858	VALOROUS
D859	VANQUISHER
D860	VICTORIOUS
D861	VIGILANT
D862	VIKING
D863	WARRIOR
D864	ZAMBESI
D865	ZEALOUS

class 43 HST power cars
specifications

THE PRODUCTION SERIES HST power cars were classified as 43s some five years after the last diesel hydraulic Class 43s were withdrawn. Initially classed as multiple units, as Classes 253/254, they were regarded as locos from the mid-1980s. Apart from three accident-damaged withdrawals, all remain in traffic. Three are with Network Rail but the other 191 are with passenger operators, and all have been re-engined. Some of the re-engined locos have been renumbered.

DETAIL DIFFERENCES

The original headlights were Bmac light clusters behind a Perspex shield. They were later changed to high intensity LED lights in a metal frame. These were fitted to all apart from 43011/019, 43173.

The bufferbeams were behind the front cowling. However, eight were converted in 1987/88 to act as DVTs to work with Class 91s and were fitted with standard buffers and drawgear, they were 43013/014/065/067/068/080/084, 43123. Of these, six have now been renumbered as 43423/465/467/468/480/484 and are used by Grand Central.

43013/014/062 have cab-mounted camera pods below their windscreens for their use with the Network Rail New Measurement Train (NMT).

They were originally built with the guard's compartment within the power car, but today this is moved to the front of the first trailer vehicle and the space remains vacant. Traction motors were differed on 43124–152, which had GEC motors as opposed to Brush.

TOPS number range:	43002–198, 43206–484		MTU 16V4000L R41R: 2,700bhp (2,010kW)
Built by:	BREL Crewe		
Years introduced:	1976–82	Power at rail:	1,770bhp (1,320kW)
Wheel arrangement:	Bo-Bo	Tractive effort:	17,980lb
Weight:	70 tons	Cont tractive effort:	10,340lb
Height:	12ft 10in (3.90m)	Cylinder bore:	Valenta: 8in (196mm) MB190: 8in (190mm) VP185: 7in (185mm) MTU4000
Length:	58ft 5in (17.80m)		
Width:	8ft 11in (2.73m)		
Wheelbase:	42ft 4in (12.90m)	Cylinder stroke:	Valenta: 8in (190mm) MB190: 8in (210mm) VP185: 8in (196mm) MTU4000
Bogie wheelbase:	8ft 7in (2.60m)		
Bogie pivot centres:	33ft 9in (10.28m)		
Wheel diameter:	3ft 4in (1.02m)	Maximum speed:	125mph (200km/h)
Min. curve negotiable:	4 chains (80.46m)	Route availability:	6
Original engine:	Paxman Valenta 12RP200L (all since removed)	Bogie type:	BP16
		Main alternator type:	Brush BA1001B
		Auxiliary ETH alternator:	Brush BAH601B
Replacement engines:	Mirrlees Blackstone MB190 Paxman 12VP185 MTU16V4000 R41R	Traction motor type:	43002–123/153–198 (Brush TMH68–46) 43124–152 (GECG417AZ)
Engine output:	Paxman Valenta 12RP200L: 2,250bhp (1,680kW) Mirrlees Blackstone MB190: 2,400bhp (1,788kW) Paxman 12VP185: 2,700bhp (2,010kW)	No. of traction motors:	4
		Gear ratio:	59:23
		Fuel tank capacity:	1,030gal (4,680ltr)
		Luggage capacity	1.5 tons, increased to 2.5 tons

OWNERSHIP

43002–005/009/010/012–015–018/020–037/040–042, 43124–152/163–165/168–172/174–177/179/181–183/185–192, 43206–208/238/239/295/296, 43304–320/366/367/378/384, 43423/465/467/468/480/484 are owned by Angel, 43013/014/043–050/052–056/058–064/066/069–071/073/075/076/078/079/081–083/086–089/091, 43156/159–162/180/ 193/195–197, 43251/257/272/274/277/285/290/299, 43300–303/321/357 are owned by Porterbrook, and 43092–094/097/098, 43122/153–155/158/194/198 are owned by First Group.

RE-ENGINEERING

All have been re-engined, and only 43011/019, which were withdrawn after accidents, retained their Valenta engines.

First withdrawal 43173 had a VP185 engine when it crashed. Some have had more than two or three different types of engine, and 43167–170 have had four different engine types over their lives.

All the GNER (later National Express and now East Coast) Class 43s were renumbered when fitted with MTU engines, with 200 being added to their numbers, so 43006 became 43206 and 43105 became 43305 and so on. Cross-Country also adopted this renumbering at re-engining. First Great Western and Network Rail did not renumber their 43s.

When the Grand Central's power cars were converted to MTU engines, they had 400 added to their number, so 43067 became 43467. However, 43123 did not become 43523, but became the more sensible 43423. However, the re-engined locos are not classed as 43/2 or 43/4s.

43053 was erroneously renumbered 43253 after its MTU conversion, an error rectified before it returned to traffic.

Conversions to Mirrlees MB190 engines: 43167 (1986); 43168–170 (1987) – all later changed to VP185s.

Conversions to Paxman VP 185s: 43170*§ (1994); 43047/075, 43167*^/169*§ (1995); 43168*§ (1996); 43173/175§/ 177§/179§/191§ (1997); 43048/049/052/ 055/072§, 43165 (2002); 43043/044/050/ 060/061/073/076/082 (2003); 43045/ 047/059/074§/075 (2005) 43046/054/

Two front ends of HST power cars show clearly some of the changes. On the left, East Coast 43239 is one of the fleet used on the ECML which have been re-engined with MTU engines and renumbered. It also features the new standard-style light clusters with LED tail-lights and now Perspex panels over the headlights. On the right is Grand Central's 43084, which had the same revised lights but still retains its original Valenta engine. However, the most noticeable change is the buffers, fitted to eight power cars to allow them to act as DVTs when the Class 91s first came in. The brake pipes are clearly visible. ANTHONY HICKS

058/066/081/083 (2008); 43064/089 (2009)

* converted from a Mirrlees MB190
§ converted to MTU
^ converted back to Valenta then MTU.

Conversions to MTU engines: 43004/ 009 (2004); 43025/026/078/092–094/ 097/098, 43125/133/141/153–155/158/ 164/165/175/183/197/198, 43290, 43300 (2006); 43005/010/012/017/018/020– 024/027–033/035–037/040/041/063/ 069/070/071/086–088/091, 43122/124/ 126–132/135/136/138–140/142/144– 152/156/159/161–163/168–172/174/ 176/177/179/181/182/185–188/191/ 192/194–196, 43208*/238*/296*, 43306*/ 309*/313*/314*/316*/318*/320*/367* (2007); 43002/003/015/016/034/042/079,43134/ 137/143/160/180/189/190/193,43206*/ 207^/239*/257*/277*/285^/295*/299*, 43301^/302*/303^/304^/305*/307*/311*/ 312*/315*/317*/319*/321^/357^/378*/384^ (2008); 43013§/014§/053/056/062§, 43251*, 43308*/310*/366^ (2009); 43465§/467§/ 468§/480§ (2010); 43272*/274*, 43423§/484§ (2011).

All were re-engined for FGW apart from * GNER/East Coast, ^ CrossCountry, § Network Rail, § Grand Central

LIVERIES

BR blue, grey and yellow: 43002–198
InterCity Executive: 43002–198
InterCity Swallow: 43002–198
InterCity with maroon stripe: 43010
InterCity with orange cab: 43028
Great Western Trains ivory and green: 43002–005/008–012/015–028/030–037/ 040–042, 43124–152/163–165/168–177/ 179/181–183/185–192
First Great Western green and gold: 43002–005/008–012/015–028/030–037/

Privatization saw Virgin, GNER, Midland Mainline and Great Western acquire HSTs, all still in InterCity colours. Shabby 43071 was one of the Virgin CrossCountry fleet, and before being repainted into red, shows off the original front-end look of an HST power car. PIP DUNN

GNER 43118 City of Kingston upon Hull *in May 2004 prior to being re-engined and renumbered 43318. The original lights are also fitted, but these have since been removed.* PIP DUNN

040–042, 43124–152/163–165/168–172/ 174–177/179/181–183/185–192
First Group (white cabs): 43003/029/ 032/137/138/140/142/165/192
First Group (blue cabs): 43002–005/ 009/010/012/015–037/040–042/063/ 071/079/088/091, 43124–152/156/161– 165/168–172/174–177/179/181–183/ 185–192/195
First Group with wavy lines: 43004/ 009
First Group all-over blue: 43002–005/ 009/010/012/015–018/020–037/040– 042/053/056/063/069–071/078/079/ 086–088/091–094/097/098, 43122/124– 156/158–165/168–172/174–177/179– 183/185–198
First Group all-over blue with Angel branding: 43009/175 (did not run in traffic like this)
Virgin red: 43006–008/013/014/062/ 063/065/067–071/078–080/084/086– 094/097–099, 43100–104/121–123/153– 162/166/178/180/184/193–198
Virgin red with yellow cab roofs: 43063/068/093

Virgin red unbranded: 43092/094, 43122/123/155/157/158
GNER with white lettering: 43096, 43109/110/113/115/167
GNER with gold lettering: 43006/008/ 038/039/051/053/056/057/067/077/ 078/080/095/096/099, 43102/105–120/ 167/197, 43208/238/290/296, 43300/ 306/309/313–315/316/318/320/367
GNER blue with London 2012 branding: 43116/120
GNER blue with Tutankhamen branding: 43051
GNER blue with online booking advert: 43039
GNER blue with Leeds-London advert: 43290, 43300
GNER blue with NatEx white stripe: 43039/051/053/056/057/077/095/099, 43105/107/110–112/117/119, 43208/ 238/296, 43306/309/313–315/316/318/ 320/367
GNER unbranded: 43039, 43108/119
MML Teal & Tangerine: 43043–061/064/ 066/072–077/081–083/085
MML Ocean Blue: 43007/043–061/063/

064/066/069–079/081–083/085–089/ 091 43104/156/159/161/166/178/180/ 184/193/195/196/198
National Express: 43039,43108,43206/ 208/238/239/251/257/277/295/290/ 296/299, 43300/302/305–320/367
NatEx East Coast: 43206/208/238/239/ 251/257/277/295/296/299, 43302/305– 320/367
CrossCountry Trains: 43207/285,43301/ 303/304/321/357/366/378/384
East Midlands Trains: 43043–050/052/ 054/055/058–061/064/066/073/075/ 076/081–083/089
Network Rail: 43013/014/062/089, 43154/196
Hornby red: 43087
Cotswold Rail silver: 43070
Grand Central black: 43065/067/068/ 080/084, 43123
Grand Central with orange solebar stripe: 43423/465/467/468/480/484
All-over black with red cab: 43101
East Coast Grey: 43206/208/238/239/ 251/257/272/274/277/290/295/296/ 299, 43300/302/305–320/367

For the launch of the new livery by First Great Western in July 2001, 43029 was unveiled in a new livery and renumbered 43001 for the occasion. The choice of a white cab was widely questioned at the press event, and after a handful of repaints, the livery was changed to a blue cab, which hid the dirt better. PIP DUNN

class 43 HST Power Cars

NAMES

43002	Top of the Pops
43002	Techni?Uest
43003	ISAMBARD KINGDOM BRUNEL
43004	Swan Hunter
43004	Borough of Swindon
43004	First for the Future
43006	Kingdom of Fife
43008	City of Aberdeen
43009	First Transforming Travel
43010	TSW Today
43011	Reader 125
43013	University of Bristol
43016	Garden Festival Wales 1992
43016	Peninsula Medical School
43017	HTV West
43018	The Red Cross
43019	City of Swansea Dinas Abertawe
43020	John Grooms
43020	MTU Power Passion Partnership
43021	David Austin – Cartoonist
43023	County of Cornwall
43024	Great Western Society 1961–2011
43025	Exeter
43025	INSTITUTION OF RAILWAY OPERATORS 2000–2010
43026	City of Westminster
43027	Westminster Abbey
43027	Glorious Devon
43030	Christian Lewis Trust
43032	The Royal Regiment of Wales
43033	Driver Brian Cooper 1947–1999
43034	The Black Horse
43034	TravelWatch South West
43037	PENYDARREN
43038	The National Railway Museum The First Ten Years 1975–1985
43038	City of Dundee
43039	The Royal Dragoon Guards
43040	Granite City
43040	Bristol St Philip's Marsh
43041	City of Discovery
43041	Meningitis Trust
43043	Leicestershire County Cricket Club
43044	Borough of Kettering
43045	The Grammar School Doncaster AD1350
43046	ROYAL PHILHARMONIC
43047	Rotherham Enterprise
43048	TCB Miller MBE
43049	Neville Hill
43051	The Duke and Duchess of York
43052	City of Peterborough
43053	County of Humberside
43053	Leeds United
43053	University of Worcester
43055	Sheffield Star
43056	University of Bradford
43056	The Royal British Legion
43057	Bounds Green
43058	MIDLAND PRIDE
43060	County of Leicestershire
43061	City of Lincoln
43062	John Armitt
43063	Maiden Voyager
43063	Rio Challenger
43064	City of York
43065	City of Edinburgh
43066	NOTTINGHAM PLAYHOUSE
43068	The Red Nose
43068	The Red Arrows
43069	Rio Enterprise
43070	Rio Pathfinder
43070	The Corps of Royal Electrical & Mechanical Engineers
43071	Forward Birmingham
43072	Derby Etches Park
43074	BBC EAST MIDLANDS TODAY
43076	BBC EAST MIDLANDS TODAY
43076	THE MASTER CUTLER 1947–1997
43076	IN SUPPORT OF HELP FOR HEROES
43077	County of Nottingham
43078	Shildon County Durham
43078	Golowan Festival Penzance
43078	Rio Crusader
43079	Rio Venturer
43081	Midland Valenta
43082	Derbyshire First
43082	Railway Children
43084	County of Derbyshire
43085	City of Bradford
43086	Rio Talisman
43087	Rio Invader
43087	11 Explosive Ordnance Disposal Regiment Royal Logistics Corps
43088	XIII Commonwealth Games Scotland 1988
43088	Rio Campaigner
43089	Rio Thunderer
43089	HAYABUSA
43091	Edinburgh Military Tattoo
43092	Highland Chieftain
43092	Institution of Mechanical Engineers 150
43093	York Festival '88
43093	Lady in Red
43095	Heaton
43095	Perth
43096	The Queen's Own Hussars
43096	The Great Racer
43096	Stirling Castle
43097	The Light Infantry
43097	Environment Agency
43098	Tyne and Wear Metropolitan County
43098	Railway Children
43099	Diocese of Newcastle
43100	Craigentinny
43100	Blackpool Rock
43101	Edinburgh International Festival
43101	The Irish Mail Tren Post Gwyddelig
43102	City of Wakefield
43102	HST Silver Jubilee
43102	Diocese of Newcastle
43103	John Wesley
43103	Helston Furry Dance
43104	County of Cleveland
43104	City of Edinburgh
43105	Hartlepool
43105	City of Inverness
43106	Songs of Praise
43106	Fountains Abbey
43107	City of Derby

One of the three Network Rail power cars, 43013, shows the nose-end camera fitted. This is one of the eight power cars that BR converted to run as DVTs, fitting buffers in the process. This loco, along with the other two NR Class 43s, have been re-engined with MTU4000-series engines. PIP DUNN

43107	*Tayside*
43108	*BBC Television Railwatch*
43108	*Old Course St Andrews*
43109	*Yorkshire Evening Post*
43109	*Scone Palace*
43109	*Leeds International Film Festival*
43110	*Darlington*
43110	*Stirlingshire*
43111	*Scone Palace*
43112	*Doncaster*
43113	*City of Newcastle upon Tyne*
43113	*The Highlands*
43114	*National Garden Festival Gateshead 1990*
43114	*East Riding of Yorkshire*
43115	*Yorkshire Cricket Academy*
43115	*Aberdeenshire*
43116	*City of Kingston upon Hull*
43116	*The Black Dyke Band*
43117	*Bonnie Prince Charlie*
43118	*Charles Wesley*
43118	*City of Kingston upon Hull*

An unusual look for an HST in 2006: after its lease with Virgin ended in 2004, 43194 was stored until it was sold to First Group in 2006, who then had it upgraded with an MTU engine and returned to traffic with its Great Western operation in 2007. It sports a First Group purple nose valance – not the same colour used to paint the FGW power cars – with its faded Virgin livery on the rest of the bodyside. ANTHONY HICKS

43119	*Harrogate Spa*
43120	*National Galleries of Scotland*
43121	*West Yorkshire Metropolitan County*
43122	*South Yorkshire Metropolitan County*
43124	*BBC Points West*
43125	*Merchant Venturer*
43126	*City of Bristol*
43127	*Sir Peter Parker 1924–2002 Cotswolds 150*
43130	*Sulis Minerva*
43131	*Sir Felix Pole*
43132	*Worship Company of Carmen*
43132	*We Save the Children – Will You?*
43134	*County of Somerset*
43135	*Quaker Enterprise*
43137	*Newton Abbot 150*
43139	*Driver Stan Martin 1950–2004*
43142	*St Mary's Hospital Paddington*
43142	*Reading Panel Signal Box*
43143	*Stroud 700*
43147	*The Red Cross*
43149	*BBC Wales Today*
43149	*University of Plymouth*
43150	*Bristol Evening Post*
43151	*Blue Peter II*
43152	*St Peter's School York AD627*
43153	*University of Durham*
43153	*THE ENGLISH RIVIERA*
43154	*InterCity*
43155	*BBC Look North*
43155	*The Red Arrows*
43155	*City of Aberdeen*
43156	*Rio Champion*
43156	*Dartington Summer School*
43157	*Yorkshire Evening Post*

43157	*HMS Penzance*
43158	*Dartmoor the Pony Express*
43159	*Rio Warrior*
43160	*Storm Force*
43160	*Porterbrook*
43160	*Sir Moir Lockhead OBE*
43161	*Reading Evening Post*
43161	*Rio Monarch*
43162	*Borough of Stevenage*
43162	*Project Rio*
43163	*Exeter Panel Signal Box 21st Anniversary 2009*
43165	*Prince Michael of Kent*
43167	*DELTIC 50 1955–2005*
43169	*THE NATIONAL TRUST*
43170	*EDWARD PAXMAN*
43173	*Swansea University*
43174	*Bristol – Bordeaux*
43175	*GWR 175th Anniversary*
43177	*University of Exeter*
43179	*Pride of Laira*
43180	*City of Newcastle upon Tyne*
43180	*Rio Glory*
43181	*Devonport Royal Dockyard*
43185	*Great Western*
43186	*Sir Francis Drake*
43188	*City of Plymouth*
43189	*Railway Heritage Trust*
43191	*Seahawk*
43192	*City of Truro*
43193	*Yorkshire Post*
43193	*Plymouth Spirit of Discovery*
43193	*Rio Triumph*
43194	*Royal Signals*
43195	*British Red Cross*
43195	*Rio Swift*
43196	*The Newspaper Society*
43196	*Rio Prince*

43197	*Railway Magazine Centenary 1897–1997*
43197	*Rio Princess*
43198	*HMS Penzance*
43198	*Rio Victorious*
43198	*Oxfordshire 2007*
43206	*Kingdom of Fife*
43208	*Lincolnshire Echo*
43238	*City of Dundee*
43290	*MTU Fascination of Power*
43296	*Stirling Castle*
43300	*Craigentinny*
43306	*Fountains Abbey*
43309	*Leeds International Film Festival*
43313	*The Highlands*
43314	*East Riding of Yorkshire*
43316	*The Black Dyke Band*
43318	*City of Kingston upon Hull*
43320	*National Galleries of Scotland*
43367	*DELTIC 50 1955–2005*
43423	*VALENTA 1972–2010*
43484	*PETER FOX 1942–2011 PLATFORM 5*

RENUMBERINGS

The GNER, CrossCountry and Grand Central power cars were renumbered as described when they were re-engined – not a renumbering as such, but some of the power cars dedicated to the Project Rio service in 2004 had an R just above their numbers.

43029 was temporarily renumbered 43001 for the launch of the first version of the First Great Western livery, but did not run in traffic as such.

specifications

TOPS number range:	44001–10
1957 BR number range:	D1–D10
Former class codes:	D23/1, later 23/1
Built by:	BR Derby
Introduced:	1959–60
Wheel arrangement:	1Co-Co1
Weight:	136 tons
Height:	12ft 10in (3.91m)
Width:	8ft 11in (2.72)
Length:	67ft 11in (20.7m)
Min. curve negotiable:	5 chains
Maximum speed:	90mph
Wheelbase:	59ft 8in (18.19m)
Bogie wheelbase:	21ft 6in (6.55m)
Bogie pivot centres:	32ft 8in (9.96m)
Wheel diameter:	Driving 3ft 9in (1.14m) Pony 3ft 0in (0.91m)
Route availability:	7
Brake force:	63 tons
Engine type:	Sulzer 12 LDA28A
Engine horsepower:	2,300bhp (1,716kW)
Power at rail:	1,800bhp (1,343kW)
Tractive effort:	70,000lb
Main generator type:	Crompton CG462A1
Auxiliary generator type:	Crompton CAG252A1
No. of traction motors:	6
Traction motor type:	Crompton C171 B1
Gear ratio:	62:17
Fuel tank capacity:	840gal (3,780ltr)

RIGHT: 44009, devoid of its SNOWDON nameplates, shows the headcode disc arrangements on the 44s, plus, unique to 44009/10, the revised bodyside grilles. At the other end, the loco sported a centre panel in the same style as some 45s/46s, a modification made after an accident. RAIL PHOTOPRINTS
BELOW: Although preserved, D8 PENYGHENT is still in original condition, aside from the MW and steam-heat pipes missing. PIP DUNN

THE MOST POWERFUL of the pilot scheme designs, the ten Class 44s were the first locos to use the Sulzer 12-cylinder engine. The locos won repeat orders for 127 locos, which became the Class 45s, and a later development became the Class 46s, of which fifty-six were ordered. Although built as mixed traffic locos, all the 44s soon lost their train heating capability and were withdrawn by 1980. None were dual-braked. Two are preserved.

DETAIL DIFFERENCES

All the 44s were built with Stones OK4625 steam-heat boilers, but these were removed *circa* 1962/63 and the locos became 'freight only'. Some retained their steam pipes for a while after, but all were soon removed and the pipe plated over.

Blue Star MW was fitted from new but also removed in the early 1960s, and all remained vacuum-braked only.

All were built with discs, but a centre-panel headcode was fitted to No. 1 end of 9 (44009) in 1969 after a collision. D9/10 were built (44009/010) with revised bodyside grilles all split into four horizontal sections.

LIVERIES

BR green: D1–10
BR green with small yellow panels: D1–10
BR green with full yellow ends: 1/3/6/10
BR blue with small yellow panels: 4 (unconfirmed)
BR blue: 44001–010
BR green with full yellow ends (special): 44004

Embellishments

White stripes and white roof: 44008
Red bufferbeams: 44004/008

NAMES

D1	44001	*SCAFELL PIKE*
D2	44002	*HELVELLYN*
D3	44003	*SKIDDAW*
D4	44004	*GREAT GABLE*
D5	44005	*CROSS FELL*
D6	44006	*WHERNSIDE*

D7	44007	*INGLEBOROUGH*
D8	44008	*PENYGHENT*
D9	44009	*SNOWDON*
D10	44010	*TRYFAN*

Nameplates were removed in the mid-1970s from some locos while still in traffic. A plan to name D8 *Schiehallion* in preservation did not happen.

NUMBERS

All were numbered from 1–10 to 44001–010.

WHILE THE PILOT scheme Sulzer-engined 1Co-Co1 designs were given their own classification (the 44s), subsequent orders for 127 more locos were given a new class – the 45s. They were steam-heat Type 4s, but fifty were later upgraded with ETH, and all were dual-braked. The locos were allocated to the LMR and ER but worked regularly on the WR and ER, and visits to the ScR and SR were not unknown.

DETAIL DIFFERENCES

All were fitted with steam heating from new using the Stones OK4625 boiler design. In 1973, fifty were converted to ETH (index 66), with their boilers removed and renumbered in the 45/1 series. Dates of conversion were 45101–118 (1973); 45119–146 (1974), 45147–150 (1975). Of these, 45105/119–/120/124–134/136/139–142/144/147 were dual-braked beforehand, and all others were dual-braked at the time of fitting with ETH.

All were built with vacuum brakes, but all were dual-braked in 1968–76. The dates they were dual-braked were as follows: 12/28/34/53/60/89, 112/129 (1968); 14–17/19/24–27/30/31 (1969); 20–23/32/33/36/38/40/41/46/55/63/64/68/70–72/74/81–83/87/88/93/95/97, 102–105/107–111/113–115/117/118/121/123/124/126/130/132/134/137 (1971); 57/75 (1972); 45001–005/007–009/055/059/077, 45101–114/116–118 (1973); 45121–123/135/137/138/143/145/146 (1974); 45023/034/035/038–040/047/053/060/061/070–072/074, 45149/150 (1975); 45033/036/043/056 (1976).

Blue Star MW was fitted to all, but removed progressively during the mid-1960s.

HEADCODE ENDS

The headcode boxes of the Peaks could fill a book in its own right. D11–30, D68–107 were built with split headcodes, but of these only D11–15 were fitted with communication doors. D11/12 differed slightly by having two vertical indentations on their communication doors to avoid collision with the headcode boxes, but this was not perpetuated on the other three locos, which had doors. The others, D31–67, D108–137, were fitted with split-centre headcodes.

Those renumbered into TOPS with split boxes were 45002/004–006/013/017/020/021/025/027–029/046–048/050/055/057–063, 45101/110/113/115/120/124/127/132/135/136/138/142/150; with split-centre boxes were 45003/007/009/010/012/014/023/030–040/042–045/065/066/068–070/072–077, 45111/116–119/123/125/126/128–131/133/135/137/140/143–149.

Some were changed to have centre panels, namely 45001/005/008/009/011/015/016/018/019/022/024/026/041/056/067, 45102–109/112/114/121/122/134/139/141.

The end of displaying train-reporting numbers led to many Class 45s having their headcode boxes totally removed, and a metal panel flush with the nose replacing it with two white lamps. The first to have this modification was accident-damaged 125, which emerged as 45071 from Derby Works in late 1975. 45071 had a unique lamp style, which were small protruding lamps; all the other 45s had larger, flatter marker lights, although 45071 was later modified to follow suit at No. 2 end.

Not all 45s received flush ends as they were withdrawn early, namely 45008/018/024/067 (centre panels), 45025/027/047/053/061 (split boxes), and 45032/035/036 (split centre panels).

Some 45s ran with different panels at each end, namely 45042 from January 1977 with a split centre panel at No. 2 end and a flush end at No. 1 end, 45056 from May 1977 with a centre panel at No. 2 end and a flush end at No. 1 end, 45031 from March 1978 with a split centre panel at No. 1 end and a flush end at No. 2 end, and 45120 from November 1978 with split boxes at No. 2 end and a flush end at No. 1 end. 45049/064 had split boxes at No. 2 end and a centre panel at No. 1 end. 45139 had a split

specifications

TOPS number range:	45001–077, 45101–150
1957 BR number range:	D11–D137
Former class codes:	D25/1, later 25/1
Built by:	BR Derby and Crewe
Introduced:	1960–62
Wheel arrangement:	1Co-Co1
Weight (operational):	138 tons 45/0 135 tons 45/1
Height:	12ft 10in (3.91m)
Width:	8ft 11in (2.72)
Length:	67ft 11in (20.7m)
Min. curve negotiable:	5 chains
Maximum speed:	90mph (144km/h)
Wheelbase:	59ft 8in (18.19m)
Bogie wheelbase:	21ft 6in (6.55m)
Bogie pivot centres:	32ft 8in (9.96m)
Wheel diameter:	Driving 3ft 9in (1.14m) Pony 3ft 0in (0.91m)
Route availability:	7
Brake force:	63 tons
Engine type:	Sulzer 12LDA28 B
Engine horsepower:	2,500bhp (1,865kW)
Power at rail:	2,000bhp (1,592kW)
Tractive effort:	55,000lb
Main generator type:	Crompton CG426A1
Auxiliary generator type:	Crompton CAG252A1
ETH alternator:	Brush BL 100-30 Mk II
No. of traction motors:	6
Traction motor type:	Crompton C172A1
Gear ratio:	62:17
Fuel tank capacity:	840gal (3,780ltr)

45068 shows a later version Class 45/0 with a flush yellow end and white marker lights. It retains its steam pipe. On the battery box covers, in between the bogies, are two X marks, which is the only external way of distinguishing a Class 45/0 from a 46, aside from the number. ANDY HOARE

centre panel at No. 1 end and a centre panel at No. 2 end, while 45147 had a split centre panel at No. 2 end and a centre panel at No. 1 end.

There were plenty of 'oddball' headcode panels seen on 45s in the late 1970s. 45019 ran with a panel with opaque lenses at No. 2 end, while 45123 ran for a period with fixed 0000 in a centre split panel and no roller blinds. Even stranger was 45128, which ran with 0O00 on its headcode but the first and last 0s had smaller Os inside the panel! 45140 ran with 0O in one split panel and a domino on the other! In the late 1960s, D101 ran in BR blue with small yellow panels but with the left-hand split box at No. 2 end in yellow, and the right-hand box frame painted blue.

Sealed beam headlights were fitted to 45/1s from 1985, and these were fitted in between the two white marker lights to 45101–146/148–150.

When new, all 45s had a lamp iron, two headboard clips and two horizontal handles. These were removed from locos when flush ends were fitted, the exceptions being 45043/071.

45119 had a centrally mounted lamp iron above the bufferbeam, while 45147 had one at the top of its nose, and 45134 retained two headboard clips and a lamp iron on the top of its nose but had lost its handrails.

LIVERIES

BR green: D11–137
BR green with small yellow panels: D11–137
BR green full yellow ends: D25/26
BR blue with small yellow panels: D47/ 50/51/55–59/61/64/71/79/91/92, D101/ 05/09/13/14/16/33/35
BR blue: 45001–077, 45101–150
BR blue with grey roof: 45114
BR green (special): 45106

No 45s ran in green with TOPS numbers (aside from 'retro' 45106 in 1988/89).

Embellishments

White solebar stripes: 45110/114/121 B
White bodyside grilles: 45013/022, 45104/107/140 B
Red bufferbeams: 45022/055, 45110/ 114 B, 45106 GY
Large numbers: 97409–413 B

Depot plaque:
Tinsley Rose: 45106 GY

NAMES

45004	77	ROYAL IRISH FUSILIER
45006	89	HONOURABLE ARTILLERY COMPANY
45007		TALIESIN˙
45012		WYVERN II˙
45013		WYVERN˙
45013		QUEEN 1˙
45014	137	THE CHESHIRE REGIMENT
45022	60	LYTHAM ST ANNES
45023	54	THE ROYAL PIONEER CORPS
45033		SIRIUS˙
45037		ECLIPSE˙
45039	49	THE MANCHESTER REGIMENT
45040	50	THE KING'S SHROPSHIRE LIGHT INFANTRY
45041	53	ROYAL TANK REGIMENT

ABOVE: Most Class 45s were built with a split centre, as seen in this view of 45075. Some were later changed to centre panels, and most were removed in favour of flush ends with white lamps. The headboard clips and lamp irons were usually removed when flush ends were fitted, but there were odd exceptions. 45075 shows the 0O00 headcode. ANDY HOARE

LEFT: One of the fifty Class 45s converted to ETH, 45114 displays a centre panel with dominos, and also a red bufferbeam, which was not the norm. The ETH Class 45/1s lost their steam-heat capability when upgraded in 1973–75. The ETH jumper is clear on the right, the large orange box and the cable that loops under the buffer and plugs into a jumper head. On the left the ETH receptacle is visible under the buffer. ANDY HOARE

ABOVE RIGHT: A picture showing the comparison of front ends after the Class 45/1s started to have headlights fitted. On the left is ETH 45128 with steam-heat 45070 next to it, although by this time all surviving 45/0s had their boilers isolated. PDC

45043	58	THE KING'S OWN ROYAL BORDER REGIMENT
45044	63	ROYAL INNISKILLING FUSILIER
45045	64	COLDSTREAM GUARDSMAN
45046	68	ROYAL FUSILIER
45048	70	THE ROYAL MARINES
45049	71	THE STAFFORDSHIRE REGIMENT (THE PRINCE OF WALES'S)
45052		SATAN*
45052		NIMROD*
45055	84	ROYAL CORPS OF TRANSPORT
45059	98	ROYAL ENGINEERS
45060	100	SHERWOOD FORESTER
45103		GRIFFON*
45104	59	THE ROYAL WARWICK-SHIRE FUSILIERS
45104		MERCURY*
45106		VULCAN*
45107		PHOENIX*
45110		MEDUSA*
45111	65	GRENADIER GUARDSMAN
45112	61	THE ROYAL ARMY ORDNANCE CORPS
45113		ATHENE*
45115		APOLLO*
45118	67	ROYAL ARTILLERYMAN
45121		PEGASUS*
45123	52	THE LANCASHIRE FUSILIERS
45124		UNICORN*
45125	123	LEICESTERSHIRE AND DERBYSHIRE YEOMANRY
45128		CENTAUR*
45134		NEPTUNE*
45135	99	3RD CARABINIER
45137	56	THE BEDFORDSHIRE AND HERTFORDSHIRE REGIMENT (T.A.)
45141		ZEPHYR*
45143	62	5TH ROYAL INNISKILLING DRAGOON GUARDS
45143	62	5TH ROYAL INNISKILLING DRAGOON GUARDS 1685-1985
45144	55	ROYAL SIGNALS
45145		SCYLLA*
45149		PHAETON*
45150		VAMPIRE*
97413		AMETHYST*

The unofficial names were painted red with white lettering and borders except 45115's, which was blue.

Many 45s lost their nameplates, either officially or they were stolen. Many had crests when named, but most of these

45120 shows the split boxes with dominos carried by several Class 45s in the late 1970s and early 1980s. The handrails, headboard clips and lamp iron remain, but these would be removed when the loco was given a flush front and two white marker lights at its next overhaul. The ETH jumper can be clearly seen on the right-hand side of the bufferbeam. PDC

were also removed, again, often illegitimately. When 45104 lost its original nameplates, replacements were made out of checkerplate, the same material to make the cab floors, by Tinsley depot staff and fitted. They were three-deck.

NUMBERS

The Class 45s were renumbered from D numbers to TOPS in the most haphazard way because locos due for overhaul in 1973 were often sent for fitting with ETH, and hence became 45/1s.

11	45122
12	45011
13	45001
14	45015
15	45018
16	45016
17	45024
18	45121
19	45025
20	45013
21	45026
22	45132
23	45017
24	45027
25	45021
26	45020
27	45028
28	45124
29	45002
30	45029
31	45030
32	45126
33	45019
34	45119
35	45117
36	45031
37	45009
38	45032
39	45033
40	45133
41	45147
42	45034
43	45107
44	45035
45	45036
46	45037
47	45116
48	45038
49	45039
50	45040
51	45102
52	45123
53	45041
54	45023
55	45144
56	45137
57	45042
58	45043
59	45104
60	45022
61	45112
62	45143
63	45044

64	45045	107	45120
65	45111	108	45012
66	45146	109	45139
67	45118	110	45065
68	45046	111	45129
69	45047	112	45010
70	45048	113	45128
71	45049	114	45066
72	45050	115	45067
73	45110	116	45103
74	45051	117	45130
75	45052	118	45068
76	45053	119	45007
77	45004	120	45108
78	45150	121	45069
79	45005	122	45070
80	45113	123	45125
81	45115	124	45131
82	45141	125	45071
83	45142	126	45134
84	45055	127	45072
85	45109	128	45145
86	45105	129	45073
87	45127	130	45148
88	45136	131	45074
89	45006	132	45075
90	45008	133	45003
91	45056	134	45076
92	45138	135	45149
93	45057	136	45077
94	45114	137	45014
95	45054		
96	45101		
97	45058		
98	45059		
99	45135		
100	45060		
101	45061		
102	45140		
103	45062		
104	45063		
105	45064		
106	45106		

Subsequent Renumberings

D95 was initially to have become 45150, but was found to be unsuitable for conversion. As a result, D78, which had been renumbered 45054 in January 1975, was selected instead, and this became 45150. D95 therefore took the vacant 45054 number in May 1975. The official renumbering of the first 45054 to 45150 is given as July 1975, although it would have been in works being converted at the same time as the second 45054 was in traffic.

In 1987 five Class 45s were selected for Departmental use, for hauling infrastructure trains in connection with the electrification of the ECML. They were all withdrawn by August 1988, the same time the last 45s were withdrawn, apart from railtour loco 45106. They were:

45022	97409
45029	97410
45034	97411
45040	97412
45066	97413

45017 was also taken into Departmental use and renumbered ADB968024.

DIFFERENCES BETWEEN THE PEAKS

The Class 44s were instantly recognizable by virtue of their headcode discs, and even the unique 44009 was easily recognizable as a 44 even when looking at its headcode panel end, by virtue of its revised grilles. The 44s also differed in that their main bodyside grille was longer than that on the 45s or 46s.

Numbers aside, the only noticeable difference between a 45/0 and 46 was on the battery boxes, which on the 45s had an X on them, whereas those on the 46s were plain.

It is often thought that one of the ways to recognize a Class 45 from a 46 is by the unplated grilles on the bodyside, but this is not correct as several 45s retained these unplated until withdrawal, namely 45008/019/022/026/041/056, 45102–109/112/114/121/122/134/141.

A split-box, vacuum-braked steam-heat D71, in the rare BR blue with a small yellow panel livery. The loco is named THE STAFFORDSHIRE REGIMENT (THE PRINCE OF WALES'S) – the second half of the name being in smaller size than the top half. The 45s had separate crests fitted on to the same backing plate that carried the nameplate. Most crests were removed (often stolen) before the locos were withdrawn, and indeed few retained their original nameplates at withdrawal. D71 became 45049 and was never converted to ETH. BILL WRIGHT

THE THIRD DEVELOPMENT of the Peak design, the locos shared the same body design as the Class 44s and 45s but had Brush electrical gear as opposed to Crompton Parkinson. All were steam heated and based on the ER and WR, but all ended their days allocated to Gateshead depot. They were withdrawn after the 44s, but all had been laid up by November 1984, ahead of the majority of the 45s.

Initially seventy-six Class 46s were ordered, but this was cut to fifty-six locos, and the engines and electrical equipment earmarked for the last twenty diverted to the first twenty Class 47s.

DETAIL DIFFERENCES

All locos had steam-heat boilers, with Stones OK4625 on D138–165 (46001–028) and Stones Mk 3 fitted to D166–193 (46029–056).

All were built with vacuum brakes, but the following were converted to dual: 166/168/169/172/173/176/182/183/186/ 188/189/193 (1970); 138/141/1439/146/ 152/155157/164/167/170/171/174/175/ 177–181/184/185/190–192 (1971); 139/ 142/144/147/148/153/154/158–163/165/ 187 (1972); 46003/008/012–014 (1973).

Blue Star MW working was fitted but removed progressively during the mid-1960s.

HEADCODES

D138–173 were new with split centre panels, while D174–193 were built with centre panels. All the former were later changed to centre panels.

As headcodes ceased to be displayed, these were changed to dominos. 46022 ran for a brief period with a rectangular black metal plate over its headcode with 0000 displayed on it.

specifications

TOPS number range:	46001–056
1957 BR number range:	D138–193
Former class code:	25/1A
Built by:	BR Derby
Year introduced:	1961–63
Wheel arrangement:	1Co-Co1
Weight:	138 tons
Height:	12ft 10in (3.91m)
Width:	8ft 10in (2.7m)
Length:	67ft 11in (20.7m)
Min. curve negotiable:	5 chains (100.58m)
Wheelbase:	59ft 8in (18.18m)
Bogie wheelbase:	21ft 6in (6.55m)
Bogie pivot centres:	32ft 8in (9.96m)
Wheel diameter:	Driving: 3ft 9in (1.14m) Pony: 3ft 0in (0.91m)
Engine type:	Sulzer 12LDA28B
Engine output:	2,500bhp (1,865kW)
Power at rail:	1,960bhp (1,460kW)
Tractive effort:	55,000lb
Maximum speed:	90mph (144km/h)
Brake force:	63 tons
Route availability:	7
Main generator type:	Brush TG160-60
Auxiliary generator type:	Brush TG69-28
Traction motor type:	Brush TM73-68
No. of traction motors:	6
Gear ratio:	62:19
Fuel tank capacity:	790gal (3,591ltr)

ABOVE LEFT: 46027 shows the standard bufferbeam layout for the class. The 46s were built with vacuum brakes and Blue Star MW, but the latter was soon removed as it was rarely, if ever, used. They were dual-braked in the early 1970s, and then spent the rest of their working lives as dual-braked, steam-heat locos. Headcodes were either split-centre or centre panels, most of which were changed to flush with white lamps, as seen here. ANDY HOARE

LEFT: In 1994 Class 46 D182 became the first preserved diesel registered to work on the national network. In 2002 it was repainted into BR blue as 46035 and retained its centre panel with roller blinds. The loco now has a high-intensity headlight, never before a feature on a 46, as well as a nose-mounted aerial for the NRN. PIP DUNN

Like the Class 45s, the Class 46s progressively lost their panels, replaced by a flush front with two white lamps. These were fitted to panels 46001–004/006–011/013–019/021–023/025–036/038–040/042–056, while 46005/012/020/024/037/041 were scrapped with domino panels. At one end, 46025 had its lenses much lower than its classmates.

When the new panels were fitted, the lamp iron, two headboard clips and two horizontal handles around the panels were removed, the exceptions being 46016/049, which retained them.

LIVERIES

All 46s, D138–193, were new in BR green with small yellow panels. A few gained full yellow nose ends, but none ran in green with TOPS numbers.

All were repainted in BR blue with at least D173/186, 46026/044 running for periods with red bufferbeams.

BR green with small yellow panels:
D138–193
BR green with full yellow ends: 138/154/155/159/166/188/193
BR blue: 46001–056
RTC red and blue: 97403

NAMES

| 46026 | 163 | *LEICESTERSHIRE AND DERBYSHIRE YEOMANRY* |
| 97403 | | *Ixion* |

NUMBERS

The Class 46s were renumbered in order from 138–193 as 46001–056. The only subsequent renumberings were for Departmental use – *see* below.

46009	97401
46023	97402
46035	97403
46045	97404

DEPARTMENTAL 46s

Four Class 46s were taken into Departmental use. The first two were for a PR stunt in July 1984 to demonstrate the robust design of a nuclear flask when 46009 was smashed into a 'derailed' flask at 100mph. For this role it was allocated the number 97401, though it was never applied. Standby 46023, allocated the number 97402, also never applied, was in reserve and was not needed.

The other two renumberings were implemented, although 97404 was again a spare loco for 97403. However, 97403 was renumbered, repainted into RTC livery of red and blue, and named *Ixion* after a mythological Greek king.

97403 was put into traffic for its new role as a test train loco in early 1985. It was withdrawn in February 1989, although not actually condemned until August 1991.

97403 featured several changes. First, it had Blue Star MW cables and receptacles mounted on its noses for working in push-pull mode with Research Centre vehicles. It also had a mesh grille fitted to the lower end of its nose, and later had a box of electronics crudely mounted on to the top left of its nose at No. 2 end.

TOP LEFT: D182 Ixion *in June 1999 in BR green with a small yellow panel. The loco has no train heating but remains dual-braked.* PIP DUNN
MIDDLE LEFT: All 46s carried centre panels at one time or another, and a handful went to the scrapyard with them, including 46037, despite it being one of the last in traffic. PDC
LEFT: Four Class 46s had roles with the Railway Technical Centre, but only one, 46035, was painted into the RTC's livery, renumbered 97403. It was also fitted with various additional cables to work with test trains, including Blue Star cables for push-pull operations. The loco is seen in 1987 in its new guise. PAUL WINTER

class 47

THE BIGGEST SINGLE class of main-line diesel loco, the Class 47s were the standard Type 4 for much of the country. 512 locos were built, although the fleet never totalled more than 510 locos at any time; 508 survived for TOPS renumbering. The rundown of the class started in 1986, but there are still thirty-five locos main-line registered today.

All had their engines downrated from 2,750bhp to 2,580bhp in the 1960s, with a further downrating to 2,400bhp in the early 2000s for selected locomotives. Five locos were originally built with Sulzer V series engines – the Class 48s (see next section). 47046 was converted to 47601 in 1976 as a testbed for the Class 56 although did not enter traffic until after the first 56s had been delivered! It was then converted to 47901 as a Class 58 test-bed loco. Thirty-three have been rebuilt as Class 57 (see later sections).

There have been numerous different numbers, liveries and modifications to the class over their fifty-year life.

TRAIN HEATING

D1500–19 were built with dual train heating, a feature also on D1960/61. The rest of the fleet were built with steam heating except D1782–1836 and D1875–1900, these eighty-one locos becoming the Class 47/3s: they had through-steam pipes and boiler water tanks fitted, although the steam pipes were soon removed.

specifications

TOPS number range:	47001–299, 47300–381, 47384–399, 47401–665, 47671–677, 47701–717, 47721–799, 47801–854, 47901, 47971–981		3,300bhp (2,455kW): 47901
		Power at rail:	2,080bhp (1,550kW) 2,400bhp (1,790kW): 47601 2,808bhp (2,089kW): 47901
1957 BR number range:	D1100–11, D1500–1999	Tractive effort:	55,000lb: 47401–420 61,400lb: 47601 57,325lb: 47901 62,000lb: rest
Former class code:	27/2	Maximum speed:	95mph (153km/h), reduced to 75mph (120km/h) or 60mph (96km/h) on selected locos 100mph (160km/h) 47701–717
Built by:	Brush, Loughborough and BR Crewe		
Years introduced:	1962–68		
Wheel arrangement:	Co-Co		
Weight:	111–121 tons		
Height:	12ft 10in (3.91m)	Brake force:	60 tons 59 tons: 47601/901
Length:	63ft 6in (19.38m)		
Width:	9ft 2in (2.79m)	Route availability:	6/7
Wheelbase:	51ft 6in (15.69m)	Main generator type:	Brush TG160-60 Mk 2, TG160-60 Mk 4 or TM172-50 Mk 1
Bogie wheelbase:	14ft 6in (4.41m)		
Bogie pivot centres:	37ft (11.27m)	Auxiliary generator type:	Brush TG69-20 or TG69-28 Mk 2
Wheel diameter:	3ft 9in (1.14m)	ETH alternator type:	Brush BL100-30
Min. curve negotiable:	4 chains (80.46m)	Main alternator type:	Brush BA1101A
Engine type:	Sulzer 12LDA28C Ruston Paxman 16RK3CT: 47601 Ruston Paxman 12RK3CT: 47901	Auxiliary alternator type:	Brush BAA602A
		Traction motor type:	Brush TM64-68 or TM64-68 Mk 1
		No. of traction motors:	6
Engine output:	2,580bhp (1,922kW) or 2,400bhp (1,790kW) 3,250bhp (2,420kW): 47601	Gear ratio:	66:17
		Fuel tank capacity:	720–1,221gal (3,273–5,550ltr)

One of the last batch of Class 47s converted from steam heat to ETH, 47641 Fife Region, not only shows off the revised fitting of ETH jumpers implemented on conversions after 47586, with the ETH jumper on the bufferbeam, but also the fitting of a full set of snowploughs, a common feature on ScR 47s. The loco has a black-painted headcode, a common cosmetic feature on Class 37s and 47s in the late 1980s. The loco has a cab-to-shore radio aerial fitted on the roof in front of the horn grilles. A Highland Rail stag logo is on the cabside, the common place for these on large logo locos. PDC

Locos were converted to either ETH (index 66) or dual heat progressively from 1971. The first batch of conversions was 1971–75, followed by another batch, 47556–585 in 1979–81, 47586–628 in 1983–85, and finally 47629–665 in 1985–87.

Dates of fitting with ETH: 1101*/02*/03*/04*/05*/06*/07*/08*/09*/10*/11*, 1975 (1971), 1520*/25*/27*/33*/34*/35/36*/41*/42*/45*/50*/77*/78*/80*/81*/86/90/95/96/98, 1601–04, 1753, 1932/36/37/40–42/44/45/46/48/49 (1972); 1531/47–49/51–61/64–69/71/74/75/87/89/93, 1607/12/16/37/62/83, 1716/60, 1930/39/43/47/51–55/58/59/68 (1973); 1563/76/79/82/84/85*/88*/94, 1600/08/27/36/41/42/46/49/51/55/57/69/78/89, 707/13/18/23/25/47/55*, 1956/57, 47260 (1974); 1592*, 1724/31, 1950*, 47126/153, (1975); 47036, 47164/169 (1979); 47024/027/028/031/034/037–039/043–045/048, 47167/172/176/180 (1980); 47020/047, 47168/170/173–175/179/181/183/184 (1981); 47026/035/042, 47165/171/177/178/182/185, 47250/251/255/263/265/267/268/271/272 (1983); 47030/070/072/076/077/080/081/082/087/090, 47134/136/138/141/

149/160/163/166, 47248/252/262/264/ 273 (1984); 47041/059/068/078/083, 47158, 47266 (1985); 47029/040/055/ 056/061/064/066/069/074/075/086/088/ 091, 47128/129/151/155, 47239/242/ 243/244/246/247/254/257/269/274 (1986); 47032, 47135, 47232/240 (1987).

* dual heat locos after conversion.

The first twenty locos had their ETH jumpers mounted on the bufferbeam. For those locos modified afterwards, of which D1101 was the first in May 1971, initially the jumper head was fixed to the bottom of the cab above the buffer-beam with a long bracket on the cab front extending to the right of the ETH jumper. For conversions from 47556–585 this bracket was shorter and the same width as the jumper head. 47535 was retro-modified to a short bracket, while 47522 had an even longer bracket extending both sides of the ETH jumper.

For conversions from 47586 onwards (modified in 1983) the jumpers were refitted to the bufferbeams in similar positions to 47401–420, although the receptacle was more angled and noticeable to the left of the drawhook.

When 47460/461/464/467/469/470/ 492, 47541/546/550/562/578 were fitted with snowploughs from the early 1980s, they had their ETH jumpers repositioned to the bufferbeam. The bracket to which the jumper had previously been affixed remained in place, although this was later removed from one end of 47461, 47470, and 47562 due to collision damage repairs, whilst 47550 and 47578 had them removed at both ends.

In 1991, 47562/586/593/595, 47604/ 616/617/643 had uprated ETH with an index of seventy-five, and were renumbered 47671–677 apart from 47643. Of these, 47671–675 changed to Class 47/ 7b or 47/8s and regained their normal ETH rating.

HEADCODES

All 47s were built with centre panels. In a trial with D1927/62/75, for a period from 1969, they had black numbers/ letters on a white background.

As headcodes were phased out, the blinds were wound round to read 0000, and then they were progressively replaced, first by dominos and later by a sheet of metal painted yellow with two opaque lenses. These were initially recessed on the cab front. At least 47256 and 47366 ran in BR two-tone green with dominos.

Those 47s that went straight from roller blinds to yellow panels and so missed out on having dominos were 47193, 47249 (No. 1 end only – flush front due to collision damage), 47282 (No. 2 end only – flush front due to collision damage), 47401/403/405/409–413/425/ 426/431–434/457–462/471, 47518–528/ 541–544/546/547/549/551–554, 47601. The first modified was 47425 in 1976.

47550 ran for a short period with a white headcode panel in the late 1970s, while 47101/103/131 had small 0000 headcodes in the mid-1970s; 47486 was similar, but had just the two outer 0 digits on display. 47499 ran with small dots on its dominos rather than the bigger size.

As Class 47s were fitted with speed-sensing equipment, at the No. 2 end only, every 47 had the lenses replaced by two white marker lights. Some locos had this modification at both ends.

Due to collision damage repairs several locos had their headcode panels removed and replaced by flush panels with two white lenses.

No. 1 end: 47019/053, 47110/117/128/ 134/150/171/197, 47204/210/230/241/ 244/249/258/270/291, 47307/324/328/ 342/345/347/356/367/379, 47413/431/ 434/443/452/460/461/471/484, 47509/ 512/521/526/567/568, 47615, 47702/ 705/707, 47846.

No. 2 end: 47011/041/054/061/066/ 070/079, 47147/165/182/193/194/218/ 219/237/239/247/282, 47321/331/333/ 334/337/375, 47421/428/438/447/449/ 470/473/477/489, 47578/589/590, 47605, 47701/703/711, 47833/835.

Both ends: 47085, 47102/141/163/190, 47299, 47458, 47501/522/535, 47790, 47813/823/832.

The following locos were renumbered but had flush panels from their earlier incarnations:

No. 1 end: 47592, 47622/640/656, 47725/ 726/738/747, 47811/841.

No. 2 end: 47598, 47620/630/649/655/ 657/661, 47742/746/764/776/788/799, 47810/812/816/825/827/830/835.

Both ends: 47610/614, 47787, 47823/ 853.

47053, 47210/244, 47477, 47846 had opaque lenses on their flush ends.

47307, 47831 had protruding lamps on a metal panel.

47079/085, 47117, 47270, 47846 had their flush fronts removed in favour of a standard cab front. 47522 had one of its flush fronts removed.

47501, 47790, 47813/832 were modified for DRS purely for aesthetics.

HEADLIGHTS AND LAMPS

Standard BR high-intensity headlights were fitted from 1983 (47208 was withdrawn before having headlights.)

Prior to standard headlights, spotlights were fitted to 47574 and 47701–712, while small sealed-beam headlights

47714 Grampian Region *shows full ScotRail livery – the same as InterCity Executive colours but with a light blue stripe instead of red. This livery was only applied to 47461 and the 47/7 push-pull locos. The TDM jumpers on the front are also seen to good effect. A Haymarket castle emblem is above the nameplate.* PDC were fitted underneath the right-hand red tail-lights to 47432/434, 47523 and 47901. In later days 47432/434 and 47523 had these lights plated over and standard headlights fitted. In the case of 47434 it was removed altogether at one end due to collision repairs. 47901 strangely never had a standard central high intensity headlight fitted, and went for scrap with its sealed beam headlights fitted.

In 1997, a trial of twin headlights was fitted at No. 2 end to 47825, but these were removed when the loco was converted to 57601.

As part of a trial, 47277 and 47373 were fitted with remote control equipment; to signify when the system was in use, roof-mounted flashing lights were fitted on their cabs. These were later removed.

Marker lights: Res started to change the red tail-lamps on most of its fleet to LED versions, and this feature was fitted to all its 47/7s bar 47704/707/716/743 and to 47474/481, 47524/543/565/566/572/574/575/576/596, 47624/627/628/634/635/640. RfD also fitted these to 47335. More recently Cotswold Rail and DRS have not only fitted these red tail-lights but also white LED marker lights to its 47s.

Buffer beam cowlings removed: Many RfD, Res 47/7s and InterCity locos had their bufferbeam cowlings removed to reduce draughts. Those modified were 47033/049–053/060/079/085/095, 47102/114/125/144/145/150/152/156/157/186/188/193/194/197, 47200/201/204–207/209–211/213/217–219/222/225/226/228–231/234/236/237/241/245/258/270/276/279–281/284–287/289–293/297–299, 47301–310/312–314/316/321/323/324/326/328/330/334/335/337–339/344/345/351/353/354/355/358/360–363/365/367/370–372/375/376/378–380, 384–399, 47452/458/473/490/491, 47500/503/517/530/531/537/541/551/559/562/565/573/578/580/581/582/589/597, 603/606/618/630/631/636/642/653, 47702/711/714/721/722/725–727/732–734/736–739/741–747/749/750/756–778/780–784, 786–793, 798, 47804–819/822/825–834/839–841/843–851/853/854. Of these, 47102, 47230, 47458 were at No. 1 end only, while 47321, 47473, 47530/565 were at No. 2 end only. 47270 later had the cowling refitted. The bufferbeam cowling was

Showing signs of fire damage, 47045 was one of the early conversions to ETH, becoming 47568 in 1979. The loco has a roller-blind headcode still in place in this 1977 view, by which time many locos were displaying dominos and some were already sporting yellow metal panels. The loco still has bufferbeam cowling. PDC

removed from 47146 but the cab fronts were not cut back.

Additional fuel tanks: These were fitted at conversion to 47701–717 and 47650–665, and retro-fitted to 47551–553/591. The twenty Class 47/4s then became 47801–820. InterCity then fitted additional tanks to 47556/560/563/570/571/577/589/590, 47602/606/607/608–614/618–623/629/632/637–639/646–649/674 – to become 47821–854. (47854 was a replacement for accident-damaged 47850)

Res also fitted additional fuel tanks – although many carried them in previous identities – to 47519, 47721/722/725–727/732–734/736–739/741–747/749/750/756–793, 798/799 and RfD/Freightliner to 47033/049–051/053/085/095, 47114/125/144/145/150/152/156/157/186/188/194, 47200/201/204/205/207/209–211/213/217–219/222/226/228/229/234/236/237/241/245/258/279–281/284–287/289–293/297–299, 47301–304/306/307/309/310/312–314/316/323/326/328/330/335/337/338/344/351/355/358/360–363/365/367/370/375/378, 47384–399. DRS added them to 47501.

Some were modified at Immingham depot in 1988/89 where an additional fuel tank was fitted inside the former boiler compartment, namely to 47054, 47115, 47212/221–224/276/294/295/299, 47319/336/373/374/379/380.

SNOWPLOUGHS

Snowplough brackets were fitted to 47003/004/006/017/018/053, 47117/118/120, 47200/206/210/245, 47316, 47460/461/464/467/469/470/492, 47541/

546/550/562/578/593/595, 47604/617/630/636/641/643/644/672*/673*/674*/675*/677*, 47756*/760*/764*/767*/773*/776*/777*/790*/791*, 47854*, 47976* (* fitted to loco in an earlier guise).

MULTIPLE WORKING

When they were built, no 47s had MW apart from D1938 (47258), which was fitted with Blue Star equipment in April 1966 with the jumpers fitted on the bufferbeam. This was for a proposed push-pull trial for Paddington-Birmingham workings, which never happened although the loco was tested in push-pull mode on the ECML. It retained the jumpers well into the 1970s.

In the late 1970s, 47370/379 had a different system fitted to allow them to work in multiple: cab-mounted cables. After the cables were removed, both locos retained the bottom pockets where the jumpers had been stored when not in use, although these were later removed.

Four of the six RTC locos, 47971/974–976, were fitted with a modified Blue Star MW with the receptacle fitted on the cab from below the headcode box. However, this was purely for push-pull working on Research trains and locos couldn't work in 'multi' with each other or any other Blue Star locos.

In 1994, Railfreight Distribution fitted MW to its fleet. This was the Green Circle system, and locos had a jumper socket on the cab fronts, in the headcode panel while the jumper cable was stored in the cab or former boiler compartment. The system was later fitted to some Freightliner, Riviera Trains and Colas locos.

Several Class 47s had their headcode panels removed and a flush front fitted with white marker lights. Dual-braked 47484 on the right shows this feature to good effect as it stands next to 47114 in a unique two-tone BR green livery with Freightliner branding. 47114 also has a Green Circle MW receptacle in its redundant headcode box; no Class 47s were built with MW, but several 47/0s and 47/3s were fitted with the system from 1994. 47114 also shows the removed bufferbeam cowling and the lack of vacuum brakes. PIP DUNN

DRS locos initially had the DRS system fitted with a receptacle on the cab on the bottom left of the headcode box, though these too have since reverted to the Green Circle system.

Locos fitted with Green Circle MW have been 47033/049/051–053/085/095, 47114/125/144–146/150/152/156/157/ 186/188/194, 47200/201/204/205/207/ 209–211/213/217–219/222/226/228/ 229/234/236/237/241/245/258/276/279 –281/284–287/289–293/297–299, 47301 –304/306–310/312–314/316/323/326/ 328/330/335/337/338/344/348/351/ 354/355/358/360–363/365/367/370/ 375/378/379, 47501, 47709/712/714/727/ 739/749/769/790, 47802/805/810/812/ 813/815/818/828/832/839/841/843/847/ 848/853. Those fitted with the DRS system have been 47237/298, 47501, 47802, of which 47237 retains it (now owned by WCR), while 47501 and 47802 have had it removed, but retain the indented squares on their cab fronts where it was fitted.

OTHER DETAIL DIFFERENCES

There were surprisingly few 'one off' changes to the 47 fleet, but worthy of mention are the bodyside grilles cut into the bodyside doors on 47295 and 47542. The latter also had its bodyside windows converted for a short time to grilles, as did 47456 and 47608.

47040, 47120, 47519 ran in traffic for a period with the occasional plated-over cabside door window.

In 1979, twelve Class 47/4s were converted to push-pull use and renumbered 47701–712. They had Railway Clearing House (RCH) time-division multiplex (TDM) jumpers mounted to their front. Later conversions 47713–717 were similar, although there were never more than sixteen locos in traffic at any one time as 47717 was a replacement for 47713, which was written off with fire damage.

RTC locos 47971–973 had two additional plug sockets above their taillights for communication cables while working Research Department trains.

In 1993, the Rail Express System's fleet of 47s were renumbered in the 477xx series, from 47721 onwards; they were also fitted with TDM cables for propelling with PCVs. These were known as Class 47/7b, while the push-pull locos were referred to as 47/7a.

The plan was for a fleet from 47721– 793, but in the event not all were modified so only 47721/722/72–727/732– 734/736–739/741/742/744–747/749/ 750/756–793 appeared with them, although in true 'nothing is ever straight-forward' style, 47566, 47624/628/635/ 640 also had them.

Freightliner's 47270 and DRS's 47237/ 298, 47501 and 47802 were fitted with high impact windscreens.

More recently DRS has been fitting Class 57-style cooler groups to some of its 47s: fitted so far have been 47501, 47813/853 at No. 1 end.

Oblong/oval buffers: The majority of the fleet had standard round buffers, but at least 47051, 47114/146, 47210/ 211/276/280, 47319/379, 47503, 47627, 47736/738/739/747/750/761/785/788/ 790 had oblong buffers, while oval buffers were fitted to at least 47222/ 276, 47336/369/380, 47648, 47802 and to 47727/772, 47850 (at No. 1 end only) and to 47492 (No. 2 end only).

LIVERIES

Green half yellow end: D1100–11, D1500–1732/34–99, D1800–1899, D1900 –52/62–99

Green full yellow end: D1100–11, 1500 –03/05–08/10–27/29/30/33–35/37–46/ 48/39/51–57/59–68/70–74/76–94/96– 99, 1600–14/17–25/27–70/71–81/83–89/ 91/93/94/96–99, 1700–11/13–17/19–22/ 24/26/27/29–31/35–43/45–53/55–83/ 85–99, 1800–99, 1900–31/33–52/66–99

Dark all-over green with full yellow ends: 47256

BR blue with small yellow panel (XP64): 1733

BR blue: 1100–11, 1500–61/63–1670/ 72–733/35–1907/09–99

BR blue with grey roof: 47003–011/ 014/016–019/052/054/055/085/093/ 097/099, 47100–102/104/105/112/114– 118/121/122/124/130/135/150/155/156/ 158/160/162–165/167/169/170/172/179/ 180/183/184, 47255/263/276–279/288/ 289/291/295/296/298, 47310/311/313/ 328/357/363, 47426/431/435/438–440/ 457/458/460/476/478/482/486/487, 47519/521/522/542–544/549/551/553/ 557/565–574/576/577/579–585/587/ 591/596, 47605, 47701–711

BR blue with black roof: 47421

BR blue with full height Union flags: 47163/164, 47580

BR blue with black windows and large numbers/badge: 47170, 47292, 47577/ 579/580

BR blue with black window surrounds: 47242, 47407

BR blue with yellow solebar: 47305/ 361

BR blue with large badges: 47401

BR blue with red buffer cowlings: 47540/581

BR 'Large Logo': 47118/120/150/170, 47291, 47341, 47401/407/411/413/422/ 424/426–428/431–434/436/438–461/ 464–468/473/479–482/485/488–490, 47501/503/512/513/515/517–519/526/ 531–541/545–547/549/550–552/563/

Six Class 47/4s were moved to the Research Department in 1989 and renumbered as Class 97s, retaining their last three digits. One, 47561, which became 97561, was painted in Midland Railway maroon, albeit with yellow wrap-around cabs. After some drivers refused to drive the locos as they were 'Class 97s', BR renumbered them as 47s in the 4797x series; this loco became 47973. PDC

564/569/571/572/574/578/580–583/585/ 587/591–593/595/597, 47603/604/614/ 616/617/629–636/638–641/644–665/ 671/674, 47711/712, 47801/802/804–820/ 847, 47971/972 (note 47291, 47439/467, 47532/545 had transposed numbers/ arrows on one side and 47445, 47526 on both sides)

BR 'Large Logo' with extended white stripes: 47583

BR 'Large Logo' with blue roofs: 47118, 47464/467, 47517/541/546/550, 47604

BR blue with yellow cabs: 47470, 47522/567/575/586, 47604,

BR 'Large Logo' with small white bodyside numbers: 47513/551, 47814

BR 'Large Logo' with no logo and small black cabside numbers: 47822/ 828/830/845/846/848/852

ScotRail: 47461, 47701717

InterCity Executive: 47406/461/471/ 487/490, 47501/509/515/525/549/553/ 555/560/593, 47606/609/611–613/618/ 620–622, 47711

InterCity Executive unbranded: 47826/835

InterCity 'Mainline': 47470/483, 47508/ 515/520/523/524/527/528/550/557/558/ 562/565–568/570/584/589/590/595, 47602/607/610/614/619/624–628/672/ 675, 47818/821/823–825/827/829/831– 833/849/853, 47973

InterCity with ScotRail branding: 47430/469/492, 47541/637/642/643

InterCity Swallow: 47509/520/586, 47801/804–823/825–851/853/854

Provincial: 47475

LNER apple green: 47522

Original Network SouthEast: 47573/ 576/581–583

Revised dark Network SouthEast: 47521/530/547/576/579/581/583/587/ 596/598, 47701/702/705/707–711/714– 716

Railfreight: 47007/010/014/016/018/ 019/099, 47107/112/119/125/186/190, 47202/211/213/215/220/235–237/280/ 285/290/297, 47318/320/325/327/331/ 337/346/348/350/356/358/362/363/365/ 366/368/370/371/374/378/379

Railfreight with no black window frames: 47050/095

Red stripe Railfreight: 47142/157/196, 47214/227/249, 47301/302/321/322/ 339/340/345/363/367/373/380

Parcels: 47458/462/474/476/479/489, 47501/522/533/535/543/559/569/572/ 574/575/582, 47634/635/640, 47703/ 712/717

Res: 47475/490–492, 47500/503/517/ 524/530–532/535–537/539/541/551/ 557–559/562/564–568/573/576/578/ 580/581/583/584/587/588/594/596– 599, 47600/603/605/606/612/615/618/ 624–628/630/631/636/642/653, 47701/ 704/705/707/709/714/716, 47721/722/ 725–727/732–734/736–739/741–747/ 749/750/756–793

GWR green: 47079, 47484, 47500, 47628

Trainload Metals: 47079, 47347/359, 47594/599

Trainload Petroleum: 47010/054/085/ 094, 47119/125/150/190/193–197, 47212/ 221/223/224/233/276–278/294/295, 47305/319/324/336/368/369/373/379– 381

Trainload Construction: 47004/006/ 007/063/079, 47114, 47210, 47328, 47430, 47901

Railfreight Distribution: 47033/049– 053/060/079/095, 47114/125/144/147/ 150/152/156/186–188/194/196, 47200/ 201/204–207/209–214/217–219/222/ 223/225/226/228/229/231/234/236– 238/241/245/256/258/276/277/279– 281/283–294/296–299, 47304–307/309– 314/316/317/319/323/326/328/330/335/ 338/339/347/349/351/354/355/357/359 –362/365/375/377/378/384/386–396/ 398/399, 47445, 47588, 47600/605/615

Railfreight Distribution European: 47033/049/051/053/079/085/095, 47125/ 146/186/188, 47200/201/217–219/228/ 234/236/237/241/245/258/285–287/ 290/293/297/299, 47306/307/310/312/ 316/323/326/338/344/348/351/360/365/ 370/375, 47525/555

Two-tone grey: 47060/085/095, 47114/ 147/150/157/187/193/197, 47201/205/ 206/211/212/223/224/225/234/236/270/ 276/279/287/289/290/292/295, 47303/ 308/313/317/321/330/339/344/347/349/ 363/367/368/378/379/385/397, 47605/ 615, 47702

Two-tone unbranded RfD European: 47287, 47370

BR blue with black window surrounds with Railfreight General logos: 47145

BR blue with RfD logos: 47145

Departmental grey: 47315/329/332– 334/343/352/353/364, 47974/976

'Dutch': 47300/308/315/329/331–334/ 339–341/343/346/352/353/357/364/366/ 372, 47540, 47974–976/981

Waterman Railways: 47488, 47703/ 705/710/712

Porterbrook: 47807/817

Royal Train (Res style): 47798/799

Royal Train with lining: 47798/799

Virgin: 47702/711/722/741/747/750/ 769, 47805–807/810/812/814/817/818/ 822/827–829/831/839–841/843–845/ 847–849/851/853/854

EWS: 47727/744/747/757/758/760/767/ 773/778/785–787/790/792/793

Celebrations maroon: 47627

Freightliner grey: 47052/060/079, 47150/152/157/197, 47204–207/209/ 212/225/231/234/270/279/283/289/290/ 296, 47301–303/305/308/309/323/330/ 334/337/339/345/349/353/354/358/361/ 367/370–372/376/377

Freightliner green: 47150/193, 47258/ 270/279/292

FM Rail: 47832

Fragonset: 47701/703/709/710/712/715

Fragonset freight: 47355

Fragonset freight unbranded: 47375

West Coast Railways light maroon with black stripe: 47854

West Coast Railways: 47237/245, 47500, 47760/786/787, 47804/826/851/854

West Coast Railways with advertising: 47826

West Coast Railways unbranded: 47500, 47854

DRS: 47237/298, 47501, 47802

DRS blue unbranded: 47791

DRS Compass: 47501, 47709/712/790, 47802/805/810/813/818/828/832/841/853

Northern Belle: 47790, 47832

Cotswold Rail: 47200, 47316, 47810/813/828

Cotswold Rail unbranded: 47033

Anglia: 47714

One: 47818

One unbranded: 47818

Advenza freight: 47237, 47375

Advenza freight unbranded: 47237, 47375

Infrastructure yellow: 47803

Blue Pullman: 47709/712

Central Services: 47972

Riviera Trains Oxford blue: 47805/839/843/848

Police: 47829

Victa Westlink: 47832

Great Western Merlin logo: 47811/813/815/830/846

First Great Western with gold band: 47811/813/815/816/830/832/846

First Great Western no gold band: 47813/816/830

White undercoat: 47846

Colas Rail: 47727/739/749

Stobart Rail: 47832

Midland Railway: 47973

BR green (specials): 47004, 47114, 47401, 47519, 47812/815/833/851

BR blue (specials): 47270, 47840

BR 'Large Logo' (specials): 47635, 47847

XP64 (special): 47643*, 47853

EMBLEMS

Small West Highland terrier: 47003–006/009/012/017/053, 47108/109/117/137/152/157, 47206/207/209–211, 47469/470, 47550/562/570/586, 47604/610/614 B; 47617 BR; 47703–710/713 SR; 47593, 47637 IC

Large dogs: 47591, 47847 B; 47118/120/150, 47552/563/578/593/595/597, 47614/617/632/633/635/636/640/641/644/649–655/657–665, 47848 BR

White castles: 47001–003/012/013/017/018/040/049/053, 47108/109/117,

47209/211/269/270, 47701–710 B; 47118, 47711/712 BR; 47701–717 SR

Red castles: 47017 B; 47708 SR

White stags: 47118/120, 47460/464, 47541, 47604 B; 47461 SC

Yellow stags: 47462, 47568 B; 47120, 47460/461/464/467/470/482, 47517/541/546/550/563/586, 47604/614/617/630/633/635/640/641 BR; 47430/492, 47541, 47637/642 IC; 47791 RX

NOTE: 47604 carried both a cabside yellow stag and a bodyside white stag for a period while in hybrid livery of BR blue with wraparound yellow cabs.

White kingfishers: 47217, 47302/303/308/346/360/361 B; 47363 FO

Coloured kingfishers: 47217, 47304 B; 47301/302/346/362 FO; 47347, 47594 FM; 47305 FP; 47361 FD

Cardiff Dragons: 47616 B (on head-code panels)

Stratford Sparrows: 47005/008/009/054/096, 47100/101/105/108/116/123/124, 47256/276/277/287–289, 47311/328/366, 47462, 47570/577/579/580/584/591, 47605 B; 47487 IC; 47007/014/016, 47366/367/374 FO; 47522 LNR; 47291, 47439/455/482, 47526/572/574/580/585, 47634/649/674 BR; 47573/576/579/581/582/596, 47711 ND; 47815 Gy; 47295 F

NSE cabside flashes: 47423/425/478 B; 47426/431/438/441/446/449/453, 47526, 47636, 47801 BR, 47573/582/583 NO, 47579, 47701/702/705/707/708/709/710/711/714/715 ND; 47706 SR; 47703/712/747 R

Freightliner logos on cabsides: 47805/812/843/848 VT; 47811/816/830 GW; 829 POL

Cast Depot Plaques

Crewe DMD cat: 47079 FM; 47010/085, 47119/125/190/193–196, 47223/233/278, 47324/368 FP; 47288, 47445 FD; 47531, 47775 RX; 47079 FA; 47288/ 47300/329/339/340/343/357, 47531, 47974-976 C; 47301/376 FF; 47974 D, 47489 had small size square plaques fitted above *Crewe Diesel Depot* nameplates R.

Eastfield West Highland terrier: 47004/006, 47114, 47210, 47328 FA

Eastleigh spitfire: 47306 FE (No. 2 end only); 47812 VT (small size plaques above nameplates)

Immingham star: 47010/054/085, 47119, 47212/221/223/224/276/278/294, 47319/336/368/373/379/380 FP; 47294 FD; 47331/346/352 C

Ripple Lane torch: 47221/223/295, 47379 FP

Southampton liner: 47095 FD (small size plaques above nameplates)

Stratford sparrow: 47007 FO (circular Sparrow plaques above nameplates); 47007, 47328, 47430 FA, 47702 F

Tinsley rose: 47052/053/060/079/095, 47152/186/194, 47205–207/209/210/212 –214/218/225/231/234/238/241/276/283/286/289/290/293/298, 47306/307/309–312/314/317/335/339/375/378/386/387/389/393/395/398, 47588, 47600/605 FD; 47214 FR*; 47033/049/051/053/079/085/095, 47125/146/186/188, 47200/201/217–219/234/236/237/241/245/258/285–287/290/293/297/299, 47306/307/310/312/323/326/338/348/351/360/365/375, 47525/555 FE; 47004/007 FA; 47085, 47290, 47308/321 F; 47145 BD; 47145 BG; 47195, 47212/224 FP; 47308, 47540 C; 47375 when first named had circular rose plaques above name-plates

Toton cooling tower: 47805 VT (small size plaques above nameplates)

Westbury horse: 47901

Cut-out Crewe cat: 47475/490/491, 47503/532/551/562/565/567/568/588/594/597, 47606/612/624/625/627/630/631/636/642, 47721/722/725–727/732/734/736–739/741/749/757/760/764–771/774/776-79/784/787/788/790–793/798/799

* on bodyside under nameplate

NUMBERS

Larger (8in) numbers: 47145, 47204, 47500/508/528/575, 47609/627 B; 47704 SR; 47471, 47555, 47637 IC

Black larger (8in): 47050, 47142, 47249/290/297, 47378 FO; 47311 FD

Large black numbers on front: 47236/237/239/242 B

Large white numbers on front: 47225/235, 47302/374 B

Small numbers (where non-standard): 47079, 47500, 47628 GWR; 47157/280, 47373/380 FR; 47277 FP; 47241/281 FD; 47487 IC

White numbers where non-standard: 47297 FO

Yellow DCE stripes: 47053, 47417/462/472 B; 47550 BR; 47366 FR

Red RTC stripes: 47472 B; 97480 BR

NSE flashes: 47703/712 R

White cant rail stripes: 47308/361 B

NAMES

D1660	CITY OF TRURO
D1661	NORTH STAR
D1662	ISAMBARD KINGDOM BRUNEL
D1663	SIR DANIEL GOOCH
D1664	GEORGE JACKSON CHURCHWARD
D1665	TITAN
D1666	ODIN
D1667	ATLAS
D1668	ORION
D1669	PYTHON
D1670	MAMMOTH
D1671	THOR
D1672	COLOSSUS
D1673	CYCLOPS
D1674	SAMSON
D1675	AMAZON
D1676	VULCAN
D1677	THOR
47001	City Of Bristol *
47002	SEA EAGLE *
47003	WILD SWAN *
47004	Old Oak Common Traction & Rolling Stock Depot
47005	HARRIER *
47007	Stratford
47008	PEREGRINE *
47009	GUILLEMOT *
47010	Xancidae
47012	MAGPIE *
47016	The Toleman Group
47016	ATLAS
47033	The Royal Logistic Corps
47049	GEFCO
47051	GREAT SNIPE *
47053	IMPALA *
47053	Cory Brothers 1842–1992
47053	Dollands Moor International
47054	Xancidae
47060	Halewood Silver Jubilee 1988
47076	CITY OF TRURO
47077	NORTH STAR
47078	SIR DANIEL GOOCH
47079	GEORGE JACKSON CHURCHWARD
47079	G. J. CHURCHWARD
47080	TITAN
47081	ODIN
47082	ATLAS
47083	ORION
47085	MAMMOTH
47085	Conidae
47085	REPTA 1893–1993
47086	COLOSSUS
47087	CYCLOPS
47088	SAMSON
47089	AMAZON
47090	VULCAN

In 1986, several Class 47s had their fuel tank capacity increased from 3,273 to 5,887 litres to allow them to work longer distance InterCity diagrams between fuelling. The last sixteen ETH conversions were 'twin tanked' at the time of their upgrade, and in 1989 these were renumbered in the 47/8 series. Later, Res and RfD locos also had increased fuel tanks. Virgin red 47831 *Bolton Wanderer* is one such loco and demonstrates a strange front end for a 47 with a flush metal plate over the headcode but two protruding white lamps. It had this feature only at No. 2 end.   PIP DUNN

In 2002, Virgin agreed for 47829 to be painted in a police livery to raise awareness of the dangers of trespassing on the railways. The striking livery is seen to good effect in this July 2002 view.   PIP DUNN

47091	THOR
47095	Southampton WRD Quality Approved
47096	ROOK *
47097	SIR PETER WHITE *
47097	FALCON *
47098	ORIOLE *
47100	MERLIN *
47102	BUZZARD *
47105	GOLDCREST *
47108	GOLDEN EAGLE *
47114	Freightlinerbulk
47116	GANNET *
47117	SPARROW HAWK *
47118	LAPWING *
47119	ARCIDAE
47120	R.A.F. Kinloss
47120	OSPREY *
47121	POCHARD *
47123	JAY *
47124	CITY OF CARDIFF *

47125	Tonnidae
47142	The Sapper
47142	TRACTION *
47145	JOSTINOT *
47145	MERDDIN EMRYS *
47145	MYRDDIN EMRYS
47146	PARIDÆ *
47146	Loughborough Grammar School
47157	Johnson Stevens Agencies
47158	Henry Ford
47167	County of Essex
47169	Great Eastern
47170	County of Norfolk
47172	County of Hertfordshire
47180	County of Suffolk
47184	County of Cambridgeshire
47186	TINSLEY TMD, SILVER JUBILEE 1965–1990 *
47186	Catcliffe Demon
47190	Pectinidae

47193	Lucinidae	47245	LINNET*	47315	Templecombe
47194	Bullidae	47245	The Institute of Export	47316	WREN*
47194	Carlisle Currock	47249	SEA HAWK*	47316	Cam Peak
47200	JACKDAW*	47258	Forth Ports Tilbury	47317	Willesden Yard
47200	Herbert Austin	47270	SWIFT*	47319	Norsk Hydro
47200	The Fosse Way	47270	Cory Brothers 1842–1992	47320	CRUSADER*
47206	The Morris Dancer	47270	SWIFT	47322	DESERT ORCHID*
47207	Bulmers of Hereford	47278	Vasidae	47323	THE JOSTINOT*
47207	The Felixstowe Partnership	47280	Pedigree	47323	ROVER GROUP QUALITY
47209	BITTERN*	47281	MERDDIN EMRYS*		ASSURED
47209	Herbert Austin	47283	Johnnie Walker	47324	Glossidae
47210	Blue Circle Cement	47284	STORM COCK/MISTLE THRUSH*	47325	RED RUM*
47213	Marchwood Military Port	47286	Port of Liverpool	47326	Saltley Depot Quality
47214	ANTAEUS*	47291	The Port of Felixstowe		Approved
47214	Tinsley Traction Depot	47293	TRANSFESA	47330	Amlwch Freighter/Trên
47214	Distillers MG	47295	BLACK PRINCE*		Nwyddau Amlwch
47217	KINGFISHER*	47297	Cobra Railfreight	47333	Civil Link
47218	FIRECREST*	47298	KESTREL*	47334	P&O Nedlloyd
47218	United Transport Europe	47298	Pegasus	47337	Herbert Austin
47219	SANDPIPER*	47299	ARIADNE*	47337	TALIESIN*
47219	Arnold Kunzler	47301	CENTURION*	47338	CORMORANT*
47220	RAPIER*	47301	Freightliner Birmingham	47338	Warrington Yard
47222	Appleby-Frodingham	47302	MERIDIAN*	47344	CHIEFTAIN*
47222	W. A. Camwell	47303	Freightliner Cleveland	47344	HUGGY BEAR*
47223	British Petroleum	47306	GOSHAWK*	47345	SCIMITAR*
47224	Arcidae	47306	The Sapper	47348	St Christopher's Railway Home
47226	SEAGULL*	47307	BUNTING*	47350	British Petroleum
47227	SALADIN*	47309	KITTIWAKE*	47350	SCORPION*
47228	axial	47309	The Halewood Transmission	47351	MADOQUA*
47229	SPRINGBOK*	47309	European Rail Operator	47352	TYNWALD*
47231	The Silcock Express		of the Year	47355	AVOCET
47233	Stombidae	47310	RAVEN*	47356	THE GURKHA*
47233	Strombidae	47310	Henry Ford	47357	The Permanent Way Institution
47236	ROVER GROUP QUALITY	47311	Warrington Yard	47358	IVANHOE*
	ASSURED	47312	Parsec of Europe	47360	FULMAR*
47238	Bescot Yard	47313	CURLEW*	47361	Wilton Endeavour
47241	The Silcock Express	47314	BLACK CAP*	47362	SARACEN*
47233	Halewood Silver Jubilee 1988	47314	Transmark	47362	TINSLEY TMD 1965 – 1998*
				47363	Billingham Enterprise
				47365	Diamond Jubilee
				47366	The Institution of Civil
					Engineers
				47366	Capital Radio's Help a
					London Child
				47367	KENNY COCKBIRD*
				47368	Neritidae
				47370	THUNDERBIRD*
				47370	Andrew A Hodgkinson
				47371	STINGRAY*
				47374	Petrolea
				47375	Tinsley Traction Depot
					Quality Approved
				47376	SKYLARK*
				47376	Freightliner 1995
				47379	Total Energy
				47380	Immingham
				47387	Transmark
				47389	The Halewood Transmission
				47390	Amlwch Freighter/Trên
					Nwyddau Amlwch

Virgin had long-term hire arrangements with EWS for Class 47s in 2000, which saw some 47/7s repainted into Virgin colours. 47747 in July 2001 shows the removed bufferbeam cowling, oblong buffers, TDM cables and also the flush front, but with the white lamps not indented, as on 47484. PIP DUNN

47393	Herbert Austin	47489	Crewe Diesel Depot	47574	LLOYD'S LIST 250TH
47392	Cory Brothers 1842–1992	47489	Crewe Diesel Depot		ANNIVERSARY
47394	Johnson Stevens Agencies		Quality Approved	47574	Benjamin Gimbert G.C.
47401	North Eastern	47490	Bristol Bath Road	47575	City of Hereford
47401	Star of the East	47490	Resonant	47576	King's Lynn
47401	North Eastern	47491	Horwich Enterprise	47577	Benjamin Gimbert G.C.
47402	Gateshead	47491	Resolve	47578	The Royal Society Of
47403	The Geordie	47492	The Enterprising Scot		Edinburgh
47404	Hadrian	47500	Great Western	47578	Respected
47405	Northumbria	47501	Craftsman	47579	James Nightall G.C.
47406	Rail Riders	47503	The Geordie	47580	County of Essex §
47407	Aycliffe	47503	Heaton Traincare Depot	47581	Great Eastern §
47408	Finsbury Park	47508	Great Britain	47582	County of Norfolk §
47409	David Lloyd George	47508	S.S. Great Britain	47583	County of Hertfordshire §
47411	The Geordie	47509	Albion	47584	County of Suffolk §
47421	The Brontës of Haworth	47510	Fair Rosamund	47584	THE LOCOMOTIVE &
47422	TRAFALGAR *	47511	Thames		CARRIAGE INSTITUTION 1911
47423	SCEPTRE *	47513	Severn	47585	County of Cambridgeshire §
47424	The Brontës of Haworth	47515	Night Mail	47586	Northamptonshire
47425	Holbeck	47517	Andrew Carnegie	47587	Ruskin College Oxford
47426	DIBATAG *	47520	Thunderbird	47588	Carlisle Currock
47431	SILURIAN *	47522	Doncaster Enterprise	47588	Resurgent
47434	Pride in Huddersfield	47523	Railfreight *	47590	Thomas Telford
47436	BUZNAK *	47524	Res Gestae	47592	County of Avon
47443	North Eastern	47526	Northumbria	47593	Galloway Princess
47444	University of Nottingham	47527	Kettering	47594	Resourceful
47446	GALTEE MORE *	47528	The Queen's Own Mercian	47595	Confederation of British
47448	Gateshead		Yeomanry		Industry
47449	ORIBI *	47531	Respite	47596	Aldeburgh Festival
47449	ORION	47532	BLUE PETER *	47597	Resilient
47450	BLACKBUCK *	47535	University of Leicester	47600	Dewi Sant/Saint David
47451	HYPERION *	47535	Saint Aidan	47602	Glorious Devon
47452	Aycliffe	47536	SOLARIO *	47603	County of Somerset
47453	ELAND *	47537	Sir Gwynedd/County	47604	Women's Royal Voluntary
47454	VELOCITY *		of Gwynedd		Service
47457	Ben Line	47539	Rochdale Pioneers	47606	ODIN §
47457	GAZELLE *	47541	The Queen Mother	47607	Royal Worcester
47458	County of Cambridgeshire	47546	Aviemore Centre	47609	FIRE FLY
47459	PERSEUS *	47547	University of Oxford	47611	Thames
47460	GREAT EASTERN *	47549	Royal Mail	47612	TITAN §
47460	TRITON *	47550	University of Dundee	47613	NORTH STAR §
47461	Charles Rennie Mackintosh	47551	Poste Restante	47615	Castell Caerffili/Caerphilly
47462	Cambridge Traction & Rolling	47555	The Commonwealth Spirit		Castle
	Stock Depot	47558	Mayflower	47616	Y Ddraig Goch/The Red
47465	MINERVA *	47559	Sir Joshua Reynolds		Dragon
47469	Glasgow Chamber of	47560	Tamar	47617	University of Stirling
	Commerce	47562	Sir William Burrell	47618	Fair Rosamund
47470	GLENLOY *	47562	Restless	47620	Windsor Castle
47470	University of Edinburgh	47563	Woman's Guild	47621	Royal County of Berkshire
47471	Norman Tunna GC	47564	COLOSSUS	47622	The Institution of Mechanical
47474	Sir Rowland Hill	47565	Responsive		Engineers
47475	Restive	47567	Red Star	47623	VULCAN §
47476	Night Mail	47567	Red Star ISO 9002	47624	CYCLOPS §
47479	Track 29	47568	Royal Engineers, Postal	47624	Saint Andrew
47480	Robin Hood		and Courier Services	47625	CITY OF TRURO §
47481	SUNSTAR *	47568	Royal Logistic Corps Postal	47625	Resplendent
47484	ISAMBARD KINGDOM BRUNEL		& Courier Services	47626	ATLAS §
47487	V. B. Menon *	47569	The Gloucestershire Regiment	47627	City of Oxford
47488	Rail Riders	47572	Ely Cathedral	47628	SIR DANIEL GOOCH §
47488	DAVIES THE OCEAN	47573	The LONDON STANDARD	47630	MENTOR *

47630	Resounding	47712	ARTEMIS	47775	Respite [§]
47631	Ressaldar	47712	Pride of Carlisle	47776	Respected [§]
47634	Henry Ford [§]	47713	Tayside Region	47777	Restored [§]
47634	Holbeck	47714	Grampian Region	47778	Irresistible
47635	The Lass O' Ballochmyle	47715	Haymarket	47778	Duke of Edinburgh's Award
47635	Jimmy Milne	47715	POSEIDON	47781	Isle of Iona
47636	Sir John De Graeme	47716	Duke of Edinburgh's Award	47783	Saint Peter
47636	Restored	47717	Tayside Region	47784	Condover Hall
47637	Springburn	47721	Saint Bede	47785	The Statesman
47638	County of Kent	47722	The Queen Mother	47785	Fiona Castle
47639	Industry Year 1986	47725	The Railway Mission	47786	Roy Castle OBE
47640	University of Strathclyde	47725	Bristol Barton Hill	47787	Victim Support
47641	COLOSSUS [§]	47726	Manchester Airport Progress	47787	Windsor Castle
47641	Fife Region	47727	Duke of Edinburgh's Award	47788	Captain Peter Manisty RN [§]
47642	Strathisla	47727	Castell Caerffili/Caerphilly	47789	Lindisfarne
47642	Resolute		Castle	47790	Saint David/Dewi Sant
47644	The Permanent Way Institution	47727	Rebecca	47790	Galloway Princess [§]
47645	Robert F. Fairlie Locomotive	47732	Restormel	47791	VENICE SIMPLON
	Engineer 1831–1885	47733	Eastern Star		ORIENT-EXPRESS
47647	THOR [§]	47734	Crewe Diesel Depot	47792	Saint Cuthbert
47654	Finsbury Park		Quality Approved	47792	Robin Hood
47671	Y Ddraig Goch/The Red	47736	Cambridge Traction	47793	Saint Augustine
	Dragon [§]		& Rolling Stock Depot	47793	Christopher Wren
47672	Sir William Burrell [§]	47737	Resurgent [§]	47798	Prince William
47673	Galloway Princess [§]	47738	Bristol Barton Hill	47799	Prince Henry
47673	York InterCity Control	47739	Resourceful [§]	47802	Pride of Cumbria
47674	Women's Royal Voluntary	47739	Robin of Templecombe	47803	Woman's Guild
	Service [§]	47741	Resilient [§]	47804	Kettering
47675	Confederation of British	47742	The Enterprising Scot	47805	Bristol Bath Road
	Industry [§]	47743	The Bobby	47805	Pride of Toton
47676	Northamptonshire [§]	47744	Saint Edwin	47805	TALISMAN
47677	University of Stirling [§]	47744	The Cornish Experience	47807	The Lion of Vienna
47701	Saint Andrew	47744	Royal Mail Cheltenham	47809	Finsbury Park [§]
47701	Old Oak Common Traction	47745	Royal London Society for the	47810	PORTERBROOK
	& Rolling Stock Depot		Blind	47810	Captain Sensible
47701	Waverley	47746	The Bobby	47810	Peter Bath MBE 1927–2006
47702	Saint Cuthbert	47747	Res Publica	47812	Pride of Eastleigh
47702	County of Suffolk	47747	Graham Farish	47813	S.S. Great Britain
47703	Saint Mungo	47747	Florence Nightingale	47813	John Peel
47703	The Queen Mother	47749	Atlantic College	47813	Solent
47703	LEWIS CARROLL	47749	Demelza	47814	Totnes Castle
47703	HERMES	47750	Royal Mail Cheltenham	47815	Abertawe Landore
47704	Dunedin	47750	ATLAS [§]	47815	GREAT WESTERN
47705	Lothian	47756	Royal Mail Tyneside	47816	Bristol Bath Road Quality
47705	GUY FAWKES	47757	Restitution		Approved
47706	Strathclyde	47757	Capability Brown	47817	The Institution of Mechanical
47707	Holyrood	47758	Regency Rail Cruises		Engineers
47708	Waverley	47760	Ribblehead Viaduct	47818	Strathclyde
47708	Templecombe	47764	Resounding [§]	47818	Emily
47709	The Lord Provost	47765	Ressaldar [§]	47822	Pride of Shrewsbury
47709	DIONYSOS	47766	Resolute [§]	47823	S.S. Great Britain
47710	Sir Walter Scott	47767	Saint Columba	47825	Thomas Telford [§]
47710	Capital Radio's Help	47767	Mappa Mundi	47826	Springburn [§]
	a London Child	47768	Resonant [§]	47828	Severn Valley Railway
47710	LADY GODIVA	47769	Resolve [§]		Kidderminster Bewdley
47710	QUASIMODO	47770	Reserved		Bridgnorth
47711	Greyfriars Bobby	47771	Heaton Traincare Depot [§]	47828	Joe Strummer
47711	County of Hertfordshire	47773	Reservist	47831	Bolton Wanderer
47712	Lady Diana Spencer	47773	The Queen Mother	47832	Tamar [§]
47712	DICK WHITTINGTON	47774	Poste Restante [§]	47832	DRIVER TOM CLARK OBE

47832	*Solway Princess*
47833	*Captain Peter Manisty RN*
47834	*FIRE FLY* §
47835	*Windsor Castle* §
47839	*Pride of Saltley*
47839	*PEGASUS*
47840	*North Star* §
47841	*The Institution of Mechanical Engineers* §
47841	*Spirit of Chester*
47843	*VULCAN* §
47844	*Derby & Derbyshire Chamber of Commerce & Industry*
47845	*County of Kent* §
47846	*Thor* §
47847	*Railway World Magazine/ Brian Morrison*
47848	*Newton Abbot Festival of Transport*
47848	*TITAN STAR*
47849	*Cadeirlan Bangor Cathedral*
47851	*Traction Magazine*
47853	*RAIL EXPRESS*
47854	*Women's Royal Voluntary Service* §
47854	*Diamond Jubilee*
47971	*Robin Hood* §
47972	*The Royal Army Ordnance Corps*
47973	*Derby Evening Telegraph*
47974	*The Permanent Way Institution*
47975	*The Institution of Civil Engineers*
47976	*Aviemore Centre* §
97480	*Robin Hood*
97561	*Midland Counties 150 1839–1989*

§ carried in an earlier guise as well
* unofficial

47844 had polished stainless-steel nameplates.

BUILD BATCHES

1962/63 D1500–D1549 Loughborough
1964/65 D1550–D1681 Crewe
1963–65 D1682–D1841 Loughborough
1965 D1842-D1861 Crewe
1965–68 D1862–D1961 Loughborough
1965/66 D1962–D1999 Crewe
1966/67 D1100–D1111 Crewe

47/0   standard locos with steam heating: 47001–020/024/026–056/059–061/063/064/066/068–070/072/074–083/085–091/0 93–126/128–131/134–138/140–153/155–160/162–252/254–258/260/262–299 *

47/3   standard locos with no train heating 47301–381

47/4   locos built with, or modified to, electric train heating 47401–547/549–665 §

* 47299 renumbered from 47216
§ locos from 47555 were previously numbered as 47/0s

Modified Batches

47/2   RfD locos with MW, twin tanks and air only various 47/0 & 47/3 (paper only classification)

47/3   'no-heat' loco converted from ETH 47468 47300

47/0 & 47/3   modified locos with Green Circle MW 47384–399 §

47/6   testbed loco with a Class 56 engine 47601

47/6   uprated ETH locos for Scottish 'sleepers' 47671–677

47/7a   push-pull locos 47701–717

47/7b   Rail Express Systems locos 47721/722/725–727/732–734/736–739/741–747/749/750/756–793/798/799^

47/4   InterCity locos with additional fuel tanks 47801–854 *

47/9   testbed loco with Class 58 engine 47901

47/4   dedicated test train locos 47971–976/981

97/4   dedicated test train locos 97472/480, 97545/561 §

^ 47798/799 were dedicated Royal Train locos
* these locos are widely referred to as '47/8s'
§ renumbered back to their original identities

Dual heat: 47401–423/425/426/428–431/435/457/458/460/461, 47517–528/541–544/552.

BRAKES

Locos built with dual brakes were D1631–81, D1758–1999, D1100–11. The remainder were converted to dual brakes except D1562, D1734, which were early withdrawals.

Two Class 47s were dedicated to the Royal Train in 1995 and repainted into a maroon version of the Res livery. In 1997 they were repainted again into this livery, which featured cast EWS logos on the cabside. 47798 Prince William *also shows the cable on the front for communication between loco and train.* PIP DUNN

One of the batch of eighty-one non-boilered Class 47s, brand new D1829 in March 1965, shows that these locos had through-steam pipes fitted, a feature rarely used. BILL WRIGHT

Conversion dates: 1576/79/82/83/87/ 89/91/96, 1608/12/53 (1968); 1501–19/ 84/85/88/91–94,1600/05/07/10/13/15– 17/91/93, 1702/19/26/27/33/36/37/43/ 48/49/51/54/56/57 (1969); 1500/33/42/ 50/80/97/99, 1606/20/21/24/95, 1703/ 06/13/52 (1970); 1521–24/26/29/30/40/ 44/61/63/83/89/92/99, 1700/04/05/07/ 08/24/25/31/35/44 (1971); 1520/25/27/ 28/32/34–39/41/43/45/46/70/72/73/78/ 81/86/90/95/98, 1601–04/26/30/94/98, 1701/09/21/46 (1972); 1531/47–49/51– 60/64–69/71/74/75, 1618/19/25/28/29, 1716 (1973); 47481, 47539–541/546/555 (1974); 47041/042/097–099, 47100–102/ 109/121–125/129/136–138/149/152 (1975); 47096, 47108/140/146–148/157 (1976).

In 1976, 47046 was rebuilt as 47601 and converted to air brakes only. Since then several Class 47s have been converted to air brakes only, namely 47033/049/ 050–053/060/079/085/095, 47114/125/ 144–146/150/152/156/157/186/188/194/ 197, 47200/201/204–207/206/209–211/ 213/217–219/222/223/225/226/228/229/ 231/234/236–238/241/245/258/270/276/ 279–281/283–287/289/290–294/5/297 –299, 47301–310/312–314/316/323/326/ 328/330/331/334/335/337–339/344/347/ 348/351/354/355/358/360–363/365/367/ 370/375/377–379, 47489, 47501/523/539/ 547, 47628/640, 47704/715/721/722/ 725–727/733/734/736–739/741/742/745/ 746/747/749/750/756–761/763/764/767/ 769/771/773/778–793/798/799, 47802/ 804–836/838–851/853/854, 47972.

In more recent times, 47237/245/292, 47746/760/773/798, 47840 have been converted back to dual-brake operation.

NUMBERS

The locos were renumbered in a random way from D numbers to TOPS because of modifications and the need to keep the batches of 'no-heat', steam heat and ETH/dual-heat locos together. Below is a full list of renumbering.

ABOVE: Four of the six RTC locos, 47971/974–976, were fitted with a modified Blue Star MW for push-pull working on Research trains; they couldn't work in 'multi' with each other or any other Blue Star locos. 47976 Aviemore Centre shows this modification. The loco has also had its ETH jumper moved; this was when, as 47546, it was fitted with snowploughs. The mounting bracket where the ETH jumper was originally located is still in place. The loco remains dual-braked. PIP DUNN

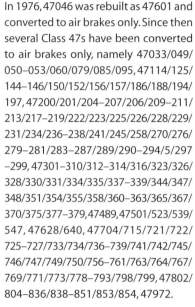

LEFT: The original version of Network South East was applied to a handful of Class 47s, but like the 50s it fared badly and showed up dirt. 47573 The London Standard, complete with Cockney Sparrow emblem, had yellow buffer cowlings that are also very dirty. Later locos from both Stratford and Old Oak Common depots had the third version of dark blue NSE applied. PDC

1100	47298		1500	47401
1101	47518		1501	47402
1102	47519		1502	47403
1103	47520		1503	47404
1104	47521		1504	47405
1105	47522		1505	47406
1106	47523		1506	47407
1107	47524		1507	47408
1108	47525		1508	47409
1109	47526		1509	47410
1110	47527		1510	47411
1111	47528		1511	47412

1512	47413
1513	47414
1514	47415
1515	47416
1516	47417
1517	47418
1518	47419
1519	47420
1520	47421
1521	47001
1522	47002
1523	47003
1524	47004
1525	47422
1526	47005
1527	47423
1528	47006
1529	47007
1530	47008
1531	47424
1532	47009
1533	47425
1534	47426
1535	47427
1536	47428
1537	47010
1538	47011
1539	47012
1540	47013
1541	47429
1542	47430
1543	47014
1544	47015
1545	47431
1546	47016
1547	47432
1548	47433
1549	47434
1550	47435
1551	47529
1552	47436
1553	47437
1554	47438
1555	47439
1556	47440
1557	47441
1558	47442
1559	47443
1560	47444
1561	47445
1562	n/a
1563	47446
1564	47447
1565	47448
1566	47449
1567	47450
1568	47451
1569	47452
1570	47017
1571	47453

1572	47018			
1573	47019			
1574	47454			
1575	47455			
1576	47456			
1577	47457			
1578	47458			
1579	47459			
1580	47460			
1581	47461			
1582	47462			
1583	47020	47556	47844	
1584	47021*	47531	47974	47531	47775
1585	47022*	47542			
1586	47463			
1587	47464			
1588	47023*	47543		
1589	47465			
1590	47466			
1591	47024	47557	47721	
1592	47025*	47544		
1593	47467			
1594	47468	47300		
1595	47469			
1596	47470			
1597	47026	47597	47741	
1598	47471			
1599	47027	47558	47722	
1600	47472	97472	47472	
1601	47473			
1602	47474			
1603	47475			
1604	47476			
1605	47028	47559	47759	
1606	47029	47635		
1607	47477			
1608	47478			
1609	47030	47618	47836	47618	47780
1610	47031	47560	47832	
1611	47032	47662	47817	
1612	47479			
1613	47033			
1614	47034	47561	97561	47973
1615	47035	47594	47739	
1616	47480	97480	47971	
1617	47036	47562	47672	47562	47760
1618	47037	47563	47831	
1619	47038	47564	47761	
1620	47039	47565		
1621	47040	47642	47766	
1622	47041	47630	47764	
1623	47042	47586	47676	
1624	47043	47566		
1625	47044	47567	47725	
1626	47045	47568	47726	
1627	47481			
1628	47046	47601	47901	
1629	47047	47569	47727	
1630	47048	47570	47849	
1631	47049			

1632	47050				
1633	47051				
1634	47052				
1635	47053				
1636	47482				
1637	47483				
1638	47054				
1639	47055	47652	47807		
1640	47056	47654	47809	47783	
1641	47057*	47532			
1642	47058*	47547			
1643	47059	47631	47765		
1644	47060				
1645	47061	47649	47830		
1646	47062*	47545	97545	47972	
1647	47063				
1648	47064	47639	47851		
1649	47065*	47535			
1650	47066	47661	47816		
1651	47067*	47533			
1652	47068	47632	47848		
1653	47069	47638	47845		
1654	47070	47620	47835	47799	
1655	47071*	47536			
1656	47072	47609	47834	47798	
1657	47073*	47537	47772		
1658	47074	47646	47852		
1659	47075	47645			
1660	47076	47625	47749		
1661	47077	47613	47840		
1662	47484				
1663	47078	47628			
1664	47079				
1665	47080	47612	47838	47612	47779
1666	47081	47606	47842	47606	47778
1667	47082	47626	47750		
1668	47083	47633			
1669	47084*	47538	ADB968035	47538	
1670	47085				
1671	n/a				
1672	47086	47641	47767		
1673	47087	47624			
1674	47088	47653	47808	47653	47781
1675	47089				
1676	47090	47623	47843		
1677	47091	47647	47846		
1678	47092*	47534			
1679	47093				
1680	47094				
1681	47095				
1682	47096				
1683	47485				
1684	47097				
1685	47098				
1686	47099				
1687	47100				
1688	47101				
1689	47486				
1690	47102				
1691	47103				
1692	47104				
1693	47105				
1694	47106				
1695	47107				
1696	47108				
1697	47109				
1698	47110				
1699	47111				
1700	47112				
1701	47113				
1702	47114				
1703	47115				
1704	47116				
1705	47117				
1706	47118				
1707	47487				
1708	47119				
1709	47120				
1710	47121				
1711	47122				
1712	47123				
1713	47488				
1714	47124				
1715	47125				
1716	47489				
1717	47126	47555			
1718	47127*	47539			
1719	47128	47656	47811		
1720	47129	47658	47813		
1721	47130				
1722	47131				
1723	47132*	47540	47975	47540	
1724	47133	47549			
1725	47490	47768			
1726	47134	47622	47841		
1727	47135	47664	47819	47784	
1728	47136	47621	47839		
1729	47137				
1730	47138	47607	47821	47786	
1731	47139*	47550			
1732	47140				
1733	47141	47614	47853		
1734	n/a				
1735	47142				
1736	47143				
1737	47144				
1738	47145				
1739	47146				
1740	47147				
1741	47148				
1742	47149	47617	47677		
1743	47150	47399	47150		
1744	47151	47648	47850		
1745	47152	47398	47152		
1746	47551	47153	47551	47801	47774
1747	47154*	47546	47976		
1748	47155	47660	47815		
1749	47156				
1750	47157				
1751	47158	47634			

1752	47159				1812	47331	
1753	47491	47769			1813	47332	
1754	47160	47605	47746		1814	47333	
1755	47161˙	47541	47773		1815	47334	
1756	47162				1816	47335	
1757	47163	47610	47823	47787	1817	47336	
1758	47164	47571	47822		1818	47337	
1759	47165	47590	47825		1819	47338	
1760	47492				1820	47339	
1761	47166	47611	47837		1821	47340	
1762	47167	47580	47732	47580	1822	47341	
1763	47168	47572			1823	47342	
1764	47169	47581	47763		1824	47343	
1765	47170	47582	47733		1825	47344	
1766	47171	47592	47738		1826	47345	
1767	47172	47583	47734		1827	47346	
1768	47173	47573	47762		1828	47347	
1769	47174	47574			1829	47348	
1770	47175	47575			1830	47349	
1771	47176	47576			1831	47350	
1772	47177	47599	47743		1832	47351	
1773	47178	47588	47737		1833	47352	
1774	47179	47577	47847		1834	47353	
1775	47180	47584			1835	47354	
1776	47181	47578	47776		1836	47355	47391	47355
1777	47182	47598	47742		1837	47187	
1778	47183	47579	47793		1838	47188	
1779	47184	47585	47757		1839	47189	
1780	47185	47602	47824	47782	1840	47190	
1781	47186				1841	47191	
1782	47301				1842	47192	
1783	47302				1843	47193	
1784	47303	47397	47303		1844	47194	
1785	47304	47392	47304		1845	47195	
1786	47305				1846	47196	
1787	47306				1847	47197	
1788	47307				1848	47198	
1789	47308				1849	47199	
1790	47309	47389	47309		1850	47200	
1791	47310				1851	47201	
1792	47311				1852	47202	
1793	47312				1853	47203	
1794	47313				1854	47204	47388	47204
1795	47314	47387	47314		1855	47205	47395	47205
1796	47315				1856	47206	
1797	47316				1857	47207	
1798	47317				1858	47208	
1799	47318				1859	47209	47393	47209
1800	47319				1860	47210	
1801	47320				1861	47211	47394	47211
1802	47321				1862	47212	
1803	47322				1863	47213	
1804	47323				1864	47214	
1805	47324				1865	47215	
1806	47325				1866	47216	47299	
1807	47326				1867	47217	
1808	47327				1868	47218	
1809	47328	47396	47328		1869	47219	
1810	47329				1870	47220	
1811	47330	47390	47330		1871	47221	

1872	47222		
1873	47223		
1874	47224		
1875	47356		
1876	47357		
1877	47358		
1878	47359		
1879	47360		
1880	47361		
1881	47362		
1882	47363	47385	47363
1883	47364	47981	
1884	47365		
1885	47366		
1886	47367		
1887	47368		
1888	47369		
1889	47370		
1890	47371		
1891	47372		
1892	47373		
1893	47374		
1894	47375		
1895	47376		
1896	47377		
1897	47378	47386	47378
1898	47379		
1899	47380		
1900	47381		
1901	47225		
1902	47226	47384	47226
1903	47227		
1904	47228		
1905	47229		
1906	47230		
1907	47231		
1908	n/a		
1909	47232	47665	47820	47785
1910	47233		
1911	47234		
1912	47235		
1913	47236		
1914	47237		
1915	47238		
1916	47239	47657	47812
1917	47240	47663	47818
1918	47241		
1919	47242	47659	47814
1920	47243	47636	47777
1921	47244	47640	
1922	47245		
1923	47246	47644	47756
1924	47247	47655	47810
1925	47248	47616	47671	47789
1926	47249		
1927	47250	47600	47744
1928	47251	47589	47827
1929	47252	47615	47747
1930	47253*	47530	
1931	47254	47651	47806

First Great Western used Class 47s on its Paddington-Penzance 'sleeper' trains but replaced them with Class 57s in 2004. The only FGW loco actually converted to 57 was 47846 Thor, although it went on to work for Virgin once rebuilt. In August 2000 it shows a short-lived period with a black-painted headcode panel, something with which it never ran in traffic. PIP DUNN

1932	47493	47701		
1933	47255	47596		
1934	47256			
1935	47257	47650	47805	
1936	47494	47706		
1937	47495	47704		
1938	47258			
1939	47496	47710		
1940	47497	47717		
1941	47498	47711		
1942	47499	47709		
1943	47500	47770	47500	
1944	47501			
1945	47502	47715		
1946	47503	47771		
1947	47504	47702		
1948	47505	47712		
1949	47506	47707		
1950	47259*	47552	47802	
1951	47507	47716		
1952	47508			
1953	47509			
1954	47510	47713		
1955	47511	47714		
1956	47260	47553	47803	
1957	47261*	47554	47705	
1958	47512			
1959	47513			
1960	47514	47703		
1961	47515			
1962	47262	47608	47833	47788
1963	47263	47587	47736	
1964	47264	47619	47829	
1965	47265	47591	47804	47792	47804
1966	47266	47629	47828	
1967	47267	47603	47745	
1968	47516	47708		
1969	47268	47595	47675	47791
1970	47269	47643		
1971	47270			
1972	47271	47604	47674	47854
1973	47272	47593	47673	47790
1974	47273	47627		
1975	47517	47758		
1976	47274	47637	47826	
1977	47275			

1978	47276		1989	47287
1979	47277		1990	47288
1980	47278		1991	47289
1981	47279		1992	47290
1982	47280		1993	47291
1983	47281		1994	47292
1984	47282		1995	47293
1985	47283		1996	47294
1986	47284		1997	47295
1987	47285		1998	47296
1988	47286		1999	47297

DRS's first four Class 47s were painted in its original livery. They were two 'no-heat' locos and two ETH locos; the former have now been disposed of, while the other two have been joined by another ten 47/4s, and all are now painted in Compass livery. In July 2002, 47802 shows off its livery complete with yellow bufferbeam cowling, which is now black. The loco also now has Green Circle MW with the DRS MW removed, leaving the indented panel on its cab front. PIP DUNN

Subsequent Renumberings

508 received TOPS numbers, and when renumberings started in 1973 there were three sub classes: 47/0 (built with boilers), 47/3 (with no train heat) and 47/4 (ETH or dual heat). Initially this involved 47001–298, 47301–381 and 47401–529. However, some 47/0s were converted to ETH in between being allocated a 47/0 number and actually renumbered, so 47530–555 were created using the locos that *should* have been 47021–023/025/057/058/062/065/067/071/073/084/092, 47127/132/133/139/154/161, 47259/261, plus, in the case of 47126/153/260, three 47/0s which did receive their original TOPS numbers for a short period in 1974.

47548 was never used because 47125, earmarked for this number, didn't receive ETH because 47126 took its train heating equipment and became 47555.

Since 1974 there have been more changes. In 1979, twelve Class 47/4s were fitted with push-pull equipment and became 47701–712. Another four were converted in 1985, and when 47713 was written off, 47497 was converted in 1988.

In 1979, additional ETH conversions started, and 47556–585 (1979–81),

47586–600/602–628 (1983–85) and 47629–665 (1985–87) appeared.

In 1976, 47046 was fitted with a Ruston 16RK3CT engine as a testbed for the forthcoming Class 56s. It was renumbered 47601. After the first 56s were delivered, 47601's role was redundant, so in September 1978 it was fitted with a Ruston 12RK3ACT engine (for the Class 58s), returning to traffic in January 1980. It stayed with its non-standard engine until withdrawal in March 1990.

In December 1981, 47216 became 47299 after a soothsayer predicted it would have a crash. In 1983, with its new number, it did.

In 1989 InterCity identified a need for a pool of fifty-three locos with additional fuel tanks, and these were renumbered 47801–853. When 47850 was damaged, 47854 was created in October 1995. In 1992–94, several 47/8s were renumbered back to their 47/4 numbers when they moved to the Res fleet.

In 1993, Res upgraded its 47s and renumbered them in the 477xx series, but with 47701–717 already taken by the push-pull locos, the new series ran from 47721–791. There were still gaps as fourteen were never modified as planned, and 47792/793 were also later

added. The decision to dedicate two 47/8s as Royal Train locos saw them become 47798/799.

In March 1994, Railfreight Distribution started to modify its 47s with multiple working so 47150/152 became 47399/398. As more were modified, more renumberings took place down to 47384 in July 1994, but as 47301–381 were already in use, the renumberings could not go beyond 47382, so 47384–399 reverted to their original numbers.

The decision to dedicate four Class 47s for test train use in 1988 saw 47472/480/545/561 become Class 97s – 97472/480/545/561 respectively. To keep them as 'Class 47s' they were renumbered 47971–973 in July 1989, 97472 having already reverted to 47472. In 1990, 47531/540/546 became 47974–976, and in November 1993 47364 became 47981.

In July 1991, eight 47/4s had their ETH uprated to work Scottish 'sleepers' and seven became 47671–677 – of which 47674 was later converted to 47854, and 47671–673/675 later became 47/7s.

47468 was withdrawn in April 1992, but the Civil Engineering sector acquired it: it removed its train heat and it became 47300 as a replacement for collision-damaged 47343.

class 48

1957 BR number range:	D1702–06	Engine type:	Sulzer 12LVA24
Built by:	Brush	Engine output:	2,650bhp (1,977kW)
Year introduced:	1965	Power at rail:	1,990bhp (1,485kW)
Wheel arrangement:	Co-Co	Tractive effort:	62,000lb
Weight:	114 tons	Maximum speed:	95mph (137km/h)
Height:	12ft 10in (3.91m)	Brake force:	60 tons
Length:	63ft 6in (19.38m)	Route availability:	6
Width:	9ft 2in (2.79m)	Main generator type:	Brush TG160-60
Wheelbase:	51ft 6in (15.69m)	Auxiliary generator type:	Brush TG69-28
Bogie wheelbase:	14ft 6in (4.41m)	Traction motor type:	Brush TM64-68
Bogie pivot centres:	37ft (11.27m)	No. of traction motors:	6
Wheel diameter:	3ft 9in (1.14m)	Gear ratio:	17:66
Min. curve negotiable:	4 chains (80.46m)	Fuel tank capacity:	850gal (3,825ltr)

DURING THE PRODUCTION of the Brush Type 4s, five were fitted with a different Sulzer engine, the 12LVA24. When TOPS came in the locos were classified as Class 48s, but in the event their engines were removed in 1969 and standard Sulzer 12LDA units were fitted, making them standard Class 47s.

DETAIL DIFFERENCES

There were no noticeable differences between a Class 47 and 48. The 48s had a Spanner Mk 3 boiler for steam heating.

LIVERIES

All were new in BR green, and all had full yellow ends added later. None were painted blue until after their conversion to Class 47s.

BR green with small yellow panels:
D1702–06
BR green with full yellow ends:
D1702–06

class 50

TOPS number range:	50001–050, 50149	Power at rail:	2,070bhp (1,540kW); 1,890bhp (1,370kW): 50149
1957 BR number range:	D400–D449		
Former class codes:	27/3	Tractive effort:	48,500lb
Built by:	English Electric Vulcan Foundry	Maximum speed:	100mph (160km/h) 80mph (128km/h): 50149 60mph (96km/h): DCWA sector locos from 1989
Years introduced:	1967–68		
Wheel arrangement:	Co-Co		
Weight:	117 tons		
Height:	12ft 11in (3.95m)	Brake force:	59 tons
Length:	68ft 6in (20.87m)	Route availability:	6
Width:	9ft 1in (2.77m)	Main generator type:	EE840-4B
Wheelbase:	56ft 2in (17.11m)	Auxiliary generator type:	EE911-5C
Bogie wheelbase:	13ft 6in (4.11m)	ETH generator type:	EE915-1B
Bogie pivot centres:	42ft 8in (13.00m)	Traction motor type:	EE538-5A
Wheel diameter:	3ft 7in (1.09m)	No. of traction motors:	6
Min. curve negotiable:	4 chains (80.46m)	Gear ratio:	53:18 (50001–050); 59:16 (50149)
Engine type:	English Electric 16CSVT	Fuel tank capacity:	1,055gal (4,797ltr)
Engine output:	2,700bhp (2,014kW) 50149 downrated to 2,450bhp (1,750kW)		

THIS WAS THE last mixed traffic design built for BR: fifty locos were initially leased by BR from English Electric. They were built for working the section of the WCML north of Crewe to Scotland prior to electrification.

After the WCML was wired they were transferred to the WR in 1972–76, named in 1978–79, and refurbished in 1979–83. They also worked on the Exeter St David's to Waterloo line, and to Birmingham from both Paddington and the West Country.

One loco was converted to a Railfreight loco in 1987 for a trial, but was changed back to a standard loco in 1989. All were withdrawn by 1994, but eighteen are preserved, of which five – 50017/031/044/049/050 – have run on the main line.

DETAIL DIFFERENCES

Train heating was ETH with an index of sixty-one. All had roof-mounted headcode boxes, but these were changed to dominos from 1977. In the mid-1970s it was common practice for the locos to show an abridged version of their TOPS number in the headcode, such as 5O39 or 5O46. The dominos were plated over with metal plates with opaque lenses on unrefurbished 50005/007/010/011/014/020/024/027/030/044/046/049 and all refurbished 50s. 50044 was at No.2 end only.

Unrefurbished 50003/035 had plated headcodes with protruding white marker lights at both ends, while 50007 had protruding opaque lenses at No.1 end.

All had snowplough brackets, but ploughs have only been carried by 50012/015/018/021/024/033/036/037 and 50007/042/049 in preservation.

Orange Square MW was fitted from new on D400/01, with the cable and receptacle mounted on the cab front. All other locos were wired for MW to be fitted at a later date, with the cab front holes plated over, and from 1970 the equipment was fitted to 402–449. In May 1969, 401 was observed with its jumper cable from No. 2 end removed and the holes plated over.

After fitting, refurbished 50010/033/041 all ran for short periods with no MW cable, but the jumper heads and receptacle still in place.

50050 was built without the horizontal handrails under the cab windows at both ends, while 50033 had the two vertical cab-front handrails at No. 1 end removed after collision damage. 50006 has its left handrail repositioned at No.2 end after a collision.

REFURBISHMENT

All were refurbished in 1979–83. The main physical detail differences were the fitting of a sealed beam headlight centrally on the cab front, the changing of one bodyside window to a grille, and the plating over of the sandboxes. The indented section at No. 2 end, which housed the cooling fans for the rheostatic brake resistors, was removed, which led to a smoother roof profile.

The locos also lost their side window deflectors; these were small glass panels fitted on the vertical pillar of the side window to deflect the wind away from the crew's face when looking out of the window at speed.

When 50006/017 were released from refurbishment, they did not have headlights fitted and the apertures were covered by blanking plates. Headlights were fitted in late 1980. 50006/017 also had their cab sandboxes retained, although these were later plated over. If locos still had dominos, these were changed to standard metal panels.

Dates of refurbishment (in order of shopping):

50006 (1979); 50017/019/001/047/013/ 023/003/004/038/032/022 (1980), 50015/ 020/035/012/010/036/040/045/039/033/ 041/031/008 (1981); 50016/009/021/037/ 044/041/029/025/005/048/028/034/024/ 026/018, (1982), 50007/046/011/043/049/ 050/027/030/002/014 (1983).

The first six were outshopped in standard BR blue with 'Large Logo' livery adopted from the seventh refurbishment, 50023.

50044 has been cosmetically restored into unrefurbished condition, although it is still a refurbished loco. It has had the right-hand tail-lights at both ends removed and changed to a sealed-beam headlight. 50002 is in the process of being cosmetically de-refurbished.

LIVERIES

BR blue: 50001–050
BR blue with wrap round yellow ends: 50023 (only for one test run)
BR 'Large Logo': 50001–050
GWR green: 50007
BR 'Large Logo' blue roof: 50010/031˙
BR 'Large Logo' black roof/blue cab roofs: 50023
BR 'Large Logo' black roof: 50002/ 003/006/008/011/014/016/024/027/028/ 031˙/042–044/046/047/049
Undercoat: 50035 (for one trip only)
Original NSE: 50002/017–019/023/025/ 026/029/032/034/035/037/044/048
Revised NSE: 50001/003/005/017/018/ 024/027/028/030/041/043/044/048–050
Dark NSE: 50002/005/009/016/017/023/ 024/027/029/033–035/037/043/045/048
Dark NSE without NSE branding: 50005
Railfreight General: 50117˙/149
'Dutch': 50015
BR blue with grey roof, black window frames ('Laira' blue): 50008/019/037
LMS Crimson: 50017˙
All-over maroon: 50008˙
Two-tone green with small yellow panels: 50044˙
Electric blue: 50002˙
Loadhaul: 50035˙

˙ in post-BR days only

ABOVE : A Class 50 in original condition in 1968, with the MW wired in but no jumper cables fitted. D402 also shows its working four-character headcode display and its sandbox filler ports below the BR badge. JIM BINNIE
RIGHT: Unrefurbished 50040 Leviathan *leads a line of five Class 50s with refurbished 50023* Howe *behind it, then 50050* Fearless, *50022* Anson *and 50039* Implacable *bringing up the rear. 50040 and 50039/050 are in nearly as-built condition apart from TOPS numbers, domino headcodes and nameplates. When built, only the first two Class 50s had their MW cables fitted, but all had them fitted by May 1970.* ANDY HOARE

ABOVE LEFT: 50007 Hercules *shows its unique headcode of protruding opaque lenses on a metal panel. The loco lacks a headlight as it is unrefurbished.* PDC

ABOVE RIGHT: Preserved 50026 Indomitable *shows a refurbished Class 50 in full detail. The main noticeable difference was the headlight, while the bodyside window above the number has been changed to a grille and the sandbox filler ports plated over. The 50s were dual-braked and fitted with ETH from new, as well as having snowplough brackets, although it was to be 1986 before a 50 was fitted with ploughs.* PIP DUNN

EMBLEMS

DCE cabside stripes: 50004/009/010/ 020/045 BR; 50019 LB

West of England crests: 50002/016/ 017/024/027/029/037/045/048 ND

Black front window frames: 50023/ 026 NO; 50024 NV (No. 1 end only)

Headcode box NSE flashes: 50031/033/ 036/038–040 BR; 50017–019/023/025/ 026/029/032/034/035/037/048 NO; 50001/003/005/017/018/024/027/028/ 030/041/044/048–050 NV; 50002/023/ 029/033/037/045 ND

Large style flashes: 50024 ND

NSE without cab flashes: 50002/017/ 018/019/023/026/032/034/037/044 NO; 50035 ND

Cast depot Laira galleon emblems: 50149 FG

Large 8in numbers: 50019/037 LB
Smaller numbers: 50008 LB

NAMES

50001	*Dreadnought*
50002	*Superb*
50003	*Temeraire*
50004	*St Vincent*
50005	*Collingwood*
50006	*Neptune*
50007	*Hercules*
50007	*SIR EDWARD ELGAR*
50008	*Thunderer*
50009	*Conqueror*
50010	*Monarch*
50011	*Centurion*
50012	*Benbow*
50013	*Agincourt*
50014	*Warspite*

50015	*Valiant*
50016	*Barham*
50017	*Royal Oak*
50018	*Resolution*
50019	*Ramillies*
50020	*Revenge*
50021	*Rodney*
50022	*Anson*
50023	*Howe*
50024	*Vanguard*
50025	*Invincible*
50026	*Indomitable*
50027	*Lion*
50028	*Tiger*
50029	*Renown*
50030	*Repulse*
50031	*Hood*
50032	*Courageous*
50033	*Glorious*

50034	*Furious*
50035	*Ark Royal*
50036	*Victorious*
50037	*Illustrious*
50038	*Formidable*
50039	*Implacable*
50040	*Leviathan*
50040	*Centurion*
50041	*Bulwark*
50042	*Triumph*
50043	*Eagle*
50044	*Exeter*
50045	*Achilles*
50046	*Ajax*
50047	*Swiftsure*
50048	*Dauntless*
50049	*Defiance*
50050	*Fearless*
50149	*Defiance*

In the revised version of Network SouthEast livery, 50018 Resolution *sports a full set of snowploughs, a relatively rare fitment for Class 50s. The loco is viewed from No. 1 end and shows the higher position of the nameplates for NSE locos (apart from 50033* Glorious*).* PDC

Notes on Nameplates

All nameplates were in BR corporate style and painted red apart from 50007 which had uppercase GWR style nameplates for its second name, and 50032 which had blue plates when in NO, and 50149 which had yellow plates when FG.

In preservation, 50044 ran with *Exeter* nameplates in GWR style when in BR green and the name in uppercase.

50045 ran for a period in ND without nameplates, while 50027 ran for about a week without plates in NV. 50035 ran without nameplates when in undercoat livery. 50040 ran for one test run only with the incorrect nameplates from 50033 *Glorious*. 50049 ran for its last days in traffic missing one nameplate.

When locos were repainted into NSE livery variants, the nameplates were moved from the centre of the body to higher up and off centre. The exception was 50033. When 50037 was repainted from NO to LB the nameplates reverted to their original position, while those in 50019 remained in the NO position. 50008 was repainted from BR to LB and retained nameplates and crests in the middle.

CRESTS

Several locos carried ship's crests. These were above the nameplates in B, BR and FG liveries, and below the nameplates in NO, NV and ND liveries. Those to carry plates were 50002 (B, BR, NO), 50004 (BR), 50005 (NV), 50008 (B, BR, BRB, LB), 50011

ABOVE: Ex-works in the first version of Network SouthEast livery with white window frames; 50034 Furious *also has NSE flashes on its headcode panel. This June 1989 picture was some three years after the livery first appeared, and shows how it did not fare too well before becoming very scruffy indeed.* PDC

BELOW: NSE 50019 Ramillies *was transferred to the Departmental sector. So bad was its paintwork that NSE demanded it be repainted, so a version of BR blue was used, albeit with a grey roof and black window frames. The nameplates were also retained in the NSE position, and NSE-size large numbers were applied.* PDC

ABOVE LEFT: In 1987, with InterCity no longer having Class 50s in its fleet, the locos were split between Network SouthEast, Parcels, Provincial and Departmental sectors, while the first withdrawals also took place. This also spared a loco for a trial with the Railfreight sector, which saw 50049 Defiance *modified using Class 37/5 CP7 bogies. The loco was restricted to 80mph, but externally, only its Railfreight General livery made it look any different to a refurbished Class 50. It ran like this from September 1987 to February 1989 when it reverted to 50049 in NSE colours.* PDC

ABOVE RIGHT: 50007 was repainted into GWR green in 1984 and lost its Hercules *name for SIR EDWARD ELGAR. Aside from the livery and brass name and numberplates, the loco was a standard refurbished loco.* PDC

(BRB), 50017 (NO⁺), 50019 (B⁺, BR⁺), 50025 (B, BR), 50027 (NV⁺), 50030 (BR⁺), 50031 (BR), 50032 (NO), 50035 (B, BR, NO, LH), 50037 (BR, NO), 50040 (BR⁺), 50042 (B⁺), 50044 (B, BR, NO, NV), 50046 (BRB), 50049 (FG¹, B⁺, BR⁺, BRB⁺), 50050 (B, BR, NV).

⁺ post-BR only
⁺ when renamed *Centurion* 7/87
¹ one side only

50007 also carried GWR crests when painted in GWR green.

NUMBERS

Locos were renumbered in series from D401–D449 to 50001–049, with D400 becoming 50050. The only subsequent renumbering was in September 1987 when 50049 emerged as 50149 as a trial Railfreight loco. It remained like this until March 1989 when converted back to a standard 50/0 as 50049, rendering the 50/1 subclass defunct.

50017/035 have both carried the numbers 50117/135 in preservation when in freight liveries.

SUBCLASSES

Livery aside, there were no distinguishable detail differences on 50149 as compared with a standard Class 50. It had re-geared bogies set for 80mph. When it was converted back to 50049 it had the 149 number on its front at No. 2 end for a period.

50033 Glorious *shows off the dark blue NSE livery applied to several Class 50s in 1989/90. The loco has lost its lower vertical grab handles after a minor collision. The nameplates were left in their original position when it was repainted – the only 50 to run like this.* PDC

In 2002, 50044 Exeter *was repainted into two-tone BR green, a livery the class had never been seen in before, but one they might well have been outshopped in if they had been built a couple of years earlier off the production line. Numbered as D444, the loco has also been cosmetically restored to its as-built unrefurbished look, with the exception of retaining the additional bodyside grille instead of a window.* PIP DUNN

A Class 50 in post-refurbished guise, but prior to NSE sectorization which saw red, white and blue flashes put on the headcode boxes of large logo locos in the NSE sector. 50039 Implacable *stands at Old Oak Common.* PDC

In March 1968, just a few weeks old, but already quite dirty, D405 shows off an 'out of the box' Class 50 look with new MW cables, a working headcode box and the side deflectors by the cab windows. BILL WRIGHT

CLASS 52s WERE the final diesel hydraulic design built for BR, with the first appearing in 1962. Withdrawals started in 1973 and ended in 1977, by which time the locos had become very popular amongst enthusiasts. They used two Maybach engines, and Voith transmissions; they had steam heating, although a few ran with isolated boilers after 1975. All but four were dual-braked, and that quartet was amongst the earlier withdrawals. Seven are preserved, one of which has returned to the main line.

DETAIL DIFFERENCES

All had split-centre panels on the cab front. As the system was phased out, it was common practice to wind the headcode round to show the loco number, such as 1O13 or 1O15.

D1023 had dominos from November 1976. D1015 has dominos on roller blinds so it can display a four-character headcode or dominos.

All were built with vacuum brakes. D1000–16/21–73 were converted to dual brakes, the dates as follows: 1013/15/26/31/55/61–63/66/69 (1968); 1004/10/24/25/27–29/32–34/38/41/49/59/65/67/70/72/73 (1969); 1001–03/06–09/14/16/30/35/42/44/45/48/54/60/68 (1970); 1011/12/21/37/39/43/46/47/50–53/56 (1971); 1000/05/22/36/40/57/64/71 (1972); 1023/58 (1973).

MW was not fitted, but all had Spanner Mk 3 boilers; these were isolated for some periods on some locos, running with the hose part of the steam pipe removed.

Front-end square ventilation panels were fitted to 1012/28/39/56/71, of which 1056 initially had four horizontal slats in its grilles.

D1025–29 were built without headboard clips on the top of the cab fronts below the windows, and these were later removed from D1003/05/40/46/49/57/63/65/71 after accidents. Trial rotary windscreen wipers were fitted to D1006/39 in the early 1960s, but soon removed.

Battery-box securing clips were fitted to locos after an accident involving 1007. They were not fitted to 1000/02/04/07/17–20/24/32/38/39/42/60, as these were withdrawn before the recommendation was made for their fitting.

Headlights have been fitted to D1015 only: they are in the headcode panel and can be covered by the roller blinds. D1015 also had radio aerials on the cab front on the top of the nose in front of the windows.

LIVERIES

Desert Sand: D1000
Desert Sand with small warning panels: D1000
BR green with small yellow panels: D1002–04/35–38
Golden Ochre with small yellow panels: D1015
BR maroon with yellow bufferbeams: D1001/05–09/39–43
BR maroon with small yellow panels: D1000–03/05–35/38–73
BR maroon with full yellow ends: D1001/02/08/12/16/25/39/41/44/45/54/56/67/68

specifications

1957 BR number range:	D1000–73
Former class codes:	D27/1, later 27/1
Built by:	BR Swindon, Crewe
Introduced:	1961–64
Wheel arrangement:	C-C
Weight (operational):	108 tons
Height:	13ft (3.96m)
Width:	9ft (2.74)
Length:	68ft (20.73m)
Min. curve negotiable:	4½ chains
Maximum speed:	90mph (144km/h)
Wheelbase:	54ft 8in (16.66m)
Bogie wheelbase:	12ft 2in (3.71m)
Bogie pivot centres:	42ft 6in (12.96)
Wheel diameter:	3ft 7in (1.09m)
Route availability:	6
Brake force:	82 tons
Engine type:	Two Maybach MD 655
Engine horsepower:	2,700bhp (2,014kW)
Power at rail:	2,350bhp (1,753kW)
Tractive effort:	72,600lb, later reduced to 70,000lb
Cylinder bore:	7¼in
Cylinder stroke:	8¼in
Transmission type:	Voith L630rU
Fuel tank capacity:	850gal (3,825ltr)

BR blue with small yellow panels: D1017/30/36/37/43/47/57
BR blue: D1000–73

NAMES

D1000   *WESTERN ENTERPRISE*
D1001   *WESTERN PATHFINDER*

ABOVE LEFT: A comparison of the only main-line registered Class 52, D1015 WESTERN CHAMPION, and the National Railway Museum's preserved D1023 WESTERN FUSILIER. While D1023 was the only 52 to have domino headcodes in BR days, D1015 now has them, but as part of its roller-blind headcodes so they can be changed. D1015 has a headlight fitted in its split centre panel, plus the equipment for the NRN radio is evident, mounted on its handrail. Both locos are dual-braked and both retain steam pipes, though D1015 no longer has a boiler. PIP DUNN

ABOVE RIGHT: Five Class 52s had air vents fitted to their cab fronts to improve ventilation for the driver. Although D1041 WESTERN PRINCE was not one of them, it carried this modification in 1998 for visual effect. PIP DUNN

D1002 WESTERN EXPLORER	D1028 WESTERN HUSSAR	D1054 WESTERN GOVERNOR
D1003 WESTERN PIONEER	D1029 WESTERN LEGIONAIRE	D1055 WESTERN ADVOCATE
D1004 WESTERN CRUSADER	D1029 WESTERN LEGIONNAIRE	D1056 WESTERN SULTAN
D1005 WESTERN VENTURER	D1030 WESTERN MUSKETEER	D1057 WESTERN CHIEFTAIN
D1006 WESTERN STALWART	D1031 WESTERN RIFLEMAN	D1058 WESTERN NOBLEMAN
D1007 WESTERN TALISMAN	D1032 WESTERN MARKSMAN	D1059 WESTERN EMPIRE
D1008 WESTERN HARRIER	D1033 WESTERN TROOPER	D1060 WESTERN DOMINION
D1009 WESTERN INVADER	D1034 WESTERN DRAGOON	D1061 WESTERN ENVOY
D1010 WESTERN CAMPAIGNER	D1035 WESTERN YEOMAN	D1062 WESTERN COURIER
D1011 WESTERN THUNDERER	D1036 WESTERN EMPEROR	D1063 WESTERN MONITOR
D1012 WESTERN FIREBRAND	D1037 WESTERN EMPRESS	D1064 WESTERN REGENT
D1013 WESTERN RANGER	D1038 WESTERN SOVEREIGN	D1065 WESTERN CONSORT
D1014 WESTERN LEVIATHAN	D1039 WESTERN KING	D1066 WESTERN PREFECT
D1015 WESTERN CHAMPION	D1040 WESTERN QUEEN	D1067 WESTERN DRUID
D1015 SIR MISHA BLACK	D1041 WESTERN PRINCE	D1068 WESTERN RELIANCE
D1016 WESTERN GLADIATOR	D1042 WESTERN PRINCESS	D1069 WESTERN VANGUARD
D1017 WESTERN WARRIOR	D1043 WESTERN DUKE	D1070 WESTERN GAUNTLET
D1018 WESTERN BUCCANEER	D1044 WESTERN DUCHESS	D1071 WESTERN RENOWN
D1019 WESTERN CHALLENGER	D1045 WESTERN VISCOUNT	D1072 WESTERN GLORY
D1020 WESTERN HERO	D1046 WESTERN MARQUIS	D1073 WESTERN BULWARK
D1021 WESTERN CAVALIER	D1047 WESTERN LORD	
D1022 WESTERN SENTINEL	D1048 WESTERN LADY	
D1023 WESTERN FUSILIER	D1049 WESTERN MONARCH	
D1024 WESTERN HUNTSMAN	D1050 WESTERN RULER	
D1025 WESTERN GUARDSMAN	D1051 WESTERN AMBASSADOR	
D1026 WESTERN CENTURION	D1052 WESTERN VICEROY	
D1027 WESTERN LANCER	D1053 WESTERN PATRIARCH	

Nameplates were red on BR green, and black on all other liveries. D1013 ran with red nameplates in BR blue from May 1976. From the early 1970s the D prefix on the number panels were painted over on some locos.

D1029 had new nameplates fitted in 1969, after it was divulged that the first set had been spelt incorrectly. D1018 ran without a nameplate from 1971–72 after it was removed because of damage.

D1010 has run as D1035 *WESTERN YEOMAN* in preservation, while D1015 frequently runs on the main-line bearing number and nameplates from other Class 52s. It spent 07/03–02/05 renamed *SIR MISHA BLACK*.

BUILD BATCHES

1961–64	D1000–29	BR Swindon
1962–64	D1030–73	BR Crewe

D1030–34 were initially intended to be built at Swindon, but the work was transferred to Crewe. Locos were not delivered in numerical order.

ABOVE: A handful of Class 52s were painted in BR blue with small yellow panels, and this livery has been replicated in preservation, such as on D1048 WESTERN LADY. *PIP DUNN*

BELOW RIGHT: All Class 52s were vacuum-braked when new, but dual-braking started in 1968. However, only seventy of the fleet were upgraded, with D1017–20 left in original condition. D1020 WESTERN HERO *shows a BR blue Class 52 with vacuum brakes only. Those Class 52s which ran in BR blue with full yellow ends while vacuum-braked only were 1000/04–06/11/17–24/26/ 29/32/33/36/40/43/48–53/ 58–60/64/65/69/71–73, while vacuum-braked 1017/30/36/37/ 43/47/57 all ran in blue with small panels. The lack of an air-brake pipe above the steam pipe is an indication of whether a Class 52 was vacuum- or dual-braked.* RAIL PHOTOPRINTS

ONE OF SEVERAL prototype Type 4s built in the early 1960s, this Brush loco had the same Maybach MD655 engines as fitted to Class 52s, but with electric traction motors. Unlike most of the other prototypes, it was sold by its makers to BR in 1970 and became Class 53 under TOPS. It was overhauled after sale, and changed from vacuum brakes to air brakes only. It retained its steam-heat boiler, although this was isolated in late 1972. It ended its days as a freight loco in South Wales until withdrawal in 1975.

A clause in the contract when it was sold by Brush stipulated that it had to be scrapped when BR had finished with it, and despite interest from preservationists, this contractual obligation was undertaken in 1976.

DETAIL DIFFERENCES

The loco had a centre panel mounted centrally on its cab front. Its Spanner

The sole Class 53 in July 1967, in its days when it was still owned by Brush and on trial with BR. It is in the second of its three liveries, two-tone green. It is vacuum-braked and has had its MW removed, but retains its operational steam-heat boiler. It was withdrawn as air-braked only, with no train heating, and in BR blue numbered 1200. RAIL PHOTOPRINTS

Mk 3 train-heating boiler was removed in 1972, and while vacuum brakes initially, it was converted to air brakes only in 1970.

MW was Blue Star at new, but whether this equipment was ever used is highly debatable. It was removed during its early 1965 overhaul and the holes plated over.

LIVERIES

Light green with light brown solebar: D0280
BR green with small yellow panels: D0280
BR blue: 1200

NAME

1200   *FALCON*

The loco had large Falcon crests above the name. The name was made of separate letters fitted to a backing plate, which was then fitted to the loco side.

NUMBER

The loco was numbered D0280 while owned by Brush, and renumbered 1200 in December 1970 after sale to BR, but it was not given the number 53001, despite lasting into the TOPS era.

Original private number:	D0280
1957 BR number:	D1200
Built by:	Brush Ltd, Loughborough
Introduced on loan:	1961
Introduced to BR stock:	1970
Wheel arrangement:	Co-Co
Weight (operational):	115 tons
Height:	12ft 10in (3.91m)
Width:	8ft 9in (2.67m)
Length:	68ft 10in (20.98m)
Min. curve negotiable:	4 chains
Maximum speed:	100mph (160km/h)
Wheelbase:	56ft 5in (17.2m)
Bogie wheelbase:	14ft 11in (4.29m)
Bogie pivot centres:	42ft (12.8m)
Wheel diameter:	3ft 7in (1.09m)
Route availability:	6
Brake force:	59 tons
Engine type:	Two Maybach MD655
Engine horsepower:	2,800bhp (2,089kW)
Power at rail:	2,165bhp
Tractive effort:	60,000lb
Main generator type:	Two Brush TG110-56 Mk 2
Auxiliary generator type:	Two Brush TAG
No. of traction motors:	6
Traction motor type:	Brush TM73-68 Mk 2
Fuel tank capacity:	1,440gal (6,480ltr)

specifications

TOPS number range:	55001–022
1957 BR number range:	D9000–021
Former class codes:	D33/1, later 33/2
Built by:	English Electric, Vulcan Foundry
Years introduced:	1961–62
Wheel arrangement:	Co-Co
Weight:	100 tons
Height:	12ft 11in (3.94m)
Length:	69ft 6in (21.18m)
Width:	8ft 10in (2.68m)
Wheelbase:	59ft 6in (18.14m)
Bogie wheelbase:	13ft 6in (4.11m)
Bogie pivot centres:	45ft (13.72m)
Wheel diameter:	3ft 7in (1.09m)
Min. curve negotiable:	4 chains (80.46m)
Engine type:	Two Napier D18.25 'Deltic'
Engine output:	3,300bhp (2,460kW)
Power at rail:	2,460bhp (1,969kW)
Tractive effort:	50,000lb
Maximum speed:	100mph (160km/h)
Brake force:	51 tons
Route availability:	5
ETH index:	66
Main generator type:	Two English Electric EE829-1A
Auxiliary generator type:	Two English Electric EE913-1A
Traction motor type:	English Electric EE538A
No. of traction motors:	6
Gear ratio:	59:21
Fuel tank capacity:	826gal (3,717ltr), 1,626gal (7,317ltr): 55022

ABOVE RIGHT: D9000 ROYAL SCOTS GREY *in its post-BR main line days was painted in original style two-tone green with small yellow panels but had features of a later Deltic, namely filled-in quarter lights, ETH jumper and dual brakes. It also has, to meet group standards for main-line running, a high-intensity headlight, an orange cant rail stripe and an aerial on its nose for the NRN.* PIP DUNN

RIGHT: 55002 THE KING'S OWN YORKSHIRE LIGHT INFANTRY *was repainted back into two-tone green in 1980 for its last year in traffic, but had a full yellow end and retained yellow headcode panels, making it unique in Deltic history. The pipes were also painted white, and TOPS numbers were retained.* PDC

AFTER A SUCCESSFUL trial with a prototype locomotive from 1955, BR ordered twenty-two Class 55 Deltics in 1960, and they were delivered in 1961/62. They were fitted with two high-speed Napier Deltic engines, and were capable of 100mph (160km/h); they were for express passenger work on the ECML. They were ousted by HSTs, withdrawals starting in 1978 and completed in January 1982. Popular with enthusiasts, six were preserved, of which five have had spells on the main line, although currently just three are main-line registered.

DETAIL DIFFERENCES

Centre panels were fitted from new, although D9021 was initially delivered with white panels until roller blinds were fitted. From 1972 dominos were fitted to all locos. From 1976 yellow metal panels were fitted to 55001–007/009–019/021; 55008/020/022 were withdrawn with dominos.

Vacuum brakes were fitted from new, but all were converted to dual brakes: 9000/02/16/19–21 in 1967, 9001/03–15/17/18 in 1968. Train heating was the Spanner Mk 2 boiler from new, and all were upgraded to dual heat with fitting of ETH (index 66): 9003/09/10/21 in 1970; 9000–02/04–08/11–20 in 1971.

All were built with warning horns under their bufferbeams, apart from D9019–21, which had them mounted on the cab roof. In June 1966 D9007 had horns mounted in its nose ends as a trial, while D9018 had them mounted on the nose in front of the windows. After trials, the D9018 position was found to be the best, and all 55s had their horns moved to this position. D9007 lost its unique horns in September 1967. The bonnet-mounted horns were originally quite big on at least D9006/08, but were later changed to a smaller design with a mesh added over the end. Two small grilles were added into the cab window frames behind the horns in the mid-1970s.

All were built with twin wipers on each windscreen, but these were changed to single wipers on 55002/007–011/013–015/017/019/022 in the mid/late 1970s. Quarterlight windows were removed from 55001–019/021/022 in

the mid-1970s. They were refitted to 55009 (1998).

When new, the locos did not have two grilles above the nameplates but these were added in the early 1960s to give improved ventilation to the engine room. Those on 55011 differed by being a plain mesh style on one side.

55017 had the footwell above its bufferbeam removed at No. 1 end after an accident in January 1980. D9000 was fitted with xenon headlights in place of its front footwells in 1961 for trials, but they were removed soon after and the loco had welded panels with footwells

fitted which protruded slightly, making it easily distinguishable.

Headlights were fitted to 55002/009/019/022 for main-line running, while 55016 had its tail-lights removed and Bmac light clusters fitted in 1999 for main-line running. These were fitted while the loco was painted in Porterbrook colours, and initially retained when it reverted to BR green in 2003. They were removed in 2006 and standard Deltic tail-lights were refitted.

Radio aerials were also fitted on the nose ends on 55002/009/016/019/022 for main-line running on NR.

LIVERIES

All were delivered in two-tone green with the exception of D9020/21, which had small yellow warning panels added from new. These were retro-applied to D9000–19.

Full yellow ends on green were applied to some, and BR blue to all.

White window surrounds were given to six Finsbury Park 55s in 1979. Of these, 55003/012 were scrapped in this guise. The others lost them in June 1981, although 55015 had them reapplied for a few days in October 1981, and again in January 1982.

Two-tone green was reapplied to 55002 in 1980 and it featured yellow headcode panels and filled-in quarter lights – the only 55 to run in this condition. Post-BR, green has been reapplied to D9000/09/15/16/19 at various stages, but with roller blinds refitted. Only D9009 has had its quarter light window refitted. D9016/19 have run in BR green with full yellow ends in preservation.

9016 was painted in Porterbrook purple in 1999 but reverted to BR green in 2003.

BR green: D9000–19
BR green with half yellow ends: D9000–21
BR green with full yellow ends: D9001/03/05/07/09/10/11/12/14/15/17/18
BR blue: 55001–022
BR blue with white windows: 55003/007/009/012/015/018
BR green with full yellow ends (special): 55002
Porterbrook: 55016

EMBELLISHMENTS

York City crests were applied above the numbers of 55002–011/013–019/021/022.

In pre-blue BR days, all locos had their numbers on all four corners. Finsbury Park 55s also had this on TOPS numbers when window frames were painted white, namely 55003/007/009/012/015/018. These were retained after the white window frames were repainted in blue after June 1981 on 55007/009/015/018. York's 55019 also had numbers on all four corners.

Silver roof grilles, red bufferbeams and white-painted pipes were applied to 55005/009/013/015/022. 55015 was

The most radical change to a Class 55 occurred in 1999 when 9016 GORDON HIGHLANDER was overhauled with sponsorship by ROSCO Porterbrook: not only was the loco repainted into the company's purple livery, it also lost its tail-lights in favour of Bmac light clusters, while still retaining a four-character headcode. It was later repainted back into green while still retaining its light clusters, but these have since been removed and the loco now has a standard Class 55 end. PIP DUNN

55017 THE DURHAM LIGHT INFANTRY shows how many Class 55s looked in their final BR days. As well as now being dual-braked and dual-heated, it also features yellow plated headcode panels, single windscreen wipers, filled-in quarterlights and horns repositioned to the top of the nose. The other front end of 55017 was unique as the footwell was plated over after an accident. ANDY HOARE

fitted with commemorative plaques on its nose ends. In the final days, 55022 had its D9000 numbers reapplied (whilst retaining 55022 numbers in the standard position).

NAMES

D9000	55022	ROYAL SCOTS GREY
D9001	55001	ST PADDY
D9002	55002	THE KING'S OWN YORKSHIRE LIGHT INFANTRY
D9003	55003	MELD
D9004	55004	QUEEN'S OWN HIGHLANDER
D9005	55005	THE PRINCE OF WALES' OWN REGIMENT OF YORKSHIRE
D9006	55006	THE FIFE & FORFAR YEOMANRY
D9007	55007	PINZA
D9008	55008	THE GREEN HOWARDS
D9009	55009	ALYCIDON
D9010	55010	THE KING'S OWN SCOTTISH BORDERER
D9011	55011	THE ROYAL NORTHUMBERLAND FUSILIERS
D9012	55012	CREPELLO
D9013	55013	THE BLACK WATCH
D9014	55014	THE DUKE OF WELLINGTON'S REGIMENT
D9015	55015	TULYAR
D9016	55016	GORDON HIGHLANDER
D9017	55017	THE DURHAM LIGHT INFANTRY
D9018	55018	BALLYMOSS
D9019	55019	ROYAL HIGHLAND FUSILIER
D9020	55020	NIMBUS
D9021	55021	ARGYLL AND SUTHERLAND HIGHLANDER

The nameplates on the six NER Class 55s (D9002/05/08/11/14/17) were in a different font to that used on the Haymarket and Finsbury Park Deltics. D9002/05/06/10/11/14/17/19/21 had double-deck nameplates. D9000/04/06/08/10/16/19/21 had regimental crests above their nameplates, all of which were removed in BR days, apart from those on 55008.

NUMBERS

Locos were renumbered keeping their last three digits, so 9001–21 became 55001–021; 9000 became 55022.

In April 1968, D9006 THE FIFE & FORFAR YEOMANRY *is in the transition phase of the Class 55s. It has been dual-braked, although the air pipe unusually has a white cock rather than a red, but it is still steam-heat only; the ETH jumper head will be added above the air-brake hose mounted to the nose front to the right of the front footwell. The loco has the warning horns in their new position on the top of the bonnet, but they are the larger style of horn rather than the smaller style that became standard. There are also no grilles behind the horns, a later addition in the 1970s. By this time most 55s had been painted into BR blue, but those still in green had full yellow ends.* BILL WRIGHT

ABOVE: *D9009* ALYCIDON *was bought from BR in 1982 and in 1991 an overhaul was started to change it back to as near as possible original condition. This meant refitting quarterlights in the cab side windows, refitting double wipers and repositioning the ETH jumper 'out of sight'. Other retro-modifications were not possible, such as removing the air brakes or the grilles from above the nameplates.* PIP DUNN

LEFT: *In 1979, Finsbury Park depot staff painted white window surrounds on their six remaining Class 55s. Showing off the livery enhancement is 55007* PINZA *in 1980. They also had numbers on all four corners, which was not standard practice on Class 55s with TOPS numbers, although 55019 also ran like this in its final years.* PDC

THE FIRST PURPOSE-BUILT heavy freight loco design, the Class 56s were born out of the 1973 oil crisis, during which it was felt there could be an increased need for coal for power stations. The locos used a modified Class 47 body with a 16-cylinder Ruston engine derived from the English Electric 16CSVT.

The first thirty locos were built under contract by Romania manufacturer Electroputere. These locos arrived with many defects that needed addressing before they could enter traffic. The remaining 105 locos were built by BREL, eighty-five at Doncaster and the last twenty at Crewe.

DETAIL DIFFERENCES

The locos were built without any headcodes. No snowplough brackets were fitted. They had no train heating and air brakes only. MW was Red Diamond, with jumpers and receptacles mounted on the cab fronts.

The Class 56s use a modified Class 47 bodyshell with an additional large body-side grille at No. 1 end. The cabs on the thirty Romanian-built 56s featured side window quarterlights mounted with rubber. Doncaster/Crewe locos had them fitted into the metal window frames.

From 56056 onwards the horn grille on the cab front was changed to a protruding design featuring a full square of mesh, as opposed to a square plate with only a small rectangle of mesh at the lower half (although some 56s ran with these upside down).

From 56061 the headlight was changed from the small rubber-mounted sealed-beam headlight to a larger light mounted in a metal frame, in the same style as the Class 50s. Also from 56056, the red tail-lights and white marker lights protruded from the flat cab front.

The first thirty-two locos were built with bufferbeam cowling in the same style as the Class 47s, which curved round the side of the bufferbeam. The top section of this cowling was retained for 56033–055, but from 56056 it was omitted.

TOPS number range:	56001–135
Built by:	56001–030 Electroputere at Craiova in Romania 56031–115 BREL Doncaster 56116–135 BREL Crewe
Years introduced:	1976–84
Wheel arrangement:	Co-Co
Weight:	126 tons
Height:	13ft (3.96m)
Length:	63ft 6in (19.39m)
Width:	9ft 2in (2.79m)
Wheelbase:	47ft 10in (14.58m)
Bogie wheelbase:	13ft 6in (4.10m)
Bogie pivot centres:	37ft 8in (11.48m)
Wheel diameter:	3ft 9in (1.14m)
Min. curve negotiable:	4 chains (80.46m)
Engine type:	Ruston Paxman 16RK3CT
Engine output:	3,250bhp (2,420kW)
Power at rail:	2,400bhp (1,790kW)
Tractive effort:	61,800lb
Maximum speed:	80mph (128km/h)
Brake force:	60 tons
Route availability:	7
Main alternator type:	Brush BA1101A
Auxiliary alternator type:	Brush BAA602A
Traction motor type:	Brush TMH73-62
No. of traction motors:	6
Gear ratio:	63:16
Fuel tank capacity:	1,150gal (5,228ltr)

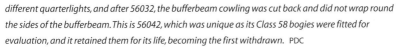

LEFT: The first thirty Class 56s were built in Romania and feature bufferbeam cowling, a small headlight, a flush horn grille, and indented tail and marker lights. The quarterlight windows were also mounted in rubber. 56001 is seven years old in this image and is still in as-built condition. PDC

BELOW: The first British-built Class 56s differed by having different quarterlights, and after 56032, the bufferbeam cowling was cut back and did not wrap round the sides of the bufferbeam. This is 56042, which was unique as its Class 58 bogies were fitted for evaluation, and it retained them for its life, becoming the first withdrawn. PDC

Due to collisions, 56004/014/029 had their cabs rebuilt to the later design – 56004 at both ends, 56014 at No. 2 end and 56029 at No. 1 end.

Roof-mounted flashing lights were fitted to 56073/074 as they were equipped with remote control for use at slow speed at power stations. The lights were removed when the locos were overhauled in 1988. 56032 had spotlamps mounted by its sealed beam headlights when used in France with Fertis.

CP1 bogies, as planned for the Class 58s, were fitted to 56042 to undergo evaluation. The 58s were then fitted with similar, but modified CP3 bogies.

Several had their headlights changed to the standard square-framed, round, high-intensity versions. Noted as such were 56003/006/031/035/037–041/043/ 045/046/049/050/052/057/068/094/095, although not always at both ends.

RIGHT: *From 56056 a new front end was devised with no bufferbeam cowling, also the tail and marker lights were no longer indented but now protruded from the body, and there was a new square horn grille which also protruded and had a bigger meshed area. From 56061 the headlight was changed to a larger, high-intensity type. 56073/074 were different in having roof-mounted flashing lights as they were fitted with trial remote-control operation, a feature that had previously been tested on 47277 and 47373. This 1984 view shows 56073, still in BR blue.* PDC

ABOVE: *The last twenty Class 56s were built by Crewe and only differed from the last Doncaster-built locos by having grey-painted bodyside grilles. 56131 is, unsurprisingly, still in as-built condition in this 1986 view, only being two years old.* PDC

RIGHT: *Trainload liveries were applied to many Class 56s, with Coal, Metals and Construction logos added – and one loco, 56036, erroneously having Trainload Petroleum logos applied. In Coal colours, 56087 is otherwise in as-built condition.* PDC

Others lost their rubber-mounted lights for the second-style lights, namely 56004/010/014/029, although all of these, apart from 56010, were as the result of having rebuilt cabs following collisions.

Buffers varied between round and oval, while some locos even had rectangular buffers such as 56030. Round buffers were fitted from new to the Romanian locos, while the British machines had oval – at least 56001/003–006/008–013/015/017–019/021/024/025/027/028 ran with oval buffers, 56007 had oblong, and 56034 had a spell with round buffers.

LIVERIES

BR blue: 56001–083
BR blue with grey roof: 56074
BR 'Large Logo': 56036/047–049/078/084–099, 56100–134
Railfreight with central badge: 56135
Railfreight: 56002/005–007/009/016–018/024/033–041/043/045/046/050/051/053/055–066/075/077/079/083–087/096, 56135

Red stripe Railfreight: 56011/019/044/048/049/052/067/068/076/088–090, 56100/107/108
Trainload Coal: 56001/005–007/009/012–018/021/023/025/027–030/047/054/066–069/071–077/079–099, 56100–102/104/106/107/109/111–135
Trainload Petroleum: 56036
Trainload Construction: 56001/016/031–035/037/039/041/043/045/046/050–053/055–060/062–065/070/078, 56103/105/110
Trainload Metals: 56032/038/040/043/044/053/054/060/061/064/069/073/076/087/097
Two-tone grey: 56011/054, 56108/121/131/133/135
'Dutch': 56031/036/046–049
'Dutch' Transrail: 56036/047/049
Loadhaul: 56003/006/021/027/034/035/045/050/055/074/077/083–085/090, 56100/102/106/107/109–112/116/118/130
Loadhaul unbranded: 56027
Transrail: 56007/010/018/022/025/029/033/037/038/040/044/052–054/056–058/060/064/066/070–073/076/079/086/092/093/099, 56101/103/113–115/119/121/123–125/127–129/132/132

EW&S: 56041/057/058/088/096, 56105/114/120
EWS: 56011/018/032/037/038/059/060/062/065/067–069/081/089/091/094/095, 56103/113/115/117/119
All-over steel blue: 56009
Fertis: 56007/018/031/032/038/049/051/059/060/062/065/069/074/078/090/091/095/096, 56103–106/113/115/117–119
Fastline Freight: 56301–303
All-over green: 56303
Hanson Traction purple: 56312
Hanson Traction grey: 56311
DCR grey: 56311/312
DCR green: 56303
Colas: 56087/094, 56302
Europhoenix: 56096

Black larger (8in) numbers; 56068 FO
Large white numbers: 56098 FR
Small numbers (where non-standard): 56055 FR
Black numbers on front: 56075 FO: 56078/079/081 B, 56086/091/093/097–099, 56101–104/110/113/119–121 BR
Red numbers on front: 56107 BR
Small numbers: 56055 FO

Cast Depot Emblems

Canton goat: 56071 FC; 56044/053/054/060/076 FM; 56001/034/044 FA; 56007/010/040/044/086/115, FT,
Leicester panther: 56060/062–065/078 FA; 56061 F
Thornaby kingfisher: 56069 FM
Toton cooling tower: 56003/005/009/012/014/017/023/025/028–030/073/075/081/082/084/085/089/090/093–100/109/112/114/115/121–123/129–132/134 FC; 56123/131/135 F; 56123/125 FT; 56047 C
Westbury horse: 56034/041/051/056 FA; 56036 FP

NAMES

56001	Whatley
56006	Ferrybridge 'C' Power Station
56012	Maltby Colliery
56028	West Burton Power Station
56030	Eggborough Power Station
56031	Merehead
56032	Sir De Morgannwg County of South Glamorgan
56033	Shotton Paper Mill
56034	Ogmore Castle Castell Ogwr
56035	Taff Merthyr
56037	Richard Trevithick
56038	Western Mail
56038	PATHFINDER TOURS 30 YEARS OF RAILTOURING 1973–2003
56039	ABP Port of Hull
56040	Oystermouth
56044	Cardiff Canton Quality Approved
56045	British Steel Shelton
56050	British Steel Teesside
56051	Isle of Grain
56052	The Cardiff Rod Mill
56053	Sir De Morgannwg Ganol County of Mid Glamorgan
56054	British Steel Llanwern
56057	British Fuels
56060	The Cardiff Rod Mill
56062	Mountsorrel

56063	Bardon Hill
56069	Thornaby TMD
56069	Wolverhampton Steel Terminal
56073	Tremorfa Steelworks
56074	Kellingley Colliery
56075	West Yorkshire Enterprise
56076	Blyth Power
56076	British Steel Trostre
56077	Thorpe Marsh Power Station
56078	Doncaster Enterprise
56080	Selby Coalfield
56086	The Magistrates Association
56087	ABP Port of Hull
56089	Ferrybridge 'C' Power Station
56091	Castle Donington Power Station
56091	Stanton
56093	The Institution of Mining Engineers
56094	Eggborough Power Station
56095	Harworth Colliery
56099	Fiddlers Ferry Power Station
56101	Mutual Improvement
56101	Frank Hornby
56103	Stora
56110	Croft
56112	Stainless Pioneer
56114	Maltby Colliery
56115	Bassetlaw
56115	Barry Needham
56117	Wilton Coalpower
56122	Wilton Coalpower
56123	Drax Power Station
56124	Blue Circle Cement

56128	West Burton Power Station
56130	Wardley Opencast
56131	Ellington Colliery
56132	Fina Energy
56133	Crewe Locomotive Works
56134	Blyth Power
56135	Port of Tyne Authority
56302	Wilson Walshe
56312	ARTEMIS

NUMBERS

The three Class 56s overhauled by Brush for Fastline Freight were renumbered in the 56/3 series on account of reliability improvements made to them. This same number series was adopted by Hanson Traction (now part of Devon and Cornwall Railways) for its resurrected ex-EWS Class 56s, although its locos started at 56311.

56301	56045	Preserved (main line registered)
56302	56124	On hire to Colas
56303	56125	Owned by DCR
56311	56057	Owned by DCR
56312	56003	Owned by DCR
56313	56128	Number not taken up, loco stored, owned by DCR
56314	56114	Number not taken up, loco since scrapped

ABOVE: 56038 was one of the earlier Doncaster-built Class 56s, but featured a number of changes aside from being in EWS livery. The tail-lights are now LED-style, though the marker lights remain the same, but the small rubber-mounted sealed-beam headlight has been swapped for a BR-style standard high-intensity version. ANTHONY HICKS

LEFT: Three Class 56s were operated by Fastline freight: two that it owned outright, and one that was leased. The first two locos were fully overhauled by Brush and renumbered in the 56/3 series. Fastline folded in 2010 and the locos were sold by the administrators and are now used for spot hire. 56302, formerly 56124, is still in as-built condition apart from its livery. It is now in traffic with Colas and has been painted in its livery. PIP DUNN

TOPS number range:	57001–012, 57301–316, 57601–605
Rebuilt by:	Brush Traction
Originally built by:	Brush
Years introduced:	1998–2005
Wheel arrangement:	Co-Co
Weight:	120.6 tons
Height:	12ft 10in (3.91m)
Length:	63ft 6in (19.38m)
Width:	9ft 2in (2.79m)
Wheelbase:	51ft 6in (15.69m)
Bogie wheelbase:	14ft 6in (4.41m)
Bogie pivot centres:	37ft (11.27m)
Wheel diameter:	3ft 9in (1.14m)
Min. curve negotiable:	4 chains (80.46m)
Engine type:	General Motors 645-12E3 (57/0) General Motors 645-12F3B (57/3)
Engine output:	2,500bhp (1,860kW) (57/0) 2,750bhp (2,051kW) (57/3)
Power at rail:	2,025bhp (1,507kW) (57/0) 2,200bhp (1,640kW) (57/3)
Tractive effort:	55,000lb
Maximum speed:	75mph (121km/h) 95mph (153km/h)
Brake force:	80 tons
Route availability:	6
Main alternator type:	Brush BA1101D (57/0) Brush BA1101F (57/3)
Auxiliary alternator type:	Brush BAA602A
ETH alternator type:	Brush BAA
Traction motor type:	Brush TM68-46
No. of traction motors:	6
Gear ratio:	66:17
Fuel tank capacity:	1,221gal (5,551ltr): 57/0; 1,308gal (5,887ltr): 57/3; 727gal (3,273ltr): 57/6

ABOVE: In April 2001, 57601 emerged from Brush's Loughborough works as the first ETH Class 57; its development and construction were financed by Porterbrook initially as a demonstrator loco to passenger TOCs. It was used by First Great Western in the beginning, but was sold to West Coast Railways in April 2003, although it was still used by FGW for some months thereafter until its own 57/6s arrived. This May 2002 view shows the loco's flush front and new-style lights – something not perpetuated on the Freightliner Class 57/0s. PIP DUNN

RIGHT: Virgin Trains ordered twelve Class 57s for Thunderbird rescue duties in early 2002, and the first, 57301, emerged in June 2002. They had a slightly uprated engine compared with 57601. Initially 57301 was painted green and was to be numbered 57611, but Virgin chose this livery and number series during the construction. It sports a Virgin Trains badge on its front. Four more 57/3s were later ordered. PIP DUNN

LEFT: It was soon decided that the 57/3s would be better suited for their role if they were able to couple directly to a Class 221 or 390, so the fleet was retro-modified with Dellner couplers. This required a section being cut into the cab front to house the retractable couplers, which were lowered through 90 degrees to allow them to hitch to a 390. 57313–316 were fitted with them at the same time as conversion from Class 47s. PIP DUNN

THE CLASS 57 was a low cost option for Freightliner to get more modern technology in its early days of operating. Using a Class 47 body and bogies, the old Sulzer engine and generator were removed and replaced by a refurbished second-hand General Motors engine married to an overhauled Class 56 alternator.

The first twelve locos – built in two batches – had no train heating and were built to order, though further orders for another eighteen locos were not taken up. Porterbrook and Brush financed the conversion of the first ETH Class 57, 57601, and this demonstrator loco went on hire to Great Western. It prompted Virgin to order twelve, and then later another four locos, and FGW to take four locos of its own. These became 57/3s and 57/6s respectively.

All the 57/3s have now been dispersed to other operators, with DRS (six), Network Rail (six) and West Coast Railways (four) now using them; FGW's four-strong fleet remains constant.

DETAIL DIFFERENCES

The original Class 57/0s retained their front ends with original tail-lights, high intensity headlights and headcode box panels. Of these, 57001/004/012 had their No.1 headcode boxes removed and replaced by a flush front, and 57009 likewise at No.2 end. All had their skirts removed if they were retained at the time of entering works for conversion.

When moved to DRS they had their tail-lights changed to LEDs, a feature also undertaken on 57001, leaving just 57005/006 with original tail-lights. All but 57001 have white LED marker lights; 57001 retains the original white lamps.

Sandboxes were fitted to 57001–012 at conversion. Green Circle MW was fitted to 57002–004/007–012 by DRS. The other three 57/0s have no multiple working.

When 57601 appeared, its front ends were tidied up with headcode boxes, lamps and tail-lights removed, and a new flush front and two large headlights just above the buffer, and two LED lights next to them which can display red tail-lights or white marker lights. This front end was adopted for the remaining 57/3 and 57/6 conversions.

Snowplough brackets have been fitted to 57602–605: they usually have only the side ploughs of a standard three-piece miniature snowplough fitted, but sometimes carry the centre ploughs. They are yellow except on 57604, which has them painted black.

The most noticeable detail change was the fitting of Dellner couplers to the Virgin locos. The first twelve locos were retro-modified with the couplers fitted to the cab fronts, with the later

four having them from new. 57301/302 were the first to be done in 2003, with 57303–313 all fitted in 2004.

57307/312–316 and 57602–605 had ETH fitted at the time of conversion, while 57001–003/005–007/009–011, 57313/314, 57603 had the vacuum brakes removed from their donor locos.

Apart from the 57/0s and 57/6s owned by WCR (57001/005/006, 57601), all 57s now have a modified cooler group with a new aluminium mesh grille fitted above the cant rail at No1.end.

57313–316 were sold to WCR in January 2013, and had their Dellner couplers removed before changing hands. It is expected they will be repainted into WCR maroon.

LIVERIES

Freightliner: 57001–012
Porterbrook silver: 57601
WCR light maroon with black stripe: 57601
WCR maroon: 57001/006, 57601
Virgin silver: 57301–316
Arriva: 57314/315
Arriva unbranded: 57313/316
Great Western green: 57602–605
First Group purple: 57602–605
GWR green: 57604
DRS Compass: 57002–004/007–012, 57302/304/307–309/311
DRS Compass with Colas logos: 57002
DRS Compass with cable thieves awareness branding: 57307
Advenza blue: 57005/006

Network Rail yellow: 57301/303/305/306/310/312

RENUMBERINGS

The Class 57s were built using bodies from Class 47s. The donor locos were as follows:

Number	Rebuilt from	Outshopped
57001	47356	1998
57002	47322	1998
57003	47317	1999
57004	47347	1999
57005	47350	1999
57006	47187	1999
57007	47332	1999
57008	47204	1999
57009	47079	1999
57010	47329	2000
57011	47231	2000
57012	47060	2000
57301	47845	2002
57302	47827	2002
57303	47705	2003
57304	47807	2003
57305	47822	2003
57306	47814	2003
57307	47225	2003
57308	47846	2003
57309	47806	2003
57310	47831	2003
57311	47817	2003
57312	47330	2003
57313	47371	2004
57314	47372	2004
57315	47234	2004

The first Class 57 conversions were for Freightliner and they kept their Class 47 front ends. Of this dozen, nine are now in use with DRS and three with WCR, one of which is withdrawn. 57004 shows the Green Circle MW receptacle in its headcode box, and the modified cooler croup grilles on the roof at No.1 end. ANTHONY HICKS

57316	47290	2004
57601	47825	2001
57602	47337	2003
57603	47349	2003
57604	47209	2004
57605	47206	2004

NAMES

57001	Freightliner Pioneer
57002	Freightliner Phoenix
57003	Freightliner Evolution
57004	Freightliner Quality
57005	Freightliner Excellence
57006	Freightliner Reliance
57007	Freightliner Bond
57008	Freightliner Explorer
57008	Telford International Railfreight Park June 2009
57009	Freightliner Venturer
57010	Freightliner Crusader
57011	Freightliner Challenger
57012	Freightliner Envoy
57301	SCOTT TRACY
57302	VIRGIL TRACY
57302	Chad Varah
57303	ALAN TRACY
57304	GORDON TRACY
57304	Pride of Cheshire
57305	JOHN TRACY
57306	JEFF TRACY
57307	LADY PENELOPE
57308	TIN TIN
57309	BRAINS
57309	Pride of Crewe
57310	KYRANO
57311	PARKER
57312	THE HOOD
57312	Peter Henderson
57313	TRACY ISLAND
57314	FIREFLY
57315	THE MOLE
57316	FAB1
57602	Restormel Castle
57603	Tintagel Castle
57604	PENDENNIS CASTLE
57605	Totnes Castle

Nameplate Styles

All the Freightliner, DRS, FGW and Network Rail locos had their names in standard BR-style font, the exceptions being 57008's second name, which was in smaller font on a double-deck nameplate, and 57604 which, when repainted in GWT green, had new plates cast in GWR style.

57602–605 had their numbers on cast plates when first overhauled, and 57602/603/605 retain these, 57604 having had them changed to GWR-style cast numberplates.

The sixteen Virgin locos all had nameplates in upper case with the red Thunderbirds logo above the name incorporated in the plate, plus a separate plaque above them with the International Rescue logo. All were black plates apart from 57307, whose plates were painted pink. All were removed when repainted into DRS, WCR or Arriva colours, apart from 57307 which retained its pink plates.

The first ETH Class 57 was a demonstrator loco financed by Porterbrook and Brush. After its role was over it was sold to charter operator West Coast Railways, which has recently acquired four Class 57/3s as well as three 57/0s. The loco was initially painted in this maroon livery with a black stripe. It is now in standard WCR maroon. ANTHONY HICKS

class 58

specifications

TOPS number range:	58001–050	Engine type:	Ruston Paxman 12RK3ACT
Built by:	BREL Doncaster	Engine output:	3,300bhp (2,460kW)
Years introduced:	1983–87	Power at rail:	2,387bhp (1,780kW)
Wheel arrangement:	Co-Co	Tractive effort:	61,800lb
Weight:	130 tons	Maximum speed:	80mph (128km/h)
Height:	12ft 10in (3.91m)	Brake force:	60 tons
Length:	62ft 10in (19.13m)	Route availability:	7
Width:	9ft 1in (2.72m)	Main alternator type:	Brush BA1101B
Wheelbase:	48ft 9in (14.85m)	Auxiliary alternator type:	Brush BAA602B
Bogie wheelbase:	13ft 9in (4.18m)	Traction motor type:	Brush TM73-62
Bogie pivot centres:	35ft 6in (10.80m)	No. of traction motors:	6
Wheel diameter:	3ft 8in (1.12m)	Gear ratio:	63:16
Min. curve negotiable:	4 chains (80.46m)	Fuel tank capacity:	927gal (4,214ltr)

A DEVELOPMENT OF the Class 56, the Class 58 freight locos were a wholly new modular design with an eye on export markers. They had a relatively short life in the UK, with withdrawals starting in 1999 and completed by 2002, although thirty-six were later moved to the Netherlands, Spain and France. Currently just nine are in use in Spain, with three more stored and twenty-four stored in France. One has been preserved and five scrapped.

DETAIL DIFFERENCES

The 58s had no headcodes, but all were fitted with snowplough brackets although none was ever fitted with three-piece snowploughs. They had no train heating and air brakes only. Red Diamond MW was mounted on the cab.

58001–014 initially had no handles on their engine-room doors. 58036–050 had small cab ventilation grilles on the cabsides to the top left of the numbers.

From 58030 onwards, a panel was added by the cabside handles to give the traincrew protection from the elements when climbing aboard. These were retro-fitted to at least 58001/005/010/013/017/025.

The first thirty-five had CP3 bogies – a development of the CP1 bogies tested under 56042 – while the last fifteen had CP3a bogies, which had sandboxes fitted on the outer sides under the cabs.

58050 – the last diesel built by a BR workshop – was fitted with separate excited traction motors from new as a trial to address wheelslip issues.

EXPORT DIFFERENCES

The three locos sent on hire to ACTS in the Netherlands – 58038/039/044 – had an additional BR-style high intensity headlight fitted on the left-hand side of the cab fronts below the marker light cluster. They then had the white marker light plated over but red tail-lights retained. They were renumbered 5814/11/12 respectively.

The locos that were moved to Spain for use with GIF – namely 58020/024/025/029–031/041/043 – had an additional spotlight fitted just below and in between the cab windows. These were not fitted to those locos that went directly to Continental Rail.

Liveries aside, there were external differences to the locos sent to France for Fertis, SECO, TSO or ETF.

LIVERIES

Red stripe Railfreight: 58001–050
Trainload Coal: 58001–050
Two-tone grey: 58001/002/004/006–008/011/014–016/018/021/023–025/027/028/031/032/034–038/040/041/043/047–049
Two-tone grey with Mainline logos: 58001–020/022/024–031/033–045/047–049
Mainline Freight blue: 58002/005/008/014/021/023/032/036/038/042/046/050

Mainline Freight blue unbranded: 58013
EW&S (high band): 58033
EW&S (middle band): 58016/024/048/049
EWS: 58030/037/039/047/050
GIF: 58020/024/025/029–031/041/043
Continental Rail: 58015/020/024/025/029–031/041/043/047/049/050
Fertis: 58004/010/011/015/016/018/021/032/034/035/046
SECO Rail: 58007/009/027/040
TSO yellow: 58033/047/049/050
ACTS blue and yellow: 58039/044
Vos Logistics black and orange: 58038
ETF yellow: 58001/005/006/013/021/032/036/038/039/042/044/048
TSO (second version): 58004/007/009–011/018/026/033–035/040/046

Door-swapping by maintenance staff also led to locos having doors in different liveries, so the Trainload Coal emblems were sometimes incomplete or separated, thus giving a haphazard appearance.

NAMES

58002	*Daw Mill Colliery*
58003	*Markham Colliery*
58005	*Ironbridge Power Station*
58007	*Drakelow Power Station*
58011	*Worksop Depot*
58014	*Didcot Power Station*
58017	*Eastleigh Depot*
58018	*High Marnham Power Station*
58019	*Shirebrook Depot*
58020	*Doncaster Works*
58021	*Hither Green Depot*
58023	*Peterborough Depot*
58031	*Caballero Ferroviario*
58032	*Thoresby Colliery*
58034	*Bassetlaw*

ABOVE: 58001, in original red stripe Railfreight colours in July 2003, has been retro-fitted with panels on the door handles to protect staff from the weather when climbing aboard. Some of the doors are from later locos as they have handles fitted; the early locos relied on standard carriage keys to open the panels and radiator grilles. PIP DUNN

RIGHT: The Class 58s, being a small fleet, were soon deemed non-standard and withdrawals started in 1999, ending in 2002. However, several have been used in the Netherlands, Spain and France on hire contracts. Twelve were sent by EWS/DBS to Spain, and the first locos were painted in GIF light blue livery, as seen on 58041. This is one of the second batch of 58s which differed by having ventilation grilles on the cabsides, and had sandboxes on their bogies. The loco also has door handles along its bodyside. PIP DUNN

ABOVE LEFT: Three Class 58s were hired to Dutch operator ACTS: two were painted in its blue and yellow colours, and a third in Vos Logistics black. 5811, formerly 58039, shows the additional headlight fitted to the left-hand side of the cab front; the white marker lights have been plated over. Other than these modifications, the loco is a standard second batch Class 58. PIP DUNN

ABOVE RIGHT: In the Trainload era all fifty Class 58s were allocated to Trainload Coal, whose livery was carried by the entire fleet. As the Trainload sectors were recast into the three regional freight companies in readiness for privatization, the 58s all moved to Mainline Freight and lost their black diamond logos for Mainline Freight locos, although several ran for periods in plain two-tone grey. In 1989, 58016 has yet to have the panels added to the door grab handles. PDC

58037	*Worksop Depot*
58039	*Rugeley Power Station*
58040	*Cottam Power Station*
58041	*Ratcliffe Power Station*
58042	*Ironbridge Power Station*
58042	*Petrolea*
58043	*Knottingley*
58044	*Oxcroft Opencast*
58046	*Thoresby Colliery*
56046	*Asfordby Mine*
58047	*Manton Colliery*
58048	*Coventry Colliery*
58049	*Littleton Colliery*
58050	*Toton Traction Depot*

58020/039–042/050 had cast Railfreight plates on their cab ends in FO and FC liveries.

Several of the nameplates had company logos incorporated within the plates. 58020 initially had plates with BRE, although they were later changed to just plain *Doncaster Works*.

58014/018/039–042 had the CEGB logo on the top left of the plates. 58002/003/019/032/047–049 had the British Coal logo. 58046, when renamed *Asfordby Mine*, had the RJB logo incorporated. 58044 also had a British Coal Opencast tree logo on its nameplate, while 58041 later had new plates with the Powergen logo instead.

The CEGB logos were later removed (by being ground out) from the *Ironbridge Power Station* nameplates when refitted to 58005 in ML.

58034 had a Bassetlaw coat of arms on a separate plaque above its nameplate, while 58007 had a Powergen logo on a separate plaque below its nameplates.

58017 was initially named with an Eastleigh spitfire diamond plaque under its nameplate, but later had cast nameplates incorporating the spitfire on the top left. 58021 was similar in having the Hither Green oast house symbol incorporated in its nameplate as well as having separate diamond oast house plaques on its cab sides.

DEPOT PLAQUES

Eastleigh spitfire: 58017 FML
Hither Green oast house: 58021 ML
Toton cooling tower: 58002/003/008–018/021–024/027/029/031–033/037/038/044/045/050 FC; 58008/038/042/046/050 ML; 58001/006/024–026/031/033/045 FML; 58001/002/008/036 F; of these, 58002/014/018/050 had small plaques fitted to bodyside doors, 58003 to the cab doors, and 58001/008–013/015–017/021/022/024–027/029/031–033/036/037/038/044–046 had small plaques on the secondman's cabside, 58023 had large plaques on the secondman's cabsides, while 58021/038/042 had their plaques moved to the driver's cabside in ML livery. 58020 had an unofficial sticky Saltley seagull diamond added to its cabside door in 2002.

BUILD BATCHES

The locos were built in two batches, 58001–035 and 58036–050, but all at the Doncaster works, and production did not stop in between the two batches.

Several 58s were painted into Mainline Freight blue, including 58005 which inherited the Ironbridge Power Station nameplates bestowed originally on 58042. The loco also has doors from a later Class 58 fitted as they have door handles. PDC

THE CLASS 59s were the first privately owned diesel locos to run on BR: four were ordered by Foster Yeoman from General Motors in the USA and delivered in 1986, and a fifth in 1989. This led to Amey Roadstone ordering four of its own; these had slight cosmetic differences. A third batch was ordered by National Power and delivered in 1995, although these were bought by EWS (now DB Schenker) in 1998. One, 59003, has been exported and now works in Germany, but the other fourteen remain in the UK, mostly working stone trains from the Mendips, although the Class 59/2s have been tried on other work.

DETAIL DIFFERENCES

The Class 59/0s had a pair of centrally mounted headlights fitted below the cab windows. The cab was mounted on a section with the MW jumper cable receptacle directly underneath it. 59s can only 'multi' with 59s, 66s and 67s.

A vertical light cluster was fitted above each of the four buffers, which had a red tail-light above a white marker light.

The Class 59/1s have Bmac-style light clusters above each buffer and no central headlights, and so the MW socket was fitted centrally on the cab front.

specifications

TOPS number range:	59001–005, 59101–104, 59201–206
Construction model (GM):	JT26CW-SS
Built by:	GM-EMD, La Grange, Illinois, USA
Years introduced:	1985/89: 59/0; 1990: 59/1; 1994–95: 59/2
Wheel arrangement:	Co-Co
Weight:	121 tons
Height:	12ft 10in (3.91m)
Length:	70ft (21.40m)
Width:	8ft 8in (2.65m)
Wheelbase:	56ft 9in (17.29m)
Bogie wheelbase:	13ft 7in (4.15m)
Bogie pivot centres:	43ft 6in (13.25m)
Wheel diameter:	3ft 6in (1.06m)
Min. curve negotiable:	4 chains (80.46m)
Engine type:	EMD 16-645E3C
Engine output:	3,000bhp (2,238kW)
Power at rail:	2,533bhp (1,889kW)
Tractive effort:	122,000lb
Maximum speed:	60mph (96km/h)
Brake force:	69 tons
Route availability:	7
Traction alternator:	EMD AR11
Companion alternator:	EMD D14A
Auxiliary alternator:	EMD 3A8147
Traction motor type:	EMD D77B
No. of traction motors:	6
Gear ratio:	62:15
Fuel tank capacity:	1,000gal (4,546ltr)

One of the original five Class 59/0s, 59005 Kenneth J Painter *sports the revised Foster Yeoman livery. The front end has two headlights above the MW receptacle, and the yellow bufferbeam is deemed to meet group standards.* PIP DUNN

The 59/2s, which were slightly different in their structural design to meet Group Standards, were all fitted with drop-head buckeye couplers from new; all these are now removed. 59001 and 59201 have bells above their cab windows at No. 1 end.

LIVERIES

Yeoman: 59001–005
ARC: 59101–104
Revised Yeoman: 59002/004
Revised ARC: 59101–104
National Power: 59201–206
EWS: 59201–206
Hanson: 59101–104
Mendip Rail: 59002
Railpower: 59003
Aggregates Industries: 59001
Aggregates Industries revised: 59001/005
DB Schenker: 59201–206

The second batch of 59s were the four 59/1s for ARC, which differed by having Bmac light clusters and now central headlights, as seen in 59101 Village of Whatley *in Hanson Aggregates livery in June 2001.* PIP DUNN

NAMES

59001	*YEOMAN ENDEAVOUR*	
59002	*YEOMAN ENTERPRISE*	
59002	*ALAN J DAY*	

59003	*YEOMAN HIGHLANDER*	
59004	*YEOMAN CHALLENGER*	
59004	*PAUL A HAMMOND*	
59005	*KENNETH J PAINTER*	
59101	*Village of Whatley*	

59102	*Village of Chantry*
59103	*Village of Mells*
59104	*Village of Great Elm*
59201	*Vale of York*
59202	*Vale of White Horse*
59203	*Vale of Pickering*
59204	*Vale of Glamorgan*
59205	*Vale of Evesham*
59205	*L Keith McNair*
59206	*Pride of Ferrybridge*
59206	*John F Yeoman Rail Pioneer*

All nameplates were fitted to the secondman's cabside, while the Class 59/0 and 59/1s had cast numberplates under the driver's windows.

These were also fitted to the 59/2s in their National Power days, but when repainted into EWS colours the nameplates were moved to the driver's cabside and the numbers applied on the bodysides. The NP 59/2s had cast data panels, which were also fitted to some 59/0s and 59/1s.

ABOVE: *The six Class 59/2s were bought by National Power and painted in its livery, which had definite similarities to Network SouthEast. 59203* Vale of Pickering *shows an as-built 59/2. In April 1998 the six locos were sold to EWS and repainted in its livery, but now all six are in DB Schenker red.* ANTHONY HICKS

RIGHT: *59101 shows off the mustard livery bestowed on the four Class 59/1s when new, a livery that is no more. The loco's Bmac light clusters are yellow and the cab is grey.* PDC

BELOW: *All six Class 59/2s have now been painted into DB Schenker red, and a handful of Class 66s – five by April 2013 – were similarly repainted. 59201, complete with its commemorative bell on the cab front, leads 59206. Although the 66s shared the same body as the 59s, there are subtle differences, namely the 59s retain the flat horn grille on the cab roof and do not have lifting points on the bufferbeam or swinghead couplers.* NATHAN SEDDON

THE LAST MAIN-LINE diesel type built for British Rail, the 100 Class 60s were bespoke freight locos for heavy haulage, and so were geared for a 62mph (99km/h) top speed. The bodies were made by Procor at Wakefield and then moved to Brush at Loughborough, where the locos were then assembled.

The first locos emerged in 1989, but it was 1991 when the last rolled off the production line, and as late as 1993 when the last were accepted by BR after teething problems.

All were acquired by EWS in 1996, but it withdrew two in 2004 after just eleven years in traffic, and withdrawals have been steady, with the fleet once down to just four working locos. However, more recently overhauls have restarted and twenty-two have been refurbished, with others following.

Liveries and names aside, detail differences between the fleet are few.

DETAIL DIFFERENCES

All locos are fitted with one-piece snow-ploughs, which are usually painted black except for 60016/039 which have yellow ploughs.

60002–005/007/009/010/012/015/017/020–028/030/037/038/041/042/046/047/049–056/058/059/064/067/070/071/077/080/081/089–091/096–098 are fitted with 1,150gal (5,228ltr) fuel tanks.

Overhauled locos as at January 2013 were 60001/007/010/015/017/019/020/039/040/054/059/062/063/074/079/091/092. Although in DBS red, 60011 has not been overhauled but has had reliability modifications, as has 60099. Due to be overhauled are 60024/044/096, 60100, and others could follow.

The MW on the 60s was within the class only and a receptacle is mounted on the cab front covered by a panel.

LIVERIES

Trainload Petroleum: 60002/003/007/013/014/024–028/033/051/053/054/062–065

Trainload Construction: 60001/005/006/009–012/015–019/039–043/048/080–085/094–099, 60100

Trainload Metals: 60008/020–023/029–031/034–038/044/049/050/052/081/093

Trainload Coal: 60004/032/045–047/055–061/066–079/086–093

Two-tone grey: 60006/010/013/015/021/028/042/046/050/067–069/079/087/095

Two-tone grey with Mainline logos: 60001/006/009–012/017–019/039–044/048/071–079/083/086–088/094/098/099, 60100

Two-tone grey with Loadhaul logos: 60050/064/070

Two-tone grey with Transrail branding and Trainload Coal symbols: 60066

Loadhaul: 60007/008/025/038/059

Mainline Freight aircraft blue: 60011/044/078

Mainline Freight aircraft blue unbranded: 60011

Transrail: 60005/015/029/032–037/045–047/055/056/058/061–063/065/066/080–082/084/085/089/092/093/096/097

Undercoat: 60022

EW&S: 60004/010/012/017/019/020/024/026/027/040/041/047/049/050/098

EWS: 60001–003/005/008/009/016/018/021–023/025/029–031/035–039/042/043/045/048/051–053/058/062/065/069/071/075/080/083/085/087/089/093/094/096/097, 60100, 60500

British Steel blue: 60006/033
Corus silver: 60006/033
GWR green: 60081
Two-tone grey/EWS logos: 60013–015/028/034/046/055–057/060/063/066–068/072–074/076/077/079/082/084/086/088/090–092/095/099
Loadhaul/EWS logos: 60007/059
Mainline/EWS logos: 60044/078
Territorial Army maroon: 60040
Teenage Cancer Trust light blue: 60074
Tata Steel silver: 60099
DBS red: 60001/010/011/015/017/019/020/039/040/054/059/062/063/079/091/092
DBS red with 'Switch on to safety' branding: 60007

Cast Depot Emblems

Canton goat: 60092 FC; 60034/035/093 FM; 60065 FP; 60015/032/033/037/063/081/096 FT
Immingham star: 60002 FP; 60090 FC; 60028 F
Stewarts Lane power station: 60018/039/040/042 FA

specifications	
TOPS number range:	60001–100, 60500
Built by:	Brush Traction, Loughborough
Years introduced:	1989–93
Wheel arrangement:	Co-Co
Weight:	129–130 tons
Height:	12ft 11in (3.95m)
Length:	70ft (21.34m)
Width:	8ft 8in (2.64 m)
Wheelbase:	56ft 3in (17.15m)
Bogie wheelbase:	13ft 7in (4.13m)
Bogie pivot centres:	42ft 10in (13.02m)
Wheel diameter:	3ft 7in (1.18m)
Min. curve negotiable:	4 chains (80.46m)
Engine type:	Mirrlees MB275T
Engine output:	3,100bhp (2,240kW)
Power at rail:	2,415bhp (1,800kW)
Tractive effort:	106,500lb
Maximum speed:	62mph (99km/h)
Brake force:	74 tons
Route availability:	7
Main alternator type:	Brush BA1000
Auxiliary alternator type:	Brush BAA700
Traction motor type:	Brush TM216
No. of traction motors:	6
Gear ratio:	19:97
Fuel tank capacity:	990gal (4,500ltr)

60004 in the first version of EWS livery with EW&S branding. Other than liveries, there have been few changes to the Class 60 fleet. PIP DUNN

Hither Green oast house: 60001 FA
Thornaby kingfisher: 60021/030/031
FM; 60021/050 F; 60050 FLH
Toton cooling tower: 60006 FML;
60006 F; 60032/092/093 FC

60081 had cast GWR-style numberplates
when repainted in GWR green in 2000.

NAMES

60001	Steadfast
60001	The Railway Observer
60002	Capability Brown
60002	High Peak
60003	Christopher Wren
60003	FREIGHT TRANSPORT ASSOCIATION
60004	Lochnagar
60005	Skiddaw
60005	BP Gas Avonmouth
60006	Great Gable
60006	Scunthorpe Ironmaster
60007	Robert Adam
60007	The Spirit of Tom Kendall
60008	Moel Fammau
60008	GYPSUM QUEEN II
60008	Sir William McAlpine
60009	Carnedd Dafydd
60010	Pumlumon Plynlimon
60011	Cader Idris
60012	Glyder Fawr
60013	Robert Boyle
60014	Alexander Fleming
60015	Bow Fell
60016	Langdale Pikes
60016	RAIL Magazine
60017	Arenig Fawr
60017	Shotton Works Centenary Year 1996
60018	Moel Siabod
60019	Wild Boar Fell
60019	PATHFINDER TOURS 30 YEARS OF RAILTOURING 1973–2003

60019	Port of Grimsby & Immingham
60020	Great Whernside
60021	Pen-y-Ghent
60021	Star of the East
60022	Ingleborough
60023	The Cheviot
60024	Elizabeth Fry
60025	Joseph Lister
60025	Caledonian Paper
60026	William Caxton
60027	Joseph Banks
60028	John Flamsteed
60029	Ben Nevis
60029	Clitheroe Castle
60030	Cir Mhor
60031	Ben Lui
60031	ABP Connect
60032	William Booth
60033	Anthony Ashley Cooper
60033	Tees Steel Express
60034	Carnedd Llewelyn
60035	Florence Nightingale
60036	Sgurr Na Ciche
60036	GEFCO
60037	Helvellyn
60037	Aberddawan Aberthaw
60038	Bidean Nam Bian
60038	AvestaPolarit
60039	Glastonbury Tor
60040	Brecon Beacons
60040	The Territorial Army Centenary
60041	High Willhays
60042	Dunkery Beacon
60042	The Hundred of Hoo
60043	Yes Tor
60044	Ailsa Craig
60045	Josephine Butler
60045	The Permanent Way Institution
60046	William Wilberforce
60047	Robert Owen
60048	Saddleback
60048	Eastern
60049	Scafell
60050	Roseberry Topping

60051	Mary Somerville
60052	Goat Fell
60052	Glofa Twr The last deep mine in Wales Tower Colliery
60053	John Reith
60053	Nordic Terminal
60054	Charles Babbage
60055	Thomas Barnardo
60056	William Beveridge
60057	Adam Smith
60058	John Howard
60059	Samuel Plimsoll
60059	Swinden Dalesman
60060	James Watt
60061	Alexander Graham Bell
60062	Samuel Johnson
60063	James Murray
60064	Back Tor
60065	Kinder Low
60065	SPIRIT OF JAGUAR
60066	John Logie Baird
60067	James Clerk-Maxwell
60068	Charles Darwin
60069	Humphry Davy
60069	Slioch
60070	John Loudon Mcadam
60071	Dorothy Garrod
60071	Ribblehead Viaduct
60072	Cairn Toul
60073	Cairn Gorm
60074	Braeriach
60074	Teenage Spirit
60075	Liathach
60076	Suliven
60077	Canisp
60078	Stac Pollaidh
60079	Foinaven
60080	Kinder Scout
60080	Cloudside Junior School, Sandiacre EWS Rail Safety Competition Winners 2001
60080	Little Eaton Primary School EWS Rail Safety Competition Winners 2002
60080	Stanley Common C of E Primary School, Ilkeston EWS Rail Safety Competition Winners 2003
60080	Bispham Drive Junior School, Toton EWS Rail Safety Competition Winners 2004
60081	Bleaklow Hill
60081	ISAMBARD KINGDOM BRUNEL
60082	Mam Tor
60083	Shining Tor
60083	Mountsorrel
60084	Cross Fell
60085	Axe Edge
60085	MINI – Pride of Oxford
60086	Schiehallion

Five Class 60s received Loadhaul livery in 1994/95, and some lasted in the livery until 2011, such is the quality of the two-pack paint techniques developed in the late 1980s. 60007 shows off the livery well.
PIP DUNN

60087	Slioch
60087	Barry Needham
60088	Buachaille Etive More
60088	Buachaille Etive Mor
60089	Arcuil
60089	THE RAILWAY HORSE
60090	Quinag
60091	An Teallach
60092	Reginald Munns
60093	Jack Stirk
60093	Adrian Harrington 1955–2003 Royal Navy/Burges Salmon
60094	Tryfan
60094	Rugby Flyer
60095	Crib Goch

60096	Ben Macdui
60097	Pillar
60097	ABP Port of Grimsby & Immingham
60098	Charles Francis Brush
60099	Ben More Assynt
60100	Boar Of Badenoch
60100	Pride of Acton
60500	RAIL Magazine

All were initially named with plates in the standard BR corporate style, painted black. The plates were applied at construction, and few had official naming ceremonies. 60032 had crests above its nameplates. All were black except 60013, which had them repainted red.

When locos were repainted into Loadhaul or Mainline Freight liveries, nameplates were removed, apart from 60044 which had them painted silver and blue. The same happened to those outshopped in EWS livery, apart from 60098.

When renamed, 60001/008/025/029/ 036/038/045/052/059/071/081/085/094/ 097/100 had plaques by the nameplates. 60008/087/098 had inscription plaques.

Some plates were cast in company typefaces, namely 60003/008/016/019/ 031/036/038/048/053/065/081/089.

RIGHT: *60018 in the revised version of the EWS livery with a different font, no ampersand, and the 'three beasties' logo on the cabside.* PIP DUNN

BELOW: *Ex-works after construction, 60044* Ailsa Craig *is in Trainload Metals colours. All 60s were painted in Trainload colours: seventeen in Petroleum, thirty-one in Construction, thirty-four in Coal and seventeen in Metals, although 60081/093 both changed sector symbols from Construction and Coal respectively to Metals – they were the only 60s to change symbols.* PDC

ABOVE: *Apart from 60001, named* Steadfast, *all Class 60s were named at construction after either famous people or mountains, although most have either been renamed or denamed. 60074 was originally named* Braeriach *but has been renamed* Teenage Spirit *after EWS repainted it in a unique light blue livery to promote the Teenage Cancer Trust. When the loco was overhauled in 2011, it kept its unique livery, albeit with DB logos on it.* PIP DUNN

Company logos were incorporated in the nameplates on 60003/017/019/048/ 053/065/089. All renamed 60s had black plates apart from 60001/019 which were light blue, and 60003/048/053 which were white.

60080 carried four nameplates for different schools which won the EWS Rail Safety Competition. The plates carried the name of the school, its location, and the inscription EWS Rail Safety Competition Winners and the year they won. The plates were 'three deck' with a decreasing font size.

On the first naming, there was a Rail Safety logo plaque to the left of the plate. When it was renamed, a 'Get a life, Track Off don't lose it' plaque was added to the right of the nameplates. The next renaming saw the first plaque removed and the second plaque repositioned to under the number, and it retained this for its fourth naming for the EWS Rail Safety Competition.

60013/014/028/032/034/046/054– 057/060/064/066–068/070/072/073/ 082/084/086/088/090/098 were laid up with both their original nameplates.

Just 60016 has been renumbered, becoming 60500 in 2004 to commemorate the 500th issue of *RAIL* magazine.

class 66

TOPS number range:	66001–250, 66301–305, 66401–434, 66501–599, 66601–625, 66701–751, 66841–850, 66951–957
Built by:	General Motors, London, Canada
Construction model (GM):	JT-42-CWR
Years introduced:	From 1998
Wheel arrangement:	Co-Co
Weight:	126 tons
Height:	12ft 10in (3.91m)
Length:	70ft 1in (21.40m)
Width:	8ft 8in (2.65m)
Wheelbase:	56ft 9in (17.29m)
Bogie wheelbase:	13ft 7in (4.15m)
Bogie pivot centres:	43ft 6in (13.25m)
Wheel diameter:	3ft 6in (1.06m)
Min. curve negotiable:	4 chains (80.46m)
Engine type:	GM 12N-710G3B-EC
Engine output:	3,300bhp (2,462kW)
Power at rail:	3,000bhp (2,238kW)
Maximum tractive effort:	92,000lb: 66/0; 105,080lb: 66/6
Continuous tractive effort:	58,390lb: 66/0; 66,630lb: 66/6
Maximum speed:	75mph (120km/h)
Brake force:	68 tons
Bogie type:	HTCR Radial
Route availability:	7
Traction alternator:	GM-EMD AR8
Companion alternator:	GM-EMD CA6
Traction motor type:	GM-EMD D43TR
No. of traction motors:	6
Gear ratio:	81:20 66/0, 83:18 66/6
Fuel tank capacity:	1,440gal (6,550ltr); except 1,145gal (5,150ltr): 66301–305, 66411–434, 66585–599, 66623–625, 66723–732, 66952–957; 1,220gal (5,546ltr): 66718–722; and 1,312gal (5,905ltr): 66951

EWS made the first order for Class 66s with 250 locos, and the first and last of this fleet stand side-by-side. There is one noticeable difference between the two locos, as 66250 has a swinghead knuckle coupler fitted, something which was retro-fitted to the entire EWS fleet apart from 66001/002. The first two of the class also have their four vertical lifting points in different positions on the bufferbeam. Other than these coupler differences, the locos are identical. PIP DUNN

FIRST ORDERED BY EWS in 1996, with the first locos arriving in 1998, the Class 66s – which share the same body design as the Class 59s – are now the standard freight loco for most operators in the UK. They have also proved popular elsewhere in the world, and have been working in Sweden, Norway, the Netherlands, Germany, Egypt, France, Belgium and Luxembourg. Ex-UK locos are now at work in Poland.

No more new locos are expected to be built, but there is a possibility that some of those built for mainland Europe could be redeployed in the UK – indeed, GBRf's 66747–751 are already ex-'Dutch' or German locos.

Three have been withdrawn – 66048, 66521 and 66734 – after collisions or derailments.

SUBCLASSES

There are three types of Class 66: the standard locos, the re-geared Freightliner locos (the Class 66/6s), and the low-emission locos. Apart from the 66/6s, whose numbers designate they are re-geared, the subclasses usually refer to the locos' users.

66/0 are DB Schenker (ordered by EWS), the 66/3 were Fastline Freight, but are now with DRS, 66/4s are DRS, 66/5s are Freightliner standard geared locos, the 66/7s are GBRf locos, and the 66/9s are the original low-emission Freightliner locos.

The 66/8s are Colas locos, the initial five were ex-DRS 66/4s which transferred to Advenza, while those in traffic now are ex-Freightliner 66/5s. There are also current examples of original and low-emission locos in both the 66/5 and 66/7 subclasses.

The first twenty DRS 66/4s have been redeployed with other users (GBRf and Freightliner), 66401–410 have been renumbered as 66/7s, while 66413–416/418–420 are in with Freightliner yet still in DRS colours, and 66411/412/417 are now abroad with Freightliner PL.

The MW receptacle is on the cab front, and the jumpers housed in the engine room when not in use. 66s can work in multiple with Class 59s, 66s, 67s and 70s.

DETAIL DIFFERENCES

66001–250 had standard Bmac light clusters, and these were fitted to 66501–537, 66601–606, 66701–707. For deliveries from 66538 new light clusters were fitted with bigger headlights; these were fitted to 66401–420, 66538–581, 66607–622, 66708–727, 66951/952.

The lights were changed again to another version of Bmac lights, and these were fitted to 66301–305, 66421–434, 66582–599, 66623–625, 66728–732, 66953–957. These have LED lights.

The design of the 66 was changed when low-emission engines were fitted. These were first seen on 66951/952, and locos fitted with these engines were 66301–305, 66401–434, 66585–599, 66623–625, 66718–732, 66953–957. These locos differ by having an extra bodyside door and a smaller fuel tank.

The DBS locos have cab wing mirrors fitted, while 66003–250 have swing-head 'knuckle' couplers fitted. 66055–059 have an additional spotlight and drawbars on their cab fronts for working

as Lickey bankers. 66001 also differs by having an additional pipe running horizontally across its bufferbeams.

OWNERSHIP

66001–250 are owned by Angel Trains; 66301–305, 66595–599, 66953–957 are owned by Beacon Rail; 66411–434, 66585–594, 66623–625 are owned by Lloyds; 66501–505/526–537/544–553, 66601–612, 66729–737 are owned by Porterbrook; 66506–520/522–525/538–543/554–572, 66613–622, 66701–728, 66951/952 are owned by Eversholt; 66738–751 are owned by GBRf; 66846–850 are owned by Colas Rail.

66033 displays the modified horn grilles retrofitted to EWS Class 66s which protrudes from the cab roof; initially they were flat on the loco. This loco has yet to have its swinghead coupler fitted, and only has two lifting points, albeit angled rather than vertical. PIP DUNN

LIVERIES

EWS: 66001–250
Freightliner: 66501–599, 66601–625, 66951–957
Shanks Waste: 66522
Bardon Aggregates: 66623
DRS Compass: 66401–434
GB Railfreight: 66701–717
Medite: 66709
Medite Sorrento: 66709
Golden Jubilee: 66705
Metronet: 66718–722
First Group: 66723–732
Fastline Freight: 66301–305, 66434
Stobart: 66048, 66411/414
DRS unbranded: 66401–404/410
DRS base blue: 66411/414
Advenza: 66841–844
Malcolm: 66405
Malcolm (second variant): 66412

Malcolm (third variant): 66434
DB Schenker: 66097, 66101/118/152
Colas: 66742–746, 66841–850
Advenza unbranded: 66843/844
Freightliner Powerhaul : 66411/412/417, 66504
DB Schenker red without yellow ends (Poland): 66163/178/189, 66220/227/248
Emily livery: 66720
GB Europorte: 66710/728–737/742–746
Freightliner unbranded: 66601/612, 66738–741

Livery Variations

Each fleet has its own standard number types. Variations have affected the GBRf fleet – 66705 had small black cabside numbers when its union flag logos were applied in the space where the running number would have been. 66709 had large cabside numbers in its first Medite livery, and 66737 had the '37' part of its number in a much larger font after its naming.

The livery on the three Stobart Rail locos all differed. The first was DRS 66411 and this had Stobart Rail branding on its bodyside with 'Rail' in upper case and only the height of half of the bodyside. The second loco, also from DRS, was 66414, which had Stobart Rail with 'Rail' in lower case but the full height of the bodyside. Both had red upper bufferbeams. 66411/414 were delivered in DRS Compass livery, and both had these decals removed and operated in base DRS blue before the Stobart wraps were applied.

66048, a DB Schenker loco, had the same bodyside lettering as 66414, but had yellow upper bufferbeams. 66048 also had the original Bmac light clusters, whereas 66411/414 had the later headlight design. It is worth mentioning that 66048 only worked one train in Stobart colours, crashing at Carrbridge just 30 miles into the journey from Inverness. It was returned to Inverness and stayed there for three months before being moved by road to Toton for component recovery. 66048 was previously in EWS livery.

The three locos with Malcolm branding also differed. All DRS locos, the first of which was 66405, had 'Malcolm Logistics Services' on the bodyside, with 'Malcolm' in upper case and the company logo in between 'Malcolm' and 'Logistics'. Underneath Logistics Services it had 'Networking with European Industry' and under

GB Railfreight's 66713 Forest City *shows the revised light clusters fitted midway through the Class 66 production line with two bigger and brighter headlights and LED tail/sidelights.* PIP DUNN

'Malcolm' it had the company's website. The DRS logos were on the cabsides under the driver's side, and behind the cab on the secondman's side.

The second loco reliveried was 66412, which had 'Malcolm' in uppercase large letters on the top of the body towards No. 1 end, and underneath the word 'Rail', also in uppercase and with triangular flashes. The company logo was behind the cab windows at No. 2 end, with small DRS Compass logos on the doors. This loco also had red and yellow stripes on the extreme bottom edge of the front valance.

66434's Malcolm livery was more striking, with 'Malcolm Rail' in the middle of the bodyside and the company's lion logo next to the grilles at No. 1 end; on the bodyside was the branding 'Committed to the environment'.

The bodyside was a light blue with a seeping dark blue which extended up behind the 'Malcolm' branding. It, too, had a yellow-/red-striped lower valance, while the cabsides had black numbers and 'Malcolm Rail' branding. This loco had previously been in DRS and then Fastline Freight liveries.

Freightliner locos branded for customers have been 66522 in Shanks Waste livery, which is actually only half the loco, the other half being in standard Freightliner green. 66623 has been branded in Bardon Aggregates blue; both the locos were reliveried from base Freightliner green.

The bogie detail on 66033. Class 66s have steering bogies which means they cause less track wear, and this is a contributing factor to allowing the locos over lines hitherto barred for large Type 5s. PIP DUNN

GBRf locos rebranded have been 66705 in Golden Jubilee livery, which is standard GBRf livery with its numbers removed and reapplied in black on the cabsides, and full height union flags on the bodyside.

66709 was rebranded in Medite livery in July 2002 with black bodysides, and MSC logos on each side of 'Medite' branding in capitals. Its nameplates were in yellow. It was reliveried in April 2012 with graphics of an MSC ship on the side.

66720 was reliveried in 2011, featuring artwork designed by six-year-old Emily Woodman, with a different design on each side.

66111 has (unofficial) Highland Rail stags on its bodyside in EWS colours.

NAMES

66002	*Lafarge Buddon Wood*
66002	*Lafarge Quorn*
66022	*Lafarge Charnwood*
66042	*Lafarge Buddon Wood*
66048	*James the Engine*
66050	*EWS Energy*
66077	*Benjamin Gimbert GC*
66079	*James Nightall GC*
66152	*Derek Holmes Railway Operator*
66172	*PAUL MELLANY*
66200	*RAILWAY HERITAGE COMMITTEE*
66411	*Eddie the Engine*
66414	*James the Engine*
66501	*Japan 2001*
66502	*Basford Hall Centenary 2001*

ABOVE: *A standard Freightliner Class 66/5. These locos do not have swinghead couplers and hence have a very clean bufferbeam. The loco has Bmac light clusters and the modified horn grilles.* PIP DUNN

RIGHT: *The front-end detail of a Freightliner Class 66 with Bmac light clusters and four lifting points. The loco also has a 55K shedplate for Leeds Midland Road. Compared with the loco bufferbeams of the 1970s, many of which were dual-braked, dual-heated and with MW, those on newer locos are much simpler as they only have air brakes, and no train heating or MW jumpers.* ANTHONY HICKS

66503	The RAILWAY MAGAZINE
66506	Crewe Regeneration
66526	Driver Steve Dunn (George)
66527	Don Raider
66532	P&O Nedlloyd Express
66533	Hanjin Express/Senator Express
66534	OOCL Express
66540	Ruby
66552	Maltby Raider
66576	Hamburg Sud Advantage
66581	Sophie
66585	The Drax Flyer
66592	Johnson Stevens Agencies
66593	3MG MERSEY MULTIMODAL GATEWAY
66594	NYK Spirit of Kyoto
66597	Viridor
66601	The Hope Valley
66612	Forth Raider
66618	Railways Illustrated Annual Photographic Awards Ian Lothian
66618	Railways Illustrated Annual Photographic Awards Derek Gorton
66618	Railways Illustrated Annual Photographic Awards Alan Barnes
66619	Derek W Johnson MBE
66623	Bill Bolsover
66701	Railtrack National Logistics
66701	Whitemoor
66702	Blue Lightning
66703	Doncaster PSB 1981–2002
66704	Colchester Power Signalbox
66705	Golden Jubilee
66706	Nene Valley
66707	Sir Sam Fay
66708	Jayne
66709	Joseph Arnold Davies
66709	Sorrento
66710	Phil Packer BRIT
66712	Peterborough Power Signalbox
66713	Forest City
66714	Cromer Lifeboat
66715	VALOUR
66716	Willesden Traincare Depot
66716	LOCOMOTIVE & CARRIAGE INSTITUTION CENTENARY 1911–2011
66717	Good Old Boy
66718	Gwyneth Dunwoody
66719	METRO-LAND
66720	Metronet Pathfinder
66721	Harry Beck
66722	Sir Edward Watkin
66723	Chinook
66724	Drax Power Station
66725	SUNDERLAND

66726	SHEFFIELD WEDNESDAY
66727	Andrew Scott CBE
66728	Institution of Railway Operators
66729	DERBY COUNTY
66730	Whitemoor
66731	InterhubGB
66732	GBRf The First Decade 1999–2009 John Smith MD
66734	The Eco Express
66736	WOLVERHAMPTON WANDERERS
66737	Lesia
66739	Bluebell Railway
66742	ABP Port of Immingham Centenary 1912–2012
66744	Crossrail
66745	Modern Railways The first 50 years
66849	Wylam Dilly
66957	Stephenson Locomotive Society 1909–2009

NAMEPLATE STYLES

The nameplate styles used on Class 66s varied: for example 66002/022/042 were in EWS style, as was also used on Class 67s, while 66050/077/079, 66152, 66501/502/506/526/527/532–534/540/552/576/581/585/592/594/597, 66601/612/619/623, 66701–710/712–714/716–724/727/728/730/732/734/737/742/745, 66849, 66957 all had their names in the standard BR corporate style font. 66618 was likewise, but had small additional nameplates for the three winners of a competition, which were changed.

66723's nameplate is in the standard font, but also had a cutout of a Chinook and three squadron crests.

66172 and 66200 had their names in uppercase in a non-standard font, 66503 had its nameplate in the same style at the magazine masthead, and 66593, 66731/744 nameplates were in company logo style.

66715 has a shaped nameplate with the inscription 'In memory of all railway employees who gave their lives for their country' in upper case. It also had separate square plaques with coats of arms to the left of the nameplates.

66716 had its second name in a circular wheel crest, with 1911/2011 in the centre.

66725/726/729/736 had the old LNER-style football curved nameplates, in upper case and with a football underneath them, albeit a flat ball rather than the half spheres the steam locos had back in their days.

66048/411/414 had their 'names' in transfers above the cab windows and on the cabsides under the windows.

Locos that have lost their names are 66022/042, 66411/414, 66576/581, 66612, 66701 (twice), 66720, while 66002, 66709/716 have been renamed.

Freightliner ordered the first two lower-emission Class 66s in 2004, numbered 66951/952, and later deliveries of 66s to DRS, GBRf, Fastline and Freightliner have been to this specification. The locos differed by having a bodyside door and a shorter fuel tank. 66434 is the last of the DRS order, and after a spell in Fastline livery as part of a long-term hire arrangement which was curtailed when Fastline went bust, it is now in a unique Malcolm Logistics livery, as seen in August 2012. PIP DUNN

Build Batches

66001–25	1998–2000	EWS now with DBS		66578–581	2005	Freightliner	now with GBRf
66301–305	2008	Fastline now with DRS		66582–594	2007	Freightliner	
6401–410	2003	DRS now with GBRf		66595–599	2008	Freightliner	
66411–420	2006	DRS now with Freightliner		66601–606	2000	Freightliner	
66421–430	2007	DRS		66607–612	2002	Freightliner	
66431–434	2008	DRS		66613–618	2003	Freightliner	
66501–505	1999	Freightliner		66619–622	2005	Freightliner	
66506–520	2000	Freightliner		66623–625	2007	Freightliner	
66521–525	2000	Freightliner		66701–707	2001	GBRf	
66526–531	2001	Freightliner		66708–712	2002	GBRf	
66532–537	2001	Freightliner		66713–717	2003	GBRf	
66538–543	2001	Freightliner		66718–722	2006	GBRf	
66544–553	2001	Freightliner		66723–727	2006	GBRf	
66554	2002	Freightliner		66728–732	2008	GBRf	
66555–566	2002	Freightliner		66747–751	2012	GBRf locos acquired from Europe	
66567–574	2003	Freightliner	66573/574 now with	66951–952	2004	Freightliner	
			Colas	66953–957	2008	Freightliner	
66575–577	2004	Freightliner	now with Colas				

Notes: 66048 written off 01/10; 66521 written off 02/01; 66734 written off 12/12; 66554 was ordered as a replacement for 66521

Renumberings

Several Class 66s have been renumbered for new users, and some locos have been renumbered twice.

Old No.	User	New No.	New user	Next user	Old No.	User	New No.	New user	Next user
66301	Fastline	-	DRS		66573	Freightliner	66846	Colas	
66302	Fastline	-	DRS		66574	Freightliner	66847	Colas	
66303	Fastline	-	DRS		66575	Freightliner	66848	Colas	
66304	Fastline	-	DRS		66576	Freightliner	66849	Colas	
66305	Fastline	-	DRS		66577	Freightliner	66850	Colas	
66401	DRS	66733	GBRf		66578	Freightliner	66738	GBRf	
66402	DRS	66734	GBRf		66579	Freightliner	66739	GBRf	
66403	DRS	66735	GBRf		66580	Freightliner	66740	GBRf	
66404	DRS	66736	GBRf		66581	Freightliner	66741	GBRf	
66405	DRS	66737	GBRf		66582	Freightliner	66009	Freightliner Poland	
66406	DRS	66841	Advenza	Colas	66583	Freightliner	66010	Freightliner Poland	
66407	DRS	66842	Advenza	Colas	66584	Freightliner	66011	Freightliner Poland	
66408	DRS	66843	Advenza	Colas	66586	Freightliner	66008	Freightliner Poland	
66409	DRS	66844	Advenza	Colas	66608	Freightliner	66603	Freightliner Poland	
66410	DRS	66845	Colas		66609	Freightliner	66604	Freightliner Poland	
66411	DRS	66012	Freightliner Poland		66611	Freightliner	66605	Freightliner Poland	
66412	DRS	66013	Freightliner Poland		66612	Freightliner	66606	Freightliner Poland	
66413	DRS	-	Freightliner		66624	Freightliner	66602	Freightliner Poland	
66414	DRS	-	Freightliner		66625	Freightliner	66601	Freightliner Poland	
66415	DRS	-	Freightliner		66841	Colas	66742	GBRf	(ex-66406)
66416	DRS	-	Freightliner		66842	Colas	66743	GBRf	(ex-66407)
66417	DRS	66014	Freightliner Poland		66843	Colas	66744	GBRf	(ex-66408)
66418	DRS	-	Freightliner		66844	Colas	66745	GBRf	(ex-66409)
66419	DRS	-	Freightliner		66845	Colas	66746	GBRf	(ex-66410)
66420	DRS	-	Freightliner						

LOCOS EXPORTED

EWS/DBS Class 66s that have spent spells working for Euro Cargo Rail in France are 66010/022/026/028/029/032/033/ 036/038/042/045/049/052/062/064/071 –073, 66123/179/190/191/195, 66202/ 203/205/208–211/214–219/222–226/ 228/229/231/233–236/239–247/249. Some of these have returned to the UK for short-term periods (mainly during the RHTT season). Some have returned for short periods of maintenance at Toton.

DBS locos moved to Poland are 66146/153/157/159/163/166/173/178/ 180/189/196, 66220/227/237/248.

Freightliner locos moved to Poland are 66411/412/417, 66582–584/586, 66608/609/611/612/624/625, of which 66411/412/417 were originally DRS locos.

Liveries aside, there have been few changes to the Class 67 fleet. 67019, still in original EWS colours, shows off its standard front end with TDM cables, MW receptacle in the centre, and Bmac lights. The bufferbeam has a swinghead knuckle coupler, ETH cables, and the standard air-brake and main reservoir pipes. ANTHONY HICKS

TOPS number range:	67001–030
Built by:	Alstom/General Motors, Valencia, Spain
Construction model (GM):	JT-42-HWHS
Years introduced:	1999–2000
Wheel arrangement:	Bo-Bo
Weight:	90 tons
Height:	12ft 9in (3.93m)
Length:	64ft 7in (19.71m)
Width:	8ft 9in (2.71m)
Wheelbase:	47ft 3in (14.43m)
Bogie wheelbase:	9ft 2in (2.80m)
Bogie pivot centres:	38ft 1in (11.63m)
Wheel diameter:	3ft 2in (965mm)
Min. curve negotiable:	3.8 chains (75m)
Engine type:	GM 12N-710G3B-EC
Engine output:	2,980bhp (2,223kW)
Maximum tractive effort:	31,750lb
Continuous tractive effort:	20,200lb
Design speed:	125mph (200km/h), restricted to 110mph (177km/h)
Brake force	78 tons
Bogie type:	Alstom high speed
Route availability:	8
Traction alternator:	GM-EMD AR9A
Companion alternator:	GM-EMD CA6HEX
Traction motor type:	GM-EMD D43FM
No. of traction motors:	4
Gear ratio:	59:28
Fuel tank capacity:	1,201gal (5,460ltr)

Two Class 67s have been painted into the Royal Plum livery work with the royal train, although the locos are still used on other trains. 67005 was the first repainted, in 2004, at Toton. The loco's Bmac light cluster housings have also been painted yellow. PIP DUNN

LIVERIES

EWS: 67001–030
WSMR grey and silver: 67010/012–015
Royal train dark plum: 67005/006
EWS managers' train silver with EWS logos: 67029
EWS managers' train silver with DB logos: 67029
DBS red: 67018
Arriva unbranded: 67001–003
Diamond Jubilee silver: 67026

NAMES

67001	*Night Mail*
67002	*Special Delivery*
67004	*Post Haste*
67005	*Queen's Messenger*
67006	*Royal Sovereign*
67010	*Unicorn*

ORDERED BY EWS in 1997, these thirty locos had a 125mph (22km/h) capability, although the reality is that this has rarely been used. They were built for mail and charter train work, but lost the former in 2004. Several are used for passenger hire contracts, which has led to new liveries. They are also now the preferred traction for the royal train, again with two dedicated locos in royal livery and a third in a Diamond Jubilee livery.

DETAIL DIFFERENCES

Liveries aside, there are no discernible detail differences across the fleet, except that 67004/007/008/009/011/030 have had RETB fitted, although this equipment has since been removed from 67008.

All have swinghead knuckle couplers, ETH (index 66), Bmac lights and standard GM-type MW to 'multi' with 59s, 66s and 67s.

67012	*A Shropshire Lad*
67013	*Dyfrbont Pontcysyllte*
67014	*Thomas Telford*
67015	*David J Lloyd*
67017	*Arrow*
67018	*Rapid*
67018	*Keith Heller*
67025	*Western Star*
67026	*Diamond Jubilee*
67027	*Rising Star*
67029	*Royal Diamond*

67012–015/026/026 have standard corporate-style nameplates on their bodysides, 67001/002/004–006/010/017/018/025/027 have EWS-style nameplates, and 67018 has a smaller flat nameplate, all mounted on the cabsides. Names from 67001/002/004/010 have been removed, while 67027 misses one plate.

Pioneer of the fleet, 67001 Night Mail, *was also the first to be named. Initially, naming of Class 67s was thought only to be possible by using thinner nameplates because of gauging concerns, but more recently standard BR-style corporate nameplates have been fitted to the locos' rippled bodysides.*
PIP DUNN

A bodyside view of 67029 Royal Diamond *in its unique silver livery. It initially ran like this with full height EWS 'three beasties' logos, but these have been removed and changed to a DB logo.* ANTHONY HICKS

The first Class 67 in the UK was 67003, delivered in October 1999. Aside from instructions on how to use the swinghead couplers that were added, the locos have not changed physically, although several now have new liveries. PIP DUNN

PENDING THE ARRIVAL of the Vossloh Class 68s in 2013, these are the UK's newest loco design. Freightliner ordered twenty locos with an option for another ten, and so far 70001–020 have been delivered. However, 70012 was dropped from the crane during unloading and badly damaged, and it has returned to the USA and will not be returning to the UK. As yet there is no clear indication from Freightliner if a twentieth loco will be supplied to replace 70012, and if so, what number it will carry.

Due to problems with the locos, namely a spate of fires, as yet there is no indication if the option to take up the extended order of 70021–030 will be realized.

In 2012, another Class 70 was built in Turkey from a kit, and this has been moved to the UK as a demonstrator loco. It is numbered 70099.

It should be noted that these are the second locos to be Class 70s, and should not be confused with the three Southern Region booster DC electric locos, numbered 20001–003, which ran in the 1960s but were all withdrawn by 1969.

DETAIL DIFFERENCES

All are fitted with MW to work with 59s, 66s, 67s and 70s, although to date none have worked in multiple other than with 70s. They are air-braked, with no train heating.

LIVERIES

Freightliner Powerhaul: 70001–020
All-over dark green: 70099

NAMES

70001	*PowerHaul*
70004	*The Coal Industry Society*

Nameplates are mounted on the solebar.

specifications

TOPS number range:	70001–020/099
Built by:	General Electric, Erie, Pennsylvania
Years introduced:	2009–12
Wheel arrangement:	Co-Co
Weight:	129 tons
Height:	3.94m
Length:	21.71m
Width:	2.64m
Wheelbase:	17.18m
Bogie wheelbase:	4.28m
Bogie pivot centres:	14.48m
Wheel diameter:	1.07m
Min. curve negotiable:	80m
Engine type:	GE Powerhaul P616LDA1
Engine output:	3,820bhp (2,848kW)
Power at rail:	2,700bhp (2,014kW)
Tractive effort:	122,000lb
Maximum speed:	75mph (120km/h)
Brake force:	96.7 tons
Route availability:	7
Main alternator type:	GE 5GTAZ6721A1
Traction motor type:	AC-GE 5GEB30B
No. of traction motors:	6
Gear ratio:	87:16
Fuel tank capacity:	1,333gal (6,000ltr)

So far twenty Class 70s have been built for Freightliner, although 70012 was written off after being dropped from the crane during unloading and has returned to the USA. To date there have been no detail differences on the fleet: the locos are similar to the 58s in having a narrow body and full-width cabs. 70001 PowerHaul *shows off the unique look of the Class 70 design.* PIP DUNN

Southern Railway numbers:	CC1/CC2
BR 1948 numbers:	20001–003
Former SR classification:	CC
Built by:	SR Ashford (20001/002); BR Brighton (20003)
Introduced:	1941/43/48
Wheel arrangement	Co-Co
Weight (operational):	100 tons (20001/002); 105 tons (20003)
Height (pan down):	12ft 6in (3.81m)
Width:	8ft 7in (2.62m)
Length:	56ft 9in (17.3m): 20001/002; 58ft 6in (17.83m): 20003
Min. curve negotiable:	5½ chains
Maximum speed:	75mph (120km/h)
Wheelbase:	43ft 6in (13.26m): 20001/002; 44ft 6in (13.56m): 20003
Bogie wheelbase:	16ft (4.88m)
Bogie pivot centres:	27ft 6in (8.38m): 20001/002; 28ft 6in (8.69m): 20003
Wheel diameter:	3ft 7in (1.09m)
Boiler water capacity:	320gal (1,440ltr)
Brake force:	85 tons (20001/002); 89 tons (20003)
Horsepower:	1,470bhp (1,097kW)
Tractive effort (max):	49,000lb (20001/002); 45,000lb (20003)
No. of traction motors:	6
Traction motor type:	EE 519A (20001/002); EE 519-4D (20003)
Control system:	DC Booster
Pantograph type:	EE cross-arm
Power supply:	660–750V DC third rail/overhead

ABOVE: *The first two Southern Railway booster locos shared the same body design, but there were noticeable differences with the third loco of the trio. 20001, seen in March 1965, shows off its front end detail well, the loco is vacuum-braked only and has steam heating. The loco's six discs for train identification are all folded either up or down. Note the vertical whistle mounted by the right-hand side window.* RAIL PHOTOPRINTS

BELOW: *20003 had an angled cab profile and a different front arrangement, clearly seen in the May 1949 view when compared with 20001. The loco has a pantograph for working in yards where high voltage live third rails were an obvious danger.* RAIL PHOTOPRINTS

THESE THREE 750V DC electric locos were built by the Southern Railway, although the last of the trio was not delivered until after nationalization in 1948. The third loco was quite different externally to the first two. Under BR they were renumbered 20001–003, but had been withdrawn by the time TOPS came in, and the Class 20 Type 1 diesels took the same numbers. They never carried E prefixes.

As they survived after 1 January 1968, they were given a TOPS classification of 70. All were condemned by the end of that year, which meant that in 2009 it was deemed acceptable for Freightliner to use the Class 70 classification for its new GE diesels.

DETAIL DIFFERENCES

The locos were vacuum-braked and fitted with Bastian & Allan steam-heating boilers. None were dual-braked.

All three locos feature differences, with the first two having a shorter body and a different cab design. The first loco was built with two character headcode panels in between the cab windows, which had the stencil-style display as used on many early SR EMUs. Four lamp irons were also fitted to allow SR-style discs to be displayed.

The headcodes and lamp irons were removed in 1945 and replaced by six white lights which had white folding discs fitted around them to display the train type. The windows were also increased in size, although the earlier window frames remained the same. In later styles the six white lamps were removed, and a roller blind, two-character headcode refitted in the centre between the windows.

The second loco was similar to the revised 20001 (with the six headcode lamps and larger windows) but differed by having two multiple working jumper receptacles mounted on its cab front; these were later removed.

The B-side was a mass of grilles, with four grilles centrally, near to the cant rail, and four close to the sole bar. On each side were two banks of parallel grilles, with six on each level. In total there were thirty sets of grilles on the B-side; the A-side had just two small grilles centrally in the body at cant-rail height. The locos also had a pantograph centrally on the roof for working in yards.

The final loco of the trio differed in many ways. Its body profile was more rounded on the roof, while the cab fronts had longer vertical windows, no head-codes, different window-wiper styles, and the six lamp and discs system. The vacuum-brake pipe was moved to the bufferbeam as opposed to being mounted to the cab front, as had been the case on the first two locos.

The cab front was also angled with a centre flat section, and the sides angled to the sides. Its grille arrangement also differed: the B-side had six sets of grilles centrally, again in two horizontal banks at cant-rail and sole-bar levels, and then just eight grilles on each side. The A-side was very similar to the first two locos.

20001 was fitted with cab roof-mounted horns and two charter roller-blind headcodes, losing its six lamps in the process in 1967.

LIVERIES

Southern green with white stripes and cab whiskers: 20001
Southern green: 20001/002
BR black: 20001–003
BR green: 20001–003
BR green with small yellow panel: 20003
BR green with full yellow end: 20002
BR blue: 20001

When new, the first two locos were numbered CC1 and CC2, and carried these numbers only on their buffer-beams. They had 'Southern', in capitals, on their bodysides.

The last loco was allocated number CC3, but this was never carried as it was delivered to British Railways numbered 20003, and with British Railways branding on the bodysides. The other two were renumbered 20001/002 and also had British Railways branding applied.

20001 was repainted into BR blue in 1967, and as it was often used on royal train duties, it sported silver buffers and white vacuum-brake and steam-heat pipes. Numbers were in standard corporate style, and BR badges were applied on the bodysides, off-centre towards No. 1 end.

class 71
specifications

THIS FLEET OF twenty-four electric locos was built for the Southern Region to work off the third rail system. They were also fitted with pantographs for working in yards when the 750V DC power supply came from overhead wires, so as to avoid dangerous live rails. Ten were converted to Class 74 electro-diesels in 1966/67 (*see* later section).

All the 71s were laid up in late 1976 and stored, but none returned to traffic, and all were condemned in November 1977. 71001 (E5001) was claimed for the National Railway Museum and has spent a spell in main-line use in the mid-1990s; however, it is not presently certified to run on Network Rail.

DETAIL DIFFERENCES

TOPS number range:	71001–014		Wheel diameter:	4ft (1.22m)
Former number range:	E5000–24		Route availability:	6
SR classification:	HA		Brake force:	41 tons
Built by:	BR Doncaster		Horsepower (continuous):	2,552bhp (1,904kW)
Introduced:	1959–60			
Wheel arrangement:	Bo-Bo		Horsepower (max):	3,000bhp (2,238kW)
Weight (operational):	77 tons		Tractive effort (max):	43,000lb
Height (pan down):	13ft 1in (3.99m)		No. of traction motors:	4
Width:	8ft 11in (2.72m)		Traction motor type:	EE 532A
Length:	50ft 7in (15.42m)		Control system:	DC Booster EE836
Min. curve negotiable:	4 chains		Auxiliary generator:	EE 910B
Maximum speed:	90mph (144km/h)		Gear ratio:	76:22
Wheelbase:	37ft 6in (11.43m)		Pantograph type:	Cross-arm
Bogie wheelbase:	10ft 6in (3.2m)		Power supply:	660–750V DC third rail/overhead
Bogie pivot centres:	27ft (8.23m)			

The locos experienced no major detail differences during their short lives, apart from a change to their bodyside grilles on B-side. Initially they had a large grille nearest to No. 2 end, and three central grilles, the middle of which was slightly shorter in depth to the full height grilles that flanked it. At No. 1 end they had two parallel horizontal banks of three grilles. On A-side they had a large window in the centre of the body flanked by two grilles. The B-side grille arrangement was changed to a smaller depth two-piece grille at No. 1 end, then the centre grille was removed, and the two grilles either side of it were shortened. A panel was also fitted at No. 1 end after the changes.

All 71s were fitted with ETH and dual train brakes; none were fitted with multiple working.

The only major changes came to the ten locos converted to Class 74s. The main external differences between a 71 and a 74 were that the latter had duplicate waist-level brake and multiple working cables on their cab fronts, and they lost the red tail-lights and front horizontal foot-step. The lamp irons were moved to just above the buffer-beam on a 74, to below the hand-rail position on a 71. The front hand-rail arrangement remained the same.

The 74s also had vestibule rubbing plates fitted, and different style ETH jumpers and buckeye couplers.

The roof profile and bodyside grilles and windows differed hugely between the Class 71s and 74s to take account of two vastly different interior layouts. On the roof the pantograph was removed and the roof made flush, but incorporating the exhaust port.

The diesel engine in a 74 was at No. 1 end. The grille arrangement on B-side was from No. 2 end, a small half-depth grille, a small window, a square half-depth grille, two larger three-quarter depth grilles, then two parallel banks of horizontal louvres, the top bank six deep, the bottom bank eight deep. There were six sets of these louvres, top and bottom. A-side comprised two windows and one small grille, a much cleaner arrangement.

LIVERIES

BR green: E5001–024
BR green with half yellow end: E5001–024
BR green with full yellow end: E5010
BR blue: 71001–014

NUMBERS

When built, the first locomotive was numbered E5000, but this was renumbered as E5024 in December 1962.

Ten Class 71s, namely E5003/05/06/15–17/19/21/23/24, were converted to Class 74s in 1966–67, gaining new E61xx numbers. This led to E5018/20/ 22 being renumbered to take up vacant numbers vacated by E5003/05/06, to keep the fleet consecutively numbered E5001–14 prior to becoming 71001–014 under TOPS.

CLASS 71/74 RENUMBERINGS

71 No.	2nd 71 No.	74 No.	TOPS No.
E5000	E5024	E6104	74004
E5001			71001
E5002			71002
E5003		E6107	74007
E5004			71004
E5005		E6108	74008
E5006		E6103	74003
E5007			71007
E5008			71008
E5009			71009
E5010			71010
E5011			71011
E5012			71012
E5013			71013
E5014			71014
E5015		E6101	74001
E5016		E6102	74002
E5017		E6109	74009
E5018	E5003		71003
E5019		E6105	74005
E5020	E5005		71005
E5021		E6110	74010
E5022	E5006		71006
E5023		E6106	74006

RIGHT: The only surviving Class 71, E5001 is in original condition apart from the addition of a yellow warning panel. The loco is dual-braked and ETH-fitted, and features a SR two-character headcode between the front cab windows. PIP DUNN

The Class 71s had a short working life, as the SR preferred to run trains using EMUs. Ten of the twenty-four were converted to Class 74 electro-diesels, and the rest were laid up in 1976. E5001 is resplendent in original condition in this 1992 view. PDC

BUILT FOR THE SR as a mixed-traffic DC electric, the Class 73s have a 600bhp EE diesel engine to allow them to run on non-electrified lines, mostly in yards or on short branches. They occasionally strayed further afield, although tended to overheat if working for long periods on diesel with a heavy load. Like the 33/2s, they were built to the Hastings line gauge.

Their incredible versatility means that not only have they proved popular even today, but their usefulness has resulted in two major engineering projects being pursued, that will lead to almost new locos using the same bodyshells and bogies. Several have been preserved.

There are noticeable detail differences between the two main batches, the six prototypes and the 43 production-series locos, but differences thereafter have been relatively few, although livery variety has been expansive. The Class 73/0s were originally to have been Class 72s.

DETAIL DIFFERENCES

There were visual differences between a 73/0 and a 73/1, with the former having two cab-mounted MW cables and the latter having only one, while on the bodysides at No. 2 end the 73/1s did not have a window, and the grille design was slightly different with an extra grille on B-side.

All locos had SR two-character head-code boxes. These were removed from 73133 in 1997, and an additional window (and wiper) fitted when it was modified as a route-learning loco. They were plated over on 73138 in 2010 in its Network Rail role.

Snowplough brackets have been fitted to 73212/213 at No. 1 end only. Three-piece snowploughs are carried all year round, although often the centre plough is detached during summer.

All were fitted with dual brakes from new, but 73138/141, 73201–213/235 have been converted to air brakes only.

TOPS number range:	73001–006, 73101–142, 73201–235, 73901/906
1957 BR number range:	E6001–E6049
Southern Region class codes:	JA 73/0; JB 73/1
Built by:	BR Eastleigh 73/0; English Electric, Vulcan Foundry 73/1
Years introduced:	1962–67
Wheel arrangement:	Bo-Bo
Weight:	76–77 tons
Height:	12ft 5in (3.79m)
Length, buffers retracted:	52ft 6in (16.00m)
Length, buffers extended:	53ft 8in (16.96m)
Width:	8ft 8in (2.64m)
Wheelbase:	40ft 9in (12.42m)
Bogie wheelbase:	8ft 9in (2.66m)
Bogie pivot centres:	32ft (11.27m)
Wheel diameter:	3ft 4in (1.01m)
Min. curve negotiable:	4 chains (80.46m)
Power supply:	660–750V DC third rail
Electric output (nom):	1,600bhp (1,193kW)
Electric power at rail (cont):	1,200bhp (895kW)
Electric power at rail (max):	2,450bhp (1,830kW)
Engine type:	English Electric 4SRKT Mk2
Engine output:	600bhp (447kW)
Diesel power at rail:	402bhp (300kW)
Electric tractive effort:	42,000lb: 73/0; 40,000lb: 73/1
Diesel tractive effort:	34,100lb: 73/0; 36,000lb: 73/1
Maximum speed:	80mph (128km/h): 73/0; 90mph (144km/h): 73/1
Brake force:	31 tons
Route availability:	6
Main generator type:	EE824-3D
Auxiliary generator type:	EE908-3C
Traction motor type:	EE542A: 73/0; EE546-1B: 73/1
No. of traction motors:	4
Gear ratio:	63:17 – 73/0; 61:19 – 73/1
Fuel tank capacity:	340gal (1,546ltr): 73/0; 310gal (1,409ltr): 73/1

Externally the first six Class 73s, classified JAs and later 73/0s, differed from the production series JBs (73/1s), having an additional MW jumper and receptacle on their cab fronts and a different window and grille arrangement. 73005 was painted in the same light blue used on the first version of Network SouthEast livery for its naming in September 1988. 73004 carried a similar livery but with wrap-round yellow ends on the lower half of its cabsides. PDC

A standard Class 73/1 in BR blue, 73119, shows the vacuum-brake pipes, buckeye coupler, vestibule rubbing plate and duplicate cab front brake and MW pipes. PDC

LEFT: In 1984 BR started painting Class 73s in 'Large Logo' colours, with the badge broken by the bodyside window. 73138 shows off the look in July 1984. PDC

RIGHT: Various styles of InterCity livery were applied to Class 73s, often regardless of which sector they were working for. 73107 was one of those painted in the IC Executive colour scheme, which had wrap-round lower yellow cabsides. This view shows the complex bufferbeam layout. The EDs could only provide ETH when working on electric power and not when working off their 600bhp EE diesel engines. PDC

Standard BR high-intensity headlights were fitted to all bar 73115 and E6027, although 73133 lost them in 1997 when it was modified with vertical Bmac light clusters which incorporated red tail-lights.

The most noticeable difference to the fleet was when Eurostar's 73118/130 were fitted with hinged Scharfenberg couplers for hauling Class 373 sets. This attachment at both ends added five feet to the locos' length. It also had a headlight attached and multiple working jumpers. These locos had large oval buffers.

When 73138 was added to the Network Rail fleet in 2010, at No. 2 it was fitted with new dual LED tail/side lights on the cab front above the bufferbeam, one on each side of the standard headlight. A third was added in the plated-over defunct headcode panel. Below it was a camera, and above it was a shield to prevent sunlight getting on the camera.

At No. 1 end the headcode panel was retained and two black modules added for fibreoptic connections for the camera, located in the centre of the cab windows at the other end.

ETH was only available while working off the third rail, and a pre-heat facility is available on Class 73/0s.

73212/213 has had their ETH removed, a feature on the 73s from new, although the 73/1s cannot provide train heat when running on diesel power.

LIVERIES

BR green: E6001–006
BR blue: 73001–006, 73101–142
BR blue, grey roof: 73001, 73100/101/121/142
BR 'Largo Logo': 73001–006, 73104/105/114/126/129/131–133/138–142
InterCity Executive with large bodyside numbers: 73123
InterCity Executive: 73101–114/116–142, 73801
InterCity Mainline: 73130/138, 73201/205
Mainline Freight blue: 73114/133/136
BR green (special): 73003
Departmental grey: 73106/108/135/136
Revised dark NSE: 73109/112/126/129/133/136
'Dutch': 73105/107/108/110/118/119/128–131/133/138
Pullman umber/cream: 73101
EW&S: 73128/131
EWS: 73128
Railtrack: 73212/213
GBRf: 73204–206/209
Network Rail: 73138/141, 73212/213
BR blue half yellow end (special): 73136
BR blue (special): 73201/208
BR 'Large Logo' (special): 73207
InterCity Executive (special): 73205
Stagecoach: 73109
South West Trains: 73109, 73201/235
Fragonset: 73107
Two-tone grey: 73107
First Group: 73141, 73212/213
Weardale Railway: 73139

NAMES

73003	*Sir Herbert Walker*
73004	*The Bluebell Railway*
73005	*Mid Hants Railway/The Watercress Line*
73101	*Brighton Evening Argus*
73101	*The Royal Alex*
73102	*Airtour Suisse*
73105	*Quadrant*
73107	*Redhill 1844–1994*
73107	*SPITFIRE*
73109	*Battle of Britain 50th Anniversary*
73112	*University of Kent at Canterbury*
73113	*County of West Sussex*
73114	*Stewarts Lane Traction Maintenance Depot*
73116	*Selhurst*
73117	*University of Surrey*
73118	*The Romney, Hythe and Dymchurch Railway*
73119	*Kentish Mercury*
73119	*Borough of Eastleigh*
73121	*Croydon 1883–1983*
73122	*County of East Sussex*
73123	*Gatwick Express*
73124	*London Chamber of Commerce*
73125	*Stewarts Lane 1860–1985*
73126	*Kent & East Sussex Railway*
73128	*O.V.S. BULLIED CBE*
73129	*City of Winchester*
73130	*City of Portsmouth*
73131	*County of Surrey*
73133	*The Bluebell Railway*
73134	*Woking Homes 1885–1985*
73136	*Kent Youth Music*

ABOVE: The Class 73 subclass was a fleet of twelve locos, later increased to fourteen, dedicated to the Gatwick Express shuttles between Victoria and Gatwick Airport. Soon after their creation they lost their vacuum brakes, and consideration was even given to removing their diesel engines, but this was not pursued. 73205 sports Gatwick Express livery, essentially the last style of InterCity colours but with GatEx branding and a maroon stripe. PDC

RIGHT: 73138 has been heavily modified for its role hauling test trains for Network Rail. Its headcode has been replaced by a camera and LED light, while two new LED lights are added to the cab front. It has lost its vacuum brakes. PIP DUNN

73136	Perseverance
73137	Royal Observer Corps
73141	Ron Westwood/David Gay (one plate each side)
73141	Charlotte
73142	Broadlands
73201	Broadlands
73202	Royal Observer Corps
73202	Dave Berry
73204	Stewarts Lane 1860–1985
73204	Janice
73205	London Chamber of Commerce
73205	Jeanette
73206	Gatwick Express
73206	Lisa
73207	County of East Sussex
73208	Croydon 1883–1983
73208	Kirsten
73209	Alison
73210	Selhurst
73211	County of West Sussex
73212	Airtour Suisse

Nameplate Styles

All were in standard BR corporate style apart from 73005, 73107/128. Of these, 73005 had a two-deck curved steam style nameplate for the Watercress line with 'Mid Hands' above it. 73107 has its *Spitfire* nameplate in upper case in the Fragonset Railways style.

73128 had *O.V.S. Bulleid C.B.E* in a scroll style with a coat of arms under it, then a separate scroll which had *1937 CME Southern Railway 1949*. Both plates were painted green.

Various locos had plaques or crests with their nameplates; 73004, 73102/105/113/118/121/122/124/129/137 had single plaques below, while 73130/133/136 had single plaques above the plates. 73126 had two crests above its nameplate, while 73142 had two plaques below.

Depot Plaques

Stewarts Lane power station: 73105/107/108/110/119/128/133 C; 73114/133/136 ML; **Hither Green oast house**: 73107 F
Yellow DCE stripes: 73103/105/109/117/118 ICE

RENUMBERINGS

E6001–006 became 73001–006, and the rest of the fleet, E6007–49, became the Class 73/1s and were numbered 73101–142, with E6027 having been scrapped in 1972 so not gaining a TOPS number.

Subsequent Renumberings

73101 was renumbered 73100 in December 1980 for its first naming – to tie in with the 100th anniversary of the *Brighton Evening Argus*; it ran with this number in traffic for three weeks.

In 1988 a dozen Class 73/1s were renumbered into the 73/2 series for their dedicated use on Gatwick Express duties. Two more conversions followed in 1991 and 1996. In July, 73101 was renumbered 73801 as part of a plan to renumber a pool of infrastructure Class 73s, but it only carried the number for a week before it reverted to 73101.

Two 73/0s were renumbered into the 73/9 series for Sandite work on Merseyrail, 73001/006 becoming 73901/906.

73001	73901	
73006	73906	73006
73101	73100	73101
73101	73801	73101
73102	73212	
73112	73213	
73113	73211	
73116	73210	
73120	73209	
73121	73208	
73122	73207	
73123	73206	
73124	73205	
73125	73204	
73127	73203	
73135	73235	
73137	73202	
73142	73201	

RE-ENGINEERING PROJECTS

There are two projects on-going that will see Class 73s re-engined: the first is at RVEL in Derby where 73104 and 73211 are being rebuilt with two Cummins QSK19 750bhp diesel engines. They will retain third rail capability, although this will be upgraded. They are for Network Rail for hauling infrastructure test trains, and further locos could follow, with 73101/139 already acquired as possible donors, plus NR's own 73138 also a candidate. 73211 is likely to become 73951, with 73104 becoming 73952.

GBRf, the biggest user of Class 73s, is also re-engining its locos with an MTU engine replacing the EE unit, again giving a 1,500bhp output. 73209 is to be the first modified, with 73204–207 to follow; if successful then 73119/136/141, 73208/212/213 could follow. Other Class 73s could be sought for these projects, either for conversion or spare parts.

LEFT: Network Rail owned three Class 73s, then sold them to GB Railfreight before acquiring 73138. While in NR ownership, 73212/213 were fitted with three-piece snowploughs but only at No. 1 end, the theory being they would work as a pair when ploughing. The bufferbeams are stripped of a lot of their unnecessary pipes as they have not only lost their vacuum brakes but also their ETH. PIP DUNN

BELOW: This image compares the two different sides of the Class 73/1s. Looking from No. 1 end is 73108, with the large vertical radiator grille clear. 73136 Kent Youth Music is viewed from No. 2 end, the diesel end. Both are owned by EWS in this 2001 view. PIP DUNN

FOLLOWING THE SUCCESS of the Class 73 electro-diesels, and a reduced need for the straight electric 750V DC Class 71s, in 1967 BR selected ten Class 71s to be converted to Class 74 EDs. The conversion work was done at Crewe Works in 1967/68, and the first appeared in late 1967 and the last in 1968.

DETAIL DIFFERENCES

The 74s were converted from 71s E5015/16/06/24/19/23/03/05/17/21. They had Blue Star MW and could also operate in multiple with 1951/57/63/66 SR EMUs when running on electric.

All had ETH, dual brakes and duplicate cab-front air-brake pipes and MW cables. In pre-TOPS guise, the locos had four bodyside numbers, each behind the doors. In TOPS numbers they had just numbers on the bodysides behind the driver's doors. They had BR double arrows on all four cabsides. Detail changes between a 71 and a 74 were detailed in the section Class 71.

LIVERIES

All carried BR blue from conversion and were withdrawn in this livery.

NUMBERS

74001	E6101	converted from E5015
74002	E6102	converted from E5016
74003	E6103	converted from E5006
74004	E6104	converted from E5024
74005	E6105	converted from E5019
74006	E6106	converted from E5023
74007	E6107	converted from E5003
74008	E6108	converted from E5005
74009	E6109	converted from E5017
74010	E6110	converted from E5021

TOPS number range:	74001–010
1957 BR number range:	E6101–10
SR classification:	HB
Rebuilt by:	BR Crewe Works
Introduced:	1967–68
Wheel arrangement:	Bo-Bo
Weight (operational):	86 tons
Height:	12ft 10in (3.91m)
Width:	9ft (2.74m)
Length, buffers extended:	50ft 6in (15.39m)
Length, buffers retracted:	49ft 4in (15.04m)
Min. curve negotiable:	4 chains
Maximum speed:	90mph (144km/h)
Wheelbase:	37ft 6in (11.43m)
Bogie wheelbase:	10ft 6in (3.2m)
Bogie pivot centres:	27ft (8.23m)
Wheel diameter:	4ft (1.22m)
Route availability:	7
Brake force:	41 tons
Power supply:	600–750V DC third rail
Engine type:	Paxman 6YJXL
Horsepower, electric:	2,552bhp (1,904kW)
Horsepower, diesel:	650bhp (485kW)
Rail horsepower, electric:	2,020bhp (1,507kW)
Rail horsepower, diesel:	315bhp (235kW)
Tractive effort, electric:	47,500lb
Tractive effort, diesel:	40,000lb
Main generator type:	EE843
No. of traction motors:	4
Traction motor type:	EE532A
Gear ratio:	76:22
Fuel tank capacity:	310gal (1,395ltr)

ABOVE: E6101 in September 1969 not long after conversion shows a Class 74 in its prime. It has bodyside numbers on all four corners, and shows the window and grille arrangement. RAIL PHOTOPRINTS

RIGHT: Withdrawn 74005 has lost its duplicate brake pipes but retains its MW cable on the cab front. These locos were converted from Class 71s and featured a Paxman diesel engine of the same design used in Class 14s. PDC

class 76

TOPS number range:	76001–057
Former number range:	E26000–057
Former class code:	EM1
Built by:	BR Doncaster and Gorton
Introduced:	1941–53
Wheel arrangement:	Bo+Bo
Weight (operational):	88 tons
Height, pan down:	13ft (3.96m)
Width:	9ft (2.74m)
Length:	50ft 4in (15.24m)
Min. curve negotiable:	6 chains
Maximum speed:	65mph (104km/h)
Wheelbase:	35ft (10.67m)
Bogie wheelbase:	11ft 6in (3.51m)
Bogie pivot centres:	23ft 6in (7.16m)
Wheel diameter:	4ft 2in (1.27m)
Route availability:	8
Brake force:	43 tons
Horsepower:	1,868bhp (1,394kW)
Tractive effort:	45,000lb
No. of traction motors:	4
Traction motor type:	MV 186
Control system:	Electro-pneumatic
Gear ratio:	17:70
Pantograph type:	MV Cross-arm
OHLE power supply:	1,500V DC overhead

THE PROTOTYPE 1,500v DC loco was built by the LNER and undertook some tests on the electrified lines to Altrincham and also on the GE lines to Shenfield. World War II prevented any further testing, and post-war with the electrification plan behind schedule, the loco was loaned to the Netherlands from 1947–52 – where it was given the nickname *Tommy* – and it was officially named as such in June 1952 on its return.

Construction of fifty-seven production series locos started in 1950, and they were delivered in 1950–53. They were used exclusively on the Manchester-Sheffield-Wath 'Woodhead' route, which was not fully electrified until 1954. Being a non-standard electrification system the line and locos fell into disrepair, losing first their passenger

services in January 1970, when the steam-heat locos lost their boilers. Full closure came in July 1981, rendering the 76s redundant. One is preserved.

DETAIL DIFFERENCES

Pioneer E26000 was noticeably different from the production series locos as it had a different cab with no quarterlight windows, and the cab doors much further along the bodyside, such that the only cabside window was in the cab door.

The production locos had a window in the doors as well as a cabside window and a quarterlight window. The front cab windows were smaller and did not have the metal rim round them; the side vertical cab pillars were also more rounded on E26000.

The cant rail where the roof was fitted was also more pronounced on the production locos, and the front horizontal handrail continued round on to the cabsides. E26000 had plaques on its front and an inscription below its nameplate. It was named 'Tommy' after the nickname given to it by 'Dutch' crews when it went to the Netherlands for trials.

Train identification was by using detachable white discs, which were placed by hand over four lamps in the

Three Class 76s, which may look the same but are not. The left and middle locos, 76012/016, are dual-braked, while 76033 on the right is air-braked only and hence has had its vacuum-brake pipe removed from the cab front. 76012 also shows the removable red discs often fitted to 76s when they were banking locos at Worsborough. All three have MW fitted, a feature exclusive to air- and dual-braked 76s. All three have their pantographs down as they are stabled. ANDY HOARE

The Class 76s not fitted with air brakes retained a clean front end with just their vacuum-brake pipes and four lamps. 76053, once named Perseus, *has changed little since construction in 1953, apart from losing its train-heating boiler and steam pipe mounted on the bufferbeam. The 76s, unlike the 77s, had their buffers fixed to their bogies, a feature only seen on Class 40/44–46s.* PDC

same inverted T formation. To show a red tail-light, a red-rimmed disc with a red lens was placed over the marker lights, and this system – most often seen on the banking locos at Worsborough – was used until the class's demise.

Bastian & Allen steam-heat boilers were fitted to E26000/046–057, but were later removed, apart from 76052–055/057, which had them isolated.

All locos were built with vacuum brakes only, but 76006–016/021–030 were converted to dual brakes in 1969/70. 76003/018/032–034/037/044/048/050 were converted to air only, and to keep them in a numerical batch, they were renumbered 76036/035/032–034/037/031/039/038 respectively. This meant the original 76036/039/038 became 76003/048/050 respectively. 76001–004/020/040/041/043/044/046–057 and E26000/005/017/019/031/035/042/045 remained vacuum-braked only until withdrawal.

All dual- and air-braked locos, 76006–016/021–039, were also fitted with MW, which was only compatible within the class.

Vacuum- and dual-braked locos had their vacuum-brake pipes mounted on the cab fronts. Dual-braked locos were noticeable as they had the MW cables on the front plus the air-brake and two main reservoir pipes on the buffer-beams. Air-braked locos looked the same as dual-braked locos, except that the vacuum pipe was removed.

LIVERIES

LNER Apple Green: 6701 (E26000)
BR black: E26000–057
BR lined green: E26000–057:
BR green with small yellow panels: E26000–057
BR green with full yellow ends: E26031
BR blue with small yellow panels: E26001/002/009/019–022/026/028/029/033/037/050
BR blue: 76001–004/006–016/018–041/043–057
BR blue with grey roof: E26002/030/046, 76025

NUMBER STYLES

76050 (later 76038) was the first BR loco of any type renumbered under TOPS in November 1971. When E26049 was initially renumbered it was incorrectly

Air-brake only 76032 stands in Reddish shed undergoing maintenance. Nine Class 76s were converted from vacuum brakes to air brakes only, while another twenty-one were converted to dual-brake operation. They were the only 1,500V DC electric locos to be renumbered under TOPS, and could only work between Manchester Piccadilly and Sheffield/Wath: when this line closed in 1981 they were redundant and sold for scrap. PDC

given the number E76049 at first, although the E was soon removed.

Despite several locos running with E numbers in the correct corporate font, some 76s also ran with TOPS numbers in serif font, namely 76044/057.

Some locos ran with numbers on all four cabs, namely 76003*/008/010–013/015/016/021–023/030/043/044/049/050/057 (* the original 76003).

The position of the BR double arrow varied depending on the side of the loco, with the badges under the nameplates on the few BR blue locos that carried nameplates (at least E26053/054/057). At least E26049–052/056 lost their plates while in green.

BR lion and wheel emblems were carried by several BR blue locos, and 76022 retained them until withdrawal in 1981. Others which had lion and wheel badges in blue were E26009/020.

NAMES

26000	*TOMMY*
26046	*ARCHIMEDES*
26047	*DIOMEDES*
26048	*HECTOR*
26049	*JASON*
26050	*STENTOR*
26051	*MENTOR*
26052	*NESTOR*
26053	*PERSEUS*
26054	*PLUTO*
26055	*PROMETHEUS*
26056	*TRITON*
26057	*ULYSSES*

Nameplates were removed *circa* 1969/70.

Dates locos dual-braked: E26007/008/010/011/016/021/023–026/030 (1969); E26006/009/012–015/022/027–029 (1970).

Dates locos air-braked only: 76034 (1975); 76018*/033/037/044* (1976); 76003*/032/048*/050* (1977); * loco renumbered upon conversion – *see* below.

RENUMBERINGS FROM E SERIES

When built in 1941, the original locomotive was numbered 6701. This was altered to 6000 and then E26000 into the main fleet.

26000/005/017/019/035/042/045 were never renumbered under TOPS. The rest of the fleet changed their E26xxx number for 76xxx numbers.

Subsequent Renumberings

To keep the nine air-braked locos together numerically, the following renumbering took place in 1975/76:

76003	76036
76018	76035
76036	76003
76038	76050
76039	76048
76044	76031
76048	76039
76050	76038

Number range:	E27000–006
Former class type:	EM2
Built by:	BR Gorton
Introduced:	1953–54
Wheel arrangement:	Co-Co
Weight:	102 tons
Height (pan down):	13ft (3.96m)
Width:	8ft 10in (2.69m)
Length:	59ft (17.98m)
Min. curve negotiable:	6 chains
Maximum speed:	90mph (144km/h)
Wheelbase:	46ft 2in (14.07)
Bogie wheelbase:	15ft 10in (4.83m)
Bogie pivot centres:	30ft 6in (9.3m)
Wheel diameter:	3ft 7in (1.09m)
Route availability:	8
Horsepower:	2,300bhp (1,716kW)
Tractive effort (max):	45,000lb
No. of traction motors:	6
Traction motor type:	MV 146
Control system:	Electro-pneumatic
Gear ratio:	17:64
Pantograph type:	MV Cross-arm
OHLE power supply:	1,500V DC overhead

Six of the seven Class 77s had an extended life working in the Netherlands from 1969 to 1986. Three were then preserved, two in the UK. 27000 Electra is now back in British Railways' black with its original number, and while the original look of a vacuum-braked 77 has been partially made by refitting pipes to the cab front, it still retains its Dutch light clusters and air brakes. PIP DUNN

Shorn of nameplates, this August 1968 image is E27002 Aurora in electric blue with a small yellow warning panel. It also shows the rotary windscreen wiper trial-fitted to this loco only. BILL WRIGHT

A CO-CO VERSION of the EM1, classified EM2s, the Class 77s shared the same cab design as their Class 76 sisters, but had a longer body. All were withdrawn in 1968 but sold to 'Dutch' state railways and shipped abroad the following year. Six of the seven were overhauled and lasted in traffic until 1985. Three have been preserved, two in the UK and one in the Netherlands.

DETAIL DIFFERENCES

The locos had the same detachable discs, fitted over marker lights, as the Class 76s to show train classification. Unlike the Class 76s, which had their buffers mounted on their bogies, the 77s had bufferbeams fixed to the body. They also had oval buffers as opposed to round.

E27002 ran with a trial rotary windscreen wiper, running for periods with one on each front cab window and then for a period with just one on the driver's front window.

All were built with vacuum brakes only, but after export E27000–04/06 were converted to air brakes only in the Netherlands. E27005 remained vacu-

um-braked only as it was scrapped for parts. All had Bastian & Allen steamheat boilers, but these were removed from the six Dutch locos that were converted to ETH.

In the Netherlands the locos had a number of changes to their front ends. The vacuum-brake pipe was removed, as were the four BR white lamps. A central headlight was fitted between, and under, the cab windows and two vertical light clusters with white marker lights at the bottom and red tail-lights at the top. The left-hand cab front lamp iron was also removed. The two crossarm pantographs were changed for single-arm versions.

LIVERIES

BR green with small yellow panels: 27000–06
Electric blue: 27001/02/04/06

Electric blue with small yellow panels: 27001/02/04
NS grey and yellow: 1501–06 (27000–04/06)

NAMES

E27000	Electra
E27001	Ariadne
E27002	Aurora
E27003	Diana
E27004	Juno
E27005	Minerva
E27006	Pandora

NETHERLANDS RENUMBERINGS

1501	E27003
1502	E27000
1503	E27004
1504	E27006
1505	E27001
1506	E27002

THE FIRST OF five designs from various manufacturers for AC electric locos for the West Coast main line, the twenty-five AL1s, later Class 81s, were built by BRCW using AEI electrical equipment at Smethwick. A batch of twenty-three passenger locos and two dedicated freight locos were planned, though the latter were shelved during their construction and all twenty-five locos ended up being the same.

The class was run down from the mid-1980s, the last loco being laid up in July 1991.

DETAIL DIFFERENCES

All had ETH and vacuum brakes from new. All were dual-braked apart from E3002/09/19, withdrawn after accidents. Dual-brake dates were E3003/05–08/10/13/18/20/96 (1972); E3001/04/11/12/14–17/21–23/97 (1973).

All were built with centre panels on their cab fronts. These were changed to dominos in the late 1970s on 81001–006/008–022, but 81007 went straight from roller blinds to yellow panels. Yellow panels with white lenses were fitted to 81001–022 from the early 1980s.

LIVERIES

Electric blue: E3001–023/096/097
BR blue: 81001–022, E3019

NUMBERS

The locos were delivered as E3001–23, and the last two were numbered E3301/02 as they were dedicated freight locos. However, only E3301 appeared as such, and E3302 actually appeared after construction as E3097. E3301 was later renumbered to E3096.

All were renumbered 81001–022, with E3002/09/19 written off before TOPS. A proposal to renumber 81020 as 81901 for ECS work was mooted but never taken up.

specifications

TOPS number range:	81001–022
Former number range:	E3001–023/096/097 (E3301–E3302)
Former class code:	AL1
Built by:	BRC&W Ltd
Introduced:	1959–64
Wheel arrangement:	Bo-Bo
Weight:	79 tons
Height:	13ft 1in (3.99m)
Width:	8ft 9in (2.67)
Length:	56ft 6in (17.22m)
Min. curve negotiable:	4 chains
Maximum speed:	100mph (160km/h)
Wheelbase:	42ft 3in (12.88m)
Bogie wheelbase:	10ft 9in (3.28m)
Bogie pivot centres:	31ft 6in (9.6m)
Wheel diameter:	4ft (1.22m)
Route availability:	6
Brake force:	40 tons
Horsepower (cont):	3,200bhp (2,387kW)
Horsepower (max):	4,800bhp (3,581kW)
Tractive effort (max):	50,000lb
No. of traction motors:	4
Traction motor type:	AEI 189
Control system:	LT tap changing
Gear drive:	Alstom Quill, single reduction
Gear ratio:	29:76
Pantograph type:	Stone-Faiveley
Rectifier type:	Originally mercury arc, modified to silicon
OHLE power supply:	25kV AC

TOP LEFT: E3007 in August 1965 is still in as-built condition, being vacuum-braked only but with ETH. It is in electric blue colours but without yellow panels. By the windows is a small vertical shield, a feature on many early electric locos (and the Class 50s) when built; it was fitted as a measure to reduce wind in the driver's face if leaning out of the window at any speed, but was soon removed. This loco later became 81006, and lost its raised aluminium digits when renumbered. BILL WRIGHT

LEFT: 81006 shows the domino headcodes adopted from the mid-1970s for Classes 81–83 but not the 84/85s. All but 81007 received this look, but all then went on to have yellow panels with marker lights fitted. PDC

class 82

TOPS number range:	82001–008
Former number range:	E3046–55
Former class code:	AL2
Built by:	Beyer Peacock
Introduced:	1960–61
Wheel arrangement:	Bo-Bo
Weight:	80 tons
Height (pan down):	13ft 1in (3.99m)
Width:	8ft 9in (2.67m)
Length:	56ft (17.07m)
Min. curve negotiable:	4 chains
Maximum speed:	100mph (160km/h)
Wheelbase:	40ft 9in (12.42m)
Bogie wheelbase:	10ft (3.05m)
Bogie pivot centres:	30ft 9in (9.37m)
Wheel diameter:	4ft (1.22m)
Route availability:	6
Brake force:	38 tons
Horsepower (cont):	3,300bhp (2,462kW)
Horsepower (max):	5,500bhp (4,103kW)
Tractive effort (max):	50,000lb
No. of traction motors:	4
Traction motor type:	AEI 189
Control system:	HT tap changing
Gear drive:	Alstom Quill, single reduction
Pantograph type:	Stone-Faiveley
Rectifier type:	Originally mercury arc, rebuilt with silicon
OHLE power supply:	25kV AC

A FLEET OF ten electric locos was built by Beyer Peacock on behalf of AEI and Metropolitan Vickers and classified AL2, later Class 82. Two were withdrawn prior to dual braking and TOPS numbering, but the other eight survived in traffic into the early 1980s. They were stored *en masse* in late 1982, although two were reinstated and moved to Willesden as 40mph ECS locos, a role they continued (along with two Class 83s) until late 1987. 82008 was repainted in InterCity colours and is now the only survivor.

DETAIL DIFFERENCES

The locos had ETH from new and vacuum brakes only. Eight were converted to dual brakes, E3049 (1971), E3047/48/50–54 (1972); E3046/55 were not dual-braked after being written off.

All were fitted with centre panels in the cab fronts, but these were changed to dominos on 82004/007/008. Yellow panels with white marker lamps were fitted to 82001/003–008. These differed to those panels fitted to 81s and 85s as they were not recessed to retain the outline shape of the redundant headcodes, and instead were plated over the whole headcode boxes.

LIVERIES

Electric blue: E3046–55
Electric blue with small yellow panel: E3046–55
BR blue: 82001–008, E3046
InterCity Executive: 82008
BR 'Large Logo' blue: 82008
(in preservation)

82006 shows the plated-over headcode panels fitted to all but 82002. These differed from the yellow panels on 81s and 85s, which had the white marker lights fitting in a recessed panel covering the headcodes. The Class 82s were also very noticeable by the large plates on the side in the middle of the bogies. PDC

class 83

TOPS number range:	83001–015	Wheel diameter:	4ft (1.22m)
Former number range:	E3024–35, E3098–100 (E3303/04)	Route availability:	6
		Brake force:	38 tons
Former class code:	AL3	Horsepower (cont):	2,950bhp (2,201kW)
Built by:	English Electric	Horsepower (max):	4,400bhp (3,283kW)
Introduced:	1960–62	Tractive effort (max):	38,000lb
Wheel arrangement:	Bo-Bo	No. of traction motors:	4
Weight:	77 tons	Traction motor type:	EE 535A
Height (pan down):	13ft 1in (3.99m)	Control system:	LT tap changing
Width:	8ft 9in (2.67m)	Gear drive:	SLM flexible, single reduction
Length:	52ft 6in (16m)		
Min. curve negotiable:	4 chains	Gear ratio:	25:76
Maximum speed:	100mph (160km/h)	Pantograph type:	Stone-Faiveley
Wheelbase:	40ft (12.19m)	Rectifier type:	Mercury arc, changed to Silicon
Bogie wheelbase:	10ft (3.05m)		
Bogie pivot centres:	30ft (9.15m)	OHLE power supply:	25kV AC

THE ENGLISH ELECTRIC offering for the early AC electric designs was a batch of fifteen locos, the AL3s. Like the Class 82s, they were all laid up by late 1982 apart from three revived for ECS work at Euston. One has been preserved.

DETAIL DIFFERENCES

All had centre panels, but these were changed in the late 1970s to dominos, although 83003/004 had been withdrawn and did not receive them. 83008/012 also avoided the change and the latter retained its original roller blinds right through to withdrawal in March 1989, even while painted in InterCity livery.

All were built with vacuum brakes, and all were dual-braked, with 83002/

004–014 in 1972, and 83001/003/015 in 1973. All were renumbered at the time of dual-braking.

LIVERIES

Electric blue: E3024–35, E3098–100
Electric blue with small yellow panels: E3024–35, E3098–100
BR blue: 83001–015
InterCity Executive: 83012

RENUMBERINGS

Like the AL1s, initially a batch of three dedicated freight locos was planned, numbered E3303–05. In the event E3305 was not numbered and took the number E3100 while E3303/04 became E3098/99. The locos were renumbered from E3024–35/98–100 to 83001–015.

The only surviving Class 83, E3035 is in near-original condition apart from now being dual-braked. The loco remarkably never lost its roller-blind headcodes despite lasting in traffic until 1989, of which the last six years were on ECS duties in the Euston area. PIP DUNN

class 84
specifications

NORTH BRITISH BUILT these ten AC electric locos, the AL4s, the only electrics it built for BR. Although all ten were dual-braked in 1972, they were the first of the early electric types to be laid up as 'life expired' and non-standard. The first two were condemned in April 1977 and the last two in November 1980.

84009 was retained for Departmental use, while 84001 was claimed by the National Railway Museum: it is the sole surviving NBL main-line loco.

DETAIL DIFFERENCES

All had centre panels, and none were changed to dominos or yellow panels, all being withdrawn with roller blinds.

All were built with vacuum brakes, and all were dual-braked in 1972 – and all were renumbered, in series, at the same time.

TOPS number range:	84001–010		Wheel diameter:	4ft (1.22m)
1957 BR number range:	E3036–45		Route availability:	6
Former class code:	AL4		Brake force:	38 tons
Built by:	North British Locomotive Co. Ltd		Horsepower (cont.):	3,300bhp (2,462kW)
			Horsepower (max):	4,900bhp (3,655kW)
Introduced:	1960–61		Tractive effort (max):	50,000lb
Wheel arrangement:	Bo-Bo		No. of traction motors:	4
Weight (operational):	77 tons		Traction motor type:	GEC WT 501
Height (pan down):	13ft 1in (3.99m)		Control system:	HT tap changing
Width:	8ft 8in (2.64m)		Gear drive:	Brown Boveri
Length:	53ft 6in (16.31m)		Gear ratio:	25:74
Min. curve negotiable:	4 chains		Pantograph type:	Stone-Faiveley
Maximum speed:	100mph (160km/h)		Rectifier type:	Mercury arc rectifiers, converted to Silicon
Wheelbase:	39ft 6in (12.04m)			
Bogie wheelbase:	10ft (3.05m)		OHLE power supply:	25kV AC
Bogie pivot centres:	29ft 6in (8.99m)			

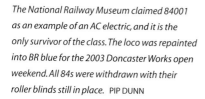

The National Railway Museum claimed 84001 as an example of an AC electric, and it is the only survivor of the class. The loco was repainted into BR blue for the 2003 Doncaster Works open weekend. All 84s were withdrawn with their roller blinds still in place. PIP DUNN

LIVERIES

Electric blue: E3036–45
Electric blue with small yellow panels: E3036–45
BR blue: 84001-010
Research Department red and blue: ADB968021 (84009)

DEPARTMENTAL USE

After withdrawal in July 1978, 84009 was transferred to Departmental use for use as a load bank to test feeder and substations during electrification projects. It was converted at the Derby RTC, which saw its headcode boxes replaced by dominos, the two grilles at No. 1 end on A-side extended the full height of the body, and on B-side the window closed to the cab at No. 1 end also being removed and replaced by two similar full-height grilles. Two other Research Department features were also added to the cab front.

A spotlamp was fitted to each cab, below the headcode boxes and in between the red tail-lights. Most striking was the livery change – into the red and blue Research Departmental livery. It was renumbered ADB968021.

84009 was taken into Departmental use as a load bank and given domino headcodes, spotlamps, extended grilles and the RTC's red and blue livery. Renumbered ADB968021, its role ended in December 1992 and it was later scrapped, although one cab was saved for posterity by the AC Loco Group. PDC

class 85

specifications

TOPS number range:	85001–040, 85101–114	Wheel diameter:	4ft (1.22m)
Former class code:	AL5	Route availability:	6
Former number range:	E3056–95	Brake force:	41 tons
Built by:	BR Doncaster	Horsepower, (cont):	3,200bhp (2,387kW)
Introduced:	1961–64	Horsepower (max):	5,100bhp (3,805kW)
Wheel arrangement:	Bo-Bo	Tractive effort (max):	50,000lb
Weight (operational):	83 tons	No. of traction motors:	4
Height (pan down):	13ft 1in (3.99m)	Traction motor type:	AEI 189
Width:	8ft 8in (2.64m)	Control system:	LT tap-changing
Length:	56ft 6in (17.22m)	Gear drive:	Alstom Quill, single reduction
Min. curve negotiable:	6 chains	Gear ratio:	29:76
Maximum speed:	100mph (160km/h)	Pantograph type:	Stone-Faiveley
Wheelbase:	42ft 3in (12.88m)	Rectifier type:	Originally mercury arc, modified to Silicon
Bogie wheelbase:	10ft 9in (3.28m)		
Bogie pivot centres:	31ft 6in (9.6m)	OHLE power supply:	25kV AC

THE FINAL DESIGN of 'early' AC electrics, the Class 85s were built by BR at Doncaster. They were the longest surviving of the AL1-5s, the last being retired from front-line traffic in late 1991, with one loco retained until 1992 as an ECS loco. A batch of ten were modified for freight use in 1989, although the locos set aside for this work varied, such that fourteen became 85/1s, but all fourteen were never in traffic together. One is preserved.

DETAIL DIFFERENCES

All were built with centre panels on their cab fronts. These were changed to yellow panels with white lenses, and were fitted to the whole fleet from the early 1980s.

All had ETH and vacuum brakes from new. All were dual-braked: E3058/65/71–74/83/85/88/89/94 in 1970; E3057/60/62/63/68/69/75–77/81/92/93/95 in 1971; E3056/59/64/66/67/70/78–80/82/84/86/87/90/91 in 1972; E3061 in 1973.

In 1989, the Railfreight sector created the 85/1s, which would have a lower top speed of 75mph (120km/h) and have their ETH isolated (usually just by removal of the jumper cables). The reduced speed did not involve any modifications.

85006/009/010/012/016/021/024/032/035/036 became 85101–110. When 85107 caught fire, 85004 became 85111, although the freight sector still had 85007/015/018/026/028/031/034/040 in its pool, all nominally 'restricted' to 80mph (129km/h) but with their ETH still operable.

As other 85/1s failed, other locos were renumbered, and 85023 was set to become 85112 to replace 85104; however, it was replaced by 85007, which took up the number in March 1990. In October 1990, 85113 was created from 85003, and this replaced 85106, while 85114, previously 85011 – another parcels sector loco – was also created the same month, in place of 85111.

LIVERIES

Electric blue: E3056–95
BR blue: 85001–040
RfD: 85101*
Two-tone grey: 85101*
Cast depot emblems; Crewe eagle:
85101 FD/F*

* in preservation

NAMES

No Class 85s were officially named in BR days, though 85030 spent many months with the unofficial name *Fell Runner* on its A-side above the BR badge. In preservation, 85101 was named *Doncaster Plant 150 1853–2003*.

SUBSEQUENT RENUMBERINGS

85006   85101
85009   85102

85010	85103
85012	85104
85016	85105
85021	85106
85024	85107
85032	85108
85035	85109
85036	85110
85004	85111
85007	85112
85003	85113
85011	85114

DETAIL DIFFERENCES BETWEEN THE AL1–5s

Although the AL1–5s and the Class 81–85s shared a similar body design, there were many detail differences between the fleets. All had ETH with an index of 66.

The Class 81s and 85s shared the same bodyshell, but the most noticeable difference was that while the bodyside grilles and windows on the 81s were flush in the body, on the 85s they were indented. The Class 85s also had a kick-step under the driver's doors, and differed in the layout of the underslung equipment.

The Class 81s had grilles on the A-side in a 1-4-3-1 formation, and four windows on the B-side.

The Class 82s when built had six grilles in a 1-4-1 layout, but when refurbished this was changed so the middle bank of four grilles were moved in pairs further down the bodyside in a 1-2-2-1 formation on the A-side. On the B-side they had a square grille, then two windows and then a grille, all similarly spaced apart.

The Class 83s had on the A-side four longer rectangular grilles that were more or less equi-distant, while on the B-side they had a large grille in the centre of the body and two larger windows, one on each side. The middle grille was originally a window when the locos were built, but changed when they were refurbished.

The Class 84s had on the A-side two grilles by the cab door, then two windows in the centre of the bodyside, and another two grilles close to the driver's door at the opposite end. On the B-side they had four windows that were two-part, unlike the other classes, where the top half could be opened by pushing it down.

The Class 85s had grilles in a 4-1-1-4 formation on the A-side and four fixed windows on the other side.

From the late 1970s dominos were fitted to some or all surviving Class 81s, 82s and 83s, but all 84s were withdrawn with roller-blind headcodes, as were

ABOVE: A Class 85 in its final guise, 85014 has yellow headcode panels, TOPS numbers and dual brakes, the air tanks for which are mounted on the roof in the space originally occupied by the second pantograph. This is the A side of the loco which had grilles in the bodyside. PDC

RIGHT: The B side of a Class 85 comprised four windows. The 85s and 81s were very similar in bodyshell, but the 81s had flush sides while the 85s had their grilles and windows indented. 85101 was the only 85 repainted into Railfreight Distribution livery, although this came after it was withdrawn and sold for preservation; however, it is a good indicator of 'what might have been' had the 85/1 trial proved a success and RfD opted to overhaul some of the locos. PIP DUNN

83003/004/008/012. No 85s had dominos.

Yellow headcode panels were added to all TOPS 81s, 85s and some 82s, but no 83s or 84s ever had them.

All locos were built with two single-arm pantographs, of which one was only ever needed at any one time, but when dual-braked the 'pan' at No. 1 end was removed and the space used to fit the three air tanks for the dual-brake modification.

The cast-raised aluminium numbers that the 81–85s had from new were removed and replaced by white transfers under the driver's cab windows. The BR lion and wheel badges and then the double arrow badges were also raised aluminium, but some of the latter were changed to transfers in later days.

Like the Class 50s when new, the AL1–5s were fitted with side window deflectors, small glass panels fitted on the vertical pillar of the side window to deflect the wind on the driver's face when looking out of his window at speed, when built. These were removed in the early 1970s, though the occasional 84, such as 84008, retained them until withdrawal.

class 86

specifications

TOPS number range:	86001–048, 86101–103, 86201–261, 86311–329, 86401–439, 86501–508, 86501, 86602–639, 86701/702, 86901/902	Traction output (max):	5,900bhp (4,400kW); 6,100bhp (4,550kW) – Class 86/2; 7,680bhp (5,860kW) – Class 86/1
		Traction output (cont):	3,600bhp (2,680kW); 4,040bhp (3,013kW) – Class 86/2; 5,000bhp (3,730kW) – Class 86/1
1957 BR number range:	E3101–E3200 series	Tractive effort:	58,000lb
Former class code:	AL6	Maximum speed:	80mph (129km/h) – Class 86/0; 100–110mph (160–180km/h) – Class 86/2; 75mph (120km/h) – Class 86/6, 86501
Built by:	English Electric Vulcan Foundry and BR Doncaster		
Years introduced:	1965–66		
Wheel arrangement:	Bo-Bo	Brake force:	40 tons
Weight:	81–87 tons	Route availability:	6
Height (pan down):	13ft 1in (3.97m)	Control system:	HT tap-changing
Length:	58ft 6in (17.83m)	Traction motor type:	AEI 282AZ, GEC G412AZ 86/1; AEI G282BZ 86/5
Width:	8ft 8in (2.64m)		
Wheelbase:	43ft 6in (13.25m)	No of traction motors:	4
Bogie wheelbase:	10ft 9in (3.27m)	Gear ratio:	22:65, 32:73 – 86/1; 18:70 - 86501
Bogie pivot centres:	32ft 9in (9.98m)		
Wheel diameter:	3ft 9¼in (1.15m)	OHLE power supply:	25kV AC overhead
Min. curve negotiable:	4 chains (80.46m)		

THE SIXTH DESIGN of AC electric loco for the WCML, the 100-strong Class 86s, entered traffic in 1965 as more of the route was electrified. They were the standard electric type for the route until the Class 87s arrived in 1973. Dual-braked and fitted with ETH, the fleet has been through many changes over the years. Sixteen remain in front-line service with Freightliner, including a unique trial loco, re-geared 86501.

DETAIL DIFFERENCES

All had centre panels on their cab fronts. 86235/251 ran with dominos, while most went from roller blinds showing 0O00 to yellow metal panels with white lamps. 86430 had its panels removed and a flush front fitted with two white lamps.

All had ETH (index 66) from new, but later isolated on 86602–615/618/620–623/627/628/631–639.

Brakes were dual from new, but the vacuum brakes were isolated on 86101/102, 86205–209/212–242/244–253/255–260, 86401/424/425, 86602–615/618/620–623/627/628/631–639 to make them air only.

86602

Freightliner is now the only user of Class 86s on a day-to-day basis. Apart from 86501, which is re-geared, the rest of its fleet are Class 86/6s, which are Class 86/4s restricted to 75mph (120km/h) and without ETH. However, in this February 2005 view, 86602 retains its ETH jumpers and the system could be reinstated relatively easily. The loco had TDM for working in multiple with other 86s, and the original multiple working cables have been removed and plated over, the mounting points being beside the top of the TDM jumpers. The loco is air-braked only and has oval buffers.
ANTHONY HICKS

Multiple-working jumpers cables for working with Class 86s and 87s were fitted on the cab fronts to 86001–005/ 008/010/031–039, 86311–315/317–323/ 325–329. Those Class 86/0s and 86/3s which did not have the equipment had it fitted when converted to Class 86/4s. The jumpers were removed in the late 1980s as TDM was fitted to the fleet. TDM was fitted to all apart from 86211.

Sealed beam headlights were fitted to the side of the red taillight on 86004/ 010/016/030/038, 86103, 86203/214, 86316/327. These were plated over on 86430/438. 86225 ran with a small spot-lamp centrally mounted above its buffer-beam. All apart from 86211 and 86429 had the standard BR high intensity head-light fitted in the mid-1980s.

Pantograph styles varied over the years. The class started with single-arm pantographs. In the 1970s some were changed to cross-arm diamond ver-sions, and then reverted to standard high-speed single-arm pantographs.

E3173 was fitted with a test cab in October 1970, with the same cab shell as were to be used on the prototype HST.

SUB-CLASS DIFFERENCES

All were built the same, but from 1972, fifty-two were converted at Crewe Works to flexicoil suspension. When TOPS came into effect, these were numbered as Class 86/2s. They differed visually from the remaining forty-eight locos – now numbered Class 86/0s – by having three vertical springs between the top of the bogies and the underside of the body. The Class 86/0s and 86/3s had a triangular frame in this area.

There were no noticeable visual dif-ferences between 86/0s and 86/3s, the latter simply having different wheelsets. The differences between the 86/2s and the three 86/1s (which were, in effect, Class 87s in a Class 86 bodyshell) were limited to below the solebar, the latter having BP9 bogies and an extra panel covering some of the underslung equipment.

When Class 86/0s and 86/3s were converted to 86/4s they had flexicoil suspension fitted, but their MW cables made them instantly different from 86/2s. Some 86/6s ran with their origi-nal MW still in place while still having TDM cables, but it was soon removed.

86252 in Anglia Railways livery. The loco is air-braked only, has TDM and a high intensity headlight, all changes made during its later life. PIP DUNN

Those Class 86/4s and 86/6s which lost their original MW cables had the holes where the equipment fitted plated over.

There have been two types of Class 86/5s. The first was a batch of eight con-verted from 86/2s in 1988/89. Initially planned for freight use only, the first loco was outshopped in InterCity colours, but 86502 onwards were in grey. However, 86506/508 were outshopped in InterCity colours by which time it was decided to convert the 86/4s to freight use as 86/6s. All eight 86/5s then reverted to their pre-vious 86/2 identities.

This led to most 86/4s being changed to 86/6s, apart from a batch retained as 86/4s for mail traffic. The 86/6s have their ETH isolated and their top speed reduced to 75mph (120km/h).

In 2000, 86608 was fitted with re-geared bogies by Freightliner, and re-numbered as 86501 with a view to a single 86/5 replacing a pair of 86/6s. While publicly the trial was a success, no more 86/6s were changed to 86/5s, although 86501 remains in traffic.

Converted from 86/2s, the two Class 86/9s are Network Rail locos used for clearing ice of OLE, while the two Class 86/7s are ETL locos available for spot hire and are 86/2s with new numbers.

LIVERIES

Electric blue with small yellow pan-els and grey cab roof: E3101–200
BR blue: 86001–048, 86101–103, 86201–261, 86311–329, 86402/420
BR blue with large numbers and body-side L&M 150th motifs: 86235

BR blue with wrap-round yellow cabs, black windows, large numbers and bodyside L&M 150th motifs: 86214/ 235
BR blue with grey cab roofs: 86233
InterCity Executive: 86101–103, 86204/ 207–210/212–221/223–229/231–236/ 238–240/242–248/250–256/259/260, 86403–425/427–439, 86501
InterCity Mainline: 86101, 86206–210/ 212–214/216/220/221/225–232/234/ 236–238/240–242/248–251/253–257/ 259–261, 86403/405/406/410/412/414– 417/419/422/424–426/428/430/431/ 434/437/439, 86506/508, 86607/609/ 620/621
InterCity: 86101–103, 86204–210/212– 238/240/242/244–253/255–260
Original NSE: 86401
Anglia: 86209/215/217/218/220/221/ 223/227/230/232/234/235/237/238/242/ 246/250/252/255/257
Parcels: 86239/241, 86419/424/425
Res: 86210/239/241/243/254/261, 86401/416/417/419/424–426/430
Virgin: 86204–206/209/212/214/222/ 226/229/231/233/236/240/242/244/245/ 247/248/251/256/258–260
Virgin Caledonian blue: 86245
Electric blue (special): 86233, 86426
Railfreight general: 86502, 86602/613/ 627
RfD: 86405/411/414/415/428/431, 86602 –615/618/620–623/627/628/631–639
RfD European: 86603–606/608/618/ 622
RfD European unbranded: 86603/608
Two-tone grey: 86502–507, 86603/607/ 612/615
EWS: 86261, 86401/426

Freightliner grey: 86604–606/611–614/618/621–623/628/633/637–639
Freightliner green: 86426/430, 86501, 86602/604/605/607–615/618/620/621/627/638/632–636
Freightliner Powerhaul: 86622/637
Network Rail yellow: 86424, 86901/902
Europhoenix: 86247
Floyd: 86215/217/218/232/248/250

NUMBERS

Standard numbers were carried in BR blue and most InterCity variations, although larger cabside numbers were on 86213/218/223/235/249/252/254, 86411/417/432/437 ICE, 86609/620 ICM.

86221 has NSE flashes under its numbers while in IO, while 86222 has NSE branding and flashes in B.

NAMES

86101	Sir William A Stanier FRS
86102	Robert A Riddles
86103	André Chapelon
86204	City of Carlisle
86205	City of Lancaster
86206	City of Stoke on Trent
86207	City of Lichfield
86208	City of Chester
86209	City of Coventry
86210	City of Edinburgh
86210	C.I.T. 75th Anniversary
86211	City of Milton Keynes
86212	Preston Guild
86212	Preston Guild 1328–1992
86213	Lancashire Witch
86214	Sans Pareil
86215	Joseph Chamberlain
86215	Norwich Cathedral
86215	Norwich & Norfolk Festival
86215	The Round Tabler
86216	Meteor
86217	Comet
86217	Halley's Comet
86217	City University
86218	Planet
86218	Harold Macmillan
86218	Year of Opera and Musical Theatre 1997
86218	NHS 50
86219	Phoenix
86220	Goliath
86220	The Round Tabler
86221	Vesta
86221	BBC Look East
86222	Fury
86222	LLOYDS LIST

86222	LLOYDS LIST 250TH ANNIVERSARY
86222	Clothes Show Live
86223	Hector
86223	Norwich Union
86224	Caledonian
86225	Hardwicke
86226	Mail
86226	Royal Mail Midlands
86226	CHARLES RENNIE MACKINTOSH
86227	Sir Henry Johnston
86227	Golden Jubilee
86228	Vulcan Heritage
86229	Sir John Betjeman
86229	Lions Club International
86230	The Duke of Wellington
86231	Starlight Express
86232	Harold Macmillan
86232	Norwich Festival
86232	Norwich & Norfolk Festival
86233	Laurence Olivier
86233	Alstom Heritage
86234	J B Priestly OM
86234	Suffolk – Relax, Refresh, Return
86235	Novelty
86235	Harold Macmillan
86235	Crown Point
86236	Josiah Wedgwood Master Potter 1736–1795
86237	Sir Charles Hallé
86237	University of East Anglia
86238	European Community
86239	L S Lowry
86240	Bishop Eric Treacy
86241	Glenfiddich
86242	James Kennedy GC

86242	Colchester Castle
86243	The Boys' Brigade
86244	The Royal British Legion
86245	Dudley Castle
86245	Caledonian
86246	Royal Anglian Regiment
86247	Abraham Darby
86248	Sir Clwyd County of Clwyd
86249	County of Merseyside
86250	The Glasgow Herald
86250	Sheppard 100
86251	The Birmingham Post
86252	The Liverpool Daily Post
86252	Sheppard 100
86253	The Manchester Guardian
86254	William Webb Ellis
86255	Penrith Beacon
86256	Pebble Mill
86257	Snowdon
86258	Ben Nevis
86258	Talyllyn – The First Preserved Railway
86258	Talyllyn 50 Years of Railway Preservation 1951–2001
86259	Peter Pan
86259	Greater Manchester The Life & Soul of Britain
86259	Les Ross
86260	Driver Wallace Oakes GC
86261	Driver John Axon GC
86261	THE RAIL CHARTER PARTNERSHIP
86311	Airey Neave
86312	Elizabeth Garrett Anderson
86328	Aldaniti
86401	Northampton Town
86401	Hertfordshire Rail Tours

EWS retained vacuum brakes on some of its 86s for working charter trains. The 86s originally had headcode panels, which were removed in the late 1970s and changed to yellow panels; only two locos had dominos. 86261 The Rail Charter Partnership *was one of three 86s painted into EWS colours.* PIP DUNN

86407	The Institution of Electrical Engineers
86408	St John Ambulance
86413	County of Lancashire
86414	Frank Hornby
86415	Rotary International
86416	Wigan Pier
86417	The Kingsman
86419	Post Haste 150 Years of Travelling Post Offices
86421	London School of Economics
86425	Saint Mungo
86426	Pride of the Nation
86427	The Industrial Society
86429	THE TIMES
86430	Scottish National Orchestra
86430	Saint Edmund
86432	Brookside

86433	Wulfruna
86434	University of London
86501	Crewe Basford Hall*
86605	Intercontainer
86620	Philip G Walton
86701	Orion
86702	Cassiopeia
86901	CHIEF ENGINEER
86902	RAIL VEHICLE ENGINEERING

* 86501 had these names fitted in error

Plaques

Crewe DMD cat: 86502/503 F
Crewe EMD eagle: 86603/604/606–615/ 618/620–623/627/628/631/633/635/637 FF; 86608 FE

BUILD BATCHES

BR Doncaster: E3101–40
EE Vulcan Foundry: E3141–99, 3200

NUMBERS

Along with the Class 45s, the Class 86s were probably the most randomly renumbered fleet when it came to applying TOPS. There have been many renumberings since.

The 100 locos were split into two subclasses when initially renumbered – forty-eight Class 86/0s and fifty-two Class 86/2s. In the mid-1980s, nine 86/0s became 86/2s, while three 86/2s became testbed Class 86/1s.

The initial E series to TOPS numbers were as follows:

Class 86/0:

86001	3199
86002	3170
86003	3115
86004	3103
86005	3185
86006	3112
86007	3176
86008	3180
86009	3102
86010	3104
86011	3171
86012	3122
86013	3128
86014	3145
86015	3123
86016	3109
86017	3146
86018	3163
86019	3120
86020	3114
86021	3157
86022	3174
86023	3152
86024	3111
86025	3186
86026	3195
86027	3110
86028	3159
86029	3200
86030	3105
86031	3188
86032	3148
86033	3198
86034	3187
86035	3124
86036	3160
86037	3130
86038	3108

86245 Caledonian was repainted into a one-off livery of light blue. The loco sparkles in the rain after its naming. It was later repainted into standard Virgin red. PIP DUNN

86247 was painted into Europhoenix livery and fitted with new light clusters and a roof-mounted headlight to woo potential export markets. However, the loco is not fully operational. PIP DUNN

86039	3153
86040	3135
86041	3118
86042	3154
86043	3139
86044	3136
86045	3137
86046	3140
86047	3142
86048	3144

Class 86/2:

86201	3191
86202	3150
86203	3143
86204	3173
86205	3129
86206	3184
86207	3179
86208	3141
86209	3125
86210	3190
86211	3147
86212	3151
86213	3193
86214	3106
86215	3165
86216	3166
86217	3177
86218	3175
86219	3196
86220	3156
86221	3132
86222	3131
86223	3158
86224	3134
86225	3164
86226	3162
86227	3117
86228	3167
86229	3119
86230	3168
86231	3126
86232	3113
86233	3172
86234	3155
86235	3194
86236	3133
86237	3197
86238	3116
86239	3169
86240	3127
86241	3121
86242	3138
86243	3181
86244	3178
86245	3182
86246	3149
86247	3192
86248	3107

Six Class 86s have been exported to Hungary for private operator Floyd, renumbered in the Class 450 series. 450.006, formerly 86217, shows the revised light clusters using LEDs, plus oval buffers and the centrally mounted headlight just below the windows. STUART WEST

86249	3161
86250	3189
86251	3183
86252	3101

Class 86/1s converted from Class 86/2s:

86101	86201
86102	86202
86103	86203

Class 86/2s converted from Class 86/0s:

86253	86044
86254	86047
86255	86042
86256	86040
86257	86043
86258	86046
86259	86045
86260	86048
86261	86041

Class 86/3s converted from Class 86/0s:

86311	86011
86312	86012
86313	86013
86314	86014
86315	86015
86316	86016
86317	86017
86318	86018
86319	86019
86320	86020
86321	86021
86322	86022
86323	86023
86324	86024
86325	86025

86326	86026
86327	86027
86328	86028
86329	86029

All these locos went on to become Class 86/4s, and most to Class 86/6s.

Class 86/4s converted from Class 86/0s:

86401	86001
86402	86002
86403	86004
86404	86004
86405	86005
86406	86006
86407	86007
86408	86008
86409	86009
86410	86010
86430	86030
86431	86031
86432	86032
86433	86033
86434	86034
86435	86035
86436	86036
86437	86037
86438	86038
86439	86039

Many of these locos went on to become Class 86/6s.

Class 86/5s converted from Class 86/2s:

86501	86258
86502	86222
86503	86503
86504	86217

86505	86246	86612	86412		
86506	86233	86613	86413		
86507	86239	86614	86414		
86508	86241	86615	86415		

Class 86/5 converted from Class 86/6:

86501	86608

All these locos reverted to their original Class 86/2 numbers.

86618	86418
86620	86420
86621	86421
86622	86422
86623	86423

Class 86/6s converted from Class 86/4s:

86602	86402
86603	86403
86604	86404
86605	86405
86606	86406
86607	86407
86608	86408
86609	86409
86610	86410
86611	86411

86627	86427
86628	86428
86631	86431
86632	86432
86633	86433
86634	86434
86635	86435
86636	86436
86637	86437
86638	86438
86639	86439

Class 86/7s converted from Class 86/2s:

86701	86205
86702	86260

Class 86/9s converted from Class 86/2s:

86901	86253
86902	86210

EXPORTED 86S

Railfreight operator Floyd in Hungary now has a fleet of 86/2s, with six locos now in use and another four expected, likely to be chosen from 86228/229/234/242/246/251. They are renumbered in the Class 450 series, and are painted in all-over black with a pink band midway on the bodyside, with FLOYD in grey – apart from the O, which is pink – midway along the body in large letters, and on the cab front in smaller letters.

A standard BR-style headlight has been fitted directly below the centre cab window, and two LED white/red lights fitted in the position of the original tail-lights.

The Floyd renumberings are :

450001–7	86248
450002–5	86250
450003–3	86232
450004–1	86218
450005–8	86215
450006–6	86217

In 2012, 86233 was exported to Bulmarket in Bulgaria, for spare parts. It retains its heritage Electric Blue livery applied by Virgin in 2001.

ABOVE: One of two Class 86/2s converted to Class 86/7s – which were no different other than being owned by ETL and available for spot hire. The loco is air-braked only but retains its ETH. It has TDM fitted, plus a BR-style standard headlight. New LED red tail-lights and marker lights (in the redundant, plated-over headcode box) are the major changes from Class 86/2s. PIP DUNN

RIGHT: E3163 shows a Class 86 in as-built condition apart from the addition of a small warning panel. The loco is dual-braked and ETH fitted, and has raised aluminium numbers on all four cabsides. It also has a raised lion and wheel emblem on its bodyside. When the loco was repainted into BR blue the BR badge was changed to a double arrow, which was also raised aluminium. When renumbered to 86018, transfers were used. The loco later became 86318, then 86418, and finally 86618. During these transitions it lost its headcode panel, and had a headlight fitted and new suspension. BILL WRIGHT

class 87

TOPS number range:	87001–035, 87101
Number range:	BREL Crewe
Years introduced:	1973–75
Wheel arrangement:	Bo-Bo
Weight:	83 tons; 79 tons – 87101
Height:	13ft 1in (3.99m)
Length:	58ft 6in (17.83m)
Width:	8ft 8in (2.64m)
Wheelbase:	43ft 6in (13.25m)
Bogie wheelbase:	10ft 9in (3.28m)
Bogie pivot centres:	32ft 9in (9.98m)
Wheel diameter:	3ft 10in (1.16m)
Min. curve negotiable:	4 chains (80.47m)
Traction output (max)	7,680bhp (5,860kW); 7,250bhp (5,401kW): 87101
Traction output (cont):	5,000bhp (3,730kW); 4,850bhp (3,620kW): 87101
Tractive effort:	58,000lb
Maximum speed:	110mph (176km/h)
Brake force:	40 tons
Route availability:	6
Control system:	HT tap-changing; Thyristor – 87101
Traction motor type:	GEC G412AZ; GEC G412BZ – 87101
No. of traction motors:	4
Gear ratio:	32:73
OHLE power supply:	25kV AC overhead

BUILT IN 1973 for the electrification of the WCML north of Crewe, the thirty-five Class 87/0s and a trial loco 87101 – fitted with thyristor control – were the mainstay of express passenger and freight on the WCML alongside the Class 86s and to a lesser extent the 81–85s.

87101 passed into freight use, while the 87/0s passed to Virgin use until withdrawal as new Class 390s came into traffic. Several 87s have been exported and are still in use in Bulgaria. Three are preserved, one of which has been main line registered.

DETAIL DIFFERENCES

All were built with ETH (index 95), air brakes and multiple working compatible only with Class 87s and those Class 86s fitted with cab-mounted jumpers – some Class 86/0s, 86/3s and all 86/4s and 86/6s. These jumpers were later replaced by the TDM system in the early 1990s, and for a period 87s ran with both systems mounted on their cab fronts; from the late 1990s the original jumpers were removed.

All had rubber-mounted headlights on the cab fronts above the buffer-beams. These were later replaced by the standard BR-style, high intensity headlights. After 87027 suffered a collision its cab was rebuilt with all trace of the original multiple-working cables removed, leaving a unique flush end at No. 2 end.

LIVERIES

Blue: 87001–035, 87101
BR blue with white windows: 87101
BR grey 'Large Logo': 87006
InterCity Executive: 87001–021/023–030/032/034
InterCity Mainline: 87001/003–005/009–014/016/018/022/028/031/033/035
InterCity: 87001–035
Virgin: 87001–035
Virgin unbranded: 87003/013/014/023/027/032/033
RfD: 87101
Porterbrook: 87002
Cotswold Rail: 87007/008
Cotswold Rail unbranded: 87007/008
DRS: 87006/022/028
DRS with blue cabsides and orange window frames (GBRf): 87022/028
DRS with orange cabsides and window frames (GBRf): 87028
Network SouthEast with Back the Bid branding: 87012
LNWR black: 87019
BR blue (retro): 87001/002/101
Bulgarian Railways: 87003/010/013/014/020/026/029/033/034
BZK silver: 87007/008
BZK blue: 87006/022/028
BZK BR blue: 87004
BSK NSE: 87012
BZK LNER: 87019
Europhoenix: 87017/023

Larger (8in) numbers: 87034 B; 87012/020/032 IC 87001 also ran with its numbers much lower on its cabsides when in B.

Cast depot emblems: Crewe eagle: 87101 FD, 87101 B

NAMES

87001	STEPHENSON
87001	Royal Scot
87002	Royal Sovereign
87002	The AC Locomotive Group
87003	Patriot
87004	Britannia
87005	City of London
87006	City of Glasgow
87006	Glasgow Garden Festival
87006	George Reynolds
87007	City of Manchester
87008	City of Liverpool
87008	Royal Scot
87009	City of Birmingham
87010	King Arthur
87010	Driver Tommy Farr
87011	The Black Prince
87011	City of Wolverhampton
87012	Cœur de Lion
87012	The Royal Bank of Scotland
87012	Cœur de Lion
87012	The Olympian
87013	John O'Gaunt
87014	Knight of the Thistle
87015	Howard of Effingham
87016	Sir Francis Drake
87016	Willesden Intercity Depot
87017	Iron Duke
87018	Lord Nelson
87019	Sir Winston Churchill
87019	ACoRP Association of Community Rail Partnerships
87020	North Briton
87021	Robert the Bruce
87022	Cock o' the North
87022	Lew Adams the Black Prince
87023	Highland Chieftain
87023	Velocity
87023	Polmadie
87024	Lord of the Isles
87025	Borderer
87025	County of Cheshire
87026	Redgauntlet
87026	Sir Richard Arkwright
87027	Wolf of Badenoch
87028	Lord President
87029	Earl Marischal
87030	Black Douglas
87031	Hal o' the Wynd
87031	Keith Harper
87032	Kenilworth
87032	Richard Fearn
87033	Thane of Fife
87034	William Shakespeare
87035	Robert Burns
87101	STEPHENSON

BULGARIA

Eighteen Class 87s were exported for Bulgarian operator BZK. They were 87012/019 (01/07), 87007/008/026 (06/08), 87010/022/028 (10/08), 87003/006/

The first-built Class 87, 87001, renamed Stephenson *and back in BR blue. The loco now has TDM instead of its original MW, the plates for which can be seen by the TDM jumpers. No changes to the bufferbeam pipe arrangement have been made to the Class 87s since their construction in 1973.* PIP DUNN

Porterbrook repainted 87002 into its striking purple livery in 2002, with the livery different on each side, one having the Porterbrook branding, the other – this side – the company's logo. The loco was later sold to Electric Traction Limited, which repainted it into BR blue and renamed it Royal Sovereign. PIP DUNN

ABOVE LEFT: 87003 Patriot *in Virgin colours with TDM, not MW, and a BR-standard high intensity headlight; this replaced the original sealed-beam headlight fitted to the class when new.* PIP DUNN
ABOVE RIGHT: In August 1988, 87032 Kenilworth *shows the transition phase when 87s retained their original MW yet the new TDM system was also added. It sports InterCity Executive livery and larger than normal cabside numbers, a feature seen on a handful of 87s.* PDC
RIGHT: Several Class 87s have been sold for use in Bulgaria, and while some have been repainted into BZK green and yellow livery, others were sent in their UK liveries. 87019 was painted in LNWR blackberry black in its final days for Virgin. Now in Bulgaria it shows the cowcatchers, revised lights and horns as well as wing mirrors. The ETH has also been removed. TONY SAYER

034 (12/08), 87020/029/033 (05/09) and 87004/013/014 (11/09).

Of these, 87008/014 are stored and used for spares – the former having been used in the Bulgaria. Locos were not always shipped in the BZK green and yellow livery, and 87006/022/028 were shipped in their GBRf-modified version of the DRS blue. 87007/008 went into Cotswold Rail livery and 87012/019 in their special NSE and LNWR liveries. 87004 was repainted into BR blue – and

renamed *Britannia* – for its move, leaving just 87003/010/013/014/020/026/029/033/034 having been repainted into BZK colours.

In September 2012, 87009/017/023/025 were moved to Bulgaria for use with a different company, Bulmarket.

With 87001/035 preserved and 87002 returned to main line use in the UK, it means that only 87005/011/015/016/018/021/024/027/030–032, 87101 have been scrapped.

The BZK Class 87s had two horns on the roof, both pointing sideways opposite to each other. Two cab roof-mounted headlights were fitted, and the central headlight above the bufferbeams was removed. Their TDM cables were retained. Cowcatchers were also fitted to the bufferbeams. They have had their ETH removed apart from 87004/026, and have been fitted with wing mirrors. Those sold to Bulmarket, 87009/023/025, retain their ETH.

SUBSEQUENT RENUMBERINGS

No Class 87s were renumbered under TOPS, although 87101 was originally going to be 87036, but the number was never used.

Those locos exported to Bulgaria have been given check digits, but still retain their TOPS numbers; they are now:

87003-0	87019-6
87004-8	87020-4
87006-3	87022-0
87007-1	87022-0
87008-9	87026-1
87010-5	87028-7
87012-1	87029-5
87013-9	87033-7
87014-7	87034-5

class 89

specifications

TOPS number:	89001	Wheel diameter:	3ft 9in (1.14m)
Built by:	BREL Crewe, as sub-contractor to Brush Traction	Min. curve negotiable:	4 chains (80.46m)
		Traction output (max):	7,860bhp (5,860kW)
Introduced:	1987	Traction output (cont):	5,745bhp (4,350kW)
Wheel arrangement:	Co-Co	Tractive effort:	46,100lb
Weight:	104 tons	Maximum speed:	125mph (200km/h)
Height (pan down):	13ft (3.97m)	Brake force:	40 tons
Length:	64ft 11in (19.76m)	Route availability:	6
Width:	9ft (2.73m)	Control system:	Thyristor
Wheelbase:	49ft 7in (15.10m)	Traction motor type:	Brush TM2201A
Bogie wheelbase:	14ft 5in (4.39m)	No. of traction motors:	6
Bogie pivot centres:	35ft 9in (10.90m)	OHLE power supply:	25kV AC

A PROTOTYPE AIMED at being suitable for ECML and WCML operations, the Class 89 was built at BREL Crewe, but was a Brush design. After initial WCML tests it was moved to the ECML where it was used until 1991, when, having failed to win any repeat orders, it soon became expensive to maintain because of its non-standard, one-off nature. It was sold to a preservationist and then sold to Sea Containers for use back on the main line by GNER from 1998.

Again it lasted only a short period when it became too expensive to retain in traffic, so it was withdrawn. It was then acquired by the AC Loco Group for preservation, and remains at Barrow Hill.

DETAIL DIFFERENCES

Being a prototype there were no detail differences and its only changes were cosmetic to its liveries. It was fitted with drophead buckeye couplings. It is air-braked only, and had ETH (index 95) and TDM.

LIVERIES

InterCity Executive: 89001
InterCity: 89001
GNER with white lettering: 89001
GNER with gold lettering: 89001

NAME

89001   *Avocet*

The nameplates were stainless steel.

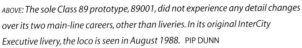

ABOVE: The sole Class 89 prototype, 89001, did not experience any detail changes over its two main-line careers, other than liveries. In its original InterCity Executive livery, the loco is seen in August 1988. PIP DUNN

RIGHT: 89001 was withdrawn and sold for preservation before being bought by GNER and returned to traffic in 1998. However, its non-standard nature and restrictions on drivers trained on it meant it soon became expensive to operate. It was then sold back into preservation. This July 2003 view shows the loco still in GNER colours with its TDM jumper cables removed. PIP DUNN

The Class 90s have been through many changes to their operations over the years, with twenty-six locos being dedicated freight locos for several years. All the fleet reverted to standard 110mph (176km/h) Class 90/0s, although some have now been withdrawn. Freightliner's 90041, one of three to receive the green and yellow livery, shows its bufferbeam, which no longer has the vestibule rubbing plates. PIP DUNN

TOPS number range:	90001–050, 90125–150, 90221–239
Built by:	BREL Crewe
Years introduced:	1987–90
Wheel arrangement:	Bo-Bo
Weight:	84.5 tons
Height (pan down):	13ft (3.96m)
Length:	61ft 6in (18.74m)
Width:	9ft (2.74m)
Wheelbase:	43ft 6in (13.25m)
Bogie wheelbase:	10ft 9in (3.27m)
Bogie pivot centres:	32ft 9in (9.98m)
Wheel diameter:	3ft 10in (1.16m)
Min. curve negotiable:	4 chains (80.43m)
Traction output (max):	7,680bhp (5,860kW)
Traction output (cont):	5,000bhp (3,730kW)
Tractive effort:	58,000lb
Maximum speed:	110mph (176km/h)
Brake force:	40 tons
Route availability:	7
Control system:	Thyristor
Traction motor type:	GEC G412CY
No of traction motors:	4
Gear ratio:	32:73
OHLE power supply:	25kV AC

INITIALLY CLASSED AS 87/2, the fact that a wholly new bodyshell was designed for these 25kV AC electric locos meant it was inevitable that a new class would be given to them, which was 90. Fifty were built, with the first twenty-five for InterCity, the next twelve for general WCML use, and the last thirteen for the Railfreight sector. Initially all were used on a common user basis, but the fleet was later split between fifteen passenger locos for InterCity, five locos for Rail express systems and the other thirty for freight. Twenty-six of the latter were renumbered as 90/1s and had their ETH isolated. It has since been reinstated and the locos reverted to their original numbers.

DETAIL DIFFERENCES

All were built to a 110mph (176km/h) passenger specification with ETH (index 95), but in 1991 90026–050 were converted to 90/1s; this saw no major physical changes other than their ETH being isolated, and their vestibule rubbing plates removed and restricted to 75mph (120km/h). They were renumbered in the 90/1 series. 90025 became 90125 in 1993.

In 1998, 90025–029 regained their ETH and original numbers, followed by 90030–040 in 1999. In 2001 Freightliner's 90142/146 had their ETH and 110mph (176km/h) capability reinstated for hire to Virgin, although they kept their 90/1 numbers until late 2001, when they reverted to 90042/046. The other eight Freightliner 90/1s reverted to 90/0s in 2002.

In 2001, nine EWS 90/0s had modified brake blocks fitted and were renumbered in the 90/2 series: they were 90021–025/027/033/038/039, which became 90221–225/227/233/238/239. They reverted to their original numbers in 2002.

LIVERIES

InterCity: 90001–025
InterCity Mainline: 90026–036
RfD: 90021–027/037–050, 90125–127/ 137–150, 90225/227/239
RfD European: 90021–024/026/031– 035/037–039
Res: 90016–020
RfD trial: 90036
SNCB: 90028, 90128
DB red: 90029, 90129
SNCF Sybic: 90030, 90130
Two-tone grey: 90022/044/047
GNER: 90024, 90224
EWS: 90017/018/020/023/026/028–032/ 034/035/037/039/040
First: 90019/021/024
Virgin: 90001–015
One: 90001–015
One unbranded: 90001–015
NatEx: 90003/009/015
Two-tone grey/EWS logos: 90036
Freightliner grey: 90041–050
Freightliner green: 90016/041/043/046
Freightliner Powerhaul: 90045/049
DBS: 90018/029

NAMES

90001	BBC Midlands Today *
90002	Girl's Brigade
90002	Mission: Impossible
90003	THE HERALD
90003	Rædwald of East Anglia
90004	The D'oyly Carte Opera Company *
90004	City of Glasgow
90004	Eastern Daily Press: 1870–2010, SERVING NORFOLK FOR 140 YEARS
90004	City of Chelmsford
90005	Financial Times *
90005	Vice-Admiral Lord Nelson
90006	High Sheriff *
90006	Roger Ford/Modern Railways Magazine
90007	Lord Stamp
90007	Keith Harper
90007	Sir John Betjeman
90008	The Birmingham Royal Ballet *
90008	The East Anglian
90009	The Economist
90009	Royal Show *
90010	275 Railway Squadron (Volunteers) *
90010	BRESSINGHAM STEAM & GARDENS
90011	The Chartered Institute of Transport *
90011	West Coast Rail 250
90011	Let's Go East of England
90012	Glasgow 1990 Cultural Capital of Europe *
90012	British Transport Police
90012	Royal Anglian Regiment
90013	The Law Society
90013	The Evening Star: PRIDE OF IPSWICH 1885–2010 – 125 YEARS OF SERVING SUFFOLK

90014	The Liverpool Phil *
90014	The Big Dish
90014	Driver Tom Clark OBE
90014	Norfolk & Norwich Festival
90015	BBC North West *
90015	The International Brigades Spain 1936–1939
90015	Colchester Castle
90017	Rail express systems Quality Assured
90019	Penny Black
90020	Colonel Bill Cockburn CBE TD
90020	Michael Heron
90020	Collingwood
90022	Freightconnection
90026	Crewe Electric Depot
90026	Crewe International Electric Maintenance Depot
90027	Allerton T&RS Depot
90028	Vrachtverbinding
90028	Hertfordshire Rail Tours
90029	Frachtverbindungen
90029	The Institution of Civil Engineers
90030	Fretconnection
90030	Crewe Locomotive Works
90031	Intercontainer
90031	The Railway Children Partnership: Working for Street Children Worldwide
90032	Cerestar
90035	Crewe Basford Hall
90037	Spirit of Dagenham
90040	The Railway Mission
90043	Freightliner Coatbridge
90126	Crewe International Electric Maintenance Depot
90127	Allerton T&RS Depot
90128	Vrachtverbinding
90129	Frachtverbindungen
90130	Fretconnection
90131	Intercontainer
90132	Cerestar
90135	Crewe Basford Hall
90143	Freightliner Coatbridge
90227	Allerton T&RS Depot

* stainless steel nameplates

PLAQUES

Crewe EMD eagle: 90021–025/027/ 037/039/040, 90125–127/138–143/145– 150 FD; 90142/143/146/148 FF; 90022/ 024/026, 90126/132–135/138/139 FE; 90128 SNCB; 90129 DB; 90130 SNCF; 90136 RDZ; **Res cut-out Crewe eagle:** 90020 RX

SUBSEQUENT RENUMBERINGS

90021	90221	90021		
90022	90222	90022		
90023	90223	90023		
90024	90224	90024		
90025	90125	90025	90225	90025
90026	90126	90026		
90027	90127	90027	90227	90027
90028	90128	90028		
90029	90129	90029		
90030	90130	90030		
90031	90131	90031		
90032	90132	90032		
90033	90133	90033	90233	90033
90034	90134	90034		
90035	90135	90035		
90036	90136	90036		
90037	90137	90037		
90038	90138	90038	90238	90038
90039	90139	90039	90239	90039
90040	90140	90040		
90041	90141	90041		
90042	90142	90042		
90043	90143	90043		
90044	90144	90044		
90045	90145	90045		
90046	90146	90046		
90047	90147	90047		
90048	90148	90048		
90049	90149	90049		
90050	90150	90050		

90024 was the only Class 90 which was painted in GNER blue, although the EWS loco did not have GNER branding. The loco has the standard bufferbeam without a vestibule rubbing plate. This loco spent a spell numbered 90224 when different brake blocks were fitted, but it has reverted to its original identity, and where the number change was made can just be made out on the bodyside. ANTHONY HICKS

EWS inherited twenty-five Class 90s at privatization, five from Res and twenty from RfD. Many were repainted into EWS colours, such as 90031. Several have now been withdrawn, although they are still used on 'sleeper' trains between England and Scotland. PIP DUNN

PURPOSE-BUILT AT Crewe for the ECML, which was electrified in 1988–91, the locos almost exclusively run with Mk 4 sets in fixed formations, with the locos at the country end. They have a raked cab at No. 1 end, with a flat front cab at No. 2, allowing the locos to run round to the other end of a train should there be a fault with a DVT. In such instances they can only run at a reduced speed of 110mph (176km/h).

They are able to haul any standard air-braked trains, but rarely do so. They were outshopped in InterCity colours after construction. The letting of the franchise to GNER in 1996 saw a new dark blue livery applied.

The fleet was refurbished in 2001–03 and renumbered as 91/1s. 91023 was involved in two fatal collisions (which did not damage the loco in either occasion), and it was decided that rather than renumber it as 91123, it would be changed to 91132. Three locos are currently in promotional liveries.

DETAIL DIFFERENCES

There were few differences between the individual locos other than liveries, but when refurbished the Class 91/1s had an additional bodyside grille just in front of the door at No. 2 (flat end). All have ETH with an index of 95.

LIVERIES

InterCity: 91001–031
GNER blue with white lettering 91004/ 008/009/014/016/018–020/022–024/ 026/028/030/031
GNER blue with gold lettering: 91001– 031, 91101–122/124–132
GNER blue with white band: 91101– 110/112–122/124–132
NatEx: 91111

East Coast Silver: 91101/106/107/109/ 110/127
East Coast Grey: 91102–105/108/111– 126/128–131/132
Flying Scotsman: 91101
Battle of Britain Memorial: 91110
Skyfall Promotional: 91107
Emblems: Cuneo mouse, 91011, 91111

NAMES

91001	Swallow˙
91002	Durham Cathedral §
91003	The Scotsman §
91004	The Red Arrows˙
91004	Grantham §
91005	Royal Air Force Regiment˙
91007	Ian Allan §
91008	Thomas Cook˙
91009	Saint Nicholas §
91009	The Samaritans §
91010	Northern Rock §
91011	Terence Cuneo˙
91012	County of Cambridgeshire
91013	Michael Faraday˙
91013	County of North Yorkshire
91014	Northern Electric˙
91014	St Mungo Cathedral
91015	Holyrood
91017	Commonwealth Institute §
91017	City of Leeds
91018	Robert Louis Stevenson §
91018	Bradford Film Festival
91019	Scottish Enterprise˙
91021	Royal Armouries §
91021	Archbishop Thomas Cranmer
91022	Robert Adley §
91022	Double Trigger
91024	Reverend W Awdry §
91025	BBC Radio 1 FM˙
91025	Berwick-upon-Tweed
91026	Voice of the North §
91026	York Minster
91027	Great North Run §
91028	Guide Dog˙
91028	Peterborough Cathedral
91029	Queen Elizabeth II˙
91030	Palace of Holyroodhouse˙
91031	Sir Henry Royce˙
91031	County of Northumberland
91101	City of London
91102	Durham Cathedral
91102	City of York §
91103	County of Lincolnshire
91104	Grantham

specifications

TOPS number range:	91001–031, 91101–122/124–132
Built by:	BREL Crewe
Years introduced:	1988–91
Wheel arrangement:	Bo-Bo
Weight:	84 tons
Height (pan down):	12ft 4in (3.75m)
Length:	63ft 8in (19.40m)
Width:	9ft (2.74m)
Wheelbase:	45ft 5in (13.85m)
Bogie wheelbase:	11ft (3.35m)
Bogie pivot centres:	34ft 6in (10.50m)
Wheel diameter:	3ft 4in (1.00m)
Min. curve negotiable:	4 chains (80.49m)
Traction output (max):	6,300bhp (4,700kW)
Traction output (cont):	6,090bhp (4,540kW)
Maximum design speed:	140mph (225km/h)
Maximum operating speed:	125mph (200km/h) restricted to 110mph (176km/h) when flat end leading
Brake force:	45 tons
Route availability:	7
Control system:	Thyristor
Traction motor type:	GEC G426AZ
No. of traction motors:	4
Gear ratio:	1.74:1
OHLE power supply:	25kV AC

The flat or blunt end of a Class 91/0, which spends most of its time coupled directly to a Mk 4 coach. 91004 shows the standard bufferbeam layout with a buckeye coupling, vestibule rubbing plate and two panels that contain the TDM cables, one of which is hanging out on the right. The loco is in InterCity livery with small numbers, later changed to be much bigger. The nameplate The Red Arrows *is in the polished stainless-steel type favoured by InterCity in the late 1980s, but soon dropped in favour of standard cast plates.* ANTHONY HICKS

91105	*County Durham*
91106	*East Lothian*
91107	*Newark on Trent*
91108	*City of Leeds*
91109	*The Samaritans*
91109	*Sir Bobby Robson* §
91110	*David Livingstone*
91110	*BATTLE OF BRITAIN MEMORIAL FLIGHT* ^
91111	*Terence Cuneo*
91112	*County of Cambridgeshire*
91113	*County of North Yorkshire*
91114	*St Mungo Cathedral*
91115	*Holyrood*
91115	*Blaydon Races* §
91116	*Strathclyde*

91117	*Cancer Research UK*
91117	*WEST RIDING LIMITED*
91118	*Bradford Film Festival*
91119	*County of Tyne & Wear*
91120	*Royal Armouries*
91121	*Archbishop Thomas Cranmer*
91122	*Double Trigger*
91122	*Tam the Gun*
91124	*Reverend W Awdry*
91125	*Berwick upon Tweed*
91126	*York Minster*
91127	*Edinburgh Castle*
91128	*Peterborough Cathedral*
91129	*Queen Elizabeth II*
91130	*City of Newcastle*
91131	*County of Northumberland*

91132	*City of Durham*

* stainless-steel nameplate; § cast BR style nameplate; ^ special cast nameplate; all other names were in transfer style

SUBSEQUENT RENUMBERINGS

All Class 91s were renumbered from the 91/0 series to the 91/1 series when refurbished in 2001–03. The locos changed from 910xx to 911xx. The exception was 91023 which became 91132. In 02/13, 91107 was renumbered 91007 for its role in promoting the James Bond film *Skyfall*.

class 92

specifications

TOPS number range:	92001–046	Traction output (max):	6,700bhp (5,000kW) – overhead power supply	
Built by:	Brush Traction			
Years introduced:	1993–95		5,360bhp (4,000kW) – third rail power supply	
Wheel arrangement:	Co-Co			
Weight:	126 tons	Tractive effort:	Normal – 81,000lb; boost – 90,000lb	
Height (pan down):	13ft (3.95m)			
Length:	70ft 1in (21.34m)	Maximum speed:	87mph (139km/h)	
Width:	8ft 8in (2.66m)	Brake force:	63 tons	
Wheelbase:	56ft 6in (17.22m)	Route availability:	8	
Bogie wheelbase:	14ft 1in (4.29m)	Control system:	Asynchronous three-phase	
Bogie pivot centres:	41ft 11in (12.75m)			
Wheel diameter:	3ft 9in (1.16m)	Traction motor type:	Brush	
Min. curve negotiable	6 chains (120.7m)	No. of traction motors:	6	
		OHLE power supply:	25kV AC or 750V DC	

THE CLASS 92 was designed solely with Channel Tunnel operation in mind. It could run off the 750V DC third rail and 25kV AC so could work trains from the electrified UK network in the north, via the third rail to the Channel Tunnel, and then return to 25kV to transit the tunnel and possibly work further into mainland Europe. However, the locos were dogged by technical issues which led to them not being allowed to operate on much of the network for several years. The fleet was split between BR's Railfreight Distribution, SNCF and Eurostar UK, with thirty, nine and seven locos respectively – though in reality the fleet was massively over-ordered.

The Eurostar and later SNCF locos have all now been sold to Europorte (part of Eurotunnel), and there is a possibility that some locos may be scrapped or rebuilt in the future. DBS, which now operates the thirty ex-RfD locos, usually needs only a third of that fleet and is now moving locos to Bulgaria.

DETAIL DIFFERENCES

Liveries aside, the fleet has been uniform since construction. A batch of DBS locos have been modified for running on HS1 with new signalling.

All have ETH with the index of 108 when on AC power, and 70 when on DC.

LIVERIES

Eurostar grey: 92001–046
Eurostar grey with RfD branding: 92009/022/030
Eurostar grey with EWS logo: 92002–005/007–009/011–013/015–017/019/022/024–027/029/030/034–037/039/041/042
Stobart: 92017
EWS: 92001/031
Stobart: 92017
Eurostar grey with Europorte branding: 92028/032/038/043
GBRf: 92032
DB Schenker: 92009/015/016/031/042

Minor Variations

SNCF cabside branding: 92006/010/014/018/023/028/033/043
DB cab logos and DB Schenker rail Bulgaria branding: 92034

EMBLEMS

All had the Crewe eagle depot plaques, which have been removed from those locos repainted into new liveries. All were fitted with three Channel Tunnel circle plaques (known as 'Polo Mint' logos) and these have been retained even on repainted locos.

NAMES

92001	*Victor Hugo*
92002	*H.G. Wells*
92003	*Beethoven*
92004	*Jane Austen*
92005	*Mozart*
92006	*Louis Armand*
92007	*Schubert*
92008	*Jules Verne*
92009	*Elgar* *
92009	*Marco Polo*

92010	Molière
92011	Handel
92012	Thomas Hardy
92013	Puccini
92014	Emile Zola
92015	D. H. Lawrence*
92016	Brahms*
92017	Shakespeare*
92017	Bart the Engine
92018	Stendhal
92019	Wagner
92020	Milton
92021	Purcell
92022	Charles Dickens
92023	Ravel
92024	J. S. Bach
92025	Oscar Wilde
92026	Britten
92027	George Eliot
92028	Saint Saëns
92029	Dante
92030	De Falla*
92030	Ashford

92031	Schiller*
92031	The Institute of Logistics & Transport*
92032	César Franck*
92032	IMechE Railway Division
92033	Berlioz
92034	Kipling
92035	Mendelssohn
92036	Bertolt Brecht
92037	Sullivan
92038	Voltaire
92039	Johann Strauss
92040	Goethe
92041	Vaughan Williams
92042	Honegger*
92043	Debussy
92044	Couperin

| 92045 | Chaucer |
| 92046 | Sweelinck |

Names were applied using transfers, except 92009/022/030–032 which had cast plates, the latter three only when renamed. 92001 retained the transfer for its name even when repainted into EWS livery. DBS red locos lost their names, although 92009 was renamed using cast plates.

LOCOS EXPORTED TO BULGARIA

92034	04/12
92025	12/12
92027	12/12

RIGHT: 92035 Mendelssohn, *in as-built condition, in the summer of 2000. Forty-six of these dual-voltage locos were built in 1993 for working through the Channel Tunnel, but the fleet has been woefully under-used. DB Schenker now owns thirty of the locos, three of which are in Bulgaria, while Europorte owns sixteen, although only a handful were in use at the start of 2013.* PIP DUNN

Two Class 92s were painted into EWS Red, and only one of those remains in this livery: 92001 Victor Hugo. *Despite the new livery, the loco retains its Channel Tunnel logos on its bodyside. The name is applied using transfers.* PIP DUNN

bibliography

To list all the texts used to research this book would be too long, but some of the key books frequently referred to are given below.

Ian Allan *At Work series*
Ian Allan *Diesel Retrospective series*
Ian Allan *In Detail series*
Booth, IRS E*x-BR diesels in industry*
Clough, Ian Allan *Diesel Pioneers*
Clough, Ian Allan *Hydraulic vs Electric*
Clough, Ian Allan *BR Standard Diesels of the 1960s*
Curtis *Western Mythology*
Curtis *Hymek Dawn*
Curtis *A Cast of Thousands*
Derrick, Strathwood *Looking back at series*
Greaves & Greengrass, Metro *Locomotive Datafile*

Harris *The Allocation History of BR Diesels and Electrics*
Howarth, LVP *Locofax*
IRS *Industrial locomotives*
Jennison, Irwell *Book of the Warships*
Lewis *The Western's Hydraulics*
Loader, Vanguard *Photofile series*
Marsden, railwaycentre.com *Modern Traction Locomotive Directory*
Marsden/Ford, Chanel AV *Encyclopaedia of Modern Traction Names*
Marsden, Ian Allan *Rail Guide*
Marsden, Ian Allan *Traction Recognition*
Neill *A Tribute to the Hymeks*
OPC *The Profile of series*
OPC *Power of series*
OPC *Life and Times series*
Platform 5 *Motive Power Pocket Book*
Strickland, D+EG *Locomotive Directory*

Sugden, Platform 5 *Diesel & Electric Loco Register*
Toms, Venture *Brush Diesel & Electric Locomotives*
various authors *Class 47 Data Files*
Walmsley, St Petroc *Shed by Shed*

The following journals were used:

Modern Locomotives Illustrated
Modem Railways
Rail Express
Rail Magazine
Railways Illustrated
Railway Magazine
Railway Observer
Railway World
Traction
Trains Illustrated

index